STUDY GUIDE TO ACCOMPANY

Psychology Today

AN INTRODUCTION

SEVENTH EDITION

Richard R. Bootzin
University of Arizona

Gordon H. Bower
Stanford University

Jennifer Crocker
SUNY at Buffalo

Elizabeth Hall

Prepared by
DANIEL PAULK

Ancillary Coordinator
MARK GARRISON
Kentucky State University

McGraw-Hill, Inc.
New York St. Louis San Francisco Auckland Bogotá
Caracas Lisbon London Madrid Mexico Milan
Montreal New Delhi Paris San Juan Singapore
Sydney Tokyo Toronto

STUDY GUIDE TO ACCOMPANY

Psychology Today: AN INTRODUCTION

4 5 6 7 8 9 0 SEM SEM 9 5 4 3 2

ISBN 0-07-006541-1

The editors were Maria Chiappetta and Christopher Rogers.
Art and design was by BOOK 1 Desktop Packagers.
The cover was designed by Armen Kojoyian.
Cover photograph by Jim Finlayson.
The production supervisor was Janelle S. Travers.
Semline, Inc., was printer and binder.

Study Guide to Accompany Psychology Today

Seventh Edition

TO THE INSTRUCTOR

Psychology Today in its seventh edition presents comprehensive coverage of major topics by integrating the findings of both classical research and new developments in the field of psychology. To help students master the wealth of ideas and information that the text puts forth, a *Study Guide* that emphasizes critical thinking and interactive learning has been created. The following elements make up this *Study Guide*.

Thinking Critically: A Psychology Student's Guide. This discussion of the processes involved in critical thinking is printed at the end of the *Study Guide,* and worth noting at the very beginning of the course. The selection is reprinted from a booklet by Robert Feldman and Steven Schwartzberg of the University of Massachusetts, Amherst. It is intended to enrich the course for both the student and instructor by helping students develop an active, analytic approach to the text content, in place of a passive, regurgitative stance.

Critical Thinking Essays. For each of the seven parts of the text, an essay is included in the *Study Guide* that describes one or more studies relevant to an issue, and offers a critical analysis of the research. The essays are written by John Vitkus of Barnard College. Each is followed by response questions that engage the student in the analysis.

A Key Term Outline summarizes the main points of the chapter and highlights many of the key terms that appear in the chapter text. In addition, charts and diagrams condense a large amount of information into a logical, concise reference aid for the student.

Major Concepts identify the most important themes of each chapter.

Learning Objectives, which are referenced to the Major Concepts, help the students focus attention on specific issues in the text. The multiple choice questions in this *Study Guide* and the *Test File* are keyed to these objectives.

Concept Builders are anchored to each major concept and set of learning objectives. Unlike many study exercises that only ask students to recall facts and definitions, Concept Builders actively involve students in learning by asking them to apply a given concept to a creative context or real-life setting. For example, in Chapter 12, Emotions, students are asked to suppose they are checking the sympathetic nervous system of a modern-day Frankenstein's monster that they created. In Chapter 14, Sexuality and Love, students are asked to pretend they are writing an advice column by answering "letters" from people with sexual problems. In Chapter 20, Health Psychology and Adjustment to Stress, students are asked to identify techniques of coping with stress as they are applied to test anxiety. As they work through the exercises, students are drawn into thinking at length about each concept and are helped in their understanding of the difficult aspects of psychology. Concept Builders may be completed independently or assigned by the instructor.

Chapter Exercises help students master the key terms found in the chapter. A wide variety of formats are used throughout the text to increase the student's motivation to learn these definitions. They include matching exercises, acrostics, crossword puzzles, anagrams, and category matching.

Practice Exams help students determine the success of their studying and practice taking tests. Each chapter includes two exams, each consisting of twelve multiple choice questions. Students' ability to recall information is tested by factual questions; their ability to apply, analyze, and synthesize the material in the chapter is tested by conceptual questions. Each question is keyed to a learning objective and text page so that students can review areas in which they do not show mastery. The difficulty level and writing style in the Practice Exam questions parallel the items in the *Test File* to ensure continuity and representativeness. Ten *Study Guide* questions from each chapter have been included in clearly marked subsections of the *Test File,* allowing the instructor convenient use of these questions when making up exams. Otherwise, there are no identical questions in these two volumes; the *Study Guide* does not give the student access to questions that will be included on the text if the test is drawn from the main body of the *Test File.*

ACKNOWLEDGMENTS

It is difficult to capture and express appreciation to all the "team" members that made this *Study Guide* a success. The editors at McGraw-Hill have been wonderful. Although Dan Alpert kicked the project off, Maria Chiappetta came into the second quarter with me and finished the game! Her relentless attention and editing ensured a high quality of content and relevance in the *Study Guide.* Her frequent contact added a much-valued camaraderie to the project as well. Thanks also to Mark Garrison for preparing the student Concepts and Learning Objectives and for reviewing the *Study Guide* manuscript in detail.

As is always the case, the family members living with an author give their priceless support by relinquishing "family time" and availability. To Lisa, I thank you and love you for being a "book-writing widow" for the last eight months. To Elliot, my two-year-old son, there really is more to daddy than the back of his head sitting at a typewriter.

Lastly, thanks to Bill Hill and Peggy Brooks at Kennesaw State College for their resource materials to keep me current in the dynamic field of psychology.

Daniel Paulk

TO THE STUDENT

Congratulations! You have made a wise investment in your psychology course by purchasing this study guide. The *Study Guide* is intended to help you study effectively and learn the basic material in *Psychology Today* in a straightforward and enjoyable manner. It will also give you practice in taking tests and provide feedback on your success. This book is meant to be used; it is a *companion* to the textbook, not a substitute for it. Along with chapter-by-chapter learning aids, the *Study Guide* offers you tools which can help you become skillful at evaluating the facts and studies you find in your text—and, for that matter, those you find anywhere else. Psychological research has shown that *how* people study greatly affects their learning and performance on tests. This *Study Guide* is meant to help you digest the text material in many ways by providing you with five learning aids for each chapter and supporting essays, all outlined below.

THINKING CRITICALLY: A PSYCHOLOGY STUDENT'S GUIDE

At the end of the *Study Guide* is a manual, or booklet, called *Thinking Critically: A Psychology Student's Guide.* Read this before you begin the first chapter. It describes techniques you can use to better assess what you read in the text—techniques which can make your study of psychology most exciting and rewarding.

CRITICAL THINKING ESSAYS

The essays which appear at the end of the *Study Guide* chapters 2, 6, 11, 14, 16, 20, and 23 treat some of the current research in psychology, and show ways in which this research can be interpreted. Reading the essays and answering the questions which follow them gives you a wider perspective on an issue relevant to the text, and also practice in approaching psychological research from a critical standpoint.

KEY TERM OUTLINE

If you flip through the *Study Guide,* you will notice a lot of charts, diagrams, and schematic depictions of psychological process. This is part of the Key Term Outline, an easy-to-read, quick summary of the main ideas in the chapter. Use this outline with the chapter summaries in the your text to review the whole chapter, and to refresh your memory of the general content of the chapter. Supplementing the written statements in the outline are several kinds of learning aids: classification charts that summarize concepts, theories, and experiments; diagrams that depict psychological processes; and "flow charts" that illustrate the order of certain variables in psychological phenomena. These visual aids can help you organize the way you recall and review the chapter's content.

MAJOR CONCEPTS AND LEARNING OBJECTIVES

Each chapter contains three to five major concepts that reflect the major ideas the authors are trying to get across. After each concept, you will notice a series of numbered learning objectives. You will find these objectives useful for two reasons: first, these statements will alert you to important ideas in the chapter. Pay attention to them; relate them to your notes. Second, the objectives will provide you with a quick reference point when you take the practice exams at the end of each chapter. Relating a test question to the objective it tests gives you feedback on whether you have mastered the objective.

CONCEPT BUILDERS

You will notice that a Concept Builder immediately follows each concept stated in the chapter. The Concept Builder lets you apply your knowledge to a "real" situation. This will help you better understand and remember the concept. I have included a whole range of exercises to get you thinking about the concepts: visual puzzles, one-act plays, identification exercises, hypothetical situations, and case studies. I have tried to make these situations both realistic and relevant to the concept being discussed. You may use an open book to help you complete these exercises or try to figure them out with what you have learned. Either way, approach these exercises with a sense of humor. Studying should be serious, but it needn't be dull!

CHAPTER EXERCISES

The Chapter Exercises will be a way to discover what you know. These exercises are oriented toward the "key terms" of each chapter. To help you pick out the key terms, the text lists them at the end of each chapter and prints them in boldface where they first appear in the text. You will find many of them appearing in your Key Term Outline as well. They are *important* words. I know studying key terms is often not very exciting, so I have devised a number of different methods, including acrostics, crossword puzzles, and anagrams, to test your recall of key terms. Try them.

PRACTICE EXAMS

You will probably find the Practice Exams in the *Study Guide* very valuable. After all, your learning is going to be measured, in part, by how well you can take tests. These Practice Exams allow you to test your knowledge of the material without the fear of being graded just yet. The answers are keyed to the learning objectives listed in the previous section of the chapter, so they are legitimate, important things to know. Answers to the questions are printed at the end of the chapter guide so that you can check your accuracy immediately. If you miss some questions, I would suggest you turn to the page in the text where the test item is discussed (the page number is also given in the answer key) and review the material. Each practice exam contains twelve test items, six factual and six conceptual. The factual items test your knowledge of specific facts, numbers, and names that appear in the text. The conceptual items test your ability to analyze, identify, and evaluate information. They're usually harder than the factual items because they involve more than just memorizing facts from the book.

I hope you get a lot of mileage out of this *Study Guide*. And you can help make subsequent editions even better by sharing any suggestions or critical comments you have. Forward your comments to:

Psychology Editor
College Division
McGraw-Hill, Inc.
215 First Street
Cambridge, MA 02142

Daniel Paulk

CONTENTS

CHAPTER ONE

Understanding Psychology: An Introduction

KEY TERM ORGANIZER

Psychology is the scientific study of mental processes and behavior. Psychology has adopted the approach of *empiricists,* scientists who verify phenomena by experiments. The earliest attempts to apply psychology relied on a technique called *introspection,* developed by Wundt. Titchener, along with Wundt, attempted to study the mind by analyzing its components (called *structuralism*). Structuralism competed with *functionalism,* studying the adaptiveness of human thought and behavior.

There are a number of modern day perspectives in psychology:

Perspective	Focus and Methods	Major Theorist(s)
Behavioral perspective	Principles governing observable activity such as *classical conditioning* and *operant conditioning*	John Watson Ivan Pavlov
Cognitive perspective	Processes of thinking and knowing	Wilhelm Wundt William James
Physiological perspective	Biological processes that underlie behavior	Hippocrates Wilhelm Wundt
Psychodynamic perspective	Unconscious inner forces that influence behavior	Sigmund Freud
Humanistic perspective	Subjective experience and the total human being	Abraham Maslow Carl Rogers

In psychology today, there are many specialties:

1. *Experimental* and *physiological psychology* investigate basic behavioral and nervous system processes. Subspecialties include:
   a. *Experimental psychology,* which investigates basic behavioral processes.
   b. *Physiological psychology* and *neuropsychology,* which explore connections between nervous and endocrine systems and behavior.
   c. *Psychopharmacology,* which studies the relationship of drugs to behavior.
2. *Developmental psychology* is concerned with behavioral development over the entire life span.
3. *Personality psychology* studies the relationship between personality and behavior, especially individual differences.
4. *Social psychology* studies the behavior of people in groups.
5. *Educational/school psychology* investigates how people learn in educational settings. Subspecialties include:
   a. *Educational psychology,* which is concerned with all the psychological aspects of the learning process.
   b. *School psychology,* which assesses and assists children with learning or emotional problems.
6. *Industrial/organizational psychology* studies the relationship between people and their jobs. This division makes the following distinctions in its discipline:
   a. *Human-factors psychology* specializes in the fit between a machine/environment and its probable user.
   b. *Personnel psychology* screens job applicants, evaluates job performance, and recommends employees for promotion.
   c. *Consumer psychology* studies consumer preferences, buying habits, and responses to advertising.
7. *Clinical psychology* focuses on studying and treating mental and behavioral disorders.
   a. *Psychiatry* is practiced by medical doctors who specialize in behavior disorders.
   b. *Counseling psychology* deals with less severe emotional problems.
   c. *Health psychology/behavioral medicine* deals with behavioral factors in health and illness.

Some of the more recent developments in psychology today have included *environmental psychology* (people and their physical settings); *forensic psychology* (psychological principles applied to law enforcement and court proceedings); *program evaluation* (evaluating the effectiveness of social programs); and the broadly defined field of *consulting,* in which the psychologist (or other professional) renders expert advice, usually for a fee.

By critically evaluating research, we are able to determine whether information is useful, relevant, and factual. Some scientific studies are sounder than others, and it is important to distinguish among them. All experimental studies are analogues to real-life phenomena and may not represent them without bias.

The relative importance of nature and nurture—heredity and environment—continues to be debated in psychology. The distinction between human beings and the animal kingdom and the existence of varying states of consciousness are still matters of interest. Whether we function as individuals or are influenced by our social roles, by persuasion, or by acts of others is a matter of continuing interest in psychology.

MAJOR CONCEPTS AND LEARNING OBJECTIVES

CONCEPT 1   The history of psychology has included several important trends of thought. From this history a number of perspectives have emerged.

1.1   Identify the subjects, aims, and goals of the science of psychology.

1.2   Describe the key contributions of Wundt, Freud, Watson, and others to the beginnings of the scientific approach to psychology.

1.3   Describe the five contemporary psychological approaches outlined in the text and how Watson, Skinner, Freud, Maslow, and Rogers contributed to them.

1.4   Discuss the main points of criticism for each of the five approaches.

Concept Builder 1

Directions: Five psychologists are interested in the reasons why people smoke cigarettes. They each go about observing and interviewing smokers. Which of the following questions would each kind of psychologist likely ask about smoking behavior?

Psychology and the Smoker

____   1.   "Is there a biological basis or mechanism involved in nicotine addiction?"

____   2.   "How is smoking reinforcing to the smoker in the short term? (Especially since the long-term effect is probable lung cancer.)"

____   3.   "Why does one person define smoking as unhealthy and detrimental while another defines it as cool and sophisticated?"

____   4.   "What might be some unconscious motivations for smoking?"

____   5.   "How does choosing to smoke—or do anything—illustrate the application of free will or choice?"

a.   Behavioral perspective
b.   Physiological perspective
c.   Cognitive perspective
d.   Psychodynamic perspective
e.   Humanistic perspective

CONCEPT 2   Contemporary psychology has a number of major fields of specialization that define both the science and the profession.

2.1   Describe the major crisis faced by the APA today.

2.2   List and describe the major areas of specialization in psychology.

2.3.   Contrast the careers of the practitioner versus the scientist in psychology.

Concept Builder 2

Directions: The following psychologists appear on a popular radio show and briefly state the kinds of things they do professionally. The listener's job (as well as yours) is to guess the specialty of each psychologist.

What's My Line?

1.   "I recently worked on the cockpit of the space shuttle. My job was to make sure the various control knobs and gauges were arranged in the most efficient location for the operator. I am a(n) _____."

2.   "I worked for a large pharmaceutical company. My job was to test drug reactions on selected medical patients and then to make recommendations to my company about its drug products. I am a(n) _____."

3.   "I teach at a large university. One of my major responsibilities is to do research; primarily I use personality tests on subjects and correlate the results with the kinds of career interest they show. I am a(n) _____."

4.   "I consult with the local court system on juvenile offender cases. My job is to compile data on court defendants and their sentences and try to reduce the number of repeat offenders. I am a(n) _____."

5.   "I work in an elementary school district. My job is to work with children who have a variety of learning problems or disabilities. I am a(n) _____."

6.   "I work at a university. My major research is studying how the media, TV in particular, affect the aggression levels of children. I am a(n) _____."

7.   "I research and evaluate employee morale. How might the job setting be more productive? What will reduce employee stress? These are important concerns to me. I am a(n) _____."

8.   "After finishing medical school, I decided I liked working with people's psychological problems more than their physical ills. I became a great therapist! I'm a(n) _____."

9.   "I work at a large corporation in which I screen new applicants as well as recommend others for promotion. It's very meaningful and valuable work to my company. I'm a(n) _____."

10.   "I'm currently working on a research grant through the university. My research focus is racial prejudice in its more subtle forms. My work is both basic science as well as applied knowledge. I'm a(n) _____."

CONCEPT 3

Critical thinking governs the direction of psychology by continuing to raise crucial questions regarding the nature and scope of the discipline. Psychologists are concerned with a wide range of enduring issues that arise in all aspects of the profession.

3.1 Describe the process of critical thinking as it applies to the science of psychology.

3.2 Describe the enduring themes that exist in psychology.

Concept Builder 3

Directions: Read each of the following "debate topics" submitted to Professor Brainbuster for possible discussion in his Introductory Psychology class. Identify the enduring theme in psychology that each represents.

The Great Debates

Debate Topic 1:

Enduring Theme: _____

Problem-solving can occur through dreams and fantasies.   *versus*   Problem-solving requires wakeful attention and alertness.

Debate Topic 2:

Enduring Theme: _____

Human communication has "animal roots."   *versus*   Human communication is a unique quality.

Debate Topic 3:

Enduring Theme: _____

Leaders are "born."   *versus*   Leaders are developed.

Debate Topic 4:

Enduring Theme: _____

Self-concept is self-defined.   *versus*   The self is defined by one's peer group.

Debate Topic 5:

Enduring Theme: _____

No two personalities are alike.   *versus*   Most people can be categorized as a given "type."

**CHAPTER
EXERCISE**

*Directions: Read each of the following definitions below and write the appropriate
terms in the spaces provided. For each answer, insert the letter from the numbered
space into the corresponding space at the top of this exercise. When you are finished, the letters should spell out the title of this book.*

Psychological Acrostics

—— —— —— —— —— —— —— —— —— ——   —— —— —— —— ——
1   2   3   4   5   6   7   8   9   10   11 12 13 14 15

1. Studies the connections between nervous systems and behavior:
    physiological psychology or __ __ __ __ __ __ __ __ __ __ __ __ __
                                              1

2. Examines the relationship between drugs and behavior:
    __ __ __ __ __ __ __ __ __ __ __ __ __ __ __ __
                                                      3

3. Studies all aspects of behavioral development over the life span:
    __ __ __ __ __ __ __ __ __ __ __ __ psychology
                                   11

4. Investigates the relationship between personality and behavior:
    __ __ __ __ __ __ __ __ __ __ psychology
              2

5. Researches the behavior of people in groups:
    __ __ __ __ __ __ psychology
          4

6. Assesses children with learning problems:
    __ __ __ __ __ __ psychology
          5

7. Investigates the psychological aspects of learning:
    __ __ __ __ __ __ __ __ __ psychology
       13

8. Investigates machine-user relationships:
    __ __ __ __ __ __ __ __ __ psychology
                          6

9. Recommends employees for promotion:
    __ __ __ __ __ __ __ __ psychology
                       7

10. Technique in which subjects report their own conscious experience:
    __ __ __ __ __ __ __ __ __ __ __
             8

11. Studies how people react when they are ill:
    __ __ __ __ __ psychology
       14

12. Studies people and their physical settings:
    __ __ __ __ __ __ __ __ __ __ __ psychology
                12

13. Applies psychology to law enforcement:
    forensic __ __ __ __ __ __ __ __
                  15

14. Evaluates the effectiveness of government programs:
    __ __ __ __ __ __ evaluation
             9

15. The study, diagnosis, and treatment of mental disorders:
    clinical __ __ __ __ __ __ __ __
                 10

PRACTICE EXAM 1

1. Wilhelm Wundt is famous for many event(s) in the history of psychology. Which of the following is *not* one of them?

   a. development of the technique of introspection
   b. establishment of the first psychological laboratory
   c. definition of psychology as the study of conscious experience
   d. outline of the elements of classical and operant conditioning

   (Factual, Obj. 1.2)

2. Which of the following statements best captures the definition of psychology?

   a. Psychology explains "why" people do the things they do.
   b. Psychology distinguishes normal from abnormal behavior.
   c. Psychology's focus is mainly on understanding the unconscious.
   d. Psychology studies anything a person does or experiences.

   (Conceptual, Obj. 1.1)

3. Which of the following perspectives represents the "third force" in the field of psychology?

   a. humanistic perspective
   b. psychodynamic perspective
   c. physiological perspective
   d. cognitive perspective

   (Factual, Obj. 1.3)

4. You are talking to a Freudian and he asks you to talk about your dreams. He then says words like "family" and "authority" and asks you to reveal your first thoughts about these words. What is this Freudian getting at?

   a. He's trying to elicit "off the wall" responses.
   b. He's trying to assess some of your unconscious thoughts and motivations.
   c. He's trying to determine your honesty or dishonesty.
   d. He's mapping your conscious thought patterns.

   (Conceptual, Obj. 1.3)

5. Physiological or neuropsychologists attempt to unravel the connections between brain functions and how we actually behave. To which general area does this specialty belong?

   a. forensic psychology
   b. applied psychology
   c. health psychology
   d. experimental psychology

   (Factual, Obj. 2.2)

6. Stanley notices that he does better on tests when he's had two cups of coffee. His teacher suggests he volunteer to be in an experiment that will study the effects of various common drugs (such as caffeine) on test performance. The specialty that would address such a concern is:

   a. behaviorism
   b. educational psychology
   c. psychopharmacology
   d. physiological psychology

   (Conceptual, Obj. 2.2)

7. The main concern of educational and school psychology is:

    a. disciplining techniques
    b. evaluation of students' performance on tests and exams
    c. the aspects and study of learning and learning problems
    d. test-taking skills and study methods

    (Factual, Obj. 2.2)

8. If the auto industry were to hire a psychologist to consult with them on effective ways to arrange dashboard controls for the driver, what kind of psychologist would they ask for?

    a. an applied psychologist
    b. a quantitative psychologist
    c. a program evaluator
    d. a human-factors psychologist

    (Conceptual, Obj. 2.2)

9. Which brand of psychology would most likely study the role of stress in the development of hypertension?

    a. an environmental psychologist
    b. an applied psychologist
    c. a neuroscientist
    d. a health psychologist

    (Factual, Obj. 2.2)

10. If you were a member of Congress concerned with the effectiveness of current job-training programs with the disadvantaged, what kind of psychology book would you have your assistant check out of the library?

    a. a book on industrial psychology
    b. a book on organizational psychology
    c. a book on quantitative psychology
    d. a book on program evaluation

    (Conceptual, Obj. 2.2)

11. As a result of a "crisis" among psychologists, some (but not all) scientific practitioners founded an organization separate from academics, intended to reflect their own special concerns. What is the name of that organization?

    a. American Psychological Association
    b. American Psychological Society
    c. American Medical Association
    d. Centers for Disease Control

    (Factual, Obj. 2.1)

12. "Are girls born without much ability in math or does society generally discourage them from showing interest in math?" This question illustrates best what enduring theme in psychology today?

    a. biological continuity and human uniqueness
    b. nature and nurture
    c. conscious and unconscious experience
    d. individual differences and universal principles

    (Conceptual, Obj. 3.2)

PRACTICE EXAM 2

1. Sigmund Freud pioneered the use of two psychological techniques, dream analysis and:

    a. introspection
    b. biofeedback
    c. free association
    d. experimental analysis

    (Factual, Obj. 1.2)

2. If Wundt were interested in the effects of cocaine on a person's mood level, he might have asked the person to take the drug and then give a detailed account of the changes that were experienced. This method is:

    a. free association
    b. controlled observation
    c. objective data gathering
    d. introspection

    (Conceptual, Obj. 1.2)

3. Which of the following names is out of place if we are talking about behaviorism?

    a. Pavlov
    b. Galton
    c. Watson
    d. Skinner

    (Factual, Obj. 1.3)

4. Skinner has been credited with a radical viewpoint that states, "If you cannot define or operationalize a concept, it has no scientific reality." This is the approach of the:

    a. cognitive psychologists
    b. structuralists
    c. empiricists
    d. functionalists

    (Conceptual, Obj. 1.3)

5. The discipline of psychology that considers the whole life span in its entirety (birth to death) is termed:

    a. social psychology
    b. developmental psychology
    c. personality psychology
    d. basic psychology

    (Factual, Obj. 2.2)

6. The Hartmans' son has been having a difficult time at school, particularly with unstructured classes, like art. It seems that little Allen doesn't have much of an attention span. What kind of psychologist might be able to help Allen?

    a. clinical psychologist
    b. developmental psychologist
    c. educational psychologist
    d. school psychologist

    (Conceptual, Obj. 2.2)

7. Which of the following psychologists would an advertising firm most likely hire to help with studying buyers' preferences?

   a. program evaluator
   b. consumer psychologist
   c. personality psychologist
   d. social psychologist

   (Factual, Obj. 2.2)

8. Jason just lost an important sale to one of his competitors. At first, he was depressed because he felt he hadn't worked hard enough on the account. He then changed his thoughts about the situation by remembering that rejection is part of selling. What perspective in psychology focuses on this aspect of behavior (thinking)?

   a. the psychodynamic perspective
   b. the behavioral perspective
   c. the cognitive perspective
   d. the humanistic perspective

   (Conceptual, Obj. 1.3)

9. If your interests included both psychology and the criminal justice system, which branch of psychology would be most appropriate?

   a. forensic psychology
   b. clinical psychology
   c. environmental psychology
   d. counseling psychology

   (Factual, Obj. 2.2)

10. What kind of psychologist might be likely to get involved in studying the role of stress in the development of cancer or AIDS?

    a. psychopharmacologist
    b. developmental psychologist
    c. forensic psychologist
    d. health psychologist

    (Conceptual, Obj. 2.2)

11. Which of the following is *not* an enduring theme in psychology today?

    a. learning by rewards and by punishment
    b. nature and nurture
    c. conscious and unconscious experience
    d. biological continuity and human uniqueness

    (Factual, Obj. 3.2)

12. If Wilhelm Wundt were alive today and applied to a postgraduate school, to which doctoral-level program would he most likely apply?

    a. Ph.D. in personality psychology
    b. Ph.D. in experimental psychology
    c. M.D. in health psychology
    d. M.D. in behavioral medicine

    (Conceptual, Obj. 2.3)

■ ANSWER KEY ■

Concept 1

1. b
2. a
3. c
4. d
5. e

Concept 2

1. human-factors psychologist
2. psychopharmacologist
3. personality psychologist
4. forensic psychologist
5. school psychologist
6. developmental psychologist
7. industrial/organizational psychologist
8. psychiatrist
9. personnel psychologist
10. social psychologist

Concept 3

1. conscious and unconscious experience
2. biological continuity and human uniqueness
3. nature and nurture
4. the individual society
5. individual differences and universal principles

Chapter Exercise

1. neuropsychology (P)
2. psychopharmacology (Y)
3. developmental (T)
4. personality (S)
5. social (C)
6. school (H)
7. educational (D)
8. human-factors (O)
9. personnel (L)
10. introspection (O)
11. health (A)
12. environmental (O)
13. psychology (Y)
14. program (G)
15. psychology (Y)

Practice Exam 1

1. d, p. 6
2. d, p. 5
3. a, p. 13
4. b, p. 13
5. d, p. 16
6. c, p. 16
7. c, p. 18
8. d, p. 18
9. d, pp. 19–20
10. d, p. 20
11. b, p. 15
12. b, pp. 24–25

Practice Exam 2

1. c, pp. 12–13
2. d, p. 6
3. b, pp. 8–9
4. c, p. 5
5. b, p. 16
6. d, p. 18
7. b, p. 18
8. c, p. 10
9. a, p. 20
10. d, pp. 19–20
11. a, pp. 23–26
12. b, pp. 6, 19

CHAPTER TWO

The Methods of Psychology

KEY TERM ORGANIZER

Psychology uses the *scientific method,* which consists of three steps: observing something of interest; formulating a *hypothesis,* or testable prediction; then collecting data to confirm or refute the hypothesis. The purpose of collecting data is to build a useful *theory.*   Hypotheses are generated and evaluated by three main types of research methods: descriptive studies, correlational research, and experiments.

Major Method	Specific Methods	Primary Use
Experimental		Used to establish a true causal relationship between one set of phenomena and another
Correlational		Used to identify systematic relationships; also to study historical relationships
Descriptive	Naturalistic observations	Used to observe behavior in natural settings without intervening
	Survey	Used to explore the characteristics, attitudes, opinions, or other behaviors of a group of people
	Case study	Used to study a single individual or a select group of individuals

When a group is large, it's impossible to survey all the members, so a *sample* is used. In order to ensure that all characteristics of the group are represented, the sample must be created through *randomization.*

In a *longitudinal study* the same group of subjects is followed over time. In a *cross-sectional study* subjects are divided into subgroups and assessed on one or more variables.

EXPERIMENTAL METHOD

An *experiment* is a method that allows scientists to establish cause and effect. Experiments must meet three requirements in order to demonstrate causality: (1) two events must vary together, called *covariation of events;* (2) a *time-order relationship* must be established; and (3) *confounding variables* must be ruled out.

An experiment explores the relationship between the *independent variable* and the *dependent variable.* It begins by *operationalizing* a *hypothesis.* Then it manipulates what is called the *experimental condition* to test the hypothesis. Experiments also contain a *control condition,* in which a *control group* is exposed to all the same factors as the experimental subjects except the experimental condition. Biases are a problem for experiments, and they must be controlled.

Problem	"Control" Procedure
Handling the independent variable:	
Confounding of the independent variable	Counterbalance
Handling the dependent variable:	
Experimenter effects	Use double-blind study
Handling the subjects:	
Demand characteristics	Keep subjects ignorant of study
Placebo effects	Randomly assign subjects
Establishing equivalent groups	Match subjects

Replication of studies is essential in science. Additionally, psychological research must have *ecological validity,* focusing on processes that occur in real-life environments.

Because psychologists have an ethical obligation to protect the dignity and welfare of the people who participate in research, the American Psychological Association has drawn up a set of ethical principles to guide research. The code sets up several conditions aimed at ensuring subjects' (1) privacy, (2) voluntary participation, (3) informed consent, and (4) freedom from harm. When research cannot ethically be done with humans, it can sometimes be performed on animals.

MAJOR CONCEPTS AND LEARNING OBJECTIVES

CONCEPT 1   Psychologists depend upon the scientific method for the development of theories and the verification of hypotheses.

1.1   Outline and describe the three steps of the scientific method.

1.2   Distinguish theory and hypothesis.

Concept
Builder 1

Directions: Read the following true story of a significant research effort that was begun over two decades ago. At the end of the story, identify the appropriate elements of the scientific process.

Science and the "Real World"

In the mid-sixties, two psychologists were perplexed at a very "odd" social phenomenon. Heinous crimes, such as rape or murder, were sometimes committed in full view of many witnesses, yet *no one* would intervene, come forward and help, or even call the police! The psychologists reasoned that maybe the sheer number of bystanders tended to inhibit any one individual from acting alone, based on the misperception that "someone else" would or should take appropriate action.

The psychologists devised ingenious situations to verify their original hunches by "staging" accidents with various number of bystanders present. Sure enough, the more bystanders, the less likely any one individual was to help. The psychologists explained their findings with a concept they called "diffusion of responsibility."

Step 1: Identify the "observation." _____

Step 2: Identify the "hypothesis." _____

Step 3: Identify the "data collection." _____

Step 4: Identify the "theory." _____

CONCEPT 2   Researchers have a variety of methods available for studying human behavior. Two of these methods are the descriptive and correlational approaches. Each has its advantages and disadvantages.

2.1   Identify and contrast the three types of descriptive research.

2.2   Discuss the advantages and disadvantages of using the descriptive approach.

2.3   Describe the relationships between variables that the correlational method allows researchers to claim.

2.4   Distinguish between a longitudinal and a cross-sectional study and discuss the advantages of each.

Concept Builder 2

Directions: Read the following brief descriptions of proposed studies and match each with the methodology most appropriate to investigate it.

Method of Choice

_____ 1. Study of whether physical attractiveness and popularity are related.

_____ 2. Investigation of how local residents feel about having a horse-racing track in their area.

_____ 3. Study of how children from inner city environments grew up and made their career choices.

_____ 4. Study of people's behavior at a shopping mall with no intervention or attempt to influence their behavior in any way.

_____ 5. Study of how musical genius developed in a retarded child.

_____ 6. Comparative study of how people at various ages score on a standard IQ test.

a. Case study
b. Correlational study
c. Longitudinal study
d. Naturalistic observation
e. Cross-sectional study
f. Survey

CONCEPT 3   The experimental method is the only method that establishes a cause-and-effect relationship. A fairly specific set of procedures must be followed in order to conduct a valid experiment.

3.1 Name and define the three requirements for establishing the cause-and-effect relationship.

3.2 Describe the components of an experimental study and discuss how control conditions are used to eliminate confounding variables.

3.3 Explain why replication of an experiment is so important to scientific research.

**Concept
Builder 3**

Directions: Read the following description of an experiment. Your task is to insert the short descriptions of the experimental procedures used into the blocks in the diagram to show the correct order of events in this experiment.

Anatomy of an Experiment

The author of this study guide decided to conduct an experiment using his class to test the effectiveness of this study guide. He divided his class into two groups by randomly picking names from a computer list. One group was given the study guide to help them prepare for an upcoming test. The other group was not. Both groups could study only during certain designated hours in the classroom. Then both groups were given identical tests on the same material, and yes, the "study-guide" group did much better on the test. This made the experimenter very happy.

Experimental Procedure

a. test scores
b. study guide
c. random assignment
d. study and test conditions (used twice)
e. no study guide
f. control group
g. experimental groups

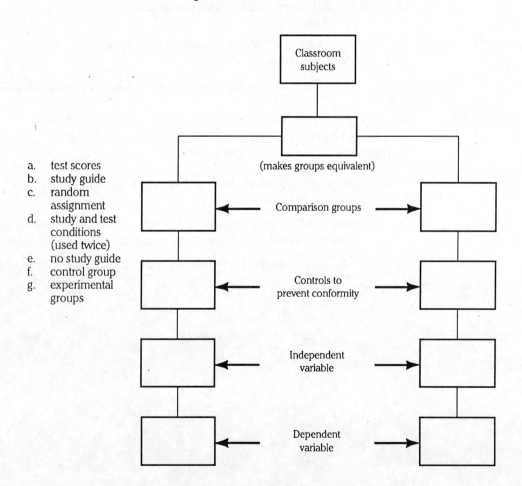

CONCEPT 4   Psychologists have an ethical obligation to protect the dignity and welfare of the people who participate in research. This obligation extends to the welfare of animal subjects as well. The APA monitors ethical standards for the profession.

4.1   Describe the four conditions that must be met in order for a scientific study with human subjects to be considered ethical.

4.2   Discuss the ethical responsibility researchers have to animal subjects.

Concept Builder 4

Directions: You are part of an ethics committee set up to identify potential ethical problems with proposed studies. Below are four situations that call into question an ethical principle. Identify the principle being violated.

Ethics Committee

1.   Experimenters go into an army boot camp and tell the platoon members they are all going to "volunteer" to be in a study on stress and performance.

Principle violated: _____

2.   Heart patients who volunteer to be in a medical study are not told about the possible (though not harmful) side effects of a new experimental drug they will be taking.

Principle violated: _____

3.   The test scores of college seniors who volunteer to take a test of leadership aptitude are secretly turned over to potential employers.

Principle violated: _____

4.   A group of volunteers agree to a physical test of muscular endurance; the test causes most subjects to have muscular cramps, pulls, and some muscle tears.

Principle violated: _____

**CHAPTER
EXERCISE**

"Word Search" Exercise

Directions: Study the following assortment of letters. In this block of letters, you will find certain "key terms." They may be spelled out vertically, diagonally, in reverse, or horizontally. Circle the key term. To help you out, there are some "clues" at the bottom of the word search diagram.

```
E  L  S  U  R  V  E  Y  O  L  U
X  A  A  T  A  A  Y  F  B  I  L
P  C  M  H  R  R  K  A  S  P  U
E  I  P  E  M  I  N  C  E  L  B
R  G  L  O  C  A  S  E  R  O  G
I  O  E  R  E  B  N  T  V  C  A
M  L  A  Y  D  L  W  D  E  K  P
E  O  B  A  D  E  M  A  N  D  T
N  C  O  N  T  R  O  L  D  E  D
T  E  O  A  S  U  C  A  S  T  X
E  H  Y  P  O  T  H  E  S  I  S
R  B  C  A  U  G  Y  E  X  P  T
```

Clues

1.   Intensive study of one individual: _____ study
2.   Compared with the experimental condition: _____ condition
3.   Subjects controlled by the research setting: _____ characteristics
4.   Bias unwittingly introduced by experimenter: _____ effects
5.   Educated "guess": _____
6.   Obtaining information by asking people: _____
7.   Representative selection from a population: _____
8.   Any measurable or observable factor: _____
9.   Fitting known facts into a logical whole: _____
10. "Real world" validity: _____ validity

**PRACTICE
EXAM 1**

1.   In the text's description of an experiment involving the testing of a learning context on classroom performance, the "same classroom" condition was called the
_____ condition.

a.   experimental
b.   control
c.   test
d.   context

(Factual, Obj. 3.2)

2.   Gasoline commercials frequently demonstrate that an additive their company adds to its gasoline helps a car travel farther than a car without the additive. In this case, "distance the car traveled" would be the:

a.   independent variable
b.   dependent variable
c.   control condition
d.   experimental condition

(Conceptual, Obj. 3.2)

3.   The major advantage of counterbalancing is that it allows the experimenter to eliminate:

a.   experimenter effects
b.   demand characteristics
c.   confounding of the independent variable
d.   the placebo effect

(Factual, Obj. 3.2)

4.   When randomization is not possible, there is still another technique available to establish equivalent groups. This technique involves:

a.   counterbalancing
b.   a double-blind procedure
c.   surveying
d.   matching subjects

(Factual, Obj. 3.2)

5.   When two sets of phenomena happen together at a rate that is significantly higher than chance, we say there is a _____ relationship between them.

a.   causal and correlational
b.   correlational and systematic
c.   systematic and hypothetical
d.   hypothetical and causal

(Factual, Obj. 3.1)

6.   To test the effectiveness of their "overcoming shyness" program, one college counseling center gave a new group of volunteers a pre-test on shyness. Then, after eight weeks of social-skill training and confidence building, a post-test was administered to measure the reduction of shyness. This experimental method involves measuring change:

a.   by participant observation
b.   by correlational research
c.   in self-selected groups
d.   by using chronological records

(Conceptual, Obj. 3.1)

7. Surveys cannot question everyone in an identified population about some behavior, attitude, or opinion. Typically, surveyors use a _____ to measure the variability of the whole population.

    a. case study
    b. sample
    c. self-selected group
    d. "matched" group   (Factual, Obj. 2.1)

8. *Sybil* was the true story of a little girl's horrible childhood history of abuse and her later personality disorder called multiple personality. As a piece of research, this information about Sybil would be classified as:

    a. a chronological record
    b. a sample (of one)
    c. a case study
    d. a correlational study   (Conceptual, Obj. 2.1)

9. In the 1930s, a psychologist named Tryon performed an ingenious experiment. He took a litter of genetically identical mice, randomly assigned them to one of two groups: "maze-bright" and "maze-dull." He warned students given the maze-dull mice that the mice would be slow, make many mistakes, and learn poorly. He told students given the maze-bright mice that these mice were fast learners, would make few errors and were alert. After two weeks of maze training, his predictions were dramatically proven: Maze-dull mice did miserably on maze tests; maze-bright mice did great. Tryon concluded that the results had nothing to do with the mice; the students communicated their expectations to the mice in the way they handled the animals and encouraged them. This experiment provides strong evidence for:

    a. demand characteristics
    b. placebo effects
    c. experimenter effects
    d. equivalent groups   (Conceptual, Obj. 3.2)

10. The old *Candid Camera* television series used to say that they filmed people "in the act of being themselves." By observing people in their natural settings without intervening, the method illustrates:

    a. naturalistic observations
    b. a field experiment
    c. a quasi-experiment
    d. participant observation   (Factual, Obj. 2.1)

11. If there is a positive correlation between participating in extracurricular activities and popularity, what does that mean?

    a. Highly popular people also participate in a lot of extracurricular activities.
    b. Participating in extracurricular activities causes people to be more popular through increased exposure.
    c. Unpopular people probably spend more time studying or working, not participating in extracurricular activities.
    d. As popularity increases, participation in extracurricular activities decreases.
                                                                  (Factual, Obj. 2.3)

12. Which of the following was *not* identified as part of the code of ethical principles the APA drew up regarding experimenting with humans?

   a. Participants in an experiment have a right to privacy.
   b. Participants' data may be shared *only* with other scientists.
   c. Participation in an experiment must be voluntary.
   d. No lasting harm should come from participating in an experiment.

                                                          (Factual, Obj. 4.1)

PRACTICE EXAM 2

1. In order for a hypothesis to be a *good* hypothesis, it must be:

   a. interesting
   b. ecologically valid
   c. naturalistic
   d. testable

                                                          (Factual, Obj. 1.2)

2. Which of the following is the major *advantage* that an experiment has over descriptive methods of study?

   a. It is less costly in time and money.
   b. It is easier to conduct.
   c. It yields more accurate correlations.
   d. It permits the experimenter to control the conditions of the study.

                                                          (Factual, Obj. 3.1)

3. In an experiment, the experimenter deliberately manipulates the:

   a. hypothesis
   b. covariation of events
   c. dependent variable
   d. independent variable

                                                          (Factual, Obj. 3.2)

4. "Any measurable or observable factor" is the definition of a(n):

   a. sample
   b. longitudinal research
   c. variable
   d. experimental group

                                                          (Factual, Obj. 2.3)

5. If a researcher gives people a test of achievement and also asks them how much money they make, she is probably conducting a(n):

   a. case study
   b. correlational study
   c. experiment
   d. naturalistic observation

                                                       (Conceptual, Obj. 2.1)

6. To find out how many incoming college freshmen were planning on taking quantum physics, one would probably use the research method of:

   a. longitudinal study
   b. cross-sectional study

c.   survey
d.   case study

(Conceptual, Obj. 2.1)

7.   If a correlational experiment were conducted on the amount of urban noise and the number of stress-related illnesses and a systematic relationship was uncovered, what would that mean?

a.   Noise causes a high number of stress-related illnesses.
b.   Eliminating noise would eliminate stress-related illnesses.
c.   Stress-related illness is caused primarily by noise in the environment.
d.   Urban noise and stress-related illness happen together at a rate higher than by chance.

(Conceptual, Obj. 2.3)

8.   Clinical psychologists often collect transcribed conversations with clients in order to help reveal particular personality problems. This technique is similar to a(n):

a.   survey
b.   experiment
c.   correlational research
d.   case study

(Conceptual, Obj. 2.1)

9.   Dr. Demento measured the nutritional "attitudes" of men when they were ten, eighteen, thirty-five and sixty years of age by interviewing a sample of men in each age category. He is conducting a(n):

a.   experiment
b.   longitudinal study
c.   correlational study
d.   cross-sectional study

(Conceptual, Obj. 2.4)

10. Which of the following illustrates the *strongest* relationship between two variables:

a.   + .63
b.   + .09
c.   − .89
d.   − .27

(Conceptual, Obj. 2.3)

11. Which of the following expresses a correlation coefficient showing that two variables are *unrelated*?

a.   + 1.0
b.   0
c.   − 1.0
d.   −.5 or +.5

(Factual, Obj. 2.3)

12. A replication would most likely consist of a study:

a.   very similar to the original study
b.   using the same subjects to test a new hypothesis
c.   expanding the conclusions of the first experimenter
d.   aimed at criticizing the experimental methods used by the first experimenter

(Factual, Obj. 3.3)

■ ANSWER KEY ■

Concept 1   Step 1:   Crimes being committed with no intervention from bystanders;
                       Step 2:   Number of bystanders may inhibit any one individual from acting;
                       Step 3:   "Staging" a number of "accidents" and recording which and how
                                   many bystanders help;
                       Theory: Diffusion of responsibility

Concept 2   1. b   4. d
                       2. f   5. a
                       3. c   6. e

Concept 3

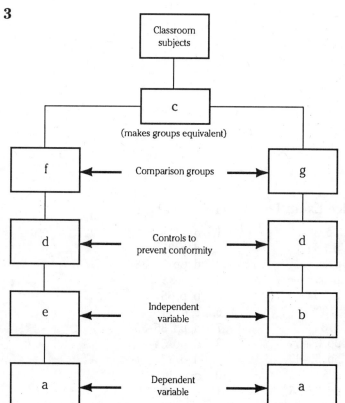

a. test scores
    (used twice)

b. study guide

c. random assignment

d. study and test conditions
    (used twice)

e. no study guide

f. control group

g. experimental groups

Concept 4   1. voluntary participation   3. privacy
                       2. informed consent   4. harm (physical)

**Chapter
Exercise**

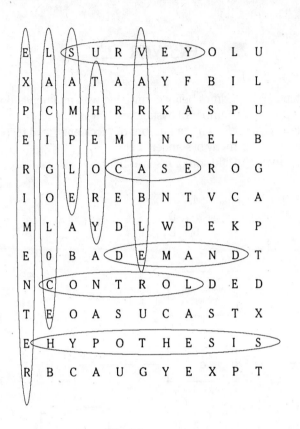

Clues:

1. case
2. control
3. demand
4. experimenter
5. hypothesis
6. survey
7. sample
8. variable
9. theory
10. ecological

Practice Exam 1

1. b, pp. 38–39
2. b, p. 38
3. c, p. 39
4. d, p. 39
5. b, p. 35
6. c, p. 39
7. b, p. 34
8. c, pp. 34–35
9. c, pp. 39–40
10. a, p. 33
11. a, pp. 35–36
12. b, pp. 41–42

Practice Exam 2

1. d, p. 30
2. d, p. 37
3. d, pp. 37–38
4. c, p. 35
5. b, p. 35
6. c, p. 34
7. d, pp. 35–36
8. d, pp. 34–35
9. d, p. 37
10. c, p. 36
11. b, p. 36
12. a, p. 40

CRITICAL THINKING ESSAY 1

Evaluating the Evidence Psychologists Give Us

Critical thinking is a process that allows us to better understand and evaluate the information we receive. In the context of psychology, critical thinking involves examining the processes involved in psychological research, assessing the various perspectives from which researchers may approach a problem, and evaluating the theoretical inferences that researchers derive from their findings. In other words, critical thinking enables us to be better judges of the quality of research studies, the approaches to research problems, and the conclusions researchers draw. This essay concentrates on the first of these aspects of critical thinking in psychology: evaluating the quality of empirical research.

Suppose the following newspaper headline catches your attention: "Psychologists Discover Miraculous New Treatment for Depression." The article reports the results of a study by two clinical psychologists at State University, Dr. X and Dr. Y, who proposed that depressed patients could be helped by listening to upbeat tunes. The researchers instructed fifty of their depressed outpatients to listen to—and sing along with—favorite songs from their childhood and adolescence. The patients compiled lists of twenty-five songs they had enjoyed, and sang along with recordings of these tunes for three hours each day, five days a week, for an average of three months. Afterward, the patients were assessed for their level of depression through questionnaires and clinical interviews. Doctors X and Y reported that their so-called Music Therapy prompted a majority of the patients to experience a statistically significant reduction in their level of depression. The newspaper article's snappy conclusion: "For some, the answer to depression may be to sing the blues away."

Depression remains the second most common psychiatric disorder among inpatients and the most common complaint among outpatients (Woodruff, Clayton, and Guze, 1975; American Psychological Association, 1987). From various studies in Europe and the United States, it is estimated that between 8 and 12 percent of men and between 18 and 23 percent of women will experience a depressive episode at some time in their lives. Certainly, then, depression is an important research topic. The proposed Music Therapy seems to promise relatively inexpensive, fast, and easy relief for many depressed people. But before this therapy is accepted (i.e., before federal grants are awarded, therapists are trained, and patients are treated), we need to know whether this therapy is truly effective. What information would help us critically evaluate the quality of this research?

Critical evaluation of a research procedure involves examining a number of factors: the qualifications of the researchers, the avoidance of experimental biases and confounding variables, the choice of appropriate samples, the generalizability of the findings, the significance of the results, and the extent of independent replication. Let's look at each of these factors in connection with the Music Therapy of Drs. X and Y.

THE QUALIFICATIONS OF THE RESEARCHERS

First, we would want to know whether the researchers are legitimate. A few researchers have been caught stealing, misrepresenting, or outright faking their results. These occurrences are quite rare, though, and without any indications to the contrary, we must assume that Drs. X and Y have the training and credentials required to qualify them to conduct this research. We must also assume that Drs. X and Y are not reporting fraudulent or fabricated data.

EXPERIMENTAL BIASES AND CONFOUNDING VARIABLES

Next, our critical analysis turns to the procedure itself—that is, to what the researchers actually did. According to the article, fifty depressed patients received music therapy and improved. The first thing we want to know is whether the patients reacted to the therapy itself or to some other aspect of the procedure. For example, simply getting attention from a therapist may have lessened the patients' depression. After all, the patients knew they were depressed, they knew they were in a clinic, and they knew they were being treated—so naturally they expected to get better. Such *confounding* could have been avoided by using an *attention control group:* subjects who received the same procedure as the treatment group except for the crucial element (in this case, music). In our example, half of the depressed patients might have been instructed to read magazines for three hours a day.

It is important to know who treated the fifty depressed patients. If Dr. X and Dr. Y did it themselves, they would have known what they expected from the procedure and might have unintentionally conveyed their expectations to the patients. To avoid this *experimenter bias,* the therapists would have had to remain unaware of the precise hypotheses of the study. But this is often difficult in practice, especially in clinical trials. After all, it is rare for a therapist to be trained in providing therapy without knowing what that therapy is supposed to do.

It would also be important for the subjects not to know the hypotheses of the study. If they had known, they might have behaved in ways they believed they *should* behave instead of behaving naturally. Like experimenter bias, these *demand characteristics* are difficult to avoid in clinical trials.

One method of avoiding demand characteristics is to assign some patients to have the therapy being studied (the *treatment group*)

and others to have some other, ineffective procedure (the *control group*). In Dr. X and Dr. Y's study neither the therapists nor the subjects should have known who was in which group. In this way, both groups should have had equal expectations, but only those who received the music therapy really should have improved. This *double-blind* procedure helps ensure that the biases of the therapists and the patients do not influence the results. Recently psychologists have considered control groups (and if possible, attention control groups) as required components of valid research designs (see Smith and Glass, 1977; Landman and Dawes, 1982).

CHOOSING APPROPRIATE SAMPLES

Who was chosen for the treatment group, and who was assigned to the control group? Basing this choice on any characteristics of the subjects themselves would make it difficult to determine whether the treatment had any effect. For instance, if the least depressed patients received the treatment, they might have shown more improvement just because they were less depressed to start with. Conversely, if the most depressed patients were picked, they might have shown little improvement—even if the treatment would really be effective for most people. *Random assignment* should be the basis for forming the treatment and control groups.

At a broader level, we must ask who was allowed to participate in the study. In this study, subjects were outpatients at the State University Medical Center. If these subjects were unusual in any way (such as because of their sex, age, occupation, or ability to take time off from work), this sample may not reflect the characteristics of outpatients as a whole (Widom, 1988). Similarly, researchers must be careful to note who volunteers for their studies. Outpatients who refuse to participate in research may differ from those who do in important ways (Frank, Shulberg, and Welsh, 1985). The researchers must be careful to choose a *random sample* of patients for the study. Of course, there are practical limits as to how random any sample can truly be.

GENERALIZABILITY AND "SAMPLES OF CONVENIENCE"

Only depressed outpatients participated in the study, yet Drs. X and Y implied that *all* depressed people would benefit from Music Therapy. This may be true, but these researchers really cannot make this claim, because they have not studied depressed *in*patients or patients in other clinics or mildly depressed people who have not sought therapy. Obviously it is difficult and costly to test samples of these groups, but without doing so, Drs. X and Y really cannot generalize their findings to these people.

Sometimes researchers use subjects drawn from available and/or captive pools—often students in introductory psychology courses. Samples that are chosen because the researcher has ready access to them, *not* because they are theoretically relevant, are called *samples of convenience.* Although the use of samples of convenience is probably unavoidable, we must remember that the effects of a treatment can be *generalized* only to people in the population who are similar to those included in the study.

STATISTICAL SIGNIFICANCE

Doctors X and Y reported that their Music Therapy resulted in a "statistically significant" reduction in their patients' level of depression. What did they mean by this? In psychology, the term *statistically significant* simply means that the observed effect is *unlikely to have happened by chance.* It does not mean that the effect is large or even meaningful; some "significant" effects are very small, and others have no theoretical importance whatsoever. It is easy to confuse "significant" with "important"; many psychologists do, either purposely or unwittingly (Smith, 1983). When you read about the results of a study, always try to determine whether the results are *important* as well as "significant."

INDEPENDENT REPLICATION

Even if Drs. X and Y followed the guidelines outlined here, we still would not know whether their results were genuine. Perhaps their findings were just a fluke, or perhaps some personal quality of these particular therapists treating these particular patients in this particular laboratory was responsible for these results. Other researchers in other labs must run similar studies in order to verify the original findings—a process known as *independent replication.* Although many studies are intriguing in their own right, the theories they claim to support should be accepted only after they have stood the test of close scrutiny by others.

To sum up, then, the quality of psychological research is judged by fairly stringent criteria. Not only must a study be well thought out and well executed, it must also be carefully controlled and free of biases and confounding variables. Within practical limits, the study must employ an appropriate randomly chosen sample. Finally, the findings must be theoretically important and repeatable. By keeping these criteria in mind, you can better judge the quality of the research studies that you will read about in the text chapters and the critical thinking essays that follow.

In addition to evaluating the quality of various research studies, the critical thinking essays that follow the remaining six units of this book will focus on the different approaches that psychologists in various fields take in examining a problem and on the conclusions that they draw from their findings. It is our hope that by employing these three aspects of critical thinking—evaluating empirical processes, comparing different approaches, and analyzing researchers' inferences—you will achieve a better understanding of psychological research and the empirical process.

REFERENCES

Frank, R. G., H. C. Schulberg, and W. P. Welch. Research selection bias and the prevalence of depressive disorders in psychiatric facilities. *Journal of Consulting and Clinical Psychology,* 1985, *53,* 370–376.

Landman, J. T. L., and R. M. Dawes, Psychotherapy outcome: Smith and Glass' conclusions stand up under scrutiny. *American Psychologist,* 1982, *37,* 504–516.

Smith, K. Tests of significance: Some frequent misunderstandings. *American Journal of Orthopsychiatry,* 1983, *53,* 315–321.

Widom, C. S. Sampling biases and implications for child abuse research. *American Journal of Orthopsychiatry,* 1988, *58,* 260–270.

Woodruff, R. A., P. J. Clayton, and S. B. Guze. Is everyone depressed? *American Journal of Psychiatry,* 1975, *132,* 627–628.

RESPONDING TO CRITICAL ESSAY 1

1. Sherlock Holmes once offered, "Whenever you eliminate the impossible, whatever remains, however improbable, must be the truth." Holmes was a master detective, of course, and relied on his deductive powers to solve crimes.

   Describe and elaborate the similarities between the scientific method and Holmes' deductive calculation.

2. Medical historians have noted that the history of medicine is a history of placebos (inert medications that "work" even though there is no known medical basis for their effectiveness; a "sugar pill").

   What similarities do you see between the apparent therapeutic effects of placebos and demand characteristics?

3. Most experimenters employ some form of deception, such as a phony "cover story," in order to avoid complications that arise when subjects do know the true intent of a research study.

   Should psychologists lie to their subjects?

CHAPTER THREE

The Brain and Behavior

KEY TERM ORGANIZER

The nervous system can be divided into two major communication networks: the *central nervous system*, which includes the *brain* and *spinal cord*, and the *peripheral nervous system*, which contains *ganglia* (collection of nerve cell bodies) and *nerves* (fiber bundles). Each of these systems is further subdivided:

CENTRAL NERVOUS SYSTEM (CNS)		PERIPHERAL NERVOUS SYSTEM (PNS)	
Spinal Cord	**Brain**	**Somatic**	**Autonomic**
Primary communications link to the outside world; brain's link to the peripheral nervous system; processes *reflex responses*.	Regulates all behavior.	Senses and acts upon the external world; voluntary control.	Regulates the internal environment; involuntary control.

	Sympathetic	**Parasympathetic**
	Dominates in emergency situations.	Dominates in relaxed situations.

The basic unit of the nervous system is the *neuron*, or nerve cell. *Glial cells* surround nerve cells, providing them with nutrients and providing a structural foundation. Some glial cells form a *myelin sheath*, a fatty covering around part of the neurons.

There are some 200 different kinds of neurons; they are classed as *sensory neurons, motor neurons,* or *interneurons.* All three types of neurons operate in a complex electrochemical manner; the chain of communication is as follows: *dendrites—cell body—axon—terminal buttons—synapse.* A *nerve impulse* is passed when a neuron's *resting potential* is changed electrically to its *action potential.* Neurons fire according to the *all-or-nothing law.* The receiving side of a synapse produces an electrical reaction called a *postsynaptic potential.*

The neuron's electrical charges are supplied by particles called *ions.* Neurons communicate with other neurons by releasing chemical substances, known as *neurotransmitters,* across the *synaptic clef.* These include:

Acetylcholine: conveys messages to muscles; affects learning.
Epinephrine: catecholamine, boosts alertness and arousal.
Norepinephrine: catecholamine involved with learning, memory, and emotion.
Dopamine: catecholamine involved with fine motor control.
Serotonin: involved in mood and emotion.
GABA: major CNS inhibitory transmitter.

The brain's basic structures, along with associated psychological functions, are summarized below.

Brain Region	Anatomical Structures	Brain Function
Lower brain regions	Brain stem (medulla, pons, reticular activating system)	Vital functions, such as breathing, circulation, consciousness.
	Cerebellum	Posture, movement, balance, fine motor control.
Central brain structures	Hypothalamus (including the suprachiasmatic nucleus)	Motivation and emotion; maintains homeostasis; controls *Circadian rhythms.*
	Limbic system	Emotions, species-specific behavior
	Amygdala	Regulates fear, anger and aggression.
	Hippocampus	Memory and emotion.
	Septum	Aggression, pleasure centers
Upper brain regions	Cerebrum (including cerebral hemispheres, corpus callosum)	Thinking, reasoning, planning, remembering
	Thalamus	Brain's "relay station."

The outer covering of the brain, the *cortex,* is divided into regions called *lobes.* Moving our bodies and detecting stimuli are handled by the *motor and sensory areas.* The *association areas* carry out most of the "higher" psychological functions. The basic pattern of brain organization is *contralateral control.*

Several areas of the brain receive sensory input. The *somatosensory cortex* is the major receiving area for skin sensations. The *visual cortex* is the primary region for receiving and initially analyzing visual information. The *auditory cortex* carries out the initial perception of sounds.

Research with split-brain patients has revealed that the two sides of the brain process different kinds of information and perform different tasks, a phenomenon known as *brain lateralization* or *hemispheric specialization.* In most people, the left side of the brain is specialized for language and the right side for visual and spatial perception and the processing of music and nonspeech sounds.

The *endocrine system* comprises the glands that secrete chemical messengers known as *hormones.* The *pituitary gland* is the "master gland" of the body.

MAJOR CONCEPTS AND LEARNING OBJECTIVES

CONCEPT 1   The nervous system is the ultimate control center for all behavior. The nervous system is divided into two major areas: the central nervous system (CNS) and the peripheral nervous system (PNS).

1.1   Outline the divisions of the nervous system and identify its major parts and functions.

1.2   Describe the autonomic nervous system and contrast the actions of the sympathetic and parasympathetic nervous systems.

Concept Builder 1

Directions: Below is an "organizational" chart of the nervous system and a list of the specific functions of each of its divisions. Match each function with the appropriate nervous system component. (Nervous system, for example, is "e.")

Mapping the Nervous System

a.   Dominates in relaxed situations.

b.   Primary communication link to the outside world.

c.   Controls involuntary functions.

d.   Transmits and stores information.

e.   Communication network among all body cells.

f.   Dominates in emergency situations.

g.   Consists of billions of neurons.

h.   Senses and acts upon the external world.

i.   Consists of nerves and ganglia.

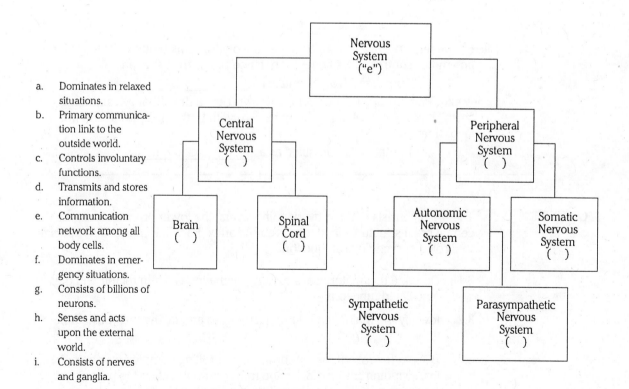

CONCEPT 2   The basic units of the nervous system are neurons, cells specifically adapted to transmit signals by means of electrochemical impulses.

2.1   Identify the parts of the neuron and describe their functions.

2.2   Describe the resting and action potentials of neurons and discuss the role of electrical signals in neuronal communication.

2.3   Name several neurotransmitters and describe how they contribute to the communication of the neuron's signal.

Concept Builder 2

Directions: The time is the year 2010; the place, a high-tech sports complex, stocked with the latest juice-drink machines that have synthetic neurochemical additives. Read what the following sports stars drink and identify the active neurotransmitter that gives each athlete the desired effect.

Better Living through Neurochemistry

1.   John Madashell, a tennis star, drinks "Chill-Out," a drink that helps keep his mood and emotions even. (He's known to throw temper tantrums.)
"Chill-Out" contains _____ .

2.   Rocky, a boxer, drinks a can of "Countdown," a drink that contains a catecholamine that boosts his alertness, arousal, and ability to throw his famous "jaw-breaker" punch.
"Countdown" contains _____ .

3.   Elton Wonder, a pianist, drinks "Ebony and Ivory," a drink that greatly helps his fine motor control so his fingers can dance across the keyboard.
"Ebony and Ivory" contains _____ .

4.   "Beefcake" Bart, a body-builder, drinks "Pump-Up," a drink that gives him a good "rush" before competition. It supplies him with both epinephrine and norepinephrine.
"Pump-Up" is classified as a _____ .

CONCEPT 3   The brain consists of three overlapping layers: the lower brain regions, the central brain structures, and the cerebral cortex. Each part has a fairly specialized role in psychological functioning.

3.1   Describe the anatomical structures of the lower brain region and their associated functions.

3.2   Identify the major central brain structures and define their basic functions.

3.3   Discuss the role of the cerebrum in controlling complex human behavior, including sensory input and motor output; define the primary functions associated with the four major lobes.

3.4   Discuss how various brain areas coordinate in the performance of higher cognitive functions.

**Concept
Builder 3**

*Directions: Unfortunately, there was a mix-up in radiology—
a number of cranial scans made on head-injury patients got
all mixed up in the laboratory. Pathology had interpreted
each area of damage, but the patients' names and symptoms
got separated from the films. Your job is to match up patient
symptoms with the correct x-ray.*

Mix-up in Radiology

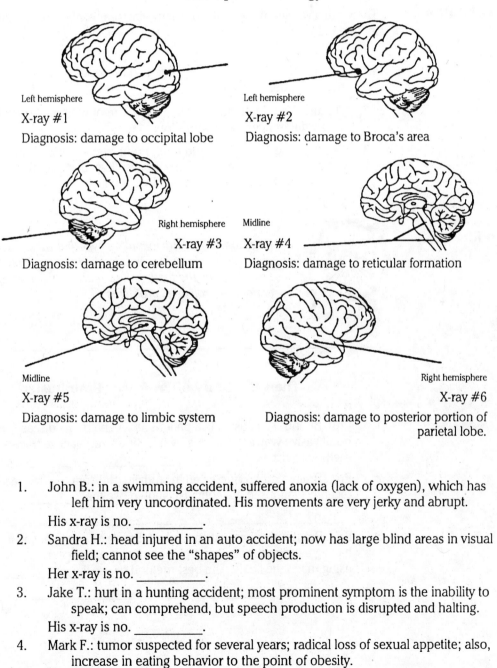

Left hemisphere

X-ray #1

Diagnosis: damage to occipital lobe

Left hemisphere

X-ray #2

Diagnosis: damage to Broca's area

Right hemisphere

X-ray #3

Diagnosis: damage to cerebellum

Midline

X-ray #4

Diagnosis: damage to reticular formation

Midline

X-ray #5

Diagnosis: damage to limbic system

Right hemisphere

X-ray #6

Diagnosis: damage to posterior portion of
parietal lobe.

1. John B.: in a swimming accident, suffered anoxia (lack of oxygen), which has
    left him very uncoordinated. His movements are very jerky and abrupt.
    His x-ray is no. _____.

2. Sandra H.: head injured in an auto accident; now has large blind areas in visual
    field; cannot see the "shapes" of objects.
    Her x-ray is no. _____.

3. Jake T.: hurt in a hunting accident; most prominent symptom is the inability to
    speak; can comprehend, but speech production is disrupted and halting.
    His x-ray is no. _____.

4. Mark F.: tumor suspected for several years; radical loss of sexual appetite; also,
    increase in eating behavior to the point of obesity.
    His x-ray is no. _____.

5. Loren W.: assault victim; beating about head and neck resulted in her becoming comatose; doesn't respond to any sensory stimulation.
    Her x-ray is no. _____.

6. Homer S.: stroke victim; cannot recognize objects by touch, even familiar objects, like keys.
    His x-ray is no. _____.

CONCEPT 4   There are a variety of methods to study living brains of both normal and injured individuals.

4.1 Describe the split-brain technique and the kinds of tasks split-brain patients can demonstrate.

4.2 Discuss the primary functions of each side of the brain as well as individual differences in lateralization.

4.3 Describe the techniques and equipment used to study and map the brain and distinguish the different physiological structures or processes observed with CT scan, MRI, and PET scan.

Concept Builder 4

Directions: Read the following hypothetical scenarios involving Professor Brainbuster, a leading neuroscientist of our time. Indicate the method he should use to investigate various neurological problems.

The Laboratory of Professor Brainbuster

1. Prof. Brainbuster suspects a patient has Alzheimer's disease. The only noninvasive way to study it is by injecting a radioactive tracer. The best method to use is _____.

2. Prof. Brainbuster is interested in studying the "brain wave" activity of a recently diagnosed epileptic. He should use the _____

    _____.

3. Prof. Brainbuster has just studied a CT scan of a patient suspected of having a brain tumor. This type of tumor can be accurately pinpointed using magnetic fields. The best method to use is _____

    _____.

CONCEPT 5   The endocrine system is closely allied with the nervous system.

5.1   Describe how the endocrine system works and how it is different from the nervous system; describe the role of hormones in behavior.

Concept Builder 5

Directions: Read the following entries in the chart below and indicate, by checking, whether the characteristic is more like a hormone, a neurotransmitter, or both.

Hormones and Neurotransmitters—Alike *and* Different

	Characteristic of hormones	Characteristic of neurotransmitters	Characteristic of both
1. Norepinephrine			
2. "Communication is swift"			
3. Works in a "lock-and-key" fashion			
4. Carried by the bloodstream			
5. Has a sustained influence			
6. Slow, but thorough, action			
7. Primarily electrical in nature			

CHAPTER EXERCISE

Directions: For each of the concepts in this chapter, there are a number of definitions on the left side of this page, with terms on the right side. Your task is to match each definition to the appropriate concept and enter the corresponding letter in the space provided. When you have finished, the letters in the left-hand column, read downward, should spell two important fields of study.

Brain Teaser Matchup

Concept 1: Major Divisions

____ 1. Neurons along spinal column
____ 2. Dominates in relaxed situations.
____ 3. Activity as being under voluntary control; acts on external world.
____ 4. Dominates in stressful situations.
____ 5. Links peripheral nervous system.

S. Sympathetic nervous system
H. Parasympathetic nervous system
P. Ganglia
Y. Somatic nervous system
I. Spinal cord

Concept 2: Neurons

____ 1. Gaps between neurons.
____ 2. Curare prevents this from acting.
____ 3. Neurotransmitters operate at these sites.
____ 4. Neurons, connecting one neuron to another.
____ 5. Initiates process of sensations.

O. Synapses (used twice)
L. Acetylcholine
Y. Sensory neurons
G. Interneurons

Concept 4: Brain Study Methodology

____ 1. Measures brain's magnetic fields.
____ 2. Good at diagnosing Alzheimer's.
____ 3. X-ray source moved in circular path around head.

D. CT scan
A. MRI
N. PET scan

Concept 3: Brain Structures

____ 1. Perception of sounds carried out here.
____ 2. Connects two hemispheres.
____ 3. Involved in "pleasure" centers.
____ 4. Regulates voluntary movements (frontal lobe).
____ 5. Wernicke discovered that damage here produces this disturbance.
____ 6. Operates on a homeostatic principle.
____ 7. Three fourths of cortex surface.

S. Corpus callosum
Y. Limbic system
H. Aphasia
O. Hypothalamus
P. Auditory cortex
C. Motor cortex
L. Association areas

Concept 5: Endocrine System

____ 1. "Master gland"
____ 2. "Chemical messengers"
____ 3. Collection of glands

G. Hormones
Y. Endocrine system
O. Pituitary gland

**PRACTICE
EXAM 1**

1.   Your text stated that the brain might be thought of as the "master control center."
     What structure functions as the "link" to the peripheral nervous system?

     a.   motor neurons
     b.   autonomic nervous system
     c.   cerebrum
     d.   spinal cord

                                                                    (Factual, Obj. 1.1)

2.   When Daniel was jogging down a normally quiet street, an unleashed dog ran up to
     him very suddenly, snarling and scaring the wits out of him. It's safe to say that his
     _____ nervous system was fully stimulated at that moment.

     a.   parasympathetic
     b.   somatic
     c.   sympathetic
     d.   peripheral

                                                                 (Conceptual, Obj. 1.2)

3.   The "receiving" sides of synapses are on what part of the neuron?

     a.   the axon
     b.   the dendrites
     c.   the myelin sheath
     d.   the cell body

                                                                    (Factual, Obj. 2.1)

4.   Which of the following makes the best analogy for how a neuronal network operates?

     a.   a digital computer
     b.   a series of computer "chips"
     c.   an electrochemical reaction
     d.   a solid-state circuit board

                                                                 (Conceptual, Obj. 2.2)

5.   It has been discovered that catecholamines play a role in Parkinson's disease. Which
     neurotransmitter seems to play a key role?

     a.   acetylcholine
     b.   epinephrine
     c.   norepinephrine
     d.   dopamine

                                                                    (Factual, Obj. 2.3)

6.   The "Craniops" are alien creatures from the planet Zenon. Craniops have a nervous
     system remarkably similar to that of humans, except for a very lopsided head. The
     right halves of their brains (and craniums) show abnormal enlargement. We would
     expect Craniops to excel in all of the following activities but one. Which one?

     a.   musical ability
     b.   visual arts
     c.   speech-giving
     d.   acting

                                                                 (Conceptual, Obj. 4.2)

7. Olds and Milner discovered that rats would perform a great deal of work in order to have electrical stimulation delivered through implanted electrodes in their "pleasure pathways." These pleasure centers are located in the:

    a. lower brain regions
    b. reticular formation
    c. pons
    d. limbic system

    (Factual, Obj. 3.2)

8. What is the best analogy for how hormones work at their receptor sites?

    a. an electrical "spark" that flips a switch
    b. dominoes knocking one another down
    c. runners running a relay race
    d. lock and key

    (Conceptual, Obj. 5.1)

9. The nervous system and the endocrine system work as complementary "partners." For example, the pituitary ("master gland") is regulated by what brain structure?

    a. the hypothalamus
    b. the amygdala
    c. the prefrontal cortex
    d. the medulla

    (Factual, Obj. 5.1)

10. If you were treating someone showing signs of botulism, what neurotransmitter would you quickly dispense from the pharmacy?

    a. dopamine
    b. GABA
    c. acetylcholine
    d. norepinephrine

    (Conceptual, Obj. 2.3)

11. Which of the following mechanisms in a house's structure operates very similarly to the way the hypothalamus functions in the nervous system?

    a. the electrical panel/fuse box
    b. the overflow valve of the water heater
    c. the thermostat
    d. the smoke alarm

    (Conceptual, Obj. 3.2)

12. Some Russian scientists claim that a kind of photography, called Kirlian photography, can capture the "electromagnetic" field surrounding living tissue. Which of the modern "imaging" techniques would the Russian scientists be most interested in?

    a. the CT scan
    b. the PET scan
    c. the MRI scan
    d. the EEG

    (Conceptual, Obj. 4.3)

**PRACTICE
EXAM 2**

1. Some modern procedures allow sufferers of migraine headaches to consciously control their own cerebral blood flow. How can this autonomic function (blood supply) be accomplished?

    a. through the aid of additional neurotransmitters
    b. by having a split-brain procedure performed
    c. by using PET scanning or CT scanning
    d. by using biofeedback procedures

    (Conceptual, Obj. 1.2)

2. When a nerve cell membrane is altered so as to make an action potential more likely (excitatory), what happens on a molecular level?

    a. Potassium ions are "shut" out of the membrane.
    b. Sodium ions can rush in through a more permeable membrane.
    c. Receptor sites become difficult to find, thus "binding" cannot take place.
    d. An outflow of potassium ions is increased because of increased membrane permeability.

    (Conceptual, Obj. 2.2)

3. Vic was involved in an auto accident and bumped the left side of his head very hard. Oddly enough, the emergency room physician was asking him about motor and sensory functions on the *right* side of his body. Why?

    a. Since the left side of the brain houses language, he wanted to see if Vic could talk coherently.
    b. The basic brain organization is contralateral in control.
    c. The physician feared a "split-brain" injury might have occurred.
    d. The physician was in error; he should have been asking about the patient's left-side capabilities.

    (Conceptual, Obj. 4.2)

4. Which of the following statements about brain lateralization is false?

    a. Left-hemisphere stroke victims are more likely to feel despondent than right-hemisphere patients.
    b. Thirty percent of left-handed people do not have their speech localized in the left hemisphere.
    c. Trained musicians process information exclusively in their right hemisphere.
    d. The female brain seems to be organized more bilaterally than the male brain.

    (Factual, Obj. 4.2)

5. The "imaging" technique that requires the use of a radioactive tracer substance is:

    a. the CT scan
    b. the PET scan
    c. the MRI scan
    d. the x-ray scan

    (Factual, Obj. 4.3)

6. Which of the following is *not* a response of the sympathetic nervous system?

    a. increased heart rate
    b. enhanced digestion
    c. increased blood-sugar level
    d. increased blood pressure

    (Factual, Obj. 1.2)

7. If a neuron is likened to an electrical wire, what part does the myelin sheath function as?

    a. the plug
    b. the insulation
    c. the copper wires
    d. the electrical outlet

                                                            (Conceptual, Obj. 2.1)

8. When a neurotransmitter effects an inhibitory connection, the electrical charge:

    a. is increased
    b. is decreased
    c. remains at resting rate
    d. is magnified

                                                            (Factual, Obj. 2.2)

9. June is a stunt woman for a popular TV series; she had a serious head injury while filming a project. She's recovered fully but has a definite intellectual deficit. Her stunts require split-second timing and executing a plan precisely in a prearranged order, but she can no longer do this. She is too easily distracted and gets "off track" very easily. Her brain damage is probably in:

    a. the temporal lobe
    b. Broca's area
    c. the prefrontal lobe
    d. the parietal lobe

                                                            (Conceptual, Obj. 3.4)

10. The corpus callosum is a bundle of neural fibers that connects:

    a. the thalamus and hypothalamus
    b. the cerebellum to the brain stem
    c. the cerebral hemispheres
    d. the lower brain to the limbic system

                                                            (Factual, Obj. 4.1)

11. The dog pound told Mr. Bateman that his vicious and very aggressive pit bulldog would either have to be impounded permanently for its attacks on pedestrians or undergo a brain operation to make it more docile and calm. The likely target area in the brain for such an operation is probably the:

    a. corpus callosum
    b. motor cortex
    c. limbic system
    d. midbrain

                                                            (Conceptual, Obj. 3.2)

12. The "relay station" of the brain's central core is the _____; it sorts information from the sensory receptors and routes it to appropriate higher brain centers.

    a. thalamus
    b. reticular formation
    c. medulla
    d. hypothalamus

                                                            (Factual, Obj. 3.3)

■ ANSWER KEY ■

Concept 1

Nervous system ("e")   Autonomic nervous system ("c")
Central nervous system ("d")   Somatic nervous system ("h")
Peripheral nervous system ("i")   Sympathetic nervous system ("f")
Brain ("g")   Parasympathetic nervous system ("a")
Spinal cord ("b")

Concept 2

1. Epinephrine   3. Dopamine
2. Serotonin   4. Catecholamines

Concept 3

John B. - no. 3   Mark F. - no. 5
Sandra H. - no. 1   Loren W. - no. 4
Jake T. - no. 2   Homer S. - no. 6

Concept 4

1. PET scan
2. EEG
3. MRI

Concept 5

Characteristics of hormones: 4, 5, 6
Characteristics of neurotransmitters: 2, 7
Characteristics of both: 1, 3

Chapter Exercise

The letters should vertically spell P H Y S I O L O G Y and P S Y C H O L O G Y

Practice Exam 1	**Practice Exam 2**
1. d, p. 49	1. d, p. 50
2. c, p. 50	2. b, pp. 52–53
3. b, p. 52	3. b, p. 64
4. c, pp. 52–53	4. c, pp. 68–70
5. d, p. 56	5. b, pp. 73–74
6. c, pp. 62, 69–70	6. b, p. 50
7. d, pp. 61–62	7. b, p. 50
8. d, p. 75	8. b, p. 55
9. a, p. 75	9. c, pp. 63–64
10. c, pp. 55–56	10. c, p. 62
11. c, p. 59	11. c, p. 60
12. c, p. 73	12. a, p. 63

CHAPTER FOUR

Sensation and the Senses

KEY TERM ORGANIZER

Psychologists have traditionally divided the process of "sensory information processing" into two parts: the process of *sensation* (activation of sensory receptors) and *perception* (interpretation of sensory input). Through the process of *transduction,* sensory reception is converted into neural activity.

Researchers have devised various concepts to measure the human limits of sensitivity.

* *Absolute threshold:* the weakest stimulus our senses can detect.

* *Difference threshold,* or *just noticeable difference* (JND): smallest change in a stimulus that produces a noticeable change in sensation.

Human sensory systems register changes in intensity proportionally (as opposed to a straightforward, one-to-one ratio). *Weber's Law* states that the JND is a constant proportion of the intensity of the original stimulus. The change of sensitivity in response to a constant, unchanging level of stimulation is called *adaptation. Afterimages* occur after a stimulus is removed.

The chart on the following page outlines the primary senses, their anatomical structures, and the basic process of sensation.

The *eye* is one of the most important and precious sense organs. Light strikes the *cornea,* passes through the *pupil* (which is surrounded by the *iris*), is focused by the *lens* through the process of *accommodation,* and impinges on the back of the eye at the *retina.* Retinal receptors, such as *rods* and *cones,* are linked by *ganglion cells,* eventually forming the *optic nerve,* which exits the eye via the *optic disk.* The optic nerves merge at a point called the *lateral geniculate nucleus* (LGN), then on to the visual cortex.

Visual information processing occurs in regions of space called *receptive fields.* The sharpness of eyesight is known as *acuity.* Acuity can be imperfect; for example, *myopia,* or nearsightedness, is the result of an abnormally long eyeball.

Color perception has been explained by two major theories.

1. *Trichromatic theory:* The eye uses three types of cones (sensitive to the primary colors); color perception is the result of the additive effects of stimulation of these cone cells.

2. *Opponent-process theory:* Cells at every stage of visual processing beyond the receptors are stimulated by one color and inhibited by its complementary color.

Sound waves are the stimulus for hearing. Pitch is determined by the *frequency* of sound waves, loudness by *amplitude.* Sound waves enter the ear, striking the *eardrum.* Little bones,

Sense	Anatomical Structures	Basic Process of Sensation
Vision	Cornea, pupil, iris, lens, retina, rods, cones, optic nerve, lateral genicular nucleus (LGN), visual cortex	Light enters eye; retina converts light to neural impulses and relays information via pathways connecting to visual cortex.
Hearing	Eardrum, ossicles, oval and round window, cochlea, hair cells, basilar membrane	Sound enters eardrum, vibrating ossicles and fluid in cochlea; hair cells produce neural signals via auditory nerve to brain.
Skin senses	Skin surface over body	Skin receptors transmit information about four kinds of sensations: pressure, warmth, cold, and pain.
Taste and smell	Olfactory epithelium; taste buds	Hair cells in nasal passages transmit messages about odors; taste buds on tongue transmit information about four taste qualities.
Vestibular senses and kinesthesis	Semicircular canals; nerve endings in and near muscles, joints, and tendons	Fluid in canals transmits information about motion; kinesthetic receptors sense bodily movements.

known as *ossicles*, form the familiar *hammer, anvil,* and *stirrup.* These ossicles transmit pressure to the *oval window* on the side of the *cochlea.* As the oval window and a second membrane, the *round window,* are vibrated, *hair cells* are stimulated inside the cochlea. Hair cells are embedded in the *basilar membrane.*

Two mechanisms seem to be involved in auditory information processing. The *place theory* of pitch says auditory information depends upon particular areas of the basilar membrane being stimulated. *Frequency theory* posits that the frequency of basilar membrane movement signals pitch to the brain. *Volley theory* is a modification of frequency theory.

Olfaction, the sense of smell, is considered a "minor" sensory ability. Olfactory receptors lie in the *olfactory epithelium.* Animals communicate by means of odors, called *pheromones.* Odor affects gustation (taste). Taste reception occurs on the *taste buds.*

Our *vestibular sense* is the sense of balance. The primary vestibular organ is the *semicircular canals.* Related to balance is *kinesthesis,* information about body position.

MAJOR CONCEPTS AND LEARNING OBJECTIVES

CONCEPT 1   Our senses respond to a limited range of stimuli, or environmental energy. The senses capture change in environmental energy and transform it into information in a form that can be processed further.

1.1   Describe the four ways sensations can differ.

1.2   Distinguish absolute threshold from difference threshold and the relation of these two concepts to sensory variability.

1.3   Discuss the approaches of Weber and Stevens to sensory scaling.

1.4   Discuss the importance of change to the process of sensory adaptation.

**Concept
Builder 1**

*Directions: Read the following situations that occur before
and during a music concert. Then match each description of
what occurs during this sensation-filled concert to the appropriate sensory principles.*

Sensational Concert

_____ 1. Before the concert, the stage crew had someone sit at
the outer edge of the auditorium and signal when they
could hear the lowest detectable sounds from the
microphone.

_____ 2. The man operating the "mixing board" for the show
knew he had to increase the volume from 60 to 66
decibels for the audience to hear the increase in
volume.

_____ 3. One thing Susan said she loved about concert music
was that it was at an "ear-splitting" volume.

_____ 4. When the auditorium lights went down, people
entering the floor area couldn't find their seats until
their eyes adjusted.

_____ 5. Each spotlight on the stage had to be adjusted at a
slightly different illumination level so that the whole
stage would appear uniformly lit to the audience.

a. Weber's Law

b. sensory
   adaptation

c. just noticeable
   difference

d. absolute
   threshold

e. intensity of
   stimulus

CONCEPT 2   Our visual systems are sensory organs that respond to changes in a very
narrow band of light wavelengths in the electromagnetic spectrum.

2.1 Describe the major structural components of the eye and the function
of each.

2.2 Describe the stages of visual information processing, from the retinal
level to higher-level brain processes.

2.3 Distinguish the trichromatic theory of color from the opponent-process
theory; explain how each accounts for color blindness.

**Concept
Builder 2**

*Directions: Here is a diagram showing the sequence of the
visual process from the retinal level all the way to the visual
cortex level, followed by a description of each component in
the process. Match the descriptions to the components.*

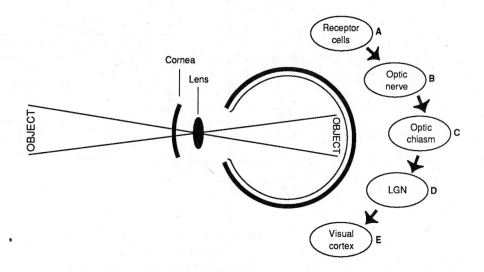

_____ 1.   Located in the thalamus region; contains ON-center and OFF-center receptive fields.

_____ 2.   Bundle of nerve fibers that leaves the eye through the optic disk.

_____ 3.   Contains all the photopigment necessary for vision.

_____ 4.   Most probably where "Gestalts" are recognized and processed, such as a mouth, nose, face, etc.

_____ 5.   Junction in brain where nerve fibers are rerouted.

CONCEPT 3   Auditory receptors of the ears respond to sound waves and transduce them to neural signals.

3.1   Describe the structures of the ear and the way physical stimuli are translated into sensory signals.

3.2   Distinguish the place theory of pitch from the volley theory and explain how these two theories work together to give an account of the different sounds we hear.

Concept Builder 3

Directions: The following is a schematic drawing of the cochlea, which has been "unfurled" so that you may see from the beginning of the basilar membrane (oval window) to the end (tip of cochlea).

Using the letter "L" (low frequency end) or "H" (high frequency end), answer the following questions, based on the drawing above. You may use L or H more than once, or use both (L+H) together.

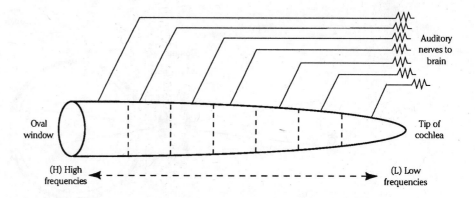

_____ 1. The elderly would tend to have more damage in this area.
_____ 2. Low, bass sounds would vibrate this area.
_____ 3. These frequencies are best explained by place theory.
_____ 4. High, treble sounds would vibrate this area.
_____ 5. These frequencies are best explained by the frequency theory.
_____ 6. Contemporary researchers subscribe to a combination of both place and frequency theories.

CONCEPT 4

The other major senses of the body (skin senses, chemical senses, and the balance senses) translate environmental energy into neural information in a manner similar to that of the visual and auditory senses.

4.1 Identify the four different sensory receptors that combine to make our sense of touch.

4.2 Describe the physiological basis for the experience of pain and distinguish it from the subjective experience of pain.

4.3 Discuss how smell and taste are related and describe the mechanisms of smell and taste sensation.

4.4 Identify the roles of the vestibular and the kinesthetic senses.

Concept Builder 4

Directions: Read the descriptions of the events that Susan experiences before and during childbirth, then match them to the terms at the right.

Sensory Events of Childbirth

_____ 1. Since becoming pregnant, Susan has had trouble with her sense of balance.

_____ 2. Susan was instructed *not* to come to the hospital until the "labor" pains became prolonged and cramp-like with no relief!

_____ 3. For the first time ever, the smell of alcohol and the hospital was a comforting sensation.

_____ 4. After Susan was prepared for the delivery room, her pain seemed to subside.

_____ 5. During the childbirth, the midwife had to use metal forceps to aid delivery; she kept the forceps at 32 degrees Centigrade so Susan would not feel the cold or warmth of the metal.

_____ 6. Upon seeing the forceps, Susan's husband said he was getting sick; the physician gave him a "tranquil-izer" to calm him. (It was really a sugar pill.)

_____ 7. During the very height of childbirth, Susan felt no pain, only an ecstatic feeling and absolutely no sense of her "body position" or orientation.

a. physiological zero

b. chronic-periodic pain

c. adaptation

d. placebo

e. olfaction

f. vestibular sense

g. kinesthetic sense

CHAPTER EXERCISE

Directions: Read the following definitions, supply the right word, then classify the word underneath the corresponding "sense" heading in the chart that follows.

Charting the Senses

1. Gives us information about our body movement and position: _____

2. What the "hair" cells are embedded in: _____

3. Also known as the optic disk: _____

4. Contains rhodopsin: _____

5. Odors used for communication: _____

6. Neurotransmitter substance P: _____

7. Another name for frequency of sound: _____

8. Sensory impressions that persist after removal of a stimulus: _____

9. Temperature at which there is *no* sensation of hot or cold: _____

10. Braille readers use this sense: _____

11. The structures responsible for vestibular senses: _____

12. Specific receptors for taste sensation: _____

13. Collective name for hammer, anvil, and stirrup: _____

14. People who are *totally* color-blind: _____

Vision	Hearing	Skin Senses	Taste and Olfaction	Balance, Posture, and Movement

PRACTICE EXAM 1

1. Which neurotransmitter has been found to be involved in the transmission and experience of pain?

    a. dopamine
    b. endorphin
    c. substance P
    d. serotonin

    (Factual, Obj. 4.2)

2. Jerome suffers a brain trauma to the visual cortex in his left hemisphere. What visual effect is he most likely to have?

    a. blindness in his right eye
    b. blindness in his left eye
    c. blindness in the left half of both eyes
    d. blindness in the left half of his left eye

    (Conceptual, Obj. 2.2)

3. Rhodopsin is:

    a. a light-sensitive chemical contained in the rods
    b. one of the three types of cones
    c. a disease of the optic disk
    d. a small pit at the back of the eye in which cones are most heavily concentrated

    (Factual, Obj. 2.1)

4. A researcher found that, when he measured the amount of bleached pigment in the retina as he shined lights of various wavelengths on the eye, much more bleaching occurred when the wavelengths corresponded to red, blue, and green light. This finding supports the:

    a. trichromatic theory
    b. monochromatic theory
    c. opponent-process theory
    d. dichromatic theory

    (Conceptual, Obj. 2.3)

5. According to trichromatic theory, we have cones that are specific for all of the following colors of light *except:*

   a. red
   b. blue
   c. green
   d. yellow

   (Factual, Obj. 2.3)

6. On a piano, the farther to the left a key is, the lower the pitch of the note produced. This example is an analogy to which theory of hearing?

   a. place theory
   b. volley theory
   c. opponent-process theory
   d. frequency theory

   (Conceptual, Obj. 3.2)

7. With light, wavelength corresponds to _____; with sound, wavelength corresponds to _____.

   a. brightness; pitch
   b. color; pitch
   c. brightness; loudness
   d. color; loudness

   (Factual, Obj. 2.1 & 3.1)

8. If someone's hearing had been impaired by listening to the whine of high-frequency jet engines, you would expect physical damage to be present at the:

   a. basilar membrane near the oval window
   b. basilar membrane at the tip of the cochlea
   c. auditory nerve
   d. LGN

   (Conceptual, Obj. 3.2)

9. Which theory would be most consistent with the engineering design of most color TV sets, which have three-color projection guns (red, green, blue) in the picture tube to produce the whole array of colors that we might perceive?

   a. Young-Helmholtz
   b. opponent-process
   c. dichromatic
   d. place theory

   (Conceptual, Obj. 2.3)

10. Which of the following is *not* one of the ossicles?

    a. hammer
    b. anvil
    c. bellows
    d. stirrup

    (Factual, Obj. 3.1)

11. Pain is transmitted through two pathways: a slow pathway and a fast pathway. The slow pathway sends what kind of information about pain?

    a. sensory
    b. kinesthetic

    c.   emotional
    d.   cognitive

(Factual, Obj. 4.2)

12.   Colognes and perfumes might be said to be the human version of other species' _____, or chemical sex attractants, since these odors are meant to communicate something.

    a.   placebos
    b.   pheromones
    c.   ossicles
    d.   olfactions

(Conceptual, Obj. 4.3)

PRACTICE EXAM 2

1.   The process of converting energy from the outside world into neural activity occurs through the process of:

    a.   signal detection
    b.   sensory adaptation
    c.   transduction
    d.   sensory scaling

(Factual, Obj. 1.1)

2.   An experienced coffee-taster can tell you just how much more of a particular coffee bean to add to make a brewed coffee taste a little different. This sensitivity in making the smallest change in coffee illustrates:

    a.   absolute threshold
    b.   difference threshold
    c.   signal detection
    d.   sensory selectivity

(Conceptual, Obj. 1.2)

3.   Weber's Law states that there is an unchanging _____ between the intensity of a stimulus and the amount the stimulus intensity has to be increased in order for a person to experience a JND in the sensation.

    a.   time interval
    b.   threshold
    c.   ratio
    d.   magnitude

(Factual, Obj. 1.3)

4.   "Motion sickness" is primarily a disturbance of the _____ sense.

    a.   kinesthetic
    b.   vestibular
    c.   sensory feedback
    d.   visual

(Factual, Obj. 4.4)

5.   Laurie can go to sleep to the most obtrusive, loud rock music you can imagine, but change it to a country and western station and she awakens immediately. Laurie is showing what kind of reaction to the rock music?

    a.   auditory streaming
    b.   Weber's Law

   c.   sensory scaling
   d.   adaptation

(Conceptual, Obj. 1.4)

6.   The process of thickening the lens to focus an image on the retina is called:

   a.   dilation
   b.   accommodation
   c.   opponent process
   d.   visual scaling

(Factual, Obj. 2.2)

7.   In frogs, there are cells in the visual cortex called "bug detectors." They "fire" only when small, bug-like objects move with irregular motions. This is very similar to the concept of:

   a.   opponent-process theory
   b.   place theory
   c.   signal detection
   d.   feature analysis

(Conceptual, Obj. 2.2)

8.   The volley principle attempts to explain how we perceive:

   a.   intensity
   b.   loudness
   c.   frequency
   d.   none of the above

(Factual, Obj. 3.2)

9.   What part of the ear operates much like a "satellite dish" for a communication system?

   a.   the outer ear
   b.   the middle ear
   c.   the inner ear
   d.   the oval window

(Conceptual, Obj. 3.1)

10.   One can play "music" by stretching a rubber band between one's fingers and plucking it. When you change the tension, you change the pitch. This primitive instrument best represents:

   a.   place theory
   b.   opponent-process theory
   c.   frequency theory
   d.   trichromatic theory

(Conceptual, Obj. 3.2)

11.   The amplitude of a sound wave is expressed in units of measurement called:

   a.   nanometers (nm)
   b.   decibels (dB)
   c.   cycles per second (Hz)
   d.   just noticeable differences (JND)

(Factual, Obj. 3.1)

12.   A plumber working underneath a house accidentally touches hot and cold water pipes simultaneously on the back of his wrist. He reports that *both* feel cold, even though one is hot. This illustrates:

a.   physiological zero
b.   paradoxical cold
c.   sensory adaptation
d.   pain threshold

(Conceptual, Obj. 4.1)

■   **ANSWER KEY**   ■

Concept 1

1. d   4. b
2. a   5. c
3. e

Concept 2

1. d   4. e
2. b   5. c
3. a

Concept 3

1. H   4. H
2. L   5. L
3. H   6. H+L

Concept 4

1. f   5. a
2. b   6. d
3. e   7. g
4. c

Chapter Exercise

Vision: 3. blind spot   4. rods   8. afterimage   14. monochromats
Hearing: 2. basilar membrane   7. pitch   13. ossicles
Skin senses: 6. neurotransmitter substance P (pain)   9. physiological zero
                 10. touch
Taste and olfaction: 5. pheromones   12. taste buds
Balance, posture, and movement: 1. kinesthetics   11. semicircular canals

Practice Exam 1	**Practice Exam 2**
1. c, p. 107	1. c, p. 81
2. c, p. 91	2. b, p. 84
3. a, p. 90	3. c, p. 85
4. a, p. 96	4. b, p. 111
5. d, pp. 96–97	5. d, pp. 86–87
6. a, p. 103	6. b, p. 88
7. b, pp. 96, 101	7. d, pp. 92–94
8. a, p. 104	8. c, p. 104
9. a, p. 96	9. a, p. 102
10. c, p. 102	10. c, p. 104
11. c, p. 107	11. b, p. 101
12. b, p. 109	12. b, p. 106

CHAPTER FIVE

Perception

KEY TERM ORGANIZER

We sense stimuli, but we perceive objects and events. *Perception* is the brain's attempt to describe objects and events in the world. The brain strives for consistency by perceiving stable properties despite variations in retinal image, as in *perceptual constancy*.

Researchers continue to deal with some basic questions surrounding the biological and psychological aspects of perception. These questions remain enduring issues:

1. How much of perception is innate and how much is learned?
2. Does the perceptual system build up its descriptions from simple sensations (feature analysis) or does it perceive an entire form (Gestalt view)?
3. Do illusions demonstrate important perceptual processes or are they simply curiosities?
4. Is perception a bottom-up or top-down process? What effect does knowledge have on perception?

The following chart depicts the basic tasks of our perceptual system.

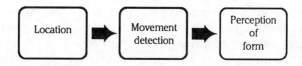

LOCATION

The perceptual system must determine "Where is it?" *Orientation* is a process that enables us to place the object in the spatial framework we project before us. *Depth perception* is constructed from several kinds of information. One source is *binocular disparity*, which gives a perception of depth, called *stereopsis*. We can also detect depth by using *monocular cues* that require information from only a single eye. Monocular cues include *motion parallax, occlusion, aerial perspective, relative size,* and *texture gradient.* Cues arising from *convergence* of the separate eyeballs also provide depth perception information.

The perceptual system must also maintain an accurate image. This is the ability to perceive objects as having certain constant properties despite great variation in their appearances. One type of perceptual constancy is *size constancy.* An *illusion* is a perception that does not correspond to a real object or event: It is produced by physical or psychological distortion.

MOVEMENT DETECTION

The perceptual system must then determine if an object is moving. The perception of movement can be caused by our own movements or the movements of objects around us. *Motion parallax,* a constant flow of what we see, produces our perception that we are moving through space. We sometimes perceive motion when no real movement is taking place. These illusions of movement include:

- *Apparent motion,* which is illustrated in the *phi phenomenon.*
- *Induced motion,* which is created by relative motion.
- The *motion aftereffect,* which is for motion as afterimages are to color perception.

FORM

The perceptual system must also determine "What kind of object is it?" The brain constructs perceptual objects from relatively small collections of features, a process known as *feature analysis.* The context, or setting in which stimuli appear, helps determine the way we see the stimuli. When the context fails to guide our perception, sensory data may be ambiguous, allowing the brain to interpret a single set of stimuli in at least two different ways.

Our expectations, past experiences, and psychological states combine, "setting" us to perceive the world in certain ways, a concept called *perceptual set.* The normal perceptual experiences of a culture may lead its members to develop perceptual biases.

Our perceptual system organizes bits of information into meaningful patterns, called *gestalts.* The brain uses *grouping* to achieve perceptual simplicity. This process allows us to perceive stimuli as coherent objects. The rules of grouping include *proximity, continuity,* and *similarity.* Perceptual processes also organize sensations by dividing stimuli into *figure,* regions that represent objects, and *ground,* the context in which figures appear.

Perception changes in predictable ways over the life span. Newborns' distance senses are not as well developed as their near senses of touch, smell, and taste. Some aspects of perception can develop only when individuals are raised in a normal visual environment.

Sensory systems begin aging during the forties, and the losses may become severe by the time people reach their seventies and eighties.

An interesting modern-day issue is whether *subliminal perception* is valid or not. Subliminal perception is the registering of sensory information by the relevant sensory system without any conscious experience of the stimulus.

MAJOR CONCEPTS AND LEARNING OBJECTIVES

CONCEPT 1   Perception refers to the process by which we make meaningful interpretations of basic sensations. Perception integrates information from all the senses.

1.1   Identify the aspects of perception that support a view of perception as an active process.

1.2   Explain the importance of perception of wholes in the Gestalt school.

1.3   Distinguish top-down from bottom-up processing and discuss the concept of perceptual set as it relates to top-down processing.

Concept Builder 1

Directions: Using the terms "TD" for top-down, or "BU" for bottom-up, identify the perceptual information process being described in the following short phrases.

The Direction of Perception

_____   1.   "expectations"
_____   2.   sensory reception
_____   3.   grouping clusters of features together
_____   4.   "context"
_____   5.   perceptual set
_____   6.   perception of speech
_____   7.   Helmholtz
_____   8.   inference in perception
_____   9.   goals and expectations
_____   10.   assumptions built on experience

CONCEPT 2   A major task of our perceptual system is the location of objects in space relative to our bodies. The perception of depth and motion is essential to this task.

2.1   Describe how depth perception is achieved through binocular disparity, or stereopsis.

2.2   List and define the monocular cues used in depth perception.

2.3   Discuss the roles of illusion in understanding the perception of depth.

2.4   Describe motion perception and the illusions of apparent motion and induced motion.

Concept Builder 2

Directions: Your text outlined a number of monocular cues to depth perception. Study the figure below and write down as many monocular cues as you can identify.

_____   _____

_____   _____

                    _____

_____

CONCEPT 3   A vital part of the perceptual process involves identifying objects and recogniz-
                     ing patterns. Several factors contribute to our ability to recognize certain
                     objects and patterns.

                     3.1   Define "feature analysis" and describe the activities or steps in feature
                            analysis that lead to the perception of particular objects.

                     3.2   List and define the organizing principles proposed by the Gestalt psy-
                            chologists.

                     3.3   Define "ambiguous figure"; identify the Gestalt principles this type of
                            figure illustrates.

**Concept
Builder 3**

_Directions: Look at the five diagrams below. Under each,
identify the Gestalt principle of form perception being
illustrated._

Seeing Is Believing

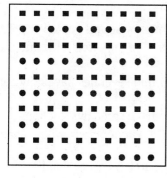

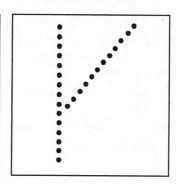

1._____ 2._____ 3._____

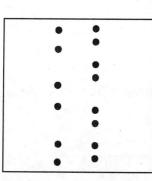

4. _____   5. _____

CONCEPT 4   Perceptual abilities change with age, and though these changes are often long term and subtle, the diminished perceptual experience becomes noticeable with advanced age.

4.1   Identify which of the senses are well developed at birth.

4.2   Outline the perceptual decline of the aging senses.

Concept Builder 4

Directions: Answer the following true-false questions on aging and the senses from what you have read in the text about age-related perceptual changes.

The Aging Senses

1. Taste perception weakens with age. T or F
2. Most people develop presbyopia. T or F
3. Presbycusis particularly affects high-frequency sound perception. T or F
4. Even middle-aged adults whose vision has been perfect may find they need to wear reading glasses. T or F
5. Seventy-five percent of people past their mid-seventies have noticeable hearing problems. T or F
6. After the age of 80, 50 percent of people have smell dysfunctions. T or F
7. The number of taste buds begins to decline in people from the age of 40 on. T or F
8. By the mid-fifties, blues and greens begin to look alike. T or F
9. Aging is associated with lens thickening and accommodation problems. T or F
10 Whatever a person's age, perception does a remarkably able job of placing the individual in touch with reality. T or F

CHAPTER EXERCISE

Directions: Match the "key" terms below the drawing with the appropriate "pillar" of perception. Each pillar represents a major function of perception (phrased in question form).

The Three Pillars of Perception

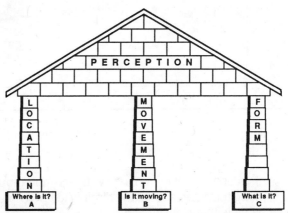

	1. relative distance		11. induced motion
____	2. continuity	____	12. feature analysis
____	3. ambiguous figures	____	13. proximity
____	4. binocular disparity	____	14. figure-ground distinction
____	5. motion parallax	____	15. "primal sketch"
____	6. motion aftereffect	____	16. absolute distance
____	7. vista paradox	____	17. stereopsis
____	8. texture gradient	____	18. sized constancy
____	9. occlusion	____	19. apparent motion
____	10. phi phenomenon	____	20. similarity

**PRACTICE
EXAM 1**

1. "Sensation" refers to the process by which our nervous system registers stimuli; "perception," by contrast, refers to the process by which our brains arrive at meaningful _____ of basic sensations.

    a. perceptions
    b. codes
    c. interpretations
    d. images

    (Factual, Obj. 1.1)

2. Several years ago, multicolored tennis balls were introduced, based on the idea that they would be most visible against all the background stimuli on the tennis court. The perceptual principle that this is based on is called:

    a. subjective contour
    b. feature analysis
    c. color constancy
    d. figure-ground

    (Conceptual, Obj. 3.2)

3. Camouflage is based upon the phi phenomenon.

    a. True
    b. False; it is based on grouping.
    c. False; it is based on figure-ground.
    d. False; it is based on size constancy.

    (Factual, Obj. 2.2)

4. Based on what we know of binocular disparity, what would you predict would be the effect, in some animals and fish, of having eyes on opposite sides of the head?

    a. They would not be affected by motion parallax.
    b. They would have increased stereopsis.
    c. They would not need monocular cues.
    d. They would be less susceptible to illusions.

    (Conceptual, Obj. 2.1)

5. The effectiveness of _____ cues is supported by the success of one-eyed airplane pilots and even a professional ballplayer.

    a. stereopsis
    b. monocular
    c. constancy
    d. perceptual set

    (Factual, Obj. 2.1)

6. Hollywood exploits _____ constancy by constructing small models of spaceships and buildings, and filming these models up close to give us the illusion of real-life size.

    a. shape
    b. location
    c. size
    d. retinal

    (Conceptual, Obj. 2.3)

7.   The basis for all motion pictures is the perceptual principle of:

     a.   induced movement
     b.   autokinetic movement
     c.   the phi phenomenon
     d.   illusory aftereffects

(Factual, Obj. 2.4)

8.   Caricatures are simple line drawings that capture a person's face with only a few, brief lines. Our ability to recognize the person depicted can be explained by:

     a.   shape constancy
     b.   grouping
     c.   perceptual constancy
     d.   feature analysis

(Conceptual, Obj. 3.1)

9.   "The whole cannot be just the sum of its parts" is a statement illustrating the power of the context according to:

     a.   the neurophysiologists
     b.   the Gestalt psychologists
     c.   Müller and Lyer
     d.   the inventor of the Ames room

(Factual, Obj. 1.2)

10.   Barry and Jane have just brought their new daughter home from the hospital. Barry's mother notes the baby's strong resemblance to her son, whereas Jane's father can see no resemblance to Barry's side of the family. To him, the baby is the "spitting image of her mother." The bias in perception shown by these proud grandparents illustrates:

     a.   perceptual set
     b.   perceptual constancy
     c.   sensory ambiguity
     d.   continuity

(Conceptual, Obj. 1.3)

11.   One kind of perceptual bias involves the readiness to perceive stimuli in specific ways, ignoring some stimuli and becoming attuned to others. This bias is called:

     a.   perceptual set
     b.   perceptual constancy
     c.   subliminal perception
     d.   the phi phenomenon

(Factual, Obj. 1.3)

12.   When listening to music, some individuals can pick out a distinctive voice in the chorus of voices and follow that voice through the music. This ability is based on the perceptual principle of:

     a.   figure-ground
     b.   continuity
     c.   perceptual set
     d.   auditory localization

(Conceptual, Obj. 3.2)

**PRACTICE
EXAM 2**

1. Binocular and monocular information answers which basic question about perception?

    a. "Is it for real?"
    b. "Where is it?"
    c. "Is it moving?"
    d. "What is it?"

    (Factual, Obj. 2.1 & 2.2)

2. Aerial photographers have been struck with the spectacular shapes of earth mounds in South America. Laid out over miles, they appear to be in shapes recognizable *only* from a high altitude. Although parts are missing, one can see what appears to be a prehistoric "runway." Archaeologists speculate that it was built as a tribute to the gods. The perceptual process that allows us to see the apparent outline, filling in the missing pieces, is called:

    a. subjective contour
    b. binocular disparity
    c. visual depth perception
    d. shape constancy

    (Conceptual, Obj. 1.2)

3. Probably the best illustration of the breakdown of size constancy is the well-known:

    a. "moon" illusion
    b. Ponzo illusion
    c. Müller-Lyer illusion
    d. phi phenomenon

    (Factual, Obj. 2.3)

4. Ancient Egyptian paintings showed an interesting, primitive artistic feature: When human figures were depicted as standing in a row, say ten across, there was no linear perspective, no corresponding reduction in size the further the person was from the foreground. The only clue to depth was the fact that one person's body partially blocked the view of another. Egyptian artists relied on what one monocular cue to imply depth?

    a. texture gradient
    b. size constancy
    c. relative size
    d. occlusion

    (Conceptual, Obj. 2.2)

5. The brain fills in "missing gaps" in our perceptual field. The example, in your text, of geometric designs illustrates the principle of:

    a. perceptual ambiguity
    b. perceptual set
    c. size constancy
    d. subjective contours

    (Factual, Obj. 1.2)

6. On movie sets, an illusion is sometimes created to portray drivers in a car: The camera holds a close-up shot of the actors while the background whizzes by them. The illusion involves the principle of:

    a.   motion aftereffects
    b.   apparent motion
    c.   induced motion
    d.   the phi phenomenon

(Conceptual, Obj. 2.4)

7.   The text explained that the anxiety of back-seat drivers may be partly attributable to an illusion known as:

    a.   vista paradox
    b.   motion parallax
    c.   aerial perspective
    d.   induced motion

(Factual, Obj. 2.4)

8.   In order to understand whether a fast talker has just said "I scream" or "ice cream," the _____ dimension of perception must be avoided.

    a.   top-down processing
    b.   bottom-up processing
    c.   part vs. whole
    d.   perceptual error

(Conceptual, Obj. 1.3)

9.   Newborns' vision is functional, but limited. What range of distances is probably most visually clear to them?

    a.   8 to 10 inches
    b.   2 to 3 feet
    c.   8 to 10 feet
    d.   All distances are the same.

(Factual, Obj. 4.1)

10.   Presbycusis is a hearing impairment that particularly affects:

    a.   young children
    b.   high-frequency reception (sound)
    c.   ability to discriminate pitch
    d.   hearing melodies in songs

(Factual, Obj. 4.2)

11.   There is an eye condition called strabismus in which the eyes don't work together in a coordinated fashion. If this condition went uncorrected from infancy on, we would expect the individual to have problems with:

    a.   pattern recognition
    b.   figure-ground relationships
    c.   normal binocular vision
    d.   sensory ambiguity

(Conceptual, Obj. 2.1)

12.   While waiting at a red light in her car, Tina was for a moment staring blankly at the car next to her. At that moment, the other car coasted backwards, and Tina suddenly slammed her brakes as hard as possible, thinking it was her car moving forward. What happened to make Tina think she was moving?

a. The phi phenomenon occurred.
b. This was an illusory aftereffect of motion.
c. Tina experienced the illusion of induced movement.
d. This was an autokinetic movement.

(Conceptual, Obj. 2.4)

■ ANSWER KEY ■

Concept 1

1.	TD	6.	TD
2.	BU	7.	TD
3.	BU	8.	TD
4.	TD	9.	TD
5.	TD	10.	TD

Concept 2

relative size, occlusion, texture gradient, linear perspective, aerial perspective

Concept 3

1. similarity
2. continuity
3. figure-ground
4. proximity
5. ambiguous figure or figure-ground reversal

Concept 4

All of these statements are true.

Chapter Exercise

1.	a	11.	b
2.	c	12.	c
3.	c	13.	c
4.	a	14.	c
5.	a	15.	c
6.	b	16.	a
7.	a	17.	a
8.	a	18.	a
9.	a	19.	b
10.	b	20.	c

Practice Exam 1

1. c, p. 118
2. d, p. 135
3. c, p. 135
4. b, p. 126
5. b, p. 127
6. c, pp. 127–128
7. c, p. 133
8. d, pp. 133–134
9. b, p. 123
10. a, p. 124
11. a, p. 124
12. a, p. 125

Practice Exam 2

1. b, p. 125
2. a, pp. 129–130
3. a, p. 128
4. d, p. 129
5. d, p. 120
6. c, p. 133
7. a, p. 130
8. a, p. 124
9. a, p. 137
10. b, p. 140
11. c, pp. 125–126
12. c, p. 133

CHAPTER 6

Consciousness

KEY TERM ORGANIZER

Although no universal definition of consciousness is accepted, the broad definition of *consciousness* includes all mental experiences, whether or not we are aware of them. Consciousness operates on a number of levels:

- *subconscious:* activities carried on outside subjective awareness;

- *preconscious:* information that can be voluntarily brought to awareness;

- *unconscious:* thoughts and images that are kept submerged.

Support for different "layers" of consciousness comes from a variety of experiments. For example, *dichotic listening* demonstrates that the brain subconsciously picks up unattended information. Likewise, *implicit memory* is a memory that results from unattended stimulation.

One uniquely human aspect of consciousness is the capacity to create alternative realities. Some daydreams, called *realistic fantasy,* are closely connected to realistic situations. Other daydreams, called *autistic fantasy,* lack any connection with reality. *Reverie* consists of unrelated images, scenes, or memories and is not under control of the fantasizer.

Between waking and sleep lie other forms of brief fantasy. When images occur as we are falling asleep, they are called *hypnogogic images.* When the images occur during the transition between sleep and waking, they are called *hypnopompic images.*

Sleep is a radically altered form of consciousness. Sleep is part of a daily biological rhythm called a *circadian rhythm.* Much of what we know about sleep comes from recording physiological activity during sleep, known as *polysomnography.*

Studies have revealed two major sleep states: *REM* (rapid eye movement) *sleep* and *NREM sleep,* in which the eyes do not move. Most dreams occur during the REM state, with the dreamer entering the REM state and alternating with stages of NREM activity on a short rhythmical cycle called an *ultradian rhythm,* with NREM sleep progressing through four stages (see diagram).

Dreams are the content of consciousness during REM sleep. Freud believed dreams had two distinct layers of content: the *manifest content* (dream's surface meaning) and the *latent content* (dream's hidden meaning). Some people report having *lucid dreams,* ones in which they realize they are dreaming. The inability to remain asleep can result in chronic sleeplessness called *insomnia.*

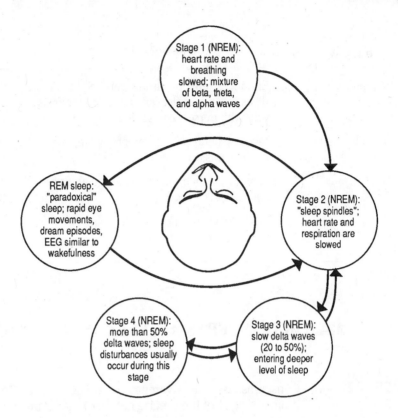

Many researchers today regard dreams as either:

1. the predictable result of a physiological process, in which the mind tries to explain the random stimulation it receives;

2. an unlearning process, in which inappropriate responses are erased to protect the brain from overload;

3. a nocturnal version of the same process that integrates perceptions during waking hours; or

4. a problem-solving activity.

There are several commonly used methods for leaving the state of consciousness. *Meditation* is a method of refocusing attention in order to enter inner consciousness. *Hypnosis* is a social interaction in which the responses of one individual to another alter perceptions, memories, and voluntary actions. Once under hypnosis, some people will carry out suggestions in the subsequent waking state, called *post-hypnotic suggestions*. By suggestion, even a memory can be suppressed, resulting in *post-hypnotic amnesia*.

Psychologists have produced two very different explanations of how hypnosis works: *Dissociation theory* says consciousness splits into several independent systems; *neodissociation theory* builds on that idea. *Role-enactment theory* contents that hypnosis is an extreme form of role playing.

Psychoactive drugs change consciousness by altering the chemistry of the brain. For example, *stimulants* act to stimulate the central nervous system (CNS). *Depressants* act on the CNS to reduce pain, tension, and anxiety. If several depressants are combined, their combined action is *synergistic*.

Hypnotics, or sleep-inducing drugs, are often taken to relieve insomnia. The *hallucinogens* produce hallucinations in the user. The following chart summarizes major forms of psychoactive drugs.

Type of Psychoactive Drug	Characteristics	Examples
Marijuana	Enhances sensory stimuli; can heighten both pleasant and unpleasant sensations; effects vary with person and setting	Marijuana, hashish
Stimulants	Increase heart rate, blood presssure, and muscle tension	Nicotine, caffeine cocaine, amphetamines
Depressants	Slow CNS functioning; decreased alertness and reaction speed	Alcohol, hypnotics tranquilizers, narcotics
Hallucinogens	Powerful visual and sensory changes; produce hallucinations	LSD, PCP, mescaline peyote, psilocybin

MAJOR CONCEPTS AND LEARNING OBJECTIVES

CONCEPT 1   Consciousness is an awareness of mental activity. Consciousness is related to brain activity, but the precise nature of the connection is not clearly known.

1.1   Define consciousness and give examples of the four separate phenomena related to consciousness.

1.2   Distinguish and contrast subjective and objective consciousness.

1.3   Name and describe the three levels of consciousness: subconscious, preconscious, and unconscious.

Concept Builder 1

Directions: Read the following statements that illustrate a process occurring during a hypothetical patient's therapy, then match that process with a level of consciousness.

___C___ 1.   While discussing her dream, Marcia "accidentally" says, "My mother lies to me" instead of "My mother likes me."

    a. subconscious
    b. preconscious
    c. unconscious

___A___ 2.   While talking to her therapist, Marcia doesn't hear the receptionist answering the phone outside the office door until the receptionist says, "Oh, yes, Marcia's in with Dr. Rosenblum now." Suddenly Marcia "hears" this message crystal clear.

___B___ 3.   Dr. Rosenblum interrupts Marcia's train of thought and asks her directly to recall what her conversation was with her mother three nights ago.

CONCEPT 2   Fantasy, sleep, and dreams are natural variations of human consciousness
                   that have great importance for psychology.

2.1   Describe fantasy and daydreaming.

2.2   Outline the stages of sleep and describe the brain activity that accompanies each stage.

2.3   Describe the function of REM sleep.

2.4   Describe and contrast the various views regarding the function of dream activity.

**Concept
Builder 2**

*Directions: Match each stage of sleep shown on the graph
with the appropriate defining characteristic from the list
below.*

Night Life

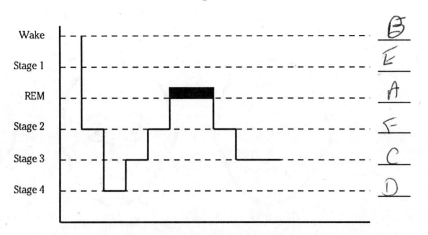

a.   Sometimes called "paradoxical sleep"
b.   When this sleeper would actually report a dream
c.   Delta waves are most prominent during this stage
d.   Deep sleep stage when night terrors most often happen
e.   Mixture of alpha, beta, and theta waves
f.   "Sleep spindles" common; slowed heart rate and respiration

CONCEPT 3   Consciousness may be altered through a variety of means that are self-imposed, such as meditation and hypnosis; others require mind-altering agents, such as psychoactive drugs.

3.1   Outline the evidence for and against considering meditation and hypnosis to be altered states of consciousness.

3.2   Describe hypnotic susceptibility and how different theories account for how hypnosis works.

3.3   Name the classes of psychoactive drugs and describe the primary effects of each.

**Concept
Builder 3**      *Directions: Match the drug listed below with the appropriate visual symbol. Each "face" represents a different physiological effect.*

Facing Up to Drugs

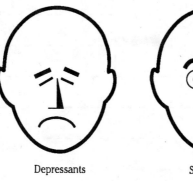      

Depressants   Stimulants   Hallucinogens

_____	_____	_____
_____	_____	_____
_____	_____	_____
_____	_____	_____

angel dust	marijuana	barbiturates
Valium	alcohol	caffeine
speed	nicotine	cocaine
peyote cactus	LSD	Librium

CHAPTER EXERCISE

Directions: Write the answers to each clue in the blank spaces provided. Then insert the letter from the numbered space in each answer into the space with the corresponding number at the top of this acrostic puzzle. When you are finished, it will spell out an important word from this chapter.

Acrostic

$$\underline{}\ \underline{}\ \underline{}\ \underline{}\ \underline{}\ \underline{}\ \underline{}\ \underline{}\ \underline{}\ \underline{}\ \underline{}\ \underline{}\ \underline{}$$
$$1\ \ 2\ \ 3\ \ 4\ \ 5\ \ 6\ \ 7\ \ 8\ \ 9\ \ 10\ \ 11\ \ 12\ \ 13$$

"Hidden" meaning of a dream is called the latent: __ __ __ __ __ __ __
1

Slows the central nervous system: __ __ __ __ __ __ __ __ __ __ __
11

Any depressant drug that induces sleep: __ __ __ __ __ __ __ __
7

Drugs that alter mood, perception, and behavior: __ __ __ __ __ __ __ __ __ __ __
5

Effect greater than sum of individual parts: __ __ __ __ __ __ __ __ __ __
6

Mental processes in which stimuli are monitored but are not registered

in subjective awareness: __ __ __ __ __ __ __ __ __ __ __
12

Caffeine, cocaine, speed: __ __ __ __ __ __ __ __
13

"Surface" meaning of dream: __ __ __ __ __ __ __
10

Explains hypnosis by multiple controls: __ __ __ __ __ __ __ __ __ __ __ __ theory
9

A fantasy that lacks any orientation toward reality: __ __ __ __ __ __ __ fantasy
8

Hearing two simultaneous but different messages: dichotic __ __ __ __ __ __ __
4

Produces hallucinations: __ __ __ __ __ __ __ __ __ __
3

Automatic images of vivid sights and intense sounds (from awake to sleeping):

forensic __ __ __ __ __ __ __ state
2

**PRACTICE
EXAM 1**

1. William James described consciousness as a succession of images and ideas that rise almost involuntarily to the surface where we become aware of them. This idea is described as:

    a. unity of consciousness
    b. self-awareness
    c. selectivity
    d. stream of consciousness

    (Factual, Obj. 1.1)

2. During the symphony, the husband of the cellist heard her every note even though everyone else in the orchestra was also playing. This closely resembles:

    a. dichotic listening
    b. reverie
    c. the cocktail party phenomenon
    d. blindsight

    (Conceptual, Obj. 1.1 & 1.3)

3. The stage of sleep that is closest to the waking state is:

    a. REM sleep
    b. Stage 1
    c. the hypnogogic state
    d. non-REM sleep

    (Factual, Obj. 2.3)

4. Steam is to boiling water as _____ is to brain activity.

    a. consciousness
    b. the neuron
    c. awareness
    d. dreaming

    (Conceptual, Obj. 1.1)

5. Which statement about REM sleep is *false*?

    a. REM is sometimes called "paradoxical sleep."
    b. REM occupies 22 percent of total sleep time.
    c. Dream recall is very high during REM sleep.
    d. REM sleep is the "deepest" level of sleep.

    (Factual, Obj. 2.3)

6. Alyson dreams that she is on the seashore collecting shells. She dreams that she places them in an aquarium and that they grow legs and come to life. She interprets the dream to mean she is pregnant. This would represent the dream's:

    a. latent content
    b. realistic fantasy
    c. manifest content
    d. subjective content

    (Conceptual, Obj. 2.4)

7.   The forerunner of modern-day hypnosis was:

    a.   role-enactment theory
    b.   Mesmerism
    c.   meditation
    d.   polysomnography

                                              (Factual, Obj. 3.1)

8.   Under hypnosis, Sarah "re-enacts" her reaction when her parents informed her that she was adopted. If, in reality, Sarah is not adopted and this incident never really happened, we have evidence for:

    a.   the neodissociation theory
    b.   role-enactment theory
    c.   an autistic fantasy
    d.   latent content

                                            (Conceptual, Obj. 3.2)

9.   Only about _____ percent of people are highly hypnotizable.

    a.   5 to 10
    b.   10 to 15
    c.   20 to 25
    d.   30 to 35

                                            (Factual, Obj. 3.2)

10.   Julie watched a film in her anthropology class that showed a man deeply concentrating with his eyes closed; he was sitting on a bed of nails yet seemed completely unaware of the pain. His state of mind would be closest to that of:

    a.   meditation
    b.   reverie
    c.   autistic fantasy
    d.   non-REM sleep

                                            (Conceptual, Obj. 3.1)

11.   The most consistent finding about marijuana is that long-term use interferes with:

    a.   sexual drive
    b.   motivation
    c.   memory
    d.   oxygen consumption

                                            (Factual, Obj. 3.3)

12.   Many pharmacists place warning labels on drug bottles to warn people not to take the medication with any form of alcohol because the effects are magnified tremendously. This illustrates the _____ property of alcohol.

    a.   sedative
    b.   synergistic
    c.   psychoactive
    d.   hallucinogenic

                                            (Conceptual, Obj. 3.3)

PRACTICE EXAM 2

1. Which of the following is *not* related to consciousness?

   a. deliberating, pondering, believing
   b. bodily sensations
   c. sleep
   d. a perception obtained through the senses

   (Factual, Obj. 1.1)

2. Which conclusion is most accurate concerning experiments with "blindsight"?

   a. Blindsight is a good illustration of the role-enactment theory.
   b. Blind people have an unusually developed sense of intuition.
   c. The visual cortex controls our awareness of sight, but does not control all functions of vision.
   d. Blindsight is apparently a reversible phenomenon.

   (Factual, Obj. 1.2)

3. The "cocktail party" phenomenon best illustrates which level of consciousness?

   a. subconscious
   b. preconscious
   c. unconscious
   d. selective attention

   (Conceptual, Obj. 1.3)

4. In what group of students would you expect to see "REM rebound"?

   a. those who nap frequently before going to bed at night
   b. the track team after competing in a 26-mile marathon
   c. the group that drove all night to get to the beach the next morning
   d. the biology students who stayed up late observing nocturnal insects

   (Conceptual, Obj. 2.3)

5. Sleep walking generally occurs within the first two hours of sleep, during:

   a. the first REM episode
   b. Stage 4
   c. Stage 1
   d. Stage 3

   (Factual, Obj. 2.2)

6. While sleeping in his hospital bed one night, Ryan dreams that mosquitoes are biting him all over his arm. What is a possible interpretation of the "manifest" content of this dream?

   a. Ryan is feeling attacked by people in his world.
   b. The nurse is giving him an injection in his arm.
   c. He feels that the "little things in life" are killing him.
   d. He feels that he is extremely vulnerable in his life.

   (Conceptual, Obj. 2.4)

7. Hypnotic susceptibility is sometimes measured with a test such as the:

   a. hypnotic induction test
   b. role-enactment inventory
   c. Stanford Hypnotic Susceptibility Scale
   d. regressive handwriting test

   (Factual, Obj. 3.2)

8. A dentist could hypnotize a patient and suggest that he will have no pain or memory of the tooth extraction. This best illustrates:

   a. polysomnography
   b. role-enactment theory
   c. post-hypnotic amnesia
   d. implicit memory

   (Conceptual, Obj. 3.2)

9. Sometimes when driving, you may have periods in which you don't pay attention to the driving; in fact, you may not recall the drive at all! This form of "highway hypnosis" best illustrates:

   a. subjective consciousness
   b. subconscious processes
   c. preconscious processes
   d. selectivity

   (Conceptual, Obj. 1.3)

10. REM/NREM sleep seems to follow a 90-minute cycle. This is an example of a(n):

    a. circadian rhythm
    b. ultradian rhythm
    c. hypnogogic phase
    d. hypnopompic phase

    (Factual, Obj. 2.2)

11. In *all* 50 states, a blood alcohol level of _____ is considered evidence of intoxication.

    a. 0.025
    b. 0.05
    c. 0.01
    d. 0.10

    (Factual, Obj. 3.3)

12. Jason goes to a rock concert and some of his friends give him a drug to take during the show. Jason soon starts to hallucinate; the walls of the auditorium seem to "breathe" and "pulsate." His sensory impressions become so bizarre that he panics, freaks out, and has to have medical attention. The medical authorities suspect he has ingested:

    a. hash
    b. cocaine
    c. amphetamine
    d. LSD

    (Factual, Obj. 3.3)

■ ANSWER KEY ■

Concept 1   1. c
                     2. a
                     3. b

Concept 2   a. REM   d. Stage 4
                     b. wake   e. Stage 1
                     c. Stage 3   f. Stage 2

Concept 3   Depressants: Valium, alcohol, barbiturates, Librium
                     Stimulants: speed, nicotine, caffeine, cocaine
                     Hallucinogens: peyote cactus, marijuana, LSD, angel dust

Chapter   Acrostic = Consciousness
Exercise
                     a. latent content   h. manifest
                     b. depressants   i. neodissociation
                     c. hypnotic   j. autistic
                     d. psychoactive   k. listening
                     e. synergistic   l. hallucinogens
                     f. subconscious   m. hypnogogic
                     g. stimulants

	Practice Exam 1	**Practice Exam 2**
1.	d, p. 146	c, pp. 146–147
2.	c, p. 150	c, p. 150
3.	a, p. 145	a, p. 150
4.	a, p. 148	c, pp. 157–158
5.	d, pp. 154–155, 158	b, p. 154
6.	a, p. 159	b, pp. 159–160
7.	b, p. 162	c, p. 163
8.	b, p. 165	c, p. 164
9.	b, p. 163	b, pp. 149–150
10.	a, p. 161	b, p. 154
11.	c, p. 166	d, p. 168
12.	b, p. 168	d, pp. 170–171

CRITICAL THINKING ESSAY 2

How Should Dreams Be Studied and Interpreted?

For thousands of years people have been fascinated by their dreams and have wondered what they meant. Many ancient cultures believed that dreams were our link with the supernatural. People who had strong, frequent, vivid, or particularly meaningful dreams were considered to be communicating with divine spirits. Some African and Micronesian tribes still ascribe religious meaning to dreams. Psychics claim that their dreams enable them to foretell the future, experience distant events, or locate lost people. In the field of psychology, dreams have a narrower use. Although a few researchers are exploring ways of using dreams to enhance creativity and to solve problems (e.g., Cartwright, 1977; LaBerge et al., 1981), for the most part only psychodynamically oriented therapists (whose viewpoint is described in Chapters 17 and 19) make extensive use of dreams, as a way of tapping their patients' unconscious processes.

THE SYSTEMATIC STUDY OF DREAMS

Until the beginning of this century, dreaming was seen by the general public and by scientists as merely the mind's response to bodily sensations (e.g., Maury, 1878; Stümpell, 1877; cited in Freud, 1900/1965). Not until the turn of the century did dreaming receive any systematic study.

Freud's Method of Dream Interpretation.   In 1900 Sigmund Freud published one of his most important works, *The Interpretation of Dreams.* In this book Freud argued that dreams were not merely "epiphenomena," as others suggested, but meaningful symbolic representations of unconscious processes. Each dream contained its *manifest content* (the frequently bizarre combinations of the dreamer's daily experiences, memories, and sensations) and its *latent content* (the unconscious meaning lying beneath the surface). Dreams were therefore "the royal road to the unconscious."

Freud devised a methodology for interpreting dreams that has been widely accepted and is still employed by thousands of therapists. Freud held that dreams should be regarded as symptoms of psychological processes, particularly the fulfillment of unconscious wish impulses. To understand these impulses the dream had to be properly interpreted. For this to happen, the dreamer (usually a patient) had to do two things: (1) concentrate on the dream as it was happening so as to be able to recall it better and to report it in as much detail as possible, and (2) eliminate self-criticism (i.e., self-evaluations that could lead to self-censoring). During sleep the barrier of unconscious defenses is lowered a bit; the dreamer should try to recall and relate as much of this original material as possible.

Interpreting dreams also entailed a few duties for the therapist. First, the therapist had to be careful to consider both the detailed aspects of each dream element and the overriding themes of the dream as a whole (and, more generally, the psychical themes of the person's life). Second, the therapist had to know the person quite well in order to determine which dream events represented important issues in that person's life. Even more important, the therapist had to look out for new, nonobvious meanings in dream events. Most modern therapists are adept at this kind of interpretation—so adept, in fact, that they often translate the manifest content of dream material into its latent content by rote. Such unthinking, "automatic" dream analysis can lead to routine interpretations and insensitivity to surface information (Margulies, 1985).

Freud (1900/1965) did not provide therapists with a precise procedure for dream interpretation. Instead, he illustrated his method through the example of a dream he himself had on the night of July 23–24, 1895. In his dream Freud was at a reception at a large hall. He pulled aside Irma, a patient of his, to chastise her for not having accepted his "solution" yet. She complained of multiple pains and a "choking" feeling. Freud called over a colleague, Dr. M., who also examined her. Dr. M. confirmed Freud's diagnosis but added that dysentery would soon cure Irma by eliminating the toxins in her body (medically a ridiculous statement). Two other young physician friends, Otto and Leopold, also examined her. Freud concluded that Otto had instigated Irma's symptoms by giving her a dangerous injection, and doing it carelessly to boot.

Freud's detailed analysis of each line of this "specimen dream" contains several noteworthy aspects. First, he is annoyed at Irma's foolish and recalcitrant attitude and wishes he could exchange her for another patient whom he finds more agreeable. Second, Dr. M., who has recently disagreed with Freud (as have Irma and Otto), is portrayed as kindly but incompetent ("an ignoramus"). Otto is seen as careless and dangerous. Like Irma, Freud wishes he could replace these two doctors with other, more competent acquaintances. Finally, Freud relates many of the dream events to his own past failings and to his need to appear competent.

Research on the Physiology of Dreaming.   In the 1950s, a group of medical researchers at the University of Chicago began their pioneering work on the physiology of sleep and dreaming. They soon observed that discrete periods of rapid eye movement (REM) sleep occurred four or five times a night (Aserinsky and Kleitman, 1955). When volunteer subjects were awakened during these periods, approximately 80 to 85 percent of them reported that they had just been dreaming (Dement and Kleitman, 1957; Dement and Wolpert, 1958). These researchers uncovered other characteristics of dreams: dream sleep is one stage of a recurring sleep cycle that lasts about 90 minutes; eye movements in REM sleep seem to correspond to how the eyes would move in the dream; the duration of a dream is roughly equal to the time it would take the events to occur in reality; when people are deprived of REM sleep, they make it up on a later night and begin to dream in non-REM (NREM) sleep. However, these findings revealed little about why people dream what they do.

In an early experiment on the content of dreams, William Dement and E. A. Wolpert (1958) tried to determine whether specific external stimuli (such as noises and lights) affect what people dream about. Sixteen volunteer subjects were presented with one of three stimuli—a steady tone, a 100-watt light, or a spray of cold water from a syringe—while they were in REM sleep. A few minutes after the stimulus was presented, subjects were awakened and asked to describe what they had just been thinking about. These reports were tape-recorded and were later transcribed verbatim, with names and other identifying information deleted. A panel of judges determined the extent of light, noise, or water in dream content. (This was not easy. For example, did dreaming of a bell indicate that the sleeper had heard the tone? Did dreaming of a sunny day mean that the light had had an effect? For the most part, only instances where the stimulus seemed to provoke a sudden *shift* in dream content were scored.) With only a few exceptions, the external stimuli had little effect on dreams. (Apparently, the exceptions are so interesting that this research is often reported as having proved that external stimuli during sleep *do* have an effect on dream content!)

Dement and Wolpert (1958) also wondered whether internal stimuli (such as hunger, thirst, and sexual urges) affect dream content. On five occasions three subjects did not have any liquids for 24 hours or longer before they slept. The experimenters expected them to dream about water or the lack of water (for example, pouring glasses of water or being in a desert), but again the external stimulus failed to have the expected effect. In a later experiment (Bokert, 1968), however, subjects ate a spicy dinner before bed. Under these conditions, most reported dreams of being thirsty.

Most theories about the role of dreams involve complex interactions between presleep stimuli and dream content. For example, do people who feel inadequate, perhaps because of a recent failure, have dreams involving themes of success or power (a wish fulfillment) or failure and humiliation (a carryover from waking life)? To test these sorts of questions, Rosalind Cartwright and her associates (Cartwright, 1977; Cartwright et al., 1969; Kling, Borowitz, and Cartwright, 1976) recruited two groups of subjects for a study of how sexual arousal affected dream content. One group consisted of heterosexual medical students who worked at the same hospital as the experimenters. The other group was composed of members of a gay activist group at a nearby, but unaffiliated, college. Both groups watched two 10-minute sexually explicit films while wearing penile strain gauges. The gauges confirmed that all subjects were sexually aroused by the movies. Subjects' sleep was monitored in the laboratory the night before they saw the films and for the four nights afterward. In this study, too, subjects were awakened during REM sleep and asked to report what they had just been thinking about, and their reports were transcribed verbatim (with identifying material deleted).

The dream reports were then interpreted psychodynamically, with an emphasis on their sexual content. The researchers expected the medical students, who were being evaluated by fellow hospital personnel, to suppress their sexual reactions and instead to present themselves as disinterested professionals. In contrast, the experimenters expected that the gay subjects would be motivated to describe their sexual thoughts in detail and to present themselves as normal, healthy individuals. These expectations were borne out: explicit sexual behavior was frequently a topic of homosexuals' dreams, but was rarely a part of the medical students' dreams. If medical students did report a sexual theme, they usually did so in a rather distant, objective

manner. Here is an example of a medical student's dream report:

> I was <u>walking through</u> a patient's room in order to get to another one, and she had just returned from the operating room and had on one of those <u>little short robes</u>. She was indignant that I had gone through her room and made some remark about it not being a thoroughfare. (<u>Like a prostitute's room, but he makes a point that he does</u> not <u>stay</u>.) [*Note:* special emphasis and parenthetical comment were added by the experimenters.]

The experimenters concluded that dreams serve two functions: First, if important issues or concerns in a person's life are not resolved, dreams provide an opportunity to tie up these loose ends (a process that psychologists call *closure*). Second, dreams allow a person to reassert his or her self-concept—as a medical professional or gay activist, for example).

Cartwright and her colleagues are also investigating the impact of important, complex real-life events such as going through psychotherapy (Melstrom and Cartwright, 1983) and getting divorced (Cartwright et al., 1984). These studies use the same basic methodology of her previous work, with the exception that the important stimulus (the therapy or the divorce) is an exterior factor and is therefore less controllable than laboratory stimuli.

CRITICAL ANALYSIS OF DREAM RESEARCH

Whenever we analyze psychological research, it is very important to look not only at what was found but also at *how* it was found. Of course, any methodology has limits, usually of an ethical or practical nature. For example, most psychodynamic therapists believe that adult neuroses stem from early childhood traumas, which can be tapped through dream analysis. But no one would have the callousness or the funds to subject an experimental group of children to severe emotional traumas and then analyze their dreams 25 years later. So psychologists work within reasonable constraints. When such limitations result in a badly flawed methodology, the validity of the conclusions is called into question. That is why we must look at *how* a conclusion was derived in order to assess whether the conclusion is reasonable or not.

Analysis of Freud's Method.   A central concept in Freud's (1900/1965) method of interpreting dreams, that dreams have not only manifest content but also latent content, advanced our understanding of dreams in two fundamental ways. First, Freud was able to provide meaning for the often disjointed and illogical events that occurred in our dreams. Dreams became less mysterious—and ultimately more readily understandable. Second, by attending both to people's day-to-day experiences and to long-standing issues in their lives, this methodology reconciled the subtle meaningfulness of dreams and their apparent disjointedness.

However, Freud's method is not without its problems. One difficulty is that the method requires the interpreter to know the dreamer very well in order to understand the symbolic connections between dream events and real experiences. The interpreter's knowledge of the subject can easily lead to experimenter bias, with the interpreter coming up with dream analyses that support his or her prior view of the subject. Conversely, a dream interpreter who does *not* know the dreamer well can make a false interpretation because he or she is not aware of the actual symbolic referent.

A second problem with Freud's method arises when the subject knows the interpreter fairly well and thus may understand what sort of dream content the experimenter expects to hear. Consciously or unconsciously, the subject may modify his or her reports to conform to this implicit expectation, or demand characteristic.

A third major problem concerns the fact that the dreamer typically decides which dream to report to the interpreter. This reporting procedure gives rise to several potential difficulties.

1. Why does the subject choose a particular dream to report? The research cited earlier (Dement and Wolpert, 1958;

Cartwright, 1977) revealed that most dreams are forgotten, some just seconds after they occur. Is there something special or unusual about dreams that end up being reported? As long as the subject is free to choose which dream to report, we will never know.

2. There is always a delay between dream and report. At best, the dream will have occurred last night, necessitating a delay of several hours. At worst, the dream may have occurred years ago. In fact, persistent memories are often seen as most clinically relevant, so the chances of a patient reporting a very old dream are not insignificant. Since our memory is not perfect and usually continues to erode over time, long reporting delays mean that many potentially important details are forgotten. Even more insidious, events in the dream may be unconsciously altered.

3. The reporting procedure gives the subject time to edit or censor the dream. This alteration may occur with or without the subject's awareness. Freud himself intentionally withholds significant material from reports. In a footnote he states, "I am obliged to add . . . that in scarcely any instance have I brought forward the *complete* interpretation of one of my own dreams, as it is known to me. I have probably been wise in not putting too much faith in my readers' discretion" (1900/1965, p. 138).

4. Subjects vary dramatically in their descriptive abilities. Some reports are terse and clipped; others are expansive and loaded with detail. It is often forgotten that an interpreter gets to interpret only the *report* of a dream, not the dream itself.

A fourth problem area is Freud's description of the interpretation process. Even a brief glance at Freud's (1900/1965) text reveals that he does not describe his method in terms of any objective standards. Rather, he explains it solely by way of an example, which makes it difficult for others to generalize from what he has done. Moreover, even in his detailed example, Freud never states exactly *how* he decides on one interpretation or another. The few specific steps or procedures that he does give are not clear, for he makes seemingly arbitrary exceptions with little support. As a result, Freud's method of interpreting dreams seems to be based on his natural talents or instincts and his description of the method is not very useful for instructing others. Accordingly, those who wish to learn the art of dream interpretation are free to adopt those associations that they see as most appropriate or fitting in any particular case. This individualistic, laissez-faire approach cannot be considered very methodical or objective.

Finally, the motives of both the dreamer and the analyst must be taken into account. Freud summarized the latent content of his dream about Irma and its relation to waking events in the following way: His treatment of Irma was only partially successful. He has discussed this case with two colleagues, Dr. M. and Otto. Freud seems to be particularly irked by Otto's comment, "She's better, but not quite well," which Freud admits is accurate. In addition, Irma, Dr. M., and Otto all disagreed with one of Freud's recent suggestions, which probably was part of Irma's treatment. In response to these comments, Freud dreams that Irma is "foolish" and "recalcitrant," Dr. M. is an "ignoramus," and Otto is "hasty" and "careless." To Freud, the motive for the dream is fulfillment of the wish to seek "revenge" for their "groundless reproaches." Freud acknowledges that this "revenge" is illogical, both in its motivation and in its execution, but he does not consider it neurotic. In fact, he chose to analyze his own dream precisely because he was not neurotic (he describes himself as an "approximately normal person"). This clearly self-serving (or self-protecting) bias is probably not limited to Freud, and the possibility of such distortion should be considered whenever dreams are analyzed by the psychodynamic method.

Analysis of Physiological Research.

In an attempt to overcome the problems of delayed reporting and the bias inherent in traditional dream interpretations, researchers turned to physiological methods to assess when dreams were taking place and when to elicit dream reports. By monitoring subjects' brain waves and eye movements, it became clear when subjects entered REM periods. By waking subjects during these periods, researchers were quite successful in minimizing subjects' forgetting, memory distortions, and dream selection biases. They also avoided experimenter bias by having dream records transcribed, made anonymous, and interpreted by independent judges. They also seemed to eliminate the demand characteristics of the procedure by simply asking subjects in an open-ended way to state what they had just been thinking about (not even making subjects acknowledge that they had been dreaming).

Although these techniques avoided many of the problems inherent in dream research, they could not eliminate all of them. Dement and Wolpert (1958) noted that subjects often forgot their dreams, sometimes within seconds after waking. For this reason it was crucial for reports to be elicited as soon after waking as possible, and definitely before subjects were distracted. In addition, subjects' dream reports varied greatly in their descriptions. One subject might simply report walking down a street, while another might describe the street itself, the buildings, the traffic signs, and so on. Another problem, one that was specific to this procedure, was that subjects were highly motivated to go back to sleep and thus might be likely to give short, terse reports. Dement and Wolpert describe a problem that is probably more potentially damaging than these other three: It is incredibly difficult to assess objectively the content of a dream. In most cases a dream is either too vague or too difficult to categorize reliably. Recall their attempts to see if external stimuli (light, sound, or water) affected dream content. Let's say that the subject dreamed about lying on the beach. This theme could indicate that any of the three stimuli was effective: the warm sun (light), the roar of the waves (sound), or the nearby ocean (water). Of course, it is just as likely that the subject would have dreamed about lying on the beach even without the external stimuli.

The experiments conducted by Cartwright and her colleagues suffered not only from the same limitations but also from a more serious problem. By attempting to analyze complex interactions between stimuli and dream content, these researchers were required to interpret subjectively the dream reports of their subjects. By highlighting the phrases "walking through" and "short little robes" (not to mention inserting the parenthetical comment) in the medical student's dream report, quoted above, the researchers indicate that they had a specific hypothesis about the meaning of the student's dream, and their intuitions led to experimenter bias. They believed that the motivation to appear professional led the medical student to reject any expression of sexual interest in the woman in his dream. However, it seems just as plausible that the woman represents the medical student himself, who feels resentment toward the experimenters for monitoring his sexual arousal with a strain gauge (represented by the "little short robe") and for constantly interrupting his REM sleep (""walking through"; "indignant that I had gone through her room"). Many other interpretations are also possible.

This final problem is reminiscent of something Yogi Berra once said: "Prediction is very difficult, especially about the future." The methods of Freud and of Cartwright and her colleagues share a common, fundamental limitation. Because both methods attempt to interpret dream content *after* the dream has occurred, they can only hope to *explain,* or interpret, dream content. Apart from the fact that any dream can be plausibly interpreted in many ways, the problem is that the task of psychology is not merely to explain behavior, but to *predict* it. Only by predicting behavior, as the scientific method demands, can we learn anything conclusive about human nature. Unfortunately, the methodology of Dement and Wolpert (1958), the only procedure discussed here that had the potential to predict dreams, failed to do so. The researchers suggested two possible reasons for this failure: (1) their hypotheses about the influence of external stimuli on dreams were incorrect and (2) the illogical, disjointed, and sometimes bizarre nature of dreams makes them very difficult to categorize reliably, and thus very difficult to predict.

CONCLUSION: WHAT DO WE KNOW ABOUT DREAMS?

The University of Chicago research group was very successful early on in identifying the physiological aspects of dreams—their periodic occurrence during REM sleep, their duration, and so on. However, neither this research group nor any other has succeeded in pinpointing the meaning of dreams. Evidence that dreams are related to internal stimuli is mixed, and proof that they are related to external stimuli is very weak. Although many theorists have suggested that dreams involve tying up life's loose ends, they have been unable to establish this with any certainty. The main stumbling block seems to be that dreams are very difficult, if not impossible, to assess without resorting to interpretation—which, as we have seen, has its own pitfalls.

Recent theories (e.g., Crick and Mitchison, 1983) propose that dreams are merely the result of the brain's attempt to make sense out of random electrical discharges. However, these theories are themselves purely speculative. Worse, they are virtually identical to those Freud (1900/1965) tried to dispel at the turn of the century. We are left with the uncomfortable feeling that we have learned nothing definite about dreams since then.

Are dreams the mind's attempt to fulfill a wish? Are they a way to provide "closure"? Do they support our self-concepts? Are they indications of "carryover" from our waking state? Are they merely random discharges of electricity in the brain? At the present stage of the young science of psychology, much of what we know about the meaning of dreams is whatever we choose to believe.

REFERENCES

Aserinsky, E., and N. Kleitman. Two types of ocular motility occurring in sleep. *Journal of Applied Physiology,* 1955, *8,* 1–10.

Bokert, E. The effects of thirst and a related verbal stimulus on dream reports. *Dissertation Abstracts,* 1968, *28,* 4753.

Cartwright, R. D. *Night life: Explorations in dreaming.* Englewood Cliffs, N. J.: Prentice-Hall, 1977.

Cartwright, R. D., N. Bernick, G. Borowitz, and A. Kling. The effect of an erotic movie on the sleep and dreams of young men. *Archives of General Psychiatry,* 1969, *20,* 262–271.

Cartwright, R. D., S. Lloyd, S. Knight, and I. Trenholme. Broken dreams: A study of the effects of divorce and depression on dream content. *Psychiatry,* 1984, *47,* 251–259.

Crick, F., and G. Mitchison. The function of dream sleep. *Nature,* 1983, *304,* 111–114.

Dement, W. C., and N. Kleitman. The relation of eye movements during sleep to dream activity: An objective method for the study of dreaming. *Journal of Experimental Psychology,* 1957, *53,* 339–346.

Dement, W. C., and E. A. Wolpert. The relationship of eye movements, body motility, and external stimuli to dream content. *Journal of Experimental Psychology,* 1958, *55,* 543–53.

Kling, A., G. Borowitz, and R. D. Cartwright. Plasma levels of 17-hydroxycorticosteroids during sexual arousal in men. *Journal of Psychosomatic Research,* 1976, *16,* 215–221.

LaBerge, S. P., L. E. Nagel, W. C. Dement, and V. P. Zarcone. Lucid dreaming verified by volitional communication during REM sleep. *Perceptual and Motor Skills,* 1987, *52,* 727–732.

Melstrom, M. A., and R. D. Cartwright. Effects of successful vs. unsuccessful psychotherapy outcome on some dream dimensions. *Psychiatry,* 1983, *46,* 51–65.

RESPONDING TO CRITICAL ESSAY 2

1. There are currently many popular texts and self-help books that teach "dream interpretation." Typically, these guides offer a lexicon, or dictionary, of prevalent dream symbols and what these symbols mean. Readers generally find a lot of intuitive appeal to such "recipe" explanations of their dream symbols. Very much like the daily horoscope, some sort of dream application can be found relevant to events in their own personal lives.

   What makes this "method" of dream interpretation unscientific and ultimately inconclusive?

2. Traditional dream interpretation (especially Freudian influenced systems) contain several serious methodological flaws. Even among highly skilled practitioners, traditional methods of dream interpretation contain problems.

   What are some examples of demand characteristics and experimenter effects that exist in dream analysis?

3. [This question is meant to be discussed with your classmates.] With the cooperation of your instructor, conduct a class survey on what seems to be the most popular explanation(s) for dream phenomena. Which do you find supportable?

CHAPTER 7
Learning

KEY TERM ORGANIZER

Learning refers to a long-lasting change in an organism's disposition to behave in certain ways as a result of experience. *Habituation* is the simplest form of learning; it means that an organism has become familiar with a particular stimulus. Each time an organism encounters a new or unexpected object, there is a "surprise reaction," known as the *orienting reflex*. After habituation, the same object causes no such reflex.

The ability to grasp time sequences is a central feature of *associative learning*. In *classical conditioning,* the organism learns to associate two specific kinds of stimuli in a temporal sense. The following chart summarizes four elements in the classical conditioning paradigm.

The process by which an organism learns an association in classical conditioning is known as *acquisition.* Once a conditioned stimulus has been established, it may in turn serve as an unconditioned stimulus for other neutral stimuli. This is known as *second-order conditioning.*

STIMULI		RESPONSES	
Unconditioned (UCS)	**Conditioned (CS)**	**Unconditioned (UCR)**	**Conditioned (CR)**
A stimulus that naturally elicits a response	A neutral stimulus that comes to elicit a response as a result of being paired with the UCS	An unlearned automatic response evoked by a UCS	A response that occurs in response to the CS in anticipation of the UCS

Extinction is a process of weakening the conditioned response by dissociating two stimuli (the CS without the UCS). If the CR has been extinguished, it may recur after a lapse in time; this is termed *spontaneous recovery*. However, after complete extinction, if the UCS is once again paired with the old CS, the extinguished response will be quickly relearned, a process called *reconditioning.*

Once an organism has been conditioned to respond to a specific stimulus, other similar stimuli or situations may elicit the same response. This response is called *stimulus generalization.* The opposing learning process is *discrimination,* in which an organism learns to distinguish among stimuli and to respond differently to each. Experiments have shown that a correlation between a CS and UCS, by itself, may not always lead to conditioning—a phenomenon known as *blocking.*

In *instrumental conditioning* (also called *operant conditioning*), we learn an association between our own response and what follows it, its consequences. When a consequence increases the likelihood or strength of repetition of the behavior that precedes it, the process is called *positive reinforcement.* When a stimulus, usually aversive or unpleasant, is removed after a response, and the removal strengthens that response, the process is called *negative reinforcement.* When the consequence of any behavior suppresses or decreases the frequency of that behavior, the process is known as *punishment.*

Reinforcement schedules are simply patterns that maintain conditioned responses. A *continuous reinforcement schedule* is one in which a reward follows each response. A *partial reinforcement schedule* rewards only some responses. For example, in a *fixed-ratio schedule,* rewards come after a specific number of responses. On a *fixed-interval schedule,* rewards come for the first response that is made after a specific time has elapsed. On a *variable-ratio schedule,* the organism is rewarded after a random number of responses since the last reward. In a *variable-interval schedule,* organisms are rewarded for their first response after a variable period of time has elapsed since the last reward.

Primary reinforcers are reinforcers that reduce basic drives or needs, such as hunger or thirst. Reinforcers that are learned and that do not reduce primary needs are known as *secondary reinforcers.* The *Premack principle* states that any activity an organism finds more preferable can be used to reinforce a less preferable activity.

Negative reinforcement and punishment are often considered together as types of *aversive conditioning.* In *escape learning,* the organism's response ends an unpleasant stimulus, enabling it to escape from an aversive situation. In *avoidance learning,* a neutral signal precedes a noxious event; the organism learns a response that allows it to escape the signal and avoid the event.

The learning of a series of movements making up a skill can be speeded by a process known as *shaping,* in which an organism is reinforced for ever-closer approximations of a desired behavior. The most efficient reinforcement when learning complex skills is immediate *feedback*—information as to whether a response is right or wrong.

Another, rather different form of learning has also been important to the survival of our species: *spatial learning,* which refers to learning where things are located in the environment. While exploring the environment, organisms construct a *cognitive map,* or an internal representation of the way objects and landmarks are arranged in their environment.

Our knowledge is not limited to what we can learn from doing or responding; we can learn by watching others by a process of *observational learning.* We observe and then imitate the behavior of others who serve as *models.* Observational learning and modeling are central concepts of *social cognitive theory,* an approach that combines learning theory with a concern for human thought processes.

MAJOR CONCEPTS AND LEARNING OBJECTIVES

CONCEPT 1   Learning refers to a long-lasting change in an organism's disposition to behave in certain ways as a result of experience. Learning must be inferred from performance.

1.1   Define habituation and describe the orienting reflex

**Concept
Builder 1**

Directions: Read the following descriptions involving infant "learning" and match them up with the appropriate learning process.

Never Too Young to Learn

C 1. Little Elliot has noticed an "interesting" relationship; every time he cries, Mommy or Daddy comes into his bedroom to comfort him. As a result, Elliot cries as frequently as possible!

B 2. Every time the radio is turned on, Elliot seems fascinated and surprised; he turns his head toward the radio and stares at his novel "music box."

A 3. Elliot seems pretty much indifferent to the radio now (a critic in the making!); the novelty seems to have worn off; the music doesn't surprise him anymore.

a. habituation
b. orienting reflex
c. learning

CONCEPT 2

Classical conditioning is a form of learning that involves development of associations between stimuli and responses. Classical conditioning seems to underlie many emotional processes.

2.1 Define conditioned response and identify the basic terminology of classical conditioning.

2.2 List and define the seven principles of classical conditioning presented in the chapter.

2.3 Explain the biological constraints on conditioning and the various genetic and physiological processes involved.

**Concept
Builder 2**

Directions: Look at the following series of charts. They are diagrams of the conditioning process as described by Pavlov. Your task is to identify each stage of the process and fill in the appropriate term from the list below.

Pavlov's Charts

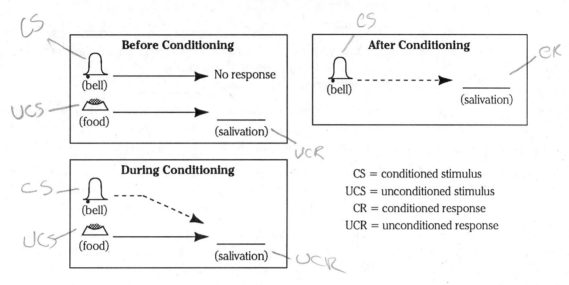

CS = conditioned stimulus
UCS = unconditioned stimulus
CR = conditioned response
UCR = unconditioned response

CONCEPT 3   Instrumental conditioning is a form of learning in which a conditioned or operant behavior precedes a reinforcing stimulus. Much of human behavior is learned and performed because of the consequences that result from such behavior.

3.1   Describe instrumental conditioning and how the basic concepts of reinforcement strengthen learning.

3.2   Describe how instrumental conditioning explains the processes of acquisition, extinction, and recovery.

3.3   Distinguish primary and secondary reinforcers.

3.4   Describe the schedules of reinforcement and outline the different rates of learning that each schedule produces.

3.5   Describe the processes of escape and avoidance learning and how they are related to punishment.

3.6   Outline the procedures of shaping and chaining.

Concept Builder 3

Directions: Read the following suggestions for training your dog to obey commands. For each description, identify the instrumental conditioning principle being illustrated.

1. "Most every dog-training technique involves giving the dog praise for getting closer and closer to the desired behavior being taught."
   Instrumental conditioning principle ___shaping___.

2. "Whenever your dog performs well, give him a pat on the head and say 'good doggie'; consistency in doing this is critical."
   Instrumental conditioning principle ___positive reinforcement___.

3. "To prevent the dog from lunging at people, knee the dog firmly in the chest when it jumps on you and say 'no' in a firm tone."
   Instrumental conditioning principle ___punishment___.

4. "If you do give your dog positive reinforcers, don't do so every time; give the dog a treat or biscuit about every fifth time it does something well."
   Instrumental conditioning principle ___fixed ratio___.

5. "While teaching the dog its name, reward it for coming only when it hears and responds to its name; when the dog approaches to other names, don't give a reward."
   Instrumental conditioning principle ___discrimination___.

6. "Remember, training is a two-way process; you are training your dog and it is training you. For example, when your dog 'begs' for food at the dinner table, you might give in to stop the whining. You have just reinforced the dog for begging and the dog has just demonstrated _____ learning on you!"
   Instrumental conditioning principle ___escape___.

CONCEPT 4   The learning required for complex cognitive tasks depends upon both classical and instrumental conditioning, as is illustrated by spatial learning and social cognitive theory.

4.1   Define and distinguish between temporal-sequence learning and spatial learning.

4.2   Define observational learning and modeling.

4.3   Name and define the four subprocesses that constitute observational learning, according to Albert Bandura.

Concept Builder 4

Directions: Read the following TV viewers' comments about the effects of TV on children. As you read each comment, identify the process of observational learning (Bandura) being emphasized.

Sound Off: The Weekly TV Editorial

_C_ 1. Mrs. H. writes: "My child sees her favorite soap-opera stars bitterly fighting with each other week after week — lying, cheating on each other, stealing, and plotting each other's demise — and being *rewarded* for their deeds. I'm afraid she will do the same thing one day in her relationships."

_A_ 2. Mr. L. writes: "Please congratulate the movie celebrities and music performers for appearing on TV and publicly condemning drinking and driving. My child will attend to them before she will attend to me on this issue."

_d_ 3. Mr. and Mrs. J.D.S. write: "When you broadcast your 'stunt' show the other night, my child attempted the same thing on his bicycle the next day, only he wound up breaking his collarbone! Remember, kids will copy what they see on TV."

_B_ 4. Mr. K. writes: "Thank you for broadcasting your public service message to children teaching them not to talk to strangers. Your little message, 'It's O.K. to say NO,' is very effective. My daughter repeats it all the time (even when I ask her to eat her vegetables!). When she's playing with her doll, she has her doll say it to make-believe strangers. I think it's working—she's formed a mental image of what to say."

a. attention
b. retention
c. motivation
d. reproduction

CHAPTER EXERCISE

Directions: Examine the four events outlined in the behavioral sequence in the box below. Then insert the four events into the appropriate spaces (within the open parentheses) in the respondent conditioning and instrumental learning diagrams.

Diagramming Learning

Behavior Sequence

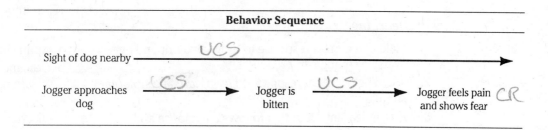

A. Respondent conditioning:

pairing $\left\{\begin{array}{l}\text{Stimulus}_1 \ (\qquad\qquad) \dashrightarrow \text{CR} \ (\qquad\qquad\qquad) \\ \text{Stimulus}_2 \ (\qquad\qquad) \longrightarrow \text{UCR} \end{array}\right.$

Result: $\text{Stimulus}_1 \ (\qquad\qquad)$ tends to elicit CR $(\qquad\qquad\qquad)$

B. Instrumental learning:

$\text{Stimulus}_1 \ (\qquad\qquad) \longrightarrow R \ (\qquad\qquad) \longrightarrow \text{Punisher} \ (\qquad\qquad\qquad)$

Result: $R \ (\qquad\qquad\qquad)$ will tend to occur less in the future!

Learning Match-ups

Classical conditioning

_d_	1.	Response learned in one situation occurring in other similar situations	a. acquisition
_A_	2.	Process by which an association is learned	b. second-order conditioning
_C_	3.	Organism eventually stops expecting UCS	c. extinction
_E_	4.	Learning to respond to one stimulus but not others	d. stimulus generalization
_B_	5.	When a second neutral stimulus (paired with CS) begins to elicit CR by itself.	e. discrimination

Operant conditioning

_D_	1.	Rewards related to lapse of time that occurs after a response	a. schedule of reinforcement
_A_	2.	Basis on which an organism is rewarded	b. superstitious behavior
_B_	3.	Result of accidental relationship between behavior and reinforcer	c. ratio schedules of reinforcement
_C_	4.	Rewards related to number of responses that occur before reinforcer is given.	d. interval schedules of reinforcement

Aversive learning

_C_	1.	Making a correct response to a signaled impending aversive stimulus to *prevent* it	a. punishment
_B_	2.	Learning a correct response to *terminate* an unpleasant stimulus	b. escape learning
_A_	3.	An unpleasant event that follows a response and *weakens* it	c. avoidance learning

Learned rewards and punishers, skills learning, and observational learning

B	1.	Reinforcing ever-closer approximations	a. primary reinforcer
D	2.	Internal representations of the way objects are arranged in their environment	b. shaping
E	3.	Learning patterns of behavior from other people	c. feedback
A	4.	A reinforcer that fulfills a basic need	d. cognitive maps
C	5.	Information as to whether a response is right or wrong	e. modeling

PRACTICE EXAM 1

1. According to the _____ psychologists, in order to define learning, the word "knowledge" would have to be included as part of the definition.

    a. behavioral
    b. cognitive
    c. gestalt
    d. learning

    (Factual, Obj. 1.1)

2. Which of the following is the best evidence of learning (versus performance)?

    a. Sarah, a ten-month-old, is learning to walk at an incredible pace.
    b. Jason raises his hand practically every time the biology teacher asks a question (whether the teacher calls on him or not).
    c. When his last relationship ended, Mark learned something: never lie about your feelings. He is now very open and direct with people he cares about.
    d. Maureen's dog amuses every new guest that comes to the house; if you find the dog's "tickle" spot, it will automatically scratch with its foot.

    (Conceptual, Obj. 1.1)

3. The simplest form of learning is:

    a. cognitive mapping
    b. perceptual/motor skills
    c. temporal sequences
    d. habituation

    (Factual, Obj. 1.1)

4. Every time Morris, the cat, hears the can opener running, he springs into the kitchen expecting food. The can opener "sound" is functioning as the _____ in this conditioned procedure.

    a. UCS
    b. UCR
    c. CS
    d. CR

    (Conceptual, Obj. 2.1)

5.   According to the text, changes in ___synaptic___ transmission along selected neural pathways could be responsible for classical conditioning.

a.   synaptic
b.   cerebral
c.   sensory
d.   motor

(Factual, Obj. 2.3)

6.   While sitting in class one day, Kimberly heard the carpenters working next door. When they started their wood drill, it made her skin crawl because it sounded like her dentist's drill. What conditioning phenomenon is she exhibiting?

a.   reconditioning
b.   stimulus generalization
c.   discrimination
d.   second-order conditioning

(Conceptual, Obj. 2.2)

7.   The test stated that one or more critical conditions must exist for conditioning to be rapid and/or strong. Which of the following is *not* conducive to rapid conditioning?

a.   The conditioned stimulus is conspicuous.
b.   The unconditioned stimulus follows soon after the conditioned stimulus.
c.   The unconditioned stimulus is of low magnitude.
d.   The animal is genetically prepared to connect a particular kind of stimulus to the reaction used as the UCR.

(Factual, Obj. 2.2)

8.   Classical conditioning is to association what instrumental conditioning is to:

a.   pairing
b.   consequences
c.   expectancies
d.   performance

(Conceptual, Obj. 2.1 & 3.1)

9.   Fixed ratio, fixed interval, variable ratio, and variable interval are all examples of:

a.   partial schedules of reinforcement
b.   operant conditioning
c.   positive reinforcement
d.   all of the above

(Factual, Obj. 3.3)

10.   Biofeedback is a procedure used to help people modify involuntary reactions such as blood pressure and heart rate. Biofeedback probably uses _____ conditioning/learning as its basis for gaining voluntary control.

a.   classical
b.   operant
c.   avoidance
d.   aversive

(Conceptual, Obj. 3.4)

11. When skills are being learned, the most *efficient* reinforcement consists of:

    a. immediate feedback
    b. primary reinforcement
    c. partial schedule of reinforcement
    d. conditioned reinforcers

    (Factual, Obj. 3.3)

12. Before Lisa, a real-estate agent, leaves her office with her clients, she "mentally" envisions the order of the houses she will show by area, so as to set up the most efficient route, with the least amount of driving. What does this kind of learning illustrate?

    a. temporal sequences
    b. cognitive maps
    c. associative learning
    d. observational learning

    (Conceptual, Obj. 3.4)

PRACTICE EXAM 2

1. Learning is a change in a behavioral disposition that is caused by:

    a. maturation
    b. reflexes
    c. experience
    d. motivation

    (Factual, Obj. 1.1)

2. Which of the following situations *best* reflects the behavioral approach to defining learning?

    a. The classroom bell rings and you, without even having to think, automatically know it's time to go to the next class.
    b. After reading this chapter's study guide, you do much better on the classroom test.
    c. The sign on the classroom door informs you that class has been moved to another building; you are basically familiar with the location of that building and have no trouble finding the new room.
    d. You have learned to figure out what will be on Dr. Fitzgerald's test; he reviews for the test the day before and practically tells you exactly what to study.

    (Conceptual, Obj. 1.1)

3. A synonym for classical conditioning is:

    a. associationism
    b. instrumental conditioning
    c. Pavlovian conditioning
    d. operant conditioning

    (Factual, Obj. 2.1)

4. Scuba diving would be an example of what kind of learning?

    a. habituation (to the water)
    b. cognitive mapping
    c. acquisition
    d. chaining and shaping

    (Conceptual, Obj. 3.4)

5.   A response that an organism has learned in one situation may occur in response to other similar stimuli or situations. This is called:

   a.   spontaneous recovery
   b.   stimulus generalization
   c.   discrimination
   d.   second-order conditioning

(Factual, Obj. 2.2)

6.   Connotations are words that trigger certain feelings when we hear them; for example, "comprehensive final examination" usually triggers unpleasant feelings in most students. Connotations derive their power from:

   a.   conditioning
   b.   extinction
   c.   habituation
   d.   causal sequences

(Conceptual, Obj. 2.1)

7.   Thorndike's famous "cat in the wooden box" experiment involved a process he called:

   a.   classical conditioning
   b.   instrumental conditioning
   c.   trial-and-error learning
   d.   the free-operant method

(Factual, Obj. 3.1)

8.   Four-year-old Nathan has a conditioned fear of thunder. Whenever he hears thunder, he gets very frightened and apprehensive. But he's not frightened of lightning. When the skies light up, whether a thunderclap occurs or not, he shows no reaction until the "boom" arrives. This appears to be a conditioning phenomenon very much like Kamin's experiments with rats, called:

   a.   generalization gradient
   b.   discrimination
   c.   CS-UCS correlation
   d.   blocking

(Conceptual, Obj. 2.2)

9.   Which of the following is *not* a disadvantage of using punishment?

   a.   Desirable as well as undesirable behavior may disappear.
   b.   Punishment gives no hint of what the person should do.
   c.   The punished person tends to avoid the person who did the punishing.
   d.   Punishment cannot be used in conjunction with positive reinforcement.

(Factual, Obj. 3.4)

10.   Before Larry makes a sales call, he always carries his "lucky" key ring with him on the call. This superstitious behavior works, sometimes. We might say that Larry is on a
   _____ schedule of reinforcement.

   a.   fixed-ratio
   b.   variable-ratio
   c.   fixed-interval
   d.   variable-interval

(Conceptual, Obj. 3.3)

11. The central concept of social cognitive theory is:

   a. spatial learning
   b. observational learning
   c. chaining
   d. cognitive mapping

(Factual, Obj. 4.2)

12. "Sea-World" trains dolphins and killer whales to do an assortment of complex "tricks" and water shows. The procedure used in training them initially involves reinforcing them for anything they do with a fish reinforcer. Gradually, however, the trainers give fish *only* when the animal gets closer and closer to doing a specific act correctly, like retrieving a water ring. This procedure illustrates:

   a. blocking
   b. partial reinforcement schedules
   c. escape training
   d. shaping

(Conceptual, Obj. 3.4)

■ ANSWER KEY ■

CONCEPT 1
1. c
2. b
3. a

CONCEPT 2
Before conditioning: bell = CS; food = UCS; salivation = UCR
During conditioning: bell = CS; food = UCS; salivation = UCR
After conditioning: bell = CS; salivation = CR

CONCEPT 3
1. shaping
2. positive reinforcement
3. punishment
4. fixed ratio
5. discrimination
6. escape

CONCEPT 4
1. c   3. d
2. a   4. b

CHAPTER EXERCISE

Diagramming Learning:

A. Respondent conditioning
   $Stimulus_1$ (sight of dog nearby)
   $Stimulus_2$ (jogger is bitten)
   CR/UCR (fear);
   Result: $Stimulus_1$ (sight of dog nearby)
   CR (fear)

B. Instrumental learning
   $Stimulus_1$ (sight of dog nearby)
   R (jogger approaches dog)
   Punisher (jogger is bitten)
   Result: R (jogger approaches dog)

Learning Match-ups:
Classical conditioning:
    1. d   2. a   3. c   4. e   5. b

Operant conditioning
    1. d   2. a   3. b   4 c

Aversive learning
    1. c   2. b   3. a
Learned rewards and punishers/skills learning/observational learning
    1. b   2. d   3. e   4. a   5. c

Practice Exam 1	**Practice Exam 2**
1. b, p. 177	1. c, pp. 176–177
2. c, p. 177	2. a, pp. 176–177
3. d, p. 177	3. c, p. 178
4. c, pp. 179–180	4. d, pp. 197–198
5. a, p. 187	5. b, p. 183
6. b, pp. 183–184	6. a, pp. 179–180
7. c, pp. 184–185	7. c, p. 187
8. b, p. 187	8. d, p. 188
9. d, pp. 192–193	9. d, pp. 196–197
10. b, pp. 198–199	10. b, p. 193
11. a, p. 198	11. b, p. 201
12. b, p. 200	12. d, pp. 197–198

CHAPTER 8

Memory

KEY TERM ORGANIZER

Memory is the cognitive process of preserving information for use now or in the future. There are three basic memory processes:

1. *Acquisition* is the process of perceiving information, encoding it, and registering it in memory.
2. *Retention* is the process of maintaining information in storage.
3. *Retrieval* is the process by which we get information from storage and bring it back into awareness.

Memory also operates in three different time frames:

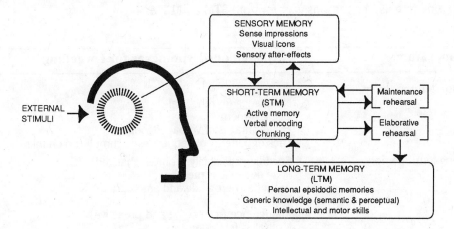

Sensory memory is the momentary lingering of sensory data after stimulation has ceased. *Short-term memory* (STM) is referred to as "working memory": the holding bin for information that a person has actively in mind. Lastly, *long-term memory* (LTM) is the unlimited repository of information we have stored away for future use.

Visual sensory storage, which is often referred to as *iconic memory,* has been studied quite extensively. Auditory sensory storage, or *echoic memory,* is more enduring that iconic memory.

Encoding involves translating data into forms that the memory system can use. *Memory traces* are believed to form physiological changes in the brain in order to record how objects appear. Since sensory representations fade rapidly, *rehearsal* "refreshes" a stimulus, reactivating it before it can fade. Rehearsal helps retain what we want to retain. During short-term memory encoding, the brain organizes incoming information into clusters called *chunks,* and the process of organizing data in this way is called *chunking.* Information is constantly being discarded from short-term memory. *Displacement* is the point at which new incoming information replaces the old. Displacement works together with *decay,* the degeneration of short-term memory traces owing to the passage of time.

In order to retain information indefinitely, we must use some sort of rehearsal to transfer it from short-term to long-term storage. Unthinking, rote repetition of information is called *maintenance rehearsal.* In *elaborative rehearsal,* we expand on the meaning of information, draw inferences about it, and relate it to other things.

Semantic memory is the portion of our knowledge that has to do with the meaning of things and the relationships among them. Long-term memory contains thousands of *schemas,* which allow us to integrate new information with old, and to make inferences about new facts. Procedural schemas, or general understandings of the various elements that schemas contain, are called *scripts.* When we see, hear, feel, smell, or taste something, we build perceptual schemas about it; memory for this type of information is called *perceptual memory.*

Long-term memory is useless unless we can retrieve stored information. *Retrieval clues* are stimuli that aid or trigger retrieval. *Recognition* is the process of identifying a piece of information as familiar. *Recall* is more difficult than recognition because it involves retrieving stored information from memory without the benefit of having that information currently before you. Retrieval can be speeded by *priming,* in which a preparatory cue is presented several seconds before memory is tested.

Sometimes we know that we know something, but we have great trouble pulling it out of memory. This experience is known as the *tip-of-the-tongue phenomenon.* Knowledge of what our memories contain and how best to use the information is known as *metamemory.* Metamemory, in turn, is an aspect of *metacognition,* our knowledge about and ability to monitor our own cognitive processes.

Everyone forgets; the reasons vary for both STM and LTM:

Time Frame	Explanations/Hypotheses for Forgetting
Short-term memory	Inattention No chance for rehearsal Displacement Disadvantages of verbal encoding Lack of patterns or sequences in stimuli (no chunks)
Long-term memory	Encoding specificity (context changed) State-dependent memory Amnesia (retrograde and anterograde) Decay Interference (retroactive and proactive) Motivated forgetting

Memories are easiest to retrieve if the retrieval situation is the same as or similar to the one in which we originally learned them; this is *encoding specificity.* *Interference* is the blurring of one memory by others that are similar to it. Interference can occur in a backward direction (*retroactive interference*) or a forward one (*proactive interference*).

Sometimes, people suffer severe memory deficits, termed *amnesia.* Some amnesics are unable to recall old information, a condition termed *retrograde amnesia.* Others have great difficulty laying down new memories, a condition known as *anterograde amnesia.*

Some drugs can promote an interesting condition known as *state-dependent memory.* Here information is more easily retrieved when a person is in the same physiological state as when he or she learned the information.

We can improve our memory by using *mnemonic systems,* strategies deliberately designed to help people remember. There are several mnemonic systems.

1. *Method of loci* uses a series of loci, or places, to organize material.
2. *Peg-word method* uses ten or more simple words as memory pegs or hooks.
3. *Key-word method* has been used successfully to learn foreign vocabulary words.
4. *PQ4R method* is a hierarchical study method that uses preview, question, read, reflect, recite, and review.

MAJOR CONCEPTS AND LEARNING OBJECTIVES

CONCEPT 1   Memory is the process of acquiring, retaining, and retrieving information. Memory also refers to the knowledge and information actually stored.

1.1   Describe the three processes, or stages, of memory.

1.2   Outline the three-store memory model and describe each of its components

1.3   Describe the sensory memory and distinguish it from short-term memory.

Concept Builder 1

Directions: Examine the definitions below the pyramid. For each definition, identify the appropriate term and write it beneath one of the three points at the base of the pyramid under the correct heading (Processes, Levels of Processing, Time Frames).

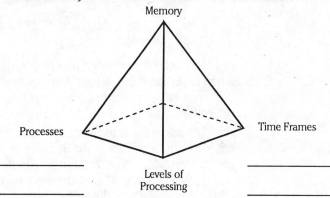

Definitions

1. The process of getting information out of storage: _retrieve_
2. What most people mean when they think of memory: _long-term memory (LTM)_
3. Focusing on the physical, surface properties of a stimulus: _shallow process_
4. Uses encoding to process information: _STM (short term memory)_
5. Stimulus is given meaning and related to other things: _deep process_
6. The process of recording and registering information: _acquisition_

CONCEPT 2

Short-term memory is composed of the currently active stimuli from the environment or from information from long-term memory. Each item in short-term memory has a fairly short duration.

2.1 Describe how the concepts of selective attention and encoding control the entrance of information into short-term memory.

2.2 Discuss the limited capacity of short-term memory and how chunking affects recall.

2.3 Distinguish between decay and displacement processes of forgetting items in short-term memory.

Concept Builder 2

Directions: As a psychology project for his General Psychology class, Professor Hill suggested that one of his students try to deal with daily living on campus without an effectively functioning short-term memory (STM). To simulate this, he walked around campus with his subject, Betty, and every time she used her STM, he called "time" and said, "That's a STM function—you don't have that, remember!" In the exercise below match each situation with the way in which STM is used.

Experiencing STM Loss for a Day

_D_ 1. Prof. Hill was talking about his wife, Barbara, when he asked Betty, "Have you met *her*?" When Betty said, "No, I haven't," Professor Hill called "time."

_A_ 2. Prof. Hill asked Betty to buy them both soft drinks while they were in the Student Union center. He said, "It's my treat; how much change will you need?" Betty paused, then said, "90 cents." Prof. Hill called "time."

Uses of STM:

a. temporary scratch pad

b. holds current intentions and strategies we wish to follow

c. maintains a seemingly smooth-flowing "movie" of our world

d. functions as our conscious awareness (e.g., our immediate conversation)

___ 3. When Prof. Hill and Betty left the Student
        Union, they walked back into the classroom,
        where a student (upon Prof. Hill's instruc-
        tions) was sitting in Betty's seat. Betty said,
        "Excuse me, but I was sitting there." Prof. Hill
        called "time."

___ 4. Prof. Hill explained his little trick to Betty and
        let her have her seat back. Prof. Hill looked at
        his watch and said, "I've got to hurry; my next
        class will be meeting in ten minutes and I've
        got to go completely across campus." Betty, in
        a switch of their roles, called "time"!

CONCEPT 3   Long-term memory refers to our relatively permanent knowledge and skills. It
                  incorporates personal memories (episodic memory), generic knowledge
                  (both semantic and perceptual), and intellectual and motor skills.

                  3.1   Compare maintenance and elaborative rehearsal.

                  3.2   Describe the role of schemas in making inferences and distortions, and
                        in formulating perceptual and sensory long-term memories.

                  3.3   Describe the various mechanisms and processes involved in retrieval of
                        long-term memories.

**Concept
Builder 3**

*Directions: After reading Chapter 8, some of the ways in
which your instructors formulate test questions may make
more sense. Look at the following "test items" and procedures and match them to the direct and indirect measures of
memory being illustrated. Correct answers to test items are
indicated in italic.*

Putting Memory Methods to the Test

___ Sample   The synonym for "primary memory" is short-term   a. free recall
    question 1   memory.   b. cued recall
                   True or false
                   Type of memory measure ___ D pair recog.   c. single-item
                                                                           recognition

___ Sample   There are two kinds of rehearsal: elaborative and   d. pair
    question 2   maintenance. The kind of rehearsal that involves a   recognition
                   "mindless" type of verbal repetition is called (*mainte-*
                   nance).   e. relearning
                   Type of memory measure ___ f priming   f. priming

___ Sample   List the three processes of memory in any order.
    question 3   (*acquisition, retention, retrieval*)
                   Type of memory measure ___ A free recall

_____ Sample
question 4

(This question is from chapter three, "The Brain and Behavior," which you had to reread for this test.)
The "language center" of the brain is located in which hemisphere? (*left*)
Type of memory measure _E relearning_

_____ Sample
question 5

The word "mnemonic" means (*memory-assisting*).
Type of memory measure _B cued recall_

_____ Sample
question 6

Which of the following is not one of the "time-perspectives" of our memory system?
  a.   sensory memory
  b.   short-term memory
  c.   *intermediate memory*
  d.   long-term memory
Type of memory measure _C single item recog._

CONCEPT 4

A variety of factors affect information in long-term memory, contributing to forgetting. However, there are a number of techniques that can be used to facilitate new learning and enhance retrieval.

4.1   Distinguish the concepts of retrieval failure, decay, interference, and motivated forgetting as explanations for forgetting.

4.2   Describe the two kinds of amnesia and the effects of drugs on memory.

4.3   Outline the major mnemonic techniques that can be used to enhance information storage and describe the active retrieval methods of recall, such as the PQ4R method.

**Concept
Builder 4**

Directions: Pretend you are a research psychologist at a university and your field of expertise is memory. You are asked to explain the reason forgetting occurs in each of the following situations. Choose your answer from the list on the right.

Ask the Memory Doctor

_____ 1.   While in New York, Curt saw one of his favorite plays, *Driving Miss Daisy*. He had seen the movie version last year and loved it, but the stage production had a different ending to it. Several weeks later he was telling his best friend about the movie version and incorrectly remembered the ending as it had been portrayed in the stage production.

_____ 2.   When Ken studies, he usually sips on coffee and smokes cigarettes steadily. The stimulants keep him alert and moving through the material briskly. He feels

a.   anterograde amnesia

b.   decay

c.   motivated forgetting

d.   retroactive interference

e.   state-dependent memory

like he accomplishes a lot of studying and remembers the information well. When he gets into a classroom situation, however, *no smoking or drinking* is allowed. He finds that although he's prepared, his recall isn't as quick or lucid as it is when he's quizzing himself at home.

___ 3. Gina's grandmother is very old and unfortunately has symptoms of Alzheimer's disease. Although her past memories of childhood and family members are good, she has great difficulty laying down new memories.

___ 4. Years after Sharon's parents were divorced, Sharon was surprised to learn that she remembered almost nothing of the divorce court battle she witnessed and even testified in. It was as if she had blocked the whole event out of her mind.

___ 5. As Andrew was reading a work by Aristotle, he was surprised by an analogy Aristotle made about the process of memory loss. Aristotle likened memory "traces" in the brain to footpaths worn in the woods. If they are well used, the path stays "open" and worn down (like a memory). If unused, the path grows over with underbrush and eventually "disappears" from lack of use (like an unused memory).

CHAPTER EXERCISE

Directions: This is a variation of an acrostic exercise in which you will read the definitions below the "crossword" boxes and put the correct term in the numbered row that corresponds to the numbered definition. When you have finished filling in all the terms, the letters in the boxes will spell out a significant memory-enhancing concept. Good luck!

10. — — — — ☐
11. — — — ☐ — — — — — — — — — —
12. — — — ☐ — -— — — — — — — —
13. — — — ☐ — — — — —
14. — — — — — -— — — — — ☐ — — — —
15. ☐ — — — — — -— — — —

Definitions:

1. The knowledge of what our memories contain.
2. The principle that memories are easiest to retrieve if the retrieval situation is similar to the one in which we originally learned. Hint: _____ specificity.
3. Forgetting owing to passage of time.
4. Mnemonic system involving a series of places that are firmly fixed in memory.
5. The loss of the ability to lay down new long-term memories.
6. _____ memory is the storage of visual sensory information.
7. A multiple choice test is an example of _____.
8. Clusters of information that the brain can recognize as a familiar pattern.
9. Clusters of interrelated concepts that provide us with general concepts of people, objects, and events.
10. The PQ4R Method helps you _____.
11. The momentary lingering of sensory data after stimulation has ceased.
12. _____-_____ memory refers to retrieving information in the same physiological state as when you learn the information.
13. The silent repetition of material in order to remember it.
14. Also called "working memory."
15. _____-_____ recognition is where you simply identify an item as one you already have in memory.

PRACTICE EXAM 1

1. Which of the following is *not* one of the stages of remembering?

    a. decoding
    b. acquisition
    c. retrieval
    d. retention

    (Factual, Obj. 1.1)

2. Memory processes are remarkably similar to information processing done by a personal computer. For example, once data are stored on a disk, it is "called up" and displayed on the screen in front of the user for review and modification. This process of taking information out of "storage" for processing is most like:

a.   acquisition
b.   storage
c.   encoding
d.   retrieval

(Conceptual, Obj. 1.2)

3.   Converting information from one form to another form before recording it in memory
     is a process called:

a.   selective attention
b.   acquisition
c.   encoding
d.   retrieval

(Factual, Obj. 1.1)

4.   Joan was in a phone booth looking up a number to dial. Just as she started to dial the
     number, a passerby asked for the time, causing her to have to look the number up
     again. This illustrates:

a.   the brevity of STM
b.   the limited use of visual icons
c.   a "fleeting sense impression"
d.   chunking

(Conceptual, Obj. 2.2)

5.   Thirty years ago, George Miller proposed that short-term memory could maintain no
     more than _____ chunks of information without error.

a.   five
b.   seven
c.   nine
d.   twelve

(Factual, Obj. 2.2)

6.   Michael called the "Galleria 8" theaters for current movie times of the eight movies
     showing there. As the recorded message was playing, he found that after about the
     fourth movie, the titles and times got all jumbled together in his mind. He couldn't
     even remember the first three—the information was presented so fast that the latter
     information just seemed to crowd out the earlier information. This STM forgetting can
     be explained by:

a.   lack of chunks in the presenting stimuli
b.   displacement
c.   selective attention to the last four movie times
d.   ambiguous verbal encoding

(Conceptual, Obj. 2.3)

7.   The text stated that chess masters can visually reproduce a chessboard with only a five-
     second look. This is explained by:

a.   chunking
b.   selective attention
c.   encoding specificity
d.   displacement

(Factual, Obj. 2.1)

8. Simon was having a hard time recalling the first five U.S. presidents until his teacher gave him a hint: "The initial letters of the last names are W A J M M." Simon immediately answered correctly. The teacher's hint brought the temporarily inaccessible information into consciousness. This stimulus is called:

    a. maintenance rehearsal
    b. metamemory
    c. schema
    d. retrieval cue

    (Conceptual, Obj. 3.3)

9. What term best fits this memory retrieval condition: "A state of mild torment, something like the brink of a sneeze"?

    a. cued recall
    b. amnesia
    c. tip-of-the-tongue phenomenon
    d. priming

    (Factual, Obj. 4.1)

10. Tony has just finished his course on real estate with a "A." Although he is thoroughly knowledgeable about the kinds of clauses that appear in sales contracts, he is temporarily unable to correct the wording of a clause on an actual contract his best friend asked him to look over. What threw him was the way the words appeared in the contract versus the way they appear in his textbook. Why was this retrieval temporarily difficult?

    a. He experienced a partial recall.
    b. He was affected by the verbal context change.
    c. He did not use elaborative rehearsal.
    d. He experienced displacement.

    (Conceptual, Obj. 4.1)

11. Sigmund Freud is credited with what concept of forgetting?

    a. interference
    b. decay
    c. motivated forgetting
    d. tip-of-the-tongue phenomenon

    (Factual, Obj. 3.2)

12. "He did badly on the test because the copies were poor." This statement is made more understandable when we add the clue "lecture notes." This exercise illustrates the role of _____ in comprehension.

    a. visual icons
    b. cued recall
    c. "nodes"
    d. schemas

    (Factual, Obj. 3.2)

PRACTICE EXAM 2

1. _____ is the memory process that is basically the same thing as "storage."

    a. acquisition
    b. retention
    c. rehearsal
    d. retrieval

    (Factual, Obj. 1.1)

2. Listeners attending to an extremely fast talker can comprehend "meaning" even though information is coming into sensory memory at a fast rate. This is best explained by:

    a. iconic memory
    b. echoic memory
    c. shallow processing
    d. deep processing

    (Factual, Obj. 1.2)

3. The text stated that one way information is kept "active" in STM is by:

    a. verbal encoding
    b. selective attention
    c. rehearsal
    d. instant retrieval

    (Factual, Obj. 2.1)

4. Which of the following would most probably *not* be in LTM before you were asked to give a response?

    a. the name of the elementary school you attended
    b. your mother's maiden name
    c. the number of the pizza parlor you just looked up
    d. your father's birthplace

    (Conceptual, Obj. 3.1)

5. The text presented an experiment on STM by Sternberg involving searching "times" for information in STM. The main findings was that the *time* a subject took to decide whether a test digit was one of the memory set increased in direct proportion to:

    a. the *time* given to learn the task set numbers
    b. the *number* of items in the task set
    c. the displacement that occurred in STM
    d. the size of the sensory aftereffects

    (Factual, Obj. 2.3)

6. As a quarterback approaches the line of scrimmage, he has to quickly scan the defensive line for familiar defensive lineups (patterns) so that signals can be relayed immediately to the offense. This process of looking for familiar sequences or patterns illustrates:

    a. verbal encoding
    b. selective attention
    c. chunking
    d. displacement

    (Conceptual, Obj. 2.1)

7. Which of the following uses a "preparatory cue" to aid retrieval?

    a. cued recall
    b. pair recognition
    c. single-item recognition
    d. priming

    (Factual, Obj. 3.1)

8. In order to remember the term "retrograde amnesia," Carla deliberately forms several associations: "retro" means "backwards"; she received "retroactive" pay once from a former employer; she visualized a person not being able to remember what happened just before a head injury, and so on. Carla is using what to strengthen the associations in LTM?

    a. maintenance rehearsal
    b. cued recall
    c. elaborative rehearsal
    d. peg-word mnemonics

    (Conceptual, Obj. 4.3)

9. The greater the change in the retrieval situation, the poorer our recall of the target memory. This principle is known as:

    a. state-dependent memory
    b. physical context
    c. verbal context
    d. encoding specificity

    (Factual, Obj. 4.1)

10. When Phil entered college, one requirement was that he take calculus for his engineering degree. Phil was very anxious about this requirement because it had been two years since he had calculus in high school. Once in the class, however, Phil found the old formulas and theorems coming back to him quickly. This phenomenon illustrates:

    a. priming
    b. relearning
    c. schema recall
    d   episodic memory

    (Conceptual, Obj. 4.1)

11. "One is a bun, two is a shoe, three is a . . ." is associated with what mnemonic technique?

    a. method of loci
    b. peg-word systems
    c. key-word system
    d. PQ4R method

    (Factual, Obj. 4.3)

12. Nalley is taking both psychology and sociology this quarter and finding that because they are so similar, she's having a hard time keeping the terms each discipline uses separate. In response to this week's psychology exam, for example, she incorrectly recalled last week's sociology terms. What is occurring?

    a. retroactive interference
    b. encoding specificity
    c. proactive interference
    d. displacement

    (Conceptual, Obj. 4.1)

■ **ANSWER KEY** ■

Concept 1
Processes: (1) retrieval (6) acquisition
Levels of processing: (3) shallow processing (5) deep processing
Time frames: (2) long-term memory (4) short-term memory

Concept 2
1. d
2. a
3. c
4. b

Concept 3
1. d
2. f
3. a
4. e
5. b
6. c

Concept 4
1. d
2. e
3 a
4. c
5. b

Chapter Exercise

1 metamemory
2. encoding
3. decay
4. method of loci
5. anterograde amnesia
6. iconic
7. pair recognition
8. chunks
9. schema
10. study
11. sensory memory
12. state-dependent
13. rehearsal
14. short-term memory
15. single-item

(*) Vertical column spells "mnemonic systems."

Practice Exam 1

1. a, p. 209
2. d, p. 209
3. c, pp. 209, 213
4. a, pp. 215–216
5. b, p. 216
6. b, p. 217
7. a, p. 216
8. d, p. 225
9. c, p. 226
10. b, p. 228
11. c, p. 230
12. d, p. 220

Practice Exam 2

1. b, p. 209
2. b, p. 212
3. c, p. 215
4. c, p. 218
5. b, p. 217
6. c, p. 216
7. d, p. 225
8. c, p. 218
9. d, pp. 227–228
10. b, p. 225
11. b, p. 234
12. c, p. 229

CHAPTER NINE

Cognition

KEY TERM ORGANIZER

Cognition includes using all the ways of using the store of knowledge that each of us possesses. Perception, learning, and memory are all components of thought. Without them, we would have no *concepts,* the general mental categories into which we group our knowledge about the world.

Most everyday concepts are fuzzy, that is, they tend not to be well-defined. For most concepts, there is a most representative member, called a *prototype.* Most families of related concepts fall into a natural hierarchy based on levels of abstraction. When we refer to ordinary objects in everyday conversation, we tend to use *basic level terms,* terms that lie somewhere in the middle of the concept hierarchy.

Reasoning, the ability to think logically, is considered one of the highest forms of human thought. In *deductive reasoning,* we conclude that certain consequences must be true if we grant that certain initial things are true. The basic model of formal deductive reasoning is the *syllogism* (two premises and a conclusion). Even when we are trying to be logical, we may misinterpret a premise and draw the wrong conclusion, as in the *atmosphere effect,* in which certain terms in the premises are carried over to the conclusion.

Another logical pitfall is the *conversion error,* in which we "convert" the premise and erroneously assume that its reverse is also true. When we try to reason logically, we apparently don't follow the laws of logic. Instead, we set up a *mental model* of the problem, using either abstract symbols or imagery.

In deductive reasoning, the conclusion is derived from general rules. In *inductive reasoning,* the general rule is inferred from specific cases. Once our beliefs are formed, we tend to avoid testing our generalizations. When we do decide to test a general belief, we may choose examples that can only confirm it and avoid harder tests which might disprove it. This form of mistaken reasoning is called *confirmation bias.*

Faced with an uncertain situation, most of us come up with an answer based on *heuristics,* quick and intuitively sensible mental rules of thumb that allow us to assess probabilities. We also make many judgments based on a comparison to some standard. The chart on the following page summarizes these major decision-making factors.

Problems differ in many ways. Some are *well-defined:* there is an accepted procedure for determining whether a proposed solution is correct. Other problems are *ill-defined:* there is not a universally accepted method for determining the "correct" answer. Whether a problem is well- or

Judgment and Decision Making

Decision-Making Heuristics	Judgmental Comparisons
Representativeness: We judge the likelihood of an event according to its similarity to the prototype of a given class.	*Framing*: The way a problem is phrased can affect the decision reached.
Availability: We estimate the likelihood of any events occurring on the basis of the availability of supporting evidence in our memory.	*Anchoring*: Our judgment is biased by the starting point from which we are making the judgment.

ill-defined, there is a five-stage process of problem solving one can use. It is known collectively as IDEAL, a handy mnemonic to remember the entire process:

I = Identify what the problem is.
D = Define the problem.
E = Explore possible strategies.
A = Act on a selected strategy.
L = Look back and evaluate the results.

Not all problems can be broken down so easily. A technique known as *means-end analysis* advocates breaking an overall problem down into sub-goals so that they can be achieved by solving smaller problems. An especially effective version of means-end analysis is *working backward* from your goal.

Sometimes the solution to a problem requires that you find an *analogy*, a parallel or correspondence between two different systems whose parts are similar in some way.

Using an inappropriate strategy in the effort to solve a problem is often the result of *fixation*—getting stuck on an ineffective approach. A specific type of fixation, called *functional fixedness*, refers to people's inability to use a familiar object to perform an unfamiliar function.

Theorists and researchers in the field of *artificial intelligence* (AI), the science that develops computer programs that behave intelligently, use the analogy between the computer and the human mind as a way of understanding human problem solving.

MAJOR CONCEPTS AND LEARNING OBJECTIVES

CONCEPT 1   Cognition refers to all ways in which we use the vast store of knowledge we each possess. Most of the higher mental processes involved in cognition require planning through the manipulation of symbols, usually to solve a problem.

1.1   Discuss the importance of concept learning in cognition.

1.2   Distinguish between the prototype approach to concept formation and the instance-storage approach.

1.3   Describe the nature of symbolic imagery and the physiological processes that are believed to be the basis for it.

**Concept
Builder 1**

Directions: Identify the following concepts illustrated in this hypothetical story. Lisa, a dynamic real estate agent with "Simply 21" realtors, recalls her early lessons in learning house architectural styles. The most difficult period for her was the Victorian era:

1. "I remember driving through old Victorian neighborhoods and being completely dumbfounded. The paradox was that each house was so unique and different, yet shared a common design period. For example, any house that could not be 'cleanly' classified as one specific style or another was simply called 'Queen Anne.'"

   Concept being illustrated: _____

2. "The 'Carpenter Gothics' were excellent representatives of the most *typical* Victorian styles: high, steep roofs, complex silhouettes, diagonal braces, lots of gingerbread trim, and exposed framing members."

   Concept being illustrated: _____

3. "The Eastlake style, by English architect Charles Eastlake, was so popular that 'Eastlake' furniture was designed and filled homes. After a while, many variations of Eastlake furniture and houses became identifiable by their characteristic ornamentations and knobs."

   Concept being illustrated: _____

CONCEPT 2

Reasoning, the ability to use logical processes, is traditionally considered one of the highest forms of human thought. Deduction and induction are two major forms of logical thought.

2.1   Define and compare deductive and inductive reasoning.

2.2   Describe the relationships between premises and conclusions in syllogistic reasoning and describe the fallacies presented in the chapter.

**Concept
Builder 2**

Directions: You are going to play a game called "Bees around the Queen." You can play with real dice or you can use the following diagram views of dice throws to play just as well. The name is a clue to the game. The object of the game is to figure out what rule is being used to play the game. For each throw, a statement is given to you that contains information useful for figuring out the rule. Once you have gotten the concept, read the following observations regarding the playing of the game and identify the cognitive concepts being illustrated. (If you don't figure out the game, don't worry; the explanation is provided at the end of the game for you!)

Bees around the Queen(s)

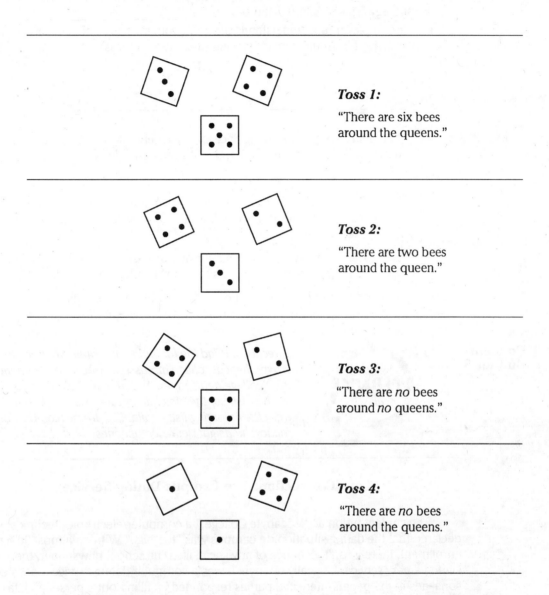

Toss 1:

"There are six bees around the queens."

Toss 2:

"There are two bees around the queen."

Toss 3:

"There are *no* bees around *no* queens."

Toss 4:

"There are *no* bees around the queens."

Have you figured out the rule by which the calls are being made? Answer: The rule is simple: you look for a center dot; if the die has one, that's the queen; the dots surrounding the center dot are the bees!

O.K., enough playing; now, back to work. Answer these questions by identifying certain cognitive processes that illustrate play during the game.

1. The easiest rule of the game is figuring out that one attribute, a center dot on a die, signifies a queen. No center dot, no queen. This general rule is inferred from observing specific rolls, a process called _____ reasoning.

2. Some observers watching the game think they know the playing rule after only a couple of rolls. Their expectations of being correct exceed their actual experience, a situation that is called _____.

3. Some players invent elaborate solutions that ultimately prove to be incorrect. Yet, despite disconfirmation, they continue to adhere to an incorrect solution strategy. This situation is termed _____.

4. Once a player fully understands the game, other rules or conclusions can now be derived from the general playing rules. This process illustrates_____reasoning.

CONCEPT 3
In judging events or making decisions, we generally use heuristics, or "rules of thumb." Heuristics are quick and intuitively sensible ways to judge probabilities.

3.1   Describe the use of the representative heuristic in decision making and explain the misunderstandings and fallacies that could result from its use.

3.2   Define the availability heuristic and discuss how it is used in making judgments and the fallacies that may result from its use.

3.3   Identify the terms "anchoring" and "framing," and discuss how both may affect our ability to make unbiased judgments.

**Concept
Builder 3**

Directions: Read the following description of two students at a hypothetical college discussing a recent experiment by their college newspaper. As you read their dialogue, identify the heuristic or the bias/fallacy that exists in their reasoning from the following list: availability, frame, conjunction fallacy, hindsight, representativeness.

Love Connection: The Campus Dating Service

The student union at "Megabyte College," a computer/electronics technical school, declared that the dating situation on campus was "the pits." With an almost 90% male enrollment, there wasn't a chance of any social life. The school newspaper, the *Printout*, started a new service. Logically enough, it was a computer dating service that listed personal ads in the paper. Interested parties responded by filling out a personal data card and checking the "profile" numbers of the ads that were of interest.

Read the following scenarios and identify the heuristic or bias that might be operating in the discussions of two Megabyte students, Louis and Arnold.

1. Louis read this ad out loud in the *Printout:* "Amanda S., 19 years old. Avid reader, very bright and articulate. Loves communicating with others and helping people. Very introspective and somewhat analytical of self and others. Sagittarius. 'Let's get together and connect.'" Louis looked cynically at his friend Arnold and said, "Oh, no! Sounds like a psych major to me. I'm not going to get 'connected' to this shrink!" Louis is basing his judgment of Amanda on the heuristic of _____.

2. Then Louis added, "She probably does a lot of community volunteer work, like a hotline or something." Louis is creating a possible fallacy called _____.

3. Now in a doubting mood, Louis says, "Why would girls advertise themselves for dates anyway; my brother said his school did the same thing once, and the only girls who ran ads were complete 'airheads,' girls so shallow and dumb, no one would tolerate them on a date." Louis is basing his portrait of a date on past supporting evidence from his brother. This heuristic is called _____.

4. Arnold quickly retorted, "Listen, you shouldn't be so critical and sexist. Don't you know other people refer to us as computer nerds? It's just as unfair. Here's how I have it figured. These girls, like us, figure that the most direct way to meet people is to openly advertise their interests and personality traits and hope that another interested, *mature* adult will read the ad and respond. It cuts out the bar scene. We're busy people, so advertising makes a lot of sense. It's very likely that we'll meet some very nice, intelligent women."

   Arnold just corrected this judgmental comparison by suggesting a more accurate way to _____ the situation.

5. One week later, after a successful date, Louis says, "I knew that checking out these ads would be a good idea. I had no doubts whatsoever, Arnold, I was merely testing you." Arnold: "Right, Louis. Whatever you say, but I think you're suffering some lapse of memory." Louis's overconfidence in recalling their "inevitable" good dating experience with this experiment illustrates _____.

CONCEPT 4   Problem solving encompasses most of the activity of thought and reason. Problems can be ill-defined or well-defined, depending upon whether there are standards by which to judge a solution as satisfactory.

4.1   Outline the steps that one follows in solving a problem and discuss how the components of the "IDEAL" approach incorporate these steps.

4.2   Outline the four problem-solving strategies—means-end analysis, search, working backward, and analogy—and distinguish them from one another.

4.3   Explain how fixation, functional fixedness, and isolation of knowledge form obstacles to problem solving.

4.4   Describe the goals of artificial intelligence (AI) and discuss Simon and Newell's general problem solver (GPS).

Concept Builder 4

Directions: Read the following situations that depict strategies used to solve different problems. Identify the solution strategy for each from this list: analogy, search, means-end, working backwards.

1. The IRS uses a computer program that sets up a "search tree" of all possible deductions that a tax filer might take. The program first examines the deductions claimed at each level (in various areas) before proceeding further along the "tree" in any one deduction category. The IRS solution strategy is _____ .

2. Before tackling the problem of tuning his car, Daniel decided to work on one particular component at a time (e.g., changing plugs, fuel filter, timing adjustments, etc.); each task would bring him a little closer to finishing the total tuning job. Daniel's strategy is very similar to a _____ – _____ analysis.

3. Benjamin needs $3,600 for next year's tuition. He makes a sketch that looks like the diagram below to list the steps he needs to take to get the money:

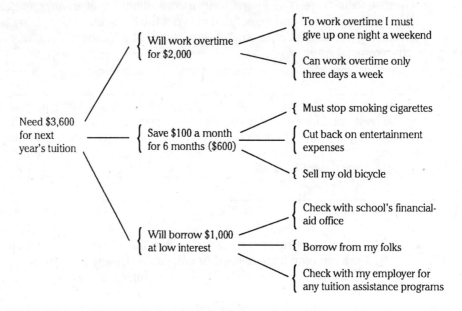

Benjamin's solution strategy is _____ .

4. While watching his hardwood floors being sanded and then coated with a hard, protective coating, Dr. Carson got a brainstorm. Why not coat teeth with a similar hard coating that would make it harder for cavities to form on the surface? Dr. Carson's solution strategy uses _____ .

CONCEPT 5   Creativity is the juxtaposition of ideas in new and unusual ways, often producing solutions to problems that are entirely new. Creative solutions may be practical and goal-oriented as well as unusual.

              5.1   Define creativity and outline the techniques discussed in the chapter for enhancing creativity.

**Concept
Builder 5**

              Directions: Read the following situations and identify the appropriate creativity concept.

Creativity at the Patent Office

1. One fellow brought in what looked like a pack of paper clips, most of which were unfolded. He said his "product" was called "Flexi-wire" and had 101 uses: a metal toothpick, a picture hanger, ornament hangers, fingernail cleaner, cheap key ring, tie clip, earring, etc. The patent officer asked him if a "paper clip" had possibly crossed his mind. The young inventor said, "Oh, yeah! You can even clip paper together as well." The patent was denied, but often a product emerges out of a lot of ideas generated (usually by a group) on novel uses of an ordinary household product. This is called _____.

2. Another person brought in a "puzzle" called "9-Dot." It looked like this:

    ● ● ●

    ● ● ●

    ● ● ●

    She hoped to patent this as a brain teaser game. The object was to connect all nine dots using four straight, continuous lines *without* retracing lines or lifting one's pen or pencil. People rarely solved the puzzle until they stopped viewing it as a "box." Once they did so, they successfully solved the problem. The obstacle embedded in this problem illustrates the role of _____ in blocking the solution.

3. Another enterprising applicant was a homemaker who brought in the compound, bicarbonate of soda (baking powder). Her product, called "Wonder Beads," had multiple uses: toothpaste, odor absorbent, mild abrasive, antacid, baking enhancer, etc. Her strategy was based upon breaking the properties of baking soda into parts and examining new possibilities for each part. Her creative process is called

    _____.

    (Patent denied, by the way; it's already used in all these ways.)

CHAPTER EXERCISE   **Anagrams**

Directions: Unscramble the letters below to match the brief definition given of each:

1. breaking problem into sub-goals: S E A M N-N E D

    _____

2. parallel is drawn: L O G N A Y A

    _____

3. "rule of thumb": H I S R U S C I T E

    _____

4. heuristic relying on similar events being remembered: A B A L I L I V I T Y

    _____

5. a "rigid" mental set: N I F A T I X O

    _____

6. most typical example: T O P T O P R Y E

    _____

7. premises and conclusions: G I S M O L Y S L

_____

8. inferring a general rule from specific cases: N O E I G R S A N

_____

9. outcome afterward seen as inevitable: D I G I N S H H T

_____

10 problem with no agreed-upon rules for solution: L I L-F I N D E E D

_____

**PRACTICE
EXAM 1**

1. The ideas underlying categories for grouping items according to their shared properties
    are called:

    a. schemas
    b. cognitions
    ⓒ concepts
    d. symbols

    (Factual, Obj. 1.1)

2. Leslie's real estate teacher was describing different roof styles for the class to learn. He
    pointed to a drawing of the gable style and said, "This is a prototype of the basic gable
    style." What does that mean?

    a. Roof styles are fuzzy categories.
    b. Roof styles are natural categories.
    c. The drawing embodied the most typical features of the roof style.
    ⓓ The gable roof style is the standard by which all other roof styles are judged.

    (Conceptual, Obj. 1.2)

3. In everyday conversation, we refer to things by a name that falls somewhere in the
    middle of a hierarchy of abstractions (not too abstract, not too concrete). Language of
    this sort is called:

    a. syllogistic
    b. attributive
    c. schematic
    ⓓ basic level

    (Factual, Obj. 1.2)

4. Kathryn was joking around with her sorority sisters one day when one of the sisters
    called her a "preppie." Kathryn was a little put off by this term and asked, "Why do
    you say that?" Her sorority buddy pulled out a "preppie" poster and said, "Don't you
    see how similar you look to this?" Her sorority friend used the _____ to make
    this judgment.

    ⓐ representativeness heuristic
    b. availability heuristic
    c. conjunction fallacy
    d. causal scenario

    (Conceptual, Obj. 3.1)

5. The availability heuristic explains the overconfidence we sometimes have in
    _____, the experience of looking back on events and feeling certain that the
    outcome was actually inevitable.

    a. non-randomness
    b. causal scenario
    c. hindsight
    d. framing

                                                                  (Factual, Obj. 3.2)

6. Morris works for the Acme Mousetrap Company. During a brainstorming session one
    day, Morris was thinking of how he might build a better mousetrap when his boss
    made this suggestion: "Rather than concentrating on building a better trap, let's look at
    the problem this way: how can we eliminate mice from the house without necessarily
    killing them?" That opened up a whole host of new possibilities. Morris's boss
    changed the perspective from which he viewed the problem. This is an example of:

    a. a well-defined problem
    b. framing
    c. the availability heuristic
    d. simplification

                                                               (Conceptual, Obj. 3.3)

7. The kinds of problems discussed in math and chemistry classes typically have neat,
    logical solutions. These problems are termed:

    a. basic-level
    b. means-end
    c. representative
    d. well-defined

                                                                  (Factual, Obj. 4.1)

8. The inventor of the old flexible ice tray did so partly by accident and partly by creative
    insight. One night he left his boots out in an ice storm; when he went to remove the
    ice from his boots the next morning, he simply twisted the boot and out came a giant
    "ice cube." Aha! The flexible ice tray was born. This cognitive process best illustrates:

    a. fractionation
    b. brainstorming
    c. analogy
    d. heuristics

                                                               (Conceptual, Obj. 5.1)

9. Saying "shellfish" rather than crustaceans or fiddler crabs best illustrates:

    a. prototypes
    b. concept hierarchies
    c. basic-level terms
    d. instance storage

                                                               (Conceptual, Obj. 1.2)

10. Some apes are vegetarians; some men are vegetarians; therefore, some men are apes.
    This syllogism illustrates a logical (and social!) error in its form. What is that?

    a. conversion error
    b. atmosphere effect
    c. representativeness
    d. wishful thinking

                                                               (Conceptual, Obj. 2.1)

11.   I-D-E-A-L is a mnemonic for remembering the stages of problem solving. Which of the following is *not* one of the five stages?

   a.   inductive reasoning about the problem
   b.   define the problem
   c.   explore possible strategies
   d.   act on selected strategy

(Factual, Obj. 4.1)

12.   The most powerful (and efficient) way to support an inductive generalization is to:

   a.   look for examples that would disconfirm the generalization
   b.   look for examples that would confirm the generalization
   c.   think in terms of probability
   d.   persevere in one's beliefs

(Factual, Obj. 2.1)

PRACTICE EXAM 2

1.   The social process of stereotyping involves treating all members of a social group as if they were like the most typical representative of the grouping. This parallels the cognitive concept of:

   a.   prototype
   b.   analogy
   c.   inductive generalization
   d.   conversion error

(Conceptual, Obj. 1.2)

2.   In recent years, prototype theory has been challenged by theories that take an opposite view of concept building. These theories assume that our minds store very detailed representations of events, as opposed to generalizations or prototypes. What is this theory called?

   a.   metacognition
   b.   instance-storage
   c.   expert systems
   d.   general problem solver

(Factual, Obj. 1.2)

3.   Kosslyn's experiments on mental images draw heavily on computer science analogies. In Kosslyn's conception, the brain builds mental images much like a:

   a.   word processor
   b.   laser printer
   c.   circuit chip
   d.   visual graphics program

(Conceptual, Obj. 1.3)

4.   A computer program that is designed to make decisions and solve problems in a specific domain is referred to as a(n):

   a.   general problem solver
   b.   heuristic
   c.   algorithm
   d.   expert system

(Factual, Obj. 4.4)

5.   Jason's class is brainstorming ways to finish college in half the normal time. Jason suggests enrolling in two colleges simultaneously and the class bursts into laughter. Why might the class's reaction stifle further suggestions from Jason?

   a.   The class is imposing implicit assumptions.
   b.   The class evaluated his idea prematurely.
   c.   The class has just become fractionated.
   d.   The class reminded Jason of the "fuzzy" nature of the problem.

                                                                (Conceptual, Obj. 5.1)

6.   The conjunction fallacy is a powerful cognitive illusion: it is based on people's use of a(n) _____ heuristic, judgment based on similarity to a stereotype or to a likely series of events.

   a.   availability
   b.   representativeness
   c.   framing
   d.   anchoring

                                                                (Factual, Obj. 3.1)

7.   Anchoring can lead to an effect in which judgment is biased by the _____ from which we are making the judgment.

   a.   starting point
   b.   ending point
   c.   frame
   d.   schema

                                                                (Factual, Obj. 3.3)

8.   If the city commissioners decided to tackle the problem of designing a "good traffic flow" pattern in the city, what kind of problem are they articulating?

   a.   an ill-defined problem
   b.   a well-defined problem
   c.   a fuzzy category
   d.   a natural category

                                                                (Conceptual, Obj. 4.1)

9.   The basic disadvantage of the General Problem Solver (GPS) program is that it cannot solve:

   a.   ill-defined problems
   b.   problems that depend on means-end analysis
   c.   reasoning problems like "hobbits and orcs"
   d.   problems requiring symbolic logic

                                                                (Factual, Obj. 4.4)

10. Jack's bulletin board was falling off the wall in his dorm room because a screw had come loose. He didn't have a screwdriver to tighten it, but his roommate suggested using a dime as a screwdriver by inserting the edge into the screw-head slot. Jack would have never thought of this because he was affected by a type of fixation called:

   a.   anchoring
   b.   framing
   c.   availability
   d.   functional fixedness

                                                                (Conceptual, 4.3)

11. Barbara has to catch a 8:45 p.m. flight. She figures out what time she has to leave home by calculating that it will take 15 minutes to check her luggage, 15 minutes to find a parking space, 30 minutes to drive to the airport, and 10 minutes to gas up. Thus, she decides to leave home at 7:35. Her problem solving reveals what strategy?

a. anchoring
b. I-D-E-A-L
c. inductive reasoning
d. working backward

(Conceptual, Obj. 4.2)

12. "Authorizer's Assistant" is a successful example of what?

a. an expert system
b. artificial intelligence
c. heuristics
d. a mental model

(Factual, Obj. 4.4)

■ ANSWER KEY ■

Concept 1	1. "fuzzy" concept		
	2. prototype		
	3. family resemblance		

| **Concept 2** | 1. inductive | 3. perseverance |
| | 2. overconfidence | 4. deductive |

Concept 3	1. representativeness	4. frame
	2. conjunction fallacy	5. hindsight
	3. availability	

| **Concept 4** | 1. search | 3. working backwards |
| | 2. means-end | 4. analogy |

Concept 5	1. brainstorming		
	2. implicit assumptions		
	3. fractionation		

Chapter Exercise

Anagrams

1. means-end	6. prototype
2. analogy	7. syllogisms
3. heuristics	8. inductive reasoning
4. availability	9. hindsight
5. fixation	10. ill-defined

Practice Exam 1

1. c, p. 242
2. c, pp. 244–245
3. d, p. 246
4. a, p. 253
5. c, p. 255
6. b, p. 256
7. d, p. 257
8. c, p. 262
9. c, p. 246
10. b, p. 249
11. a, p. 258
12. a, p. 252

Practice Exam 2

1. a, pp. 244–245
2. b, p. 245
3. d, p. 247
4. d, p. 266
5. b, p. 270
6. b, p. 255
7. a, p. 256
8. a, p. 257
9. a, p. 266
10. d, p. 265
11. d, p. 262
12. a, p. 267

CHAPTER TEN

Language

KEY TERM ORGANIZER

All human languages have the properties of expressive power, productivity, and displacement. *Expressive power* refers to a language's ability to communicate almost any situation, feeling, internal state, idea, thought, or any slice of time. *Productivity* grows out of the rule-governed nature of language. What gives language its productive power is the set of rules called *grammar*, which governs how elements, such as words and phrases, can be combined to form sentences. *Displacement*, or the ability to talk about something that is not present, is the aspect of language that makes civilization possible.

The discipline of *linguistics* has as its goal the description of knowledge. Language knowledge is thought to be organized into several components: a sound component, a syntactic component, and a semantic component.

The component of language that contains our knowledge of sound is known as the *phonological component*. The rules in this component are called *phonological rules*, and they are applied to *phonemes*, the basic units of sound.

The second component of language is called the *syntactic component*. The rules of this component, called *syntax*, determine how the basic units of meaning in a language, called *morphemes*, can be combined to form sentences. Syntactic rules are of two kinds: phrase-structure rules and transformation rules. *Phrase-structure rules* are those that describe the ways in which words are grouped hierarchically to form a sentence, and the ways in which the various elements of a sentence relate to one another. The hierarchical structure of the constituents of a particular sentence can be exhibited in a *phrase-structure tree*.

Transformation rules operate on what is called the deep structure of a sentence to turn it into its surface structure. The surface structure of a sentence is the actual sequence of words that one hears or produces. In contrast, the *deep structure* of a sentence is an abstract representation of the grammatical relations of the subject to the verb and the verb to the objects.

The third component of language and grammar is called the *semantic component*. Semantics is the study of meaning, and *semantic* applies to anything having to do with meaning or with differences in meaning. In general, those who study word meaning find it useful to distinguish between sense and reference. The *sense* of a word is simply its definition. A word's *reference* indicates the sense in which the word points to a tangible object in the external world. The meaning of a sentence also depends on the meanings of its *propositions*—the basic conceptual units that make up the sentence and that can be either true or false.

Chomsky argued that the three components of linguistic knowledge constitute the *language competence* of the speaker. Our ability to produce and understand sentences has its foundation in our language competence, but this competence must be implemented by a *performance system,* an information processor that constructs mental representations of sentences. One feature of syntax is called *recursion,* which permits us to embed sentences within sentences or phrases within phrases.

UNDERSTANDING SPOKEN LANGUAGE

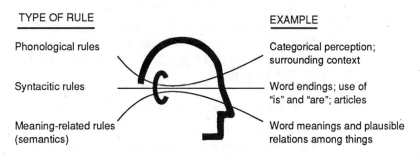

TYPE OF RULE	EXAMPLE
Phonological rules	Categorical perception; surrounding context
Syntacitic rules	Word endings; use of "is" and "are"; articles
Meaning-related rules (semantics)	Word meanings and plausible relations among things

Psycholinguistics is primarily concerned with describing the mental processes involved in using and understanding language—the performance system. We choose what to say in order to achieve certain goals. For this reason, utterances can be viewed as *speech acts.* A speech act is made in a physical and social context. Items discussed in a conversation, such as mutual surroundings, friends, beliefs, and recent topics of conversation, make up the *common ground* between speaker and listener. Making use of common ground is one example of the operation of a more general agreement that holds between speaker and listener called the *cooperative principle.*

Speech errors, sometimes called Freudian slips, or *slips of the tongue,* result from anxiety-provoking unconscious thoughts that interfere with our speech processing. In general, psychologists tend to believe that most slips occur as a result of a breakdown in speech planning. The *speech plan* begins with the selection of a syntactic structure, proceeds with the insertion of morphemes into this structure, and ends with a translation of these morphemes into phonetic segments that can be articulated.

Discourse is any connected series of statements in written or spoken form. When we listen to the speech stream, we must try to segment speech into units which can be identified as words; this is known as the *segmentation problem.*

When we read, our goal is the same as when we listen—to construct a mental model of the discourse in written material. Pattern recognition for written words is known as *decoding.*

When speakers communicate, they have an implicit agreement to deal with new information in such a way that it can be easily linked with old (or given) information. This is known as the *given-new contract.*

When children acquire a language, they simultaneously acquire a world view, according to Benjamin Whorf. The idea that language determines thought is *linguistic determinism.* This was illustrated in Rosch's work on *focal colors* —shades at the center of a group of colors all given the same label (usually a single word).

Our ability to use spoken language is closely related to our biological structure. Damage to the left hemisphere of the brain can cause various forms of aphasia, a disruption in the ability to produce or understand language. *Expressive aphasia* is the disruption of the ability to produce coherent speech as a result of damage to the left frontal lobe of the brain. *Receptive aphasia* is a condition in which the ability to comprehend spoken and written language is seriously disrupted, as is the ability to generate coherent speech.

Other animal species communicate. However, some people in the past have mistakenly interpreted an animal's behavior as evidence for knowledge of language. This type of mistake has been named the *"Clever Hans" phenomenon.*

MAJOR CONCEPTS AND LEARNING OBJECTIVES

CONCEPT 1   Human language is an advanced system of social communication that represents the highest achievement of human cognition. Human language is a complicated structure and has characteristics that make it unique among animal signaling systems.

1.1   Describe three universal features of human language.

1.2   Identify the major components of phonology and syntax and describe the difference between phonemes and morphemes.

1.3   Distinguish word meaning and sentence meaning in semantics and describe the transformational and phrase structure rules that generate sentences from combinations of words.

Concept Builder 1

Directions: You are a bright, budding linguist who has been asked to demonstrate some of the "basics" of language analysis. For each question below, supply the correct answer(s).

Diagramming Language

1.   How many *phonemes* are there in the word "pot"? _____

2.   How many *morphemes* are there in the word "disembody"? _____

3.   In the space provided below and on the following page, outline two phrase-structure trees for the following sentence: "They are visiting scholars."

CONCEPT 2   As a tool for social communication, language coordinates the thoughts and actions of the speaker and the listener. The field of psycholinguistics addresses the function of language.

2.1   Identify the characteristics of a speech act and explain the role of common ground and the cooperative principle in communication.

2.2   Distinguish direct from indirect speech.

2.3   Define discourse and identify the three processes involved in understanding discourse.

2.4   Describe the differences between recognizing words in speech and recognizing written words.

2.5   Describe how schemas govern the way we interpret or identify propositions contained in language.

Concept Builder 2

Directions: Suppose you heard the following "slips of the tongue" made by various members of a family. Your task is to identify the type of speech "error" each illustrates.

All in the Family

_____ 1. "You can cake my car."

_____ 2. "Mommy, my laps are chipped."

_____ 3. "I've already walked the wog."

_____ 4. "May I sow you to your sheats?" (said deliberately as a joke)

a.   anticipation

b.   perseveration

c.   reversals

d.   spoonerism

CONCEPT 3   The relationship between thought and language has been debated extensively. One group believes that language determines thought, others that thought determines language.

3.1   Explain the concept of linguistic determinism and its consequences.

3.2   Discuss both the cross-cultural evidence for the relationship between perception and language and the experimental evidence suggesting a possible relationship between memory and language.

Concept Builder 3

Directions: Read the following observations and research findings and match them to the appropriate component of the language-thought continuum.

Language and Thought—A Matter of Degree

A	B	C
Language *determines* thought	**Language *influences* thought**	**Language and thought are *independent***

_____ 1. There is an old Czechoslovakian saying that states, "Learn a new language and gain a new soul."

_____ 2. The first concepts children learn the world over are virtually the same.

_____ 3. Despite having only two color terms, the Dani (in your text) perceive similar color categories with hues similar to those perceived by Americans.

_____ 4. How we label something influences the way we remember it (an ambiguous figure labeled "eyeglasses" will be remembered differently from the same figure labeled "dumbbell").

_____ 5. Although they are described with different labels, there seem to be six basic, primary emotions that are universal.

_____ 6. Although it is modifiable, when one thinks of "doctor" and "nurse" one tends to think automatically of a male and a female (respectively).

_____ 7. Studies of deaf mutes show that they have the ability to use reasoning and analytic skills.

CONCEPT 4   Human physiology makes much of the verbal range and flexibility of language possible, and our large brains make the complexity of our communication possible.

4.1   Discuss why brain specialization is important for the human ability to communicate.

4.2   Outline the evidence for nonhuman language production and identify the competing views regarding nonhuman communication.

**Concept
Builder 4**

Directions: Read the following three "neurological" descriptions and identify the psycholinguistic concept being illustrated.

Brains and Language

1. Jeremy M. produces incoherent speech. His speech is halting and limited to content words (nouns, verbs). Brain damage is thought to be in Broca's area.
   Psycholinguistic concept: _____

2. When a patient's left hemisphere is anesthetized in surgery, she cannot speak or sing the words to a familiar song, but she can hum it. By contrast, when her right hemisphere is anesthetized, she cannot hum the melody but she can recite the words.
   Psycholinguistic concept: _____

3. A patient is known to have suffered damage to the left temporal lobe of the brain. Although the patient's speech is fluent, it makes no sense.
   Psycholinguistic concept: _____

**CHAPTER
EXERCISE**

Directions: Review the following key terms and identify the primary concept each pertains to (following the four major concepts of this chapter). Write the number associated with each term in the appropriate quadrant.

Sorting Language Concepts

1 HUMAN LANGUAGE HAS A COMPLICATED LINGUISTIC STRUCTURE:	

2 UNDERSTANDING LANGUAGE AND SPEECH IN DAILY LIFE:	

3 LANGUAGE AND THOUGHT ARE RELATED:	

4 LANGUAGE HAS A BIOLOGICAL BASIS:	

1. focal colors	11. slip of the tongue
2. aphasia	12. sense
3. syntax	13. decoding
4. recursion	14. propositions
5. segmentation problem	15. expressive power
6. "Clever Hans" phenomenon	16. receptive aphasia
7. displacement	17. given-new contract
8. morphemes	18. transformation rules
9. common ground	19. perseveration
10. linguistic determinism	20. ambiguity

PRACTICE EXAM 1

1. Which of the following is *not* one of the characteristics that distinguish human language from animal signaling systems?

   a. expressive power
   b. productivity
   c. pragmatics
   d. displacement

   (Factual, Obj. 1.1)

2. As Donna stepped into the elevator, she noticed and heard a feature designed to help blind people. At each floor, an electronically synthesized voice announced the floor number. The device accomplished this by making a series of overlapping speech sounds. These speech sounds correspond to:

   a. morphemes
   b. phonemes
   c. phrases
   d. utterances

   (Conceptual, Obj. 1.2)

3. The rules that govern how words and phrases are combined into sentences are called grammar. Psycholinguists call this aspect of language:

   a. phonology
   b. pragmatics
   c. linguistics
   d. syntax

   (Factual, Obj. 1.2)

4. Jonathan's first baby words always referred to what was right in front of him. At this stage, his language lacked the characteristic of:

   a. displacement
   b. productivity
   c. discreteness
   d. meaningfulness

   (Conceptual, Obj. 1.1)

5. During brain surgery, Mr. H. had his right hemisphere anesthetized. What would Mr. H. be *unable* to do?

    a. talk
    b. recite words to an old familiar song
    c. hum the melody of an old familiar song
    d. recite recently learned words

    (Conceptual, Obj. 4.1)

6. After three years of intensive training, Savage-Rumbaugh and her colleagues showed that two chimpanzees could grasp the idea that objects have names. This indicates that they could understand the _____ use of symbols.

    a. displacement
    b. referential
    c. discrete
    d. pragmatic

    (Factual, Obj. 4.2)

7. In the alien culture of "Spectrum," there exist only three color terms. What would those color terms be?

    a. black, white, gray
    b. black, white, red
    c. red, green, yellow
    d. mauve, rose, magenta

    (Conceptual, Obj. 3.2)

8. Nathan is two years old now and his parents are continually amazed at his ability to come up with unlimited ways to express thoughts. This ability illustrates the language characteristic of:

    a. discreteness
    b. meaningfulness
    c. productivity
    d. displacement

    (Conceptual, Obj. 1.1)

9. While Lucy was watching an old "Perry Mason" episode on TV, she recognized a language principle being illustrated. Perry objected to the D.A.'s question to the witness: "Did you see *the* pistol in your husband's overcoat?" The judge sustained the objection and the D.A. rephrased the question to "Did you see *a* pistol in your husband's overcoat?" This objection illustrated the:

    a. cooperative principle
    b. given-new contract
    c. categorical perception principle
    d. adjacency pair principle

    (Conceptual, Obj. 2.3)

10. Read the following sentence: "Jan's boyfriend purchased an engagement ring." Which of the following is *not* a proposition contained in this sentence?

    a. Jan has a boyfriend.
    b. The ring is an engagement ring.
    c. Jan and her boyfriend are getting married soon.
    d. Jan's boyfriend bought a ring.

    (Conceptual, Obj. 2.5)

11. An utterance is as much an instrumental act as opening a door, and for this reason utterances can be viewed as:

 a. speech acts
 b. commands
 c. constituents
 d. categorical perceptions

(Factual, Obj. 2.1)

12. If you were to conduct a "chimp language learning" project for the anthropology department, what strategy would be sure to fail?

 a. teaching them sign language
 b. using small plastic symbols for words
 c. using a computer controlled keyboard
 d. actually teaching them to speak simple words

(Conceptual, Obj. 4.2)

PRACTICE EXAM 2

1. Which of the following clues in language comprehension helps the listener decide if a word is functioning as a main noun, a verb, or in some other role?

 a. phonological clues
 b. syntactic clues
 c. meaning-related clues
 d. knowledge schemas

(Factual, Obj. 1.2)

2. Which of the following phonemes is different from the others?

 a. the c in silence
 b. the s in silence
 c. the s in cats
 d. the c in cats

(Conceptual, Obj. 1.2)

3. "Car tuned well ran the" is a sentence that violates the rules of:

 a. semantics
 b. phonology
 c. recursion
 d. syntax

(Conceptual, Obj. 1.2)

4. Finding that English-speaking people are not as capable as Vietnamese people of distinguishing among different kinds of rice would _____ the linguistic determinism hypothesis (Whorf's theory).

 a. support
 b. cast serious doubts upon
 c. be irrelevant to
 d. illustrate the power of context rather than

(Conceptual, Obj. 3.1)

5. A sentence is *ambiguous* if it has _____ surface structure(s) and _____ phrase structure(s).

a. 1; 1
b. 1; 2 or more
c. 2 or more; 1
d. 3 or more; 3 or more

(Conceptual, Obj. 1.3)

6. Roseanne is often accused of being wordy, long-winded, and tangential because her sentences typically contain several "sentences within sentences." Roseanne's speech could be said to contain:

a. deep structures
b. structural ambiguities
c. recursions
d. expressive power

(Conceptual, Obj. 1.3)

7. "Would you mind holding that door open for me, please?" is an example of a speech act where it is *expected* that the listener will comply. This is called:

a. the cooperative principle
b. indirect speech
c. linguistic meaning
d. speaker's meaning

(Conceptual, Obj. 2.1)

8. Pattern recognition for written words is known as:

a. a speech plan
b. segmentation
c. decoding
d. fixation

(Factual, Obj. 2.4)

9. Suppose your secretary said, "Someone called this morning but I forgot to take their message. It was from either Ron Dolinsky or Rhonda Linsky; I'm not sure." This illustrates a language problem known as a:

a. segmentation problem
b. referential problem
c. semantic problem
d. recursion problem

(Conceptual, Obj. 2.3)

10. Rosch's experiments with the Dani tribe involved identifying "basic" colors (like red, blue, brown)—one-word prototypes. These colors are called:

a. focal
b. common ground
c. surface structure
d. mental models

(Factual, Obj. 3.2)

11. As a consulting psychologist with the judicial system, what is your basic opinion of eyewitness testimony?

a. Eyewitness testimony is about 98% accurate.
b. Eyewitness testimony is extremely unreliable and biased.

c.   Verbal "cues" can affect the content of what we recall, thus making eyewitness testimony less than accurate.

d.   Verbal recall is inaccurate but visual recall is highly accurate in eyewitness testimony.

(Factual, Obj. 3.2)

12.   The text stated that if an infant's left hemisphere were injured, eventually:

a.   lateralization would cease
b.   the right hemisphere would take over language function
c.   seizures would develop
d.   visual processing would be interrupted

(Factual, Obj. 4.1)

■ ANSWER KEY ■

Concept 1
1.   3, or P/O/T
2.   3, or DIS-EM-BODY

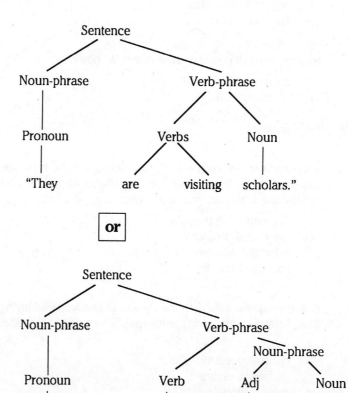

Concept 2
1.   a   3.   b
2.   c   4.   d

Concept 3

1.	a	5.	c
2.	c	6.	b
3.	c	7.	c
4.	b		

Concept 4

1. expressive aphasia
2. brain lateralization
3. receptive aphasia

Chapter Exercise

1	HUMAN LANGUAGE HAS A COMPLICATED LINGUISTIC STRUCTURE:	3, 4, 7, 8, 12, 14, 15, 18, 20

2	UNDERSTANDING LANGUAGE AND SPEECH IN DAILY LIFE:	5, 9, 11, 13, 17, 19

3	LANGUAGE AND THOUGHT ARE RELATED:	1, 10

4	LANGUAGE HAS A BIOLOGICAL BASIS:	2, 6, 16

Practice Exam 1	Practice Exam 2
1. c, pp. 276–278	1. b, p. 279
2. b, pp. 278–279	2. d, pp. 278–279
3. d, p. 279	3. d, p. 279
4. a, p. 278	4. a, p. 296
5. c, pp. 300–301	5. b, p. 281
6. b, pp. 284, 303	6. c, p. 282
7. b, pp. 297–298	7. b, pp. 286–287
8. c, p. 277	8. c, p. 290
9. b, p. 295	9. a, p. 289
10. c, pp. 293–294	10. a, p. 297
11. a, p. 285	11. c, pp. 298–299
12. d, pp. 302–304	12. b, pp. 300–301

CHAPTER ELEVEN

Intelligence and Intelligence Testing

KEY TERM ORGANIZER

Intelligence consists of general abilities that help people achieve their goals in life. Two pioneers, Binet and Simon, developed the concept of *mental age,* or grouping intelligence test items according to age. Stern combined the concepts of chronological age and mental age to form a ratio. Terman multiplied this ratio by 100, thus setting the formula for the modern-day intelligence quotient, or IQ.

IQ scores do not correlate particularly well with artistic success, measures of creativity, or types of manual or other expertise.

The *Stanford-Binet* is still one of the most widely used tests of intelligence. It includes nonverbal subtests called *performance tests.*

The Wechsler scales were modifications of the Stanford-Binet. For adults, Wechsler developed the *Wechsler Adult Intelligence Scale* (WAIS), the *Wechsler Intelligence Scale for Children* (WISC) for ages 6 through 16, and the *Wechsler Preschool and Primary Scale of Intelligence* (WPPSI) for children 4 to 6 1/2.

Many common group tests exist today.

Type of Test	Content Measured	Examples
Intelligence (or ability)	General problem-solving ability and verbal knowledge	Stanford-Binet, WAIS, WISC, WPPSI
Achievement	Evaluates what a person knows	Group tests, final exams
Aptitude	Predicts how successful a person will be in certain situations	Scholastic Aptitude Test (SAT)

There have been many attempts to describe intelligence. Spearman proposed that there was a *general intelligence factor* (*g factor*) that underlay *all* types of abilities. His theory was based on the statistical techniques of *factor analysis.*

Cattell proposed two basic types of intelligence: *fluid intelligence*—the ability to learn and perform—and *crystallized intelligence* —acquired knowledge. More recently, Sternberg has proposed a "triarchic" view of intelligence; *componential intelligence,* the ability to process information; *experiential intelligence,* the ability to learn from experience; and *contextual intelligence,* the ability to adapt to the world.

A good test must be both reliable and valid. *Reliability* provides consistent measurement; *validity* indicates that tests are measuring what they purport to measure. If a test is valid, it must also be reliable.

There are several different forms of reliability and validity.

Reliability

Kind of Reliability	Test Characteristic
Internal consistency	Different parts of the test must produce the same results.
Test-retest	Repeated administrations of the same test to the same group of people produce the same results.
Interjudge	Scoring by different judges produces the same results.

Validity

Kind of Validity	Test Characteristic
Content	The test covers a representative sample of the measured attribute.
Predictive	A test produces scores that show a relationship to future performance.
Concurrent	A test produces scores that correlate highly with other existing measures or standards.
Construct	A test measures the hypothetical construct it claims to measure.

Before tests are put into general use, testers establish norms by giving the test to a large, well-defined sample group called a *standardization group.* Test scores are commonly presented in a *percentile system* of 100 equal-sized parts or a *standard score system,* reflecting a normal curve distribution.

Mental retardation involves a decreased ability to function in the world as well as decreased intellectual performance. Mental retardation is described in terms of four levels:

- *Mild retardation:* IQ range of 50–69
- *Moderate retardation:* IQ range of 35–49
- *Severe retardation:* IQ range of 20–34
- *Profound retardation:* IQ below 20

Although retardation has many causes, *Down syndrome* is one of the most common causes. Ability tests can be somewhat useful for diagnosing different levels of mental retardation. The *heritability* of IQ is an estimate of the genetic contributions to individual differences in IQ scores.

MAJOR CONCEPTS AND LEARNING OBJECTIVES

CONCEPT 1   Intelligence consists of those general abilities that help people reach their goals. A variety of measures of intelligence have been developed, and a number of purposes have been served by these different tests.

    1.1   Discuss the goals of the early investigators of intelligence: Galton, Cattell, Binet, and Stern.

    1.2   Define "intelligence quotient" (IQ) and describe the individual and group intelligence tests in use today.

Concept Builder 1

Directions: You are asked to act as a test consultant for your school's counseling department. Your job, as a student assistant, is to determine which test would be most appropriate in each situation.

Test Questions

_____ 1.   "Which IQ test would you recommend for my little brother, who's in junior high school?"

_____ 2.   "My French professor said that I should take a standardized test of French to determine if I should register for intermediate or advanced French. What kind of a test would you recommend?"

_____ 3.   "I'm a junior in high school, and I'm thinking about going to college. What kind of test would show me whether I'm college material?"

_____ 4.   "I'd like to take a test that would specifically measure my verbal and performance abilities. What test should I take?"

_____ 5.   "I don't know what I want to be when I grow up. What sort of test might help me see what kinds of capacities and career interests I might have?"

a.   intelligence test: WAIS

b.   intelligence test: WISC

c.   achievement test

d.   aptitude test

e.   SAT

CONCEPT 2   A variety of competing theories have been proposed to define intelligence. To date, no specific definition has been accepted.

2.1   Explain factor analysis and the correlation coefficient.

2.2   Discuss the evidence supporting concepts of a "g factor" of fluid intelligence and of crystallized intelligence.

2.3   Describe the three components of the triarchic view of intelligence.

Concept Builder 2

Directions: Identify each of the following abilities and attributes as illustrating either Cattell's fluid intelligence (F) or his crystallized intelligence (C).

Two Faces of Intelligence

1.   vocabulary use   _____
2.   problem solving   _____
3.   memory span   _____
4.   social reasoning   _____
5.   ability to copy symbols   _____
6.   ability to solve abstract problems   _____
7.   declines with age   _____
8.   measures knowledge   _____
9.   increases with age   _____
10. represents abilities   _____

CONCEPT 3   A psychological test must be an objective and standardized measure of a sample of behavior which provides a systematic basis for making inferences about people. Intelligence tests must meet these criteria.

3.1   Define reliability, validity, and standardization and discuss how each of these criteria is applied to the evaluation of an IQ test.

3.2   Discuss the effectiveness of IQ and other ability tests, such as the SAT, in the prediction of job performance and academic success.

3.3   Describe the degrees of retardation and the definition of giftedness.

**Concept
Builder 3**

Directions: The students at Borderline College have been having trouble passing the school's tests of reading and writing competency. This is particularly puzzling to the school's president, Dr. Emily Wordsworth Bronte, who must uphold a 200-year-old tradition of excellence in liberal arts education at this school. She decides to call in the world-famous test consultant, Professor Ignatius Q. Tester, to help the school out. Read his suggestions below and match each suggestion with the appropriate terms.

The Travels of Professor I.Q. Tester

a. test-retest reliability
b. interjudge reliability
c. content validity
d. predictive validity
e. concurrent validity
f. construct validity

[Setting: The faculty meeting room; Dr. Bronte, four faculty members, and four student representatives, one from each class year.]

Dr. Bronte: "Thank you so much for coming to help us out, Professor Tester."

Prof. Tester: "Please, call me Iggy. You're welcome. Well, as I understand it, over a third of the students do not pass your required literature test, which involves both reading and writing skills. Is that correct?"

Dr. Bronte: "Yes, that's correct, Professor. Our English faculty is concerned. They have been told, and it's documented, that these tests correlate highly with future ability to read information and write about it clearly."

Testing point 1: Dr. Bronte is referring to what property of the test? ____

Freshman student: "Professor Tester, have you seen these dumb tests? I've taken them twice now, and I got the same low score both times!"

Prof. Tester: "That's not altogether bad, young man. In fact, a test—even a poor one—should yield consistent results."

Testing point 2: What is Tester referring to? ____

Senior student: "Sir, maybe it has something to do with the fact that that test seems to ask questions in only a few, narrow areas of literature. We cover a broad range of authors and eras, but the test doesn't test us on those."

Testing point 3: What is this senior saying that the test lacks? ____

Prof. Tester: "Ah, so! The test doesn't represent what you've studied?"

All four students *[loudly]*: "Right!"

English teacher *[defensively]*: "Well, Brian, my driver's license picture doesn't look anything like my real face. Does that make it invalid?"

Prof. Tester: "Good teacher, that makes it low in 'face' validity." *[Only the students laugh.]* "A little joke. But they may be on to something. Let's check that out. Now, is the test graded and who does it?"

Dr. Bronte: "Well, we have a panel of four teachers—the ones present here—who grade the exams. There is a high level of agreement on the scoring."

Testing point 4: What does this illustrate? ____

[One student whispering to another]: "God, those four couldn't pass their own blood tests!" *[Laughter erupts.]*

Prof. Tester: "That's good. High agreement. Well, I think the problem lies mainly in the area of validity. The first thing I want to do is compare your test with another known test of writing and reading ability to see if the two correlate."

Testing point 5: What is this characteristic called? ____

Dr. Bronte: "What can we do at this end, Professor?"

Prof. Tester: "Collect information on both your passing and failing students. See if you find any independent evidence, like performance in other courses such as history, oral presentations, or term papers that might corroborate good or poor performance on the standardized test."

Testing point 6: This characteristic is called ____ .

Prof. Tester: "We'll get this problem licked or I'll change my name."

CONCEPT 4   There continues to be debate concerning the innate differences among groups of people. A person's IQ score reflects not only his or her genetic potential for intellectual development (heredity), but also what he or she has learned from the environment.

4.1   Outline the different perspectives concerning intelligence and racial differences.

4.2   Describe the evidence for the role of the environment in intelligence and discuss whether education or practice can improve intelligence test performance.

Concept Builder 4

Directions: To understand the concepts of heritability and reaction range, pretend you are a botanical researcher who is experimenting with various seed strains and soil properties. Study the following diagrams and answer the questions that follow.

Heritability in the Hothouse

Chart 1　　　　　　　　　　　　　　**Chart 2**

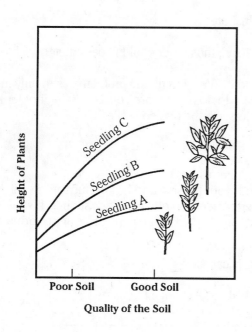

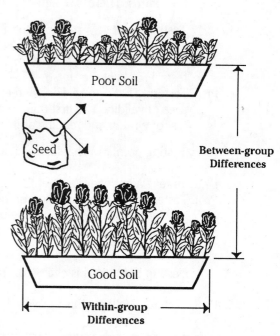

____ 1. Look at chart 2. Notice that the soil condition is identical for all plants in each pan, yet the plants are of different heights. The varying plant heights reflect different seeds and their capabilities for growth. The seeds, in this case, produce a kind of variation called

_____.

____ 2. Look at chart 1. It looks as if improving the soil condition benefits all seedlings in terms of growing taller, particularly seedling C. What does the height of the plants to the right of the curved lines represent?

____ 3. In chart 2, notice that the differences between groups are produced by a difference in soil quality. In this example, what would soil represent?

____ 4. Chart 2 also illustrates something called "within-group" differences. These height variations reflect the genetic differences among seeds within a constant environment (soil). What is another way of describing this?

a. genetic-environment interactions

b. heritability

c. genetic contributions

d. environmental contributions

**CHAPTER
EXERCISE**

*Directions: Complete the crossword puzzle below by filling in the correct terms
from the list of definitions below.*

Across:

3. Established by giving a test to a standardization group of people: _____
5. The extent to which the scoring or interpretation of a test by different judges will produce the same results: _____ reliability
7. Measuring what a test purports to measure: _____
8. Selective breeding of humans: _____
9. Mental retardation in which the IQ is between 52 and 67: _____
10. A test that measures both verbal and performance ability of children from 6 to 16 years of age: _____
12. A test must have both validity and _____.
13. Tests designed to find out about an individual's talent or capacity for particular lines of work: _____

Down:

1. Intelligence test for preschoolers: _____
2. The extent to which observed variation of a trait can be attributed to genetic differences: _____
4. A system of scoring tests in which the group of scores is divided into 100 equal parts: _____
6. A test designed to measure "aptitude for college studies": _____
11. Intelligence that declines with age: _____

PRACTICE EXAM 1

1. The text stated that one should expect high test-retest reliability when _____ is/are being measured.

   a. intelligence
   b. math ability
   c. attitudes and moods
   d. vocabulary use

   (Factual, Obj. 3.1)

2. Human Dynamics Corporation called on a consultant to develop a "placement" test that would identify potential managers. The consultant, in this case, would want to make certain the placement test would be high in:

   a. predictive validity
   b. concurrent validity
   c. internal consistency reliability
   d. face validity

   (Conceptual, Obj. 3.1)

3. What standardization procedure divides a group of scores into 100 equal parts?

   a. standard score system
   b. percentile system
   c. rational, deductive system
   d. factor analytic approach

   (Factual, Obj. 3.1)

4. Sandra's five-year-old daughter is already showing exceptional intellectual skill. She would like to have her daughter tested. What would be the most appropriate test to use?

   a. WAIS
   b. WISC
   c. WPPSI
   d. WISC-R

   (Conceptual, Obj. 1.2)

5. What piece of information is a more valid predictor of college grades than the SAT?

   a. WAIS
   b. any of the group intelligence tests
   c. college placement exams
   d. high school class rank

   (Factual, Obj. 3.2)

6. Dr. Bradford has been testing his own theory of intelligence on high school students. In addition to measuring their knowledge of various fields, he also assesses their musical ability, watches them play video games, and even assesses dancing and pantomiming skill. This theory is very similar to:

   a. Gardner's theory of multiple intelligences
   b. Sternberg's information-processing theory of intelligence
   c. Stanford-Binet
   d. WAIS

   (Conceptual, Obj. 2.3)

7. Tyrone is mentally retarded. Through training, however, he has been able to work for a restaurant by cleaning tables. He is very reliable and dependable doing this simple job and can lead a somewhat normal personal life. Tyrone's mental retardation would be classified as:

    a. mild
    b. moderate
    c. severe
    d. profound

    (Conceptual, Obj. 3.3)

8. The original purpose of the intelligence test, as developed by Binet, was to:

    a. predict job success
    b. measure interpersonal knowledge
    c. measure vocabulary
    d. identify mental retardation in schoolchildren

    (Factual, Obj. 1.1)

9. If it is true that dietary changes reduce the incidence of coronary heart disease in those individuals who are genetically predisposed to develop the disease, what effect can we say diet is having on the heritability of heart disease?

    a. It has done nothing to affect it.
    b. It has increased the heritability of heart disease.
    c. It has decreased the heritability of heart disease.
    d. That is impossible to answer from the information given.

    (Conceptual, Obj. 4.2)

10. Which of the following is *not* one of Sternberg's triarchic components of intelligence?

    a. crystallized intelligence
    b. componential intelligence
    c. experiential intelligence
    d. contextual intelligence

    (Factual, Obj. 2.3)

11. Spearman's "g factor" involved the use of a sophisticated statistical procedure that came to be known as:

    a. the percentile system
    b. the correlation coefficient
    c. factor analysis
    d. standard scores

    (Factual, Obj. 2.2)

12. The "Critical Thinking Essays" that appear throughout this study guide most actively encourage:

    a. creative thinking
    b. open-minded thinking
    c. fluid intelligence
    d. crystallized intelligence

    (Conceptual, Obj. 2.2)

PRACTICE
EXAM 2

1. During the high-dive competition trials of the "goodwill" games, the American and Russian judges kept differing sharply over the scores given to the Romanian divers. This difference in rating reflects a lack of:

    a. test-retest reliability
    b. interjudge reliability
    c. predictive validity
    d. concurrent validity

                                                                    (Conceptual, Obj. 3.1)

2. Which of the following is the *most* correct statement?

    a. Reliable tests are always valid.
    b. One cannot have reliability without validity.
    c. Valid tests measure nothing but reliability.
    d. Valid tests are always reliable.

                                                                    (Factual, Obj. 3.1)

3. At Raymond's fitness center, physical assessments are made on new members and their results are reported in percentiles. Raymond's cardiovascular index was reported at 95 percent in relation to his standardization group. What does that mean?

    a. Only 5 percent in Raymond's standardization group scored higher than he did.
    b. Raymond is in the bottom 5 percent, who are not very fit.
    c. Raymond is scoring at 95 percent of his peak level of efficiency.
    d. Out of 100 people, Raymond did better than only 5 people

                                                                    (Conceptual, Obj. 3.1)

4. The text stated that modern IQ tests no longer represent the ratio of mental age to chronological age. What do modern scores represent?

    a. percentile scores
    b. norms
    c. "deviation IQs"
    d. an intelligence quotient

                                                                    (Factual, Obj. 1.2)

5. Laura is finishing up her degree in early childhood education, but before she can teach she must pass what is called a competency exam, which measures her knowledge as a teacher. This exam would be most like:

    a. the SAT
    b. an achievement test
    c. the Stanford-Binet
    d. a creativity test

                                                                    (Conceptual, Obj. 1.2)

6. There are approximately _____ million people in the United States who are mentally retarded.

    a. 1.2 to 3.5
    b. 5.6 to 6.7
    c. 8.1 to 8.9
    d. 9.5 to 10

                                                                    (Factual, Obj. 3.3)

7.   Jane Mercer developed a "nonacademic" test of intelligence. She measured such things as the ability of an individual to button clothes, put away toys, go to movies, etc. Her scale is called the:

    a.   WPPSI
    b.   Mercer-Binet
    c.   Adaptive Behavior Scale
    d.   Social Aptitude Scale

                                                                (Factual, Obj. 3.3)

8.   Laverne is 10 years old. Her IQ has been measured as 120. According to Binet's original IQ formula, what is Laverne's mental age?

    a.   6
    b.   8
    c.   10
    d.   12

                                                                (Conceptual, Obj. 1.2)

9.   Suppose you are research director at a major city zoo and you are directing three trained observers to record aggressive behavior exhibited by "Spike," a feisty little gorilla. What kind of reliability are you most interested in?

    a.   concurrent reliability
    b.   interjudge reliability
    c.   split-half reliability
    d.   test-retest reliability

                                                                (Conceptual, Obj. 3.1)

10.   Gomer, 12 years old, cannot read, write, or do arithmetic. He needs constant supervision, but he can communicate and, with practice, has learned to dress himself and brush his teeth. The best estimate of Gomer's condition is:

    a.   mild retardation
    b.   profound retardation
    c.   severe retardation
    d.   moderate retardation

                                                                (Conceptual, Obj. 3.3)

11.   Which of the following is *not* an environmental influence on IQ?

    a.   malnutrition
    b.   family size (number of siblings)
    c.   level of cognitive stimulation in the home
    d.   heritability

                                                                (Factual, Obj. 4.2)

12.   A personnel director wants to develop a test to use for placing job applicants in jobs where they will do well. She would be most interested in:

    a.   predictive validity
    b.   concurrent validity
    c.   content validity
    d.   construct validity

                                                                (Conceptual, Obj. 3.2)

■ ANSWER KEY ■

Concept 1
1. b   4. a
2. c   5. d
3. e

Concept 2
1. C   6. F
2. C   7. F
3. F   8. C
4. C   9. C
5. F   10. F

Concept 3
1. d   4. b
2. a   5. e
3. c   6. f

Concept 4
1. c   3. d
2. a   4. b

**Chapter
Exercise**

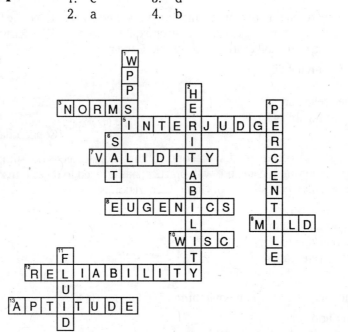

Practice Exam 1

1. a, p. 322
2. a, p. 323
3. b, p. 324
4. c, p. 314
5. d, p. 326
6. a, p. 319
7. a, p. 326
8. d, p. 311
9. b, p. 331
10. a, pp. 317–318
11. c, p. 317
12. b, p. 336

Practice Exam 2

1. b, p. 323
2. d, p. 323
3. a, p. 324
4. c, p. 324
5. b, p. 315
6. b, p. 326
7. c, p. 328
8. d, pp. 311–312
9. b, p. 323
10. d, p. 326
11. d, pp. 334–336
12. a, p. 323

CRITICAL THINKING ESSAY 3

Looking for the Sources of Creativity

Since the time of Plato, the search for the sources of creativity has been a central concern for philosophers and psychologists (Galton, 1883; Freud, 1908; Weisberg, 1987; Mumford and Gustafson, 1988). Over the years researchers have proposed numerous explanations of creativity, but there has been little agreement among them. A fundamental reason for this lack of agreement is the *criterion problem*, the absence of a clear definition of creativity and of appropriate assessment techniques to measure it (Amabile, 1982a). Thus, a better way to approach the question "What does it take to be creative?" may be to begin by answering the question "What does it *mean* to be creative?"

TWO BASIC VIEWS OF CREATIVITY

The bulk of the work in this field has focused on two operating definitions of what constitutes creativity. One notion, which some have labeled the "genius" view, states that true creativity is a rare and infrequent quality or cluster of qualities possessed by unusually talented people (see, e.g., Weisberg, 1987). To be considered truly creative, one must produce highly original works—such as art, literature, scientific theories, and technological inventions—that one's society recognizes as important (Mumford and Gustafson, 1988).

Other psychologists take a more "everyday" view, seeing creativity as a collection of qualities possessed in varying degrees by virtually everyone. One need not publish a classic novel or patent a revolutionary invention to be creative; creativity can also be expressed through originality in relatively mundane activities like daydreams and hobbies (e.g., Richards et al., 1988). Accordingly, "creativity can be regarded as the quality of products or responses (or the processes that produce them) judged to be creative by appropriate observers" (Amabile, 1982a, p. 1001).

Each of the two views of creativity employs a particular method of research with its own focus on specific aspects. Each also has its own inherent limitations and biases. Let us take a look at one study, chosen for its simplicity, from each view, then at the limitations of each approach.

STUDYING CREATIVITY FROM THE "GENIUS" VIEW

Some researchers believe there is a price to pay for being creative. For example, a recent article on the front page of the *APA Monitor*, the American Psychological Association's professional newspaper, reported an association between musical creativity and mental illness (DeAngelis, 1989). The diaries of five famous composers—Berlioz, Handel, Mahler, Schumann, and Wolf—contained passages that clearly indicated the presence of bipolar disorder (commonly called manic-depressive illness). This report, jointly sponsored by the National Institute of Mental Health, the Johns Hopkins University Department of Psychiatry, and the Manic-Depressive Illness Foundation with the Eleanor Naylor Dana Charitable Trust, concluded that bipolar disorder, or at least a history of dramatic mood swings, may have enhanced the creativity of these artists. It clearly did make their lives more painful.

Because researchers who adhere to the genius view see creativity as pertaining to only a few extraordinary individuals, they concentrate on examining the abilities of a small group of recognized creative people such as composers (DeAngelis, 1989), writers (Freud, 1908; Andreasen, 1987), artists (Simonton, 1984), distinguished electrical engineers (Lehman, 1966), eminent scientists (Zuckerman, 1974), and Nobel laureates (Clark and Rice, 1982). By focusing on small, select samples, these researchers are able to gather quite comprehensive information on their subjects. These investigators often administer lengthy questionnaires and conduct personal, in-depth interviews. Sometimes this research is longitudinal, spanning years or even decades. Some researchers, such as the author of the *APA Monitor* article, make use of secondary sources—diaries, letters, biographies, autobiographies, and official citations and awards—to gather data about subjects who are deceased or otherwise unavailable for direct study.

STUDYING CREATIVITY FROM THE "EVERYDAY" VIEW

Researchers who hold the view that creativity stems from fairly normal processes typically rely on volunteers for their subjects. These volunteers are randomly selected; that is, they are chosen without regard to their talents or abilities. Subjects may be children (Amabile, 1982b), college students (Amabile, 1979; Hocevar, 1981), or adults drawn from the general population (Sternberg and Davidson, 1982; Richards et al., 1988). Because such subjects are not part of a special group, they usually cannot give the experimenters a great deal of time. As a result, most experimental procedures are limited to those that subjects can do relatively quickly and easily, such as completing questionnaires (Hocevar, 1981; McCrea, 1987), solving puzzles (Weisberg and Suls, 1973; Sternberg and Davidson, 1982), and making small collages (Amabile, 1979, 1982b).

Partly because their range of procedures is limited, these researchers also have relatively limited aims. Most studies attempt to demonstrate or isolate a *component* of creativity, not creativity itself. Some of the many different components that have received attention are cognitive skills such as divergent thinking (Guilford, 1950) and problem solving (Weisberg, 1987); personality factors such as risk taking (Sternberg, 1985) and openness to experience (McCrea, 1987); motivational factors such as extrinsic justification (Amabile, 1982a); and environmental factors such as public support (Sternberg, 1989). Only recently have researchers attempted to incorporate these components into complex models of creativity itself (e.g., Amabile, 1983; Mumford and Gustafson, 1988; Sternberg, 1989).

One example of this type of research is a study of motivation and creativity in children (Amabile, 1982b). Twenty-two girls between the ages of seven and eleven were invited to attend one of two "art parties." At the parties the girls were each provided with a piece of cardboard, small pieces of colored paper, and glue and were asked to make a collage. They were also told that they would have a chance to win one of three prizes.

At the first party, the prizes were raffled off. Each girl was given a raffle ticket and told that she would have the same chance of winning a prize as everyone else; no connection was made between the prizes and the collages. The fifteen girls who attended this party constituted the control group. At the other party, the girls were told that the prizes would be awarded to the three "best" collages. This instruction gave the girls a clear reason for making their collages; to win a prize. These seven girls constituted the experimental group. A panel of expert judges recruited from a university art department then rated both groups' collages (without knowing which collages had been made by members of which group) in terms of their level of creativity and their technical quality.

The collages from the experimental group were rated as less original but technically more proficient than those from the control group. The researcher concluded that (1) external justification inhibits creativity, although it may enhance task orientation; and (2) more generally, environmental factors like rewards may have a significant effect on creativity, so creativity may not be a wholly innate, personal quality.

CRITICAL ANALYSIS OF CREATIVITY RESEARCH

The two studies just described were chosen because they are straightforward and easy to summarize. It would be unfair to judge the merits of the "genius" and "everyday" approaches to creativity solely on the basis of these two studies. Instead, let's focus on the problems common to most studies that investigate creativity from these viewpoints.

In its own way, each type of study offers interesting insights into creativity. The genius view provides rich, detailed information about how the most creative among us go about their work and their lives. Studies of everyday creativity shed light on the personal factors that make some of us more creative than others and on the environmental factors that may enhance or inhibit creativity in all of us. Nevertheless, both paradigms have their problems, the bulk of which concern issues of validity and center on problems of sampling.

Analysis of the "Genius" View.   The discovery of an association between musical creativity and manic-depressive illness in five famous composers (DeAngelis, 1989) is certainly intriguing and merits further study. But what are the weaknesses of this report?

First, by choosing small, specially selected samples, researchers limit the generalizability of their results. It may very well be that five composers suffered from bipolar disorder. But is this also true for the thousands of composers who were *not* described? Is it true for other types of creative people—artists, musicians, writers, or scientists? Generally speaking, are the thousands of people who suffer from bipolar disorder more creative than nonsufferers? With such *anecdotal evidence*— just a few examples that support an already existing hypothesis—we cannot answer these sorts of questions.

Even studies that randomly select subjects have problems with generalizability. For example, one researcher (Andreasen, 1987) randomly chose a sample of thirty published authors from those who attended the prestigious University of Iowa Writers' Workshop. She found their rate of mood disorders to be twice that of a matched control sample of thirty people from the community (lawyers, hospital administrators, and the like). However, this study tells us more about writers than about creativity per se (Flach, 1988). Since the study

focused on the characteristics of a group of carefully chosen subjects, we cannot tell whether other creative people have this problem. In fact, there is evidence that measures of psychiatric problems are unrelated, or even negatively related, to standard measures of creativity (Klein and Cooper, 1986; Schubert, in press, cited in Flach, 1988).

A second difficulty with many reports about creativity is the unreliable nature of much of the evidence. In the study of writers, the level of the subjects' mental problems was derived from interviews with the subjects themselves. It is possible that the writers and the controls had different biases. For example, the writers may have been more sensitive to mental problems in themselves, or perhaps the nonwriters were more knowledgeable about mood disorders. In either case, these biases would result in different reports even if the actual rates of psychiatric problems were similar.

This problem gets much worse when researchers base their data on secondary sources such as biographies and historical documents. It is a common belief that many famous creative people produced their works by some inexplicable flash of insight, and many researchers employ historical documents to support this notion (Weisberg, 1987). Mozart, for instance, wrote letters (Ghiselin, 1952) describing how fully completed musical pieces came to him almost effortlessly; when composing, he said, he merely transcribed already finished works. However, musicologists have known for some time that these self-reports are not trustworthy. Analyses of Mozart's first drafts show signs of extensive reworking (Sloboda, 1984), and some people even doubt that Mozart actually wrote the letters in question (Deutsch, 1964). Nevertheless, this evidence contradicting Mozart's self-reported creative style has not affected the popular culture to any great degree, as evidenced by the film *Amadeus,* which portrayed an obnoxious and immature Mozart who almost magically produced finished compositions of unbelievable beauty.

Analysis of the "Everyday" View.
The problems with research into everyday creativity, too, involve validity and sampling—

specifically, external validity, or the extent to which the study approximates real-life phenomena. True creativity has been defined as the production of "novel, socially valued products" of two types: major contributions and minor contributions (Mumford and Gustafson, 1988). Major contributions are masterpieces that revolutionize a particular field; Edison's electric light and Dali's surrealism would both be considered in this category. In contrast, minor contributions are new and insightful extensions of an existing line of thought. Developing the three-way light bulb and drawing cartoon caricatures are examples of minor contributions. According to this definition, then, even a minor contribution requires extensive work and public recognition. It is not clear what proportion of the general population makes even a "minor" contribution, so that it becomes impossible to select a random sample of subjects to objectively measure the characteristics of true creativity.

A second problem with investigations of everyday creativity is the validity of the creativity measurement. Do any of the cognitive, personality, or environmental factors studied (e.g., divergent thinking, problem solving, risk taking, and external justification) really tap true creativity? For example, are the collages made by the girls at the "art parties" (Amabile, 1982b) truly creative "products" in the same way that art masterpieces are?

Other measures of creativity have similar problems. Many psychologists have assessed creativity by measuring *divergent thinking* (Guilford, 1950), the ability to come up with many solutions to a problem. Typically, the subject is given an object or a word and asked to generate a list of uses, synonyms, or meanings. Usually the results are scored in terms of frequency—the number of responses. But investigators (Romaniuk and Romaniuk, 1981; Owen and Baum, 1985) have found measures of divergent thinking to be influenced by noncreativity factors such as the task instructions (instructional set), the subjects' typical response style (response set), and test anxiety. Thus, it is not clear whether constructs such as divergent thinking actually measure creativity;

it is even unclear whether tests of divergent thinking really measure divergent thinking.

CONCLUSION: WHAT DO WE KNOW ABOUT THE SOURCES OF CREATIVITY?

What we know about the sources of creativity depends on what we believe creativity is. Research based on the genius view seems to indicate that true creativity is a collection of different factors that combine in unique ways to produce extraordinary people. However, when you read about the characteristics of especially creative people, ask yourself: Does the sample in the study relate to creative people in general? Is the evidence based on trustworthy sources? Are the conclusions valid in their interpretation and generalizability?

Everyday creativity is also seen as a result of a combination of processes. The difference is that these factors are ones that most people possess (or at least are capable of possessing). Yet because of the limited range of most researchers' work, it is unclear how these factors combine or which of them are most important. When you read studies of this sort, ask yourself: Does this measure really relate to creativity in a meaningful way? How does this factor combine with other factors to produce true creativity?

So, what does it take to be creative? To this question researchers have provided many different answers: energy; knowledge; intelligence; insight; an eccentric nature; a predisposition toward mood disorders; a creative cognitive style; a willingness to take risks; an openness to new ideas; intrinsic motivation; and a supportive professional, educational, or public environment. Unfortunately, despite all this research, our understanding of creativity has not been advanced by any great degree. Researchers still disagree about which of these factors are truly related to creativity, which are important to the development of creativity, and how these factors combine to produce creative behavior.

REFERENCES

Amabile, T. M. External justification and creativity. *Journal of Personality and Social Psychology,* 1979, *37,* 221–233.

Amabile, T. M. The social psychology of creativity: A consensual assessment. *Journal of Personality and Social Psychology,* 1982a, *43,* 997–1013.

Amabile, T. M. Children's artistic creativity: Detrimental effects of competition in a field setting. *Personality and Social Psychology Bulletin,* 1982b, *8,* 573–78.

Amabile, T. M. The social psychology of creativity: A componential conceptualization. *Journal of Personality and Social Psychology,* 1983, *43,* 997–1013.

Andreasen, N. C. Creativity and mental illness: Prevalence rates in writers and their first-degree relatives. *The American Journal of Psychiatry,* 1987, *144,* 1288–1292.

Clark, R. D., and G. A. Rice. Family constellations and eminence: The birth orders of Nobel prize winners. *The Journal of Psychology,* 1982, *110,* 281–287.

DeAngelis, T. Mania, depression, and genius. *The APA Monitor,* 1989, *20,* 1, 24.

Deutsch, O. E. Spurious Mozart letters. *Music Review,* 1964, *25,* 120–123.

Flach, F. Mental illness and creativity. *The American Journal of Psychiatry,* 1988, *145,* 771.

Freud, S. Creative writers and day-dreaming. *Collected Papers.* Vol. 4. London: Hogarth, 1908.

Galton, F. Inquiries into human faculty and its development. London: Macmillan, 1883.

Ghiselin, B. (Ed.) The creative process. New York: Mentor, 1952.

Guilford, J. P. Creativity. *American Psychologist,* 1950, *5,* 444–454.

Hocevar, D. Measurement of creativity: Review and critique. *Journal of Personality Assessment,* 1981, *45,* 450–464.

Lehman, H. C. The most creative years of engineers and other technologists. *Journal of Genetic Psychology,* 1966, *108,* 263–270.

McCrea, R. B. Creativity, divergent thinking, and openness to experience. *Journal of Personality and Social Psychology,* 1987, *52,* 1258–1265.

Mumford, M. D., and S. B. Gustafson. Creativity syndrome: Integration, application, and innovation. *Psychological Bulletin,* 1988, *103,* 27–43.

Owen, S. V., and S. M. Baum. The validity of the measurement of originality. *Educational and Psychological Measurements,* 1985, *45,* 939–944.

Richards, R., D. K. Kinney, M. Benet, and A. P. C. Merzel. Assessing everyday creativity: Characteristics of the lifetime creativity scales and validation with three large samples. *Journal of Personality and Social Psychology,* 1988, *54,* 476–485.

Romaniuk, J. G., and M. Romaniuk. Creativity across the life span: A measurement perspective. *Human Development,* 1981, *24,* 366–381.

Simonton, D. K. Artistic creativity and interpersonal relationships across and within generations. *Journal of Personality and Social Psychology,* 1984, *46,* 1273–1286.

Sloboda, J. *The musical mind.* New York: Oxford University Press, 1984.

Sternberg, R. J., Implicit theories of intelligence, creativity, and wisdom. *Journal of Personality and Social Psychology,* 1985, *49,* 607–627.

Sternberg, R. J. An investment model of creativity. Paper presented at Teachers College, New York, March 1989.

Sternberg, R. J. and J. E. Davidson. The mind of the puzzler. *Psychology Today,* 1982, *16,* 37–44.

Weisberg, R. W. Problem solving and creativity. In R. J. Sternberg (Ed.), *The nature of creativity.* Cambridge: Cambridge University Press, 1987, pp. 148–176.

Weisberg, R. W., and J. Suls. An information-processing model of Duncker's candle problem. *Cognitive Psychology,* 1973, *4,* 255–276.

Zuckerman, H. The scientific elite: Nobel laureates' mutual influence. In R. S. Albert (Ed.), *Genius and eminence.* New York: Pergamon Press, 1974, pp. 171–186.

RESPONDING TO CRITICAL ESSAY 3

1. The bulk of work in the study of creativity has focused on two operating definitions of creativity, the "genius" view and the "everyday" view. Each view offers interesting insights about creativity.

    Draw a parallel between the major views of creativity and one of the enduring themes in psychology, nature vs. nurture.

2. There is an ancient myth that "genius is next to insanity." Indeed, this critical essay observes that musical creativity and manic-depressive illness has been associated in five famous composers.

    What's wrong, methodologically, with reports of this sort?

3. Creativity is a fascinating topic to study. Many explanations have been offered for creativity, but there is widespread disagreement on what creativity "means."

    [This is a two-part question.] (a) What is the reason for such diverse definitions of creativity? and (b) What components of the creative process would you include?

CHAPTER TWELVE
Emotions

KEY TERM ORGANIZER

A useful working definition states that *emotion* is a pattern of responses, involving arousal and impulses to action, thoughts, and behavioral expression (including actions, facial expressions, and vocal qualities), to an event relevant to our needs, desires, and goals.

The physiological changes that constitute *arousal* are controlled by the autonomic nervous system. The *galvanic skin response* (GSR) is a measure of arousal.

The *James-Lange theory* stated that arousal, or the perception of it, is the emotion being experienced. Schachter proposed in his *two-factor theory* that emotion is composed of both physiological arousal and a content-based cognitive interpretation of that arousal.

In order to account for the swiftness with which emotion can descend, Cannon proposed that there must also be a subjective experience of emotion occurring simultaneously with the triggering of arousal, and probably controlled by the cortex.

Ekman's studies found important differences among emotional states, including physiological differences and clear distinctions between positive and negative emotions.

As it is now understood, arousal serves to intensify the emotional state. The impulse to act seems to be a central element of emotion and may account for arousal. This impulse also may illustrate that emotion is functional and adaptive; it motivates us to fight or flee.

Darwin believed that much of human emotional expression has an evolutionary basis. Evidence for this theory comes from striking similarities in the expression and interpretation of basic emotions around the world and from the presence of emotional expressions in very young infants.

The *facial feedback hypothesis* holds that the subjective experience of emotion results from an awareness of our facial expressions. The *vascular theory* attempts to explain how facial feedback works. This theory proposes that changes in facial muscles alter patterns of blood flow to the brain, which then dictate the specific emotion.

Whatever the biological basis or component of emotion may be, it is clear that *appraisal*—cognitive interpretation of events with respect to personal needs and goals—plays a large role in human emotional expression. Appraisal often takes place unconsciously.

Negative and positive appraisals are probably the most basic types made. Certain specific appraisals trigger certain emotions, and people around the world agree on what appraisals elicit which basic emotions.

Cognitive control of emotion can be achieved through religious training or therapy. Other ways to control emotion include altering our goals and desires, altering our appraisals by reevaluating events or situations, and suppressing unwanted emotions. Cognition and emotion are closely intertwined.

Happiness is not usually determined by objective circumstances; it is transitory and relative. Agreed-upon appraisals that elicit happiness include those that involve achievement, positive surprises bringing a high degree of pleasure, and satisfaction of interpersonal concerns.

MAJOR CONCEPTS AND LEARNING OBJECTIVES

CONCEPT 1   Emotions are patterns of responses to events that are relevant to the goals and needs of an organism. Emotions serve to arouse the individual and are essential for individual survival, for maintaining a community, and for the development of civilization.

(handwritten margin notes: arousal is physio + cognitive; perception of emotion; James Lange; general increase of arousal by many emotions; Cannon; 2 factor - cognitive interpretation of arousal; biological offsprings of basic)

1.1   Distinguish between basic and subordinate emotions.

1.2   Describe the theories of emotion that depend in some way upon arousal.

1.3   List the five problems identified by Ekman that have historically prevented the development of a theory of emotions.

1.4   Describe how arousal relates to the "impulse to act."

Concept Builder 1

Directions: You are making some "fine-tuning" adjustments on a modern-day Frankenstein's monster. While you have this creature on the operating table, you give it a little jolt of electricity to check the wiring of its sympathetic nervous system. Igor, your assistant, is keeping a checklist of the responses. What will his list look like if "Frankie, Jr." passes the sympathetic nervous system check with 100 percent?

Frankenstein's Monster Returns

1. Heart rate: increase _____ decrease _____
2. Blood diverted to: skeletal muscles _____   GI tract _____
3. Liver: conserves sugar _____   releases sugar _____
4. Breathing: deepens _____   remains even _____
5. Pupils: dilate _____ constrict _____
6. Salivary glands: work profusely _____   stop working _____
7. "Monster" (goose) bumps   rise _____ disappear _____

CONCEPT 2   While emotions are indeed important for arousal and action, they are also key elements of human expression. The facial features of emotion have been described for a number of emotions.

[handwritten, left margin: a personal experience of emotion results in facial expression]

[handwritten, right margin: People from different cultures express emotions similarily even though emotions are same; present at birth recognition]

2.1   Describe the contemporary evidence supporting Darwin's view that emotions have a genetic basis and play a key role in the survival of the species.

2.2   Describe the facial feedback hypothesis and the vascular theory of emotions and discuss the evidence supporting these views.

[handwritten: blood flow]

Concept Builder 2

Directions: Read the following "facts" gleaned from around the world regarding the expression of emotions. Some facts support the biological foundation of emotion, some the learning foundation. You decide which supports each theory.

[handwritten: cognition   physiological]

Emotions around the World

Observation 1:   There are several reports of children blind and deaf from birth exhibiting anger, sorrow, and joy just like normally sighted children.

Observation 1 supports ____biological____.

Observation 2:   In China, tradition has it that when a good meal is finished, the guests show their appreciation by belching loudly. Unlike Americans, Chinese hosts take pride in hearing these sounds at the dinner table.

Observation 2 supports ____learning____.

Observation 3:   In some countries, males are socialized to suppress the display of emotions and women are encouraged to be expressive. In other countries the reverse is true: women are coolly rational and inexpressive while men are emotional and very expressive.

Observation 3 supports ____learning____.

Observation 4:   New Guinea tribesmen can readily label the emotion being displayed by facial expressions in photographs of Americans, even though they have had little or no contact with Americans and their characteristic patterns of expression.

Observation 4 supports ____biological____.

CONCEPT 3   The cognitive interpretation of events is also an essential component of emotional expression and experience.

→ 3.1   Explain the relationship of cognitive appraisal to emotions.

3.2   Distinguish between unconscious and cognitive appraisal in emotional expression.

Concept Builder 3

Directions: Look at the following diagram of the process of appraisal:

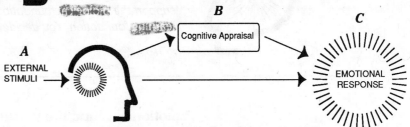

Now identify the following events and situations that illustrate the three elements of appraisal. Note your answers by using an "A," "B," or "C," or some combination of the three.

The Power of Appraisal

"There is nothing either good or bad, but thinking makes it so."
—Shakespeare

(SAMPLE)   In response to an upcoming job interview (A), Gina thinks, "I'll blow it. I just know I'll blow it!" (B) Indeed, she gets herself worked up and feels apprehensive (C).

1.   Emmanuel's teacher announced that there would be a comprehensive final exam in his chemistry course (A). He immediately felt lightheaded and dizzy (C) because he could just visualize himself sitting at his desk and his mind going blank on final exam day (B).

2.   Annette feels queasy (C) every time she enters a dentist's office and hears the drill (A). She is unaware of why she thinks and feels this way (B).

3.   When Richard was told he had cancer (A), he said, "I'm going to fight this disease and beat it with a positive attitude" (B); he immediately felt better and more positive (C).

4.   Laura's therapist reminded her that her mother's critical remarks (A) didn't make Laura feel guilty (C); she *allowed* herself to interpret the criticism as valid and true (B).

CONCEPT 4   Emotions have been examined in great depth in both laboratory settings and in cross-cultural settings, revealing universal characteristics.

4.1   Give a detailed account of the research into happiness. *contentment satisfaction.*

4.2   Describe the cultural differences and regularities that have been identified in emotions. *They have universal characteristics,*

Concept Builder 4

Directions: Read the three statements given by three different people "on the street." For each, identify the appropriate kind of appraisal that elicits happiness.

"Pardon Me, How Do You 'Spell' Happiness?"

1.   "Happiness is the love of warm family; a place where 'everybody knows your name,' as the old song goes. A place where I'm accepted."

      satisfied with interpersonal concerns

2.   "Happiness is reaching your goals in life: buying a house, getting a degree, retiring early."

      accomplishment of goal

3.   "Happiness is winning the lottery!"

      reality exceeds your expectations

CHAPTER EXERCISE   *Directions: Study the five flow charts below and the series of events they depict in the ultimate expression of emotion. Match each diagram with the appropriate theory.*

Emotion Flow Charts

Theories

a.   Cannon's theory
b.   vascular theory
c.   James-Lange theory
d.   facial-feedback theory
e.   two-factor theory

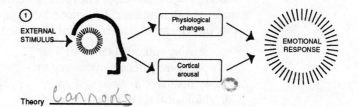

Theory *Cannon's*

Theories

a. Cannon's theory
b. vascular theory
c. James-Lange theory
d. facial-feedback theory
e. two-factor theory

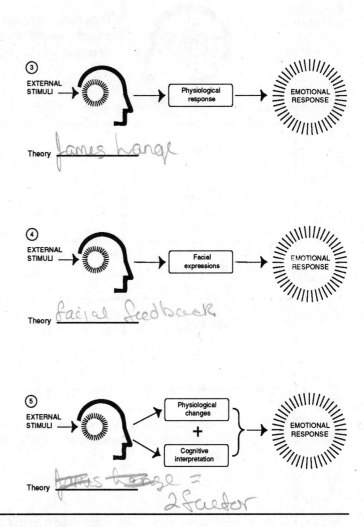

Theory *vascular*

Theory *James Lange*

Theory *facial feedback*

Theory ~~James Lange~~ = 2 factor

PRACTICE EXAM 1

1. Shana's English professor unexpectedly announced a quiz on some assigned reading material, catching almost everyone by surprise. The anxiety level of the class suddenly shot up. The arousal level of most class members was being affected by the:

   a. sensory source of emotion
   b. parasympathetic nervous system
   c. sympathetic nervous system
   d. biological source of emotion

   (Conceptual, Obj. 1.2)

2.   Which part of the face dominates our interpretation of another person's facial expression?

    a.   the eyes and eyelids
    b.   the mouth and lower face
    c.   the eyebrows and forehead
    d.   all portions are equally expressive

                                                 (Factual, Obj. 2.2)

3.   Which of the following statements would be most damaging to the argument that the foundation of emotions is primarily biological?

    a.   Emotional expression develops as early as two months in infants.
    b.   Our means of expressing emotions are similar to those of other animals.
    c.   People the world over express emotions in a consistently similar manner.
    d.   The manner of expressing emotions depends on one's cultural background.

                                               (Conceptual, Obj. 2.1)

4.   Arnold's theory about depression is that if you smile and make yourself laugh a lot, the depression will go away after a while. His theory is most similar to:

    a.   the James-Lange theory
    b.   Cannon's theory
    c.   facial-feedback hypothesis
    d.   the Schachter-Singer two-factor theory

                                               (Conceptual, Obj. 2.2)

5.   Darwin argued that many of our patterns of emotional expression are inherited because they:

    a.   serve a vascular function
    b.   have survival value
    c.   have cultural significance
    d.   serve as self-regulation mechanisms

                                               (Factual, Obj. 2.1)

6.   Twelve-year-old Jason was watching a news special one night on cosmetic facial surgery and was very distressed by the procedure being used. The patient was being operated on yet seemed awake and conscious the whole time. After his dad explained that the anesthesia caused the patient to feel no pain, Jason felt comfortable watching the rest of the program. The difference in his emotional reaction can be explained by:

    a.   a difference in his cognitive appraisal of the situation
    b.   the chance to decrease his level of arousal
    c.   his lack of direct experience with minor surgery
    d.   the temporary nature of the distress reaction

                                               (Conceptual, Obj. 3.1)

7.   Which of the following is *not* a criticism of the James-Lange theory?

    a.   Physiological change alone cannot produce emotion.
    b.   Emotions are often felt rapidly.
    c.   Many of the same bodily changes accompany different emotions.
    d.   Physiological changes precede the actual emotional response.

                                               (Factual, Obj. 1.2)

8.   Annette was thrilled that an old silent-movie actress was visiting her drama class and instructing them in some of the tricks of acting in front of the camera. The actress spent a lot of time on facial expressions, particularly concerning:

   a.   visual intensity
   b.   head orientation
   c.   mouth expressiveness
   d.   facial makeup

(Conceptual, Obj. 4.2)

9.   The Schachter-Singer experiments demonstrated the importance of what factor(s) in the experience of emotions?

   a.   physiological changes
   b.   cognitive interpretations of change
   c.   sensory changes
   d.   both *a* and *b*

(Factual, Obj. 2.2)

10.   Recent research shows that if you give subjects tonic water in orange juice and tell them it is alcohol, they start to show all the classic symptoms of intoxication after several drinks. This observation supports which theory of emotion?

   a.   the James-Lange theory
   b.   Cannon's theory
   c.   the facial-feedback hypothesis
   d.   the Schachter-Singer two-factor theory

(Conceptual, Obj. 2.2)

11.   Waynbaum proposed a vascular theory of emotion earlier in this century. His main thesis was that emotions served a(n) _____ function.

   a.   regulatory
   b.   expressive
   c.   arousal
   d.   cognitive

(Factual, Obj. 2.2)

12.   Which of the following is *least* like the other two?

   a.   James-Lange theory
   b.   Waynbaum's vascular theory
   c.   two-factor theory
   d.   all three are basically similar

(Conceptual, Obj. 2.2)

PRACTICE EXAM 2

1.   In a fear-arousing situation, a person's:

   a.   blood-sugar level decreases
   b.   salivary glands may stop working
   c.   breathing slows
   d.   digestion speeds up

(Factual, Obj. 1.2)

2. When you are at home, relaxed in front of the TV, you are likely to feel very little emotion. At this time, the component of your nervous system that is probably controlling your activities is the:

    a. somatic system
    b. limbic system
    c. parasympathetic system
    d. sympathetic system

(Conceptual, Obj. 1.2)

3. William James hypothesized that the reason emotions such as fear and rage differ from one another is that:

    a. different patterns of physiological activity are triggered
    b. we learn to apply different labels to them
    c. they register in different receptor sites in the brain
    d. they are produced by different situations

(Factual, Obj. 1.2)

4. If you said that we experience emotions too quickly to allow physiological changes to occur, you would be in agreement with:

    a. Walter Cannon
    b. Stanley Schachter
    c. William James
    d. Carl Lange

(Conceptual, Obj. 1.2)

5. The broadest categories into which emotions can be divided are positive emotions and negative emotions. These categories are referred to as:

    a. subordinate
    b. midlevel
    c. superordinate
    d. basic

(Factual, Obj. 1.1)

6. Which of the following statements describes Schachter's theory of emotion?

    a. Emotion produces physiological arousal.
    b. The situation produces physiological arousal, which produces emotion.
    c. The situation produces emotion, which produces physiological arousal.
    d. Physiological arousal and situational cues interact to produce emotion.

(Conceptual, Obj. 3.1)

7. According to Schachter's two-factor theory, the two components of emotion are a physiological change and:

    a. an emotional change
    b. a psychological change
    c. the opportunity to demonstrate that change
    d. a cognitive (situational) interpretation of that change

(Factual, Obj. 3.1)

8. Which of the following theories of emotion appears to be essentially correct?

    a. the James-Lange theory
    b. Schachter's two-factor theory
    c. Cannon's theory
    d. there appears to be support for each of these theories

                                                        (Conceptual, Obj. 2.2, 3.1)

9. Shaver and Schwartz have studied cultural aspects of emotion and concluded that subordinate emotions are _____ determined.

    a. genetically
    b. hormonally
    c. culturally and cognitively
    d. neurologically

                                                        (Factual, Obj. 4.2)

10. According to adaptation-level theory, if people receive a large sum of money (say, from a lottery), they would generally be no happier than others because:

    a. they begin associating with people who have even more money than they do
    b. they habituate to the new level
    c. money generally brings unhappiness
    d. one can never satiate oneself with money

                                                        (Conceptual, Obj. 4.1)

11. According to the text, what is the point of *cognitive* therapies?

    a. to feel happy
    b. to learn how to be emotionally expressive
    c. to learn how to express negative emotions, such as anger
    d. to alter thoughts, thus adjusting emotions

                                                        (Factual, Obj. 3.2)

12. Suppose you are very poor, want your children to be happy, and believe in the downward-comparison theory of happiness. You would:

    a. give your children the same things your neighbors had
    b. send your kinds to the best schools so they can see the wonderful things rich kids have
    c. make them save money for their future
    d. move to a neighborhood where everyone else is even poorer than you are

                                                        (Conceptual, Obj. 4.1)

■ ANSWER KEY ■

Concept 1
1. increases
2. skeletal muscles
3. releases sugar
4. deepens
5. dilate
6. stop working
7. rise

Concept 2

Observation 1: biological
Observation 2: learning
Observation 3: learning
Observation 4: biological

Concept 3
1. a-c-b
2. c-a-b
3. a-b-c
4. a-c-b

Concept 4
1. satisfaction of interpersonal concerns
2. completing a task successfully
3. reality exceeds your expectations

Chapter Exercise
1. a
2. b
3. c
4. d
5. e

Practice Exam 1
1. c, p. 346
2. b, p. 353
3. d, pp. 354–355
4. c, p. 356
5. b, pp. 352–354
6. a, pp. 359–360
7. d, p. 348
8. c, p. 353
9. d, pp. 348–349
10. d, pp. 348–349
11. a, pp. 357–359
12. c, pp. 347–349, 357–359

Practice Exam 2
1. b, p. 346
2. c, p. 346
3. a, p. 347
4. a, pp. 347–348
5. c, p. 368
6. d, pp. 348–349
7. d, pp. 348–349
8. d, pp. 347–349
9. c, p. 368
10. b, p. 367
11. d, p. 364
12. d, p. 367

CHAPTER 13

Motivation

KEY TERM ORGANIZER

To psychologists, the term *motivation* refers to processes that energize, maintain, and direct behavior toward goals. Unlike humans, much of the behavior of lower animals seems to be the result of *instincts*—innate, fixed responses characteristic of a species. Psychologists have replaced the term "instinct" with *fixed action pattern,* which is a stereotyped and often-repeated pattern of movement.

In contrast to instinct theories, *drives* are motivational states that result from physiological deficits or needs and instigate behaviors to reduce those needs. The goal of drive reduction is *homeostasis*—maintaining a balanced or constant physiological state. Drive-reduction theories acknowledge that external stimuli, known as *incentives,* can serve as anticipated rewards for certain behaviors.

self actualizat.. (handwritten note)

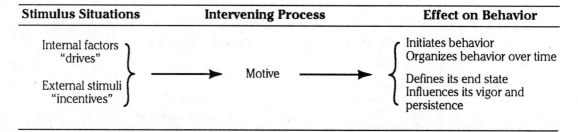

Stimulus Situations	Intervening Process	Effect on Behavior
Internal factors "drives" } External stimuli "incentives" } →	Motive →	Initiates behavior Organizes behavior over time Defines its end state Influences its vigor and persistence

Expectancy-value theories are one type of theory that includes cognitive activity in motivational processes. Eating behavior is a good example of how motivation is affected by external stimuli. People who are particularly susceptible to food cues are known as *externals.* The body has a remarkable ability to maintain a steady weight. People differ in their *basal metabolism rate,* the rate at which they expend calories when resting. Each person's body seems to have a *set point,* a weight that the body seems "set" to maintain.

In contrast to biologically based needs, many of our activities involve acquired or learned motivation. For example, *optimal-level theories* suggest we have a built-in tendency to seek a certain level of stimulation and activity. In *opponent-process theory,* two forces are involved in acquired or learned motivation—a primary process that is an intense response to a stimulus and a secondary process that opposes the first.

The study of human social motives is complex. One social motive that has been heavily researched is the *achievement motive*, the need to attain some standard of excellence. Psychologists have analyzed achievement strivings by considering whether the rewards sought are internal or external. Behavior undertaken for the sake of some external reward is considered to be *extrinsically motivated*. Behavior undertaken for its own sake is considered to be *intrinsically motivated*.

A more encompassing motive that has been studied is our need for self-esteem. For example, depressed people seem to exhibit a pattern of thought called *depressive realism*, in which self-serving, positive biases are absent. Even potentially destructive behavior can be used to protect our favorable self-views, as in the deliberate *self-handicap*.

How do social motives regulate behavior? In part, through *behavioral self-regulation*, a monitoring of our own behavior.

Maslow believed that there is a hierarchy of human motives. The *basic needs* are physiological in origin (like thirst and hunger). Intermediate motivational needs are known as *deficiency needs;* when they are not met, people seek to satisfy them in whatever way is feasible. The highest needs are called *metaneeds*, which include needs for intellectual accomplishment, creativity, and "self-actualization."

MOTIVES		
Biological	**Social**	
Primary Drives		
Thirst	Achievement	
Hunger	Self-esteem	
Acquired Motives		
Motives explained by optimal-level and opponent-process theories		
Hierarchical		
Basic needs	Deficiency needs	Metaneeds

MAJOR CONCEPTS AND LEARNING OBJECTIVES

CONCEPT 1   Motivation refers to the processes that energize, maintain, and direct behavior toward goals. Instinct, drive-reduction, and cognitive theories have been offered to account for the regulation of behavior in these processes.

1.1   Define motivation, instinct, and drive.

1.2   List and describe the main concepts of the instinct, drive-reduction, and cognitive theories of motivation.

Concept
Builder 1

Directions: Read the following quotations from sales managers who are commenting on their views of motivation and the motivated salesperson. Then match each comment to the aspect of motivation the manager is focusing on.

Sales and Motivation

_____ Sales Manager 1:
"I look for salespeople who set goals for themselves: monthly, weekly, or even daily goals. This gives the salesperson something to aim for and even surpass if possible. Take away the goal and I think you take away the motivation to succeed."

_____ Sales Manager 2:
"I look for salespeople who get *started* immediately; that shows motivation. Getting started on a project is half the sale; slow starters don't get ahead in sales."

_____ Sales Manager 3:
"I look for salespeople who see beyond just the immediate sale. Motivation, to me, should influence a whole pattern of responses: selling, planning for new accounts, follow-ups on old accounts, positioning a product for long-term advantage. That's motivation at its best!"

a. Initiates
   behavior

b. Organizes
   behavior
   over time

c. Defines end
   states

CONCEPT 2 Body equilibriums like thirst and hunger are controlled through basic biological mechanisms. Regulation of these processes is crucial to the survival of the organism.

2.1 Outline and describe the mechanisms that regulate the induction and satiation of thirst.

2.2 Outline and describe the mechanisms that regulate hunger and weight and explain the role diet and exercise play in the process.

Concept
Builder 2

Directions: Dr. Rotundo, a leading authority on obesity, has developed a special diagnostic test that he playfully dubbed "B.L.O.A.T." (Body Leanness-Obesity Assessment Test). Look at his list of "critical" factors below and check whether they would most likely be associated with a normal-weight person or with a potentially obese person.

B.L.O.A.T. Checklist

	Indicative of a normal-weight person	Indicative of a potentially obese person
1. Heightened responsiveness to food cues		
2. Highly efficient body metabolism		
3. Burns up more calories while resting		
4. High level of insulin in blood		
5. Faster metabolism (needs more calories)		
6. More "fat cells" in the body		

CONCEPT 3   Motivation may be acquired through adaptation to environmental conditions or to levels of arousal that seem unrelated to meeting specific needs. These behaviors reflect efforts to cope with stress and danger.

3.1   Define acquired motivation and distinguish optimum-level theory from opponent-process theory.

Concept Builder 3

Directions: Below are four situations that reflect different aspects of motivation in real life. Label each situation as reflecting either opponent-process theory (A) or optimal-level theory (B).

Motivation: Two Mini-theories

_____ 1. Would be used to explain the "rush" a novice drug user gets when taking a drug, followed by the aversive aftereffect (which increases over time).

_____ 2. Would be used to explain why veteran videogame players seek out new games that offer some new challenge at a level just above their own.

_____ 3. Might be used to explain Zuckerman's "sensation seekers," whose need for stimulation is higher than the average person's.

_____ 4. Would be used to explain the phenomenon in parachute jumpers in which a novice's terror during the first few jumps is gradually replaced by the veteran's exhilaration.

CONCEPT 4   Social motivation governs a wide range of human behavior crucial to our survival in groups. Social motives include achievement, affiliation, power, and self-esteem.

4.1   Define achievement motivation and discuss the means by which individual differences in achievement are measured.

4.2   Describe the attribution theory of achievement motivation.

4.3   Distinguish between intrinsic and extrinsic motivation and how these motives may affect behavior and performance.

4.4   Define self-esteem and discuss the importance to self-esteem of beliefs about the self.

4.5   Identify the reactions individuals may have to information about themselves and how they may then seek ways to protect self-esteem.

**Concept
Builder 4**

Directions: Read the comments below, made by students as they receive their test results. After you have read each response, categorize that response by placing the letter of the comment in the appropriate quadrant of the achievement "window."

What'd Ya Get? Listening to Student Reactions

ACHIEVEMENT WINDOW

	High Achiever	**Low Achiever**
Success	1. Ability, effort Student_____	2. Luck, easy task Student_____
Failure	3. Lack of effort Student_____	4. Lack of ability Student_____

A.   "Wow! I got an 'A' on the test! I can't believe it; it must be a mistake. Well . . . luck was on my side this time."

B.   "Hmmmmm. C+; that might as well be an F in my book, I can do much better; I didn't put in the effort I should have on this exam. I'm not going to let this happen again—110 percent effort for the next test."

C.   "All right! A + + on the exam and a big fat 'excellent' written on my answer sheet from Dr. Demento. I deserved it; I studied hard for this exam and psychology is my field. Beer and pizza, here I come!"

D.   "Oh no, not another F! I guess I just don't have what it takes for college. Boy, Dad will for sure accuse me of being adopted now; 'All of the Davis men made dean's list in college,' he chirps all the time. I'll just slither out of here."

CONCEPT 5   Social motives are powerful regulators of human behavior, and the mechanisms of self-regulation cannot be explained entirely by physiological and adaptive mechanisms.

    5.1   Define behavioral self-regulation and discuss how this concept accounts for social motivation.

    5.2   Outline and describe Maslow's need hierarchy.

**Concept
Builder 5**

Directions: Each picture below represents a level of needs in Maslow's hierarchy of needs. Under each picture, write the type of need it represents.

Visualizing Maslow

Now write each level of needs in its appropriate place in the diagram below.

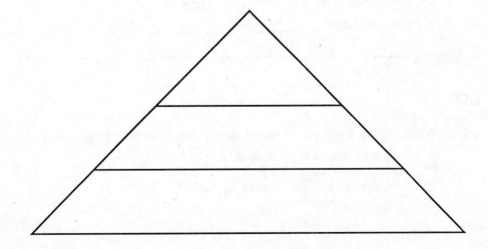

CHAPTER EXERCISE

Directions: Read the following short descriptions plucked from the files of Jessica Flasher, super-sleuth detective and mystery writer. Match each criminal's description with an appropriate motivational concept.

Murder, She Wrote

1. "Luis seemed to extract inherent pleasure from the act of killing, as inborn in him as his desire to breathe air."

   Motivation concept: _____Instinct._____

2. "The small-town sheriff was no knave when it came to solving crime. His mind was methodical: what initiated the brutal act, what forces moved the assailant to plot and plan, what led to that awful conclusion, the final act of demise?"

   Motivation concept: _____motivation_____

3. "Her motives were purely mercenary; she was motivated simply, unashamedly by the desire to collect his insurance money."

   Motivation concept: _____extrinsic_____

4. "After he had done the dirty deed, he discovered that it wasn't nearly as satisfying, as fulfilling as the pleasure he got out of planning the crime, rehearsing the 'script,' fantasizing about every element; he'd do it again because of the private pleasure he got out of it, whether paid or not."

   Motivation concept: _____intrinsic_____

5. "The poor, young man. One felt almost sorry for him. The temptations were always so great—favors, status, money—all were offered as inducements to engage him in cold extermination."

   Motivation concept: _____incentives_____

6. "It's tempting to characterize the criminal as depraved and lacking. Living only to fulfill the most base and animalistic urges that course through all of us. The depravity—a result of not feeling intellectually alive, creative, actualized—connected to life!"

   Motivation concept: _____metaneeds_____

7. "In reality, the actual commission of crime, of any kind, made Hank feel sick and repulsed. As bizarre as it may sound, he committed crimes only because it felt so good (and relieving) when it (the crime) was over."

   Motivation concept: _____opponent-process_____

PRACTICE EXAM 1

1. Which of the following is *not* one of the characteristics of a motive?

   a. causes behavior to be initiated
   b. maintains behavior over time
   c. prevents an end state from being reached
   d. regulates behavior

   (Factual, Obj. 1.1)

2. Drives are to internal stimuli as _____ are to external stimuli.

    a. basic needs
    b. metaneeds
    c. incentives
    d. primary drives

    (Conceptual, Obj. 1.1)

3. One of the primary cues used to signal satiated thirst is:

    a. salt ratio in the bloodstream
    b. stomach distention
    c. urine level
    d. body temperature

    (Factual, Obj. 2.1)

4. According to Tesser, it would be most difficult to maintain self-esteem when:

    a. your closest office mate wins "salesperson of the month," narrowly beating you out
    b. the company brings in an outsider, Joey "Dynamo" Rizzo, a veteran supersalesman who continues his unrivaled sales record
    c. the airport skycap consistently makes more money than you, a computer programmer
    d. your best friend wins a free trip to Iowa

    (Conceptual, Obj. 4.5)

5. In opponent-process theory, there are two processes: a primary process and a secondary process. The secondary process is a reaction of what part of the body?

    a. the circulatory system
    b. the central nervous system
    c. the endocrine system
    d. the lymphatic system

    (Factual, Obj. 3.1)

6. The TAT is based on an idea by Sigmund Freud that people express their motives more freely when they are:

    a. angry
    b. dreaming
    c. free-associating
    d. completely relaxed

    (Conceptual, Obj. 4.1)

7. According to research findings, which one of the following indicates high achievement motivation?

    a. high test anxiety
    b. a preference for either very easy or very difficult jobs
    c. attribution of "success" to external factors
    d. low test anxiety

    (Factual, Obj. 4.2)

8. Suppose you were working for McClelland's research team investigating achievement motivation. If he sent you out to an elementary school to look for an indication of achievement motivation for that generation, what would you be observing and analyzing?

    a.   the way the children played games with each other
    b.   how often books were checked out of the library
    c.   how active the P.T.A. is
    d.   the themes in children's books

                                                                        (Conceptual, Obj. 4.1)

9. Self-reflection, or momentarily paying attention to ourselves, may lead us to engage in a monitoring process called:

    a.   self-actualization
    b.   self-handicapping
    c.   depressive realism
    d.   behavioral self-regulation

                                                                        (Factual, Obj. 5)

10. Which theory of motivation most logically explains why people race autos, skydive, and even take drugs?

    a.   optimal-level theory
    b.   opponent-process theory
    c.   Maslow's hierarchy theory
    d.   Weiner's theory of attribution

                                                                        (Factual, Obj. 3.1)

11. Phil Zimbardo, a famous social psychologist, tells the humorous story of his father, a shopkeeper, who used to be pestered by local boys who threw rocks at his shop windows. One day, Mr. Zimbardo offered the boys 50 cents to carry out the same deed, and said he would do so every day if they threw rocks! One day, he abruptly said he was out of money, and he asked if the boys would continue to throw rocks anyway. Well, as you might have guessed, the boys were not going to throw rocks if they didn't get paid! What explains this change in their motivation?

    a.   illusion of control
    b.   opponent-process theory
    c.   overjustification effect
    d.   behavioral self-regulation

                                                                        (Conceptual, Obj. 4.3)

12. What would Maslow predict about a group of children who have not yet satisfied their need for love and belonging (safety needs)?

    a.   They would have a strong need for creativity and expression.
    b.   They would be less ready to engage in helping behavior than more mature children.
    c.   These children would show symptoms of dysphoria.
    d.   These children would be primarily extrinsically motivated.

                                                                        (Conceptual, Obj. 5.1)

**PRACTICE
EXAM 2**

1. Most detectives have a standard line of inquiry when investigating a crime. One of the most essential facts to learn is the "reason" a crime was committed. This involves establishing a(n):

    a.   incentive
    b.   primary drive
    c.   basic need
    d.   motive

    (Conceptual, Obj. 1.1)

2. Which of the following does *not* belong in Weiner's theory of attribution?

    a.   distinctiveness
    b.   locus
    c.   stability
    d.   controllability

    (Factual, Obj. 4.2)

3. Sylvia is an intern in training at a local hospital. Her training includes emergency room duty. One night while she was on duty, a victim of a serious auto accident was admitted. The chief resident said the victim lost a lot of blood, then asked her how that would affect the patient's physiological needs. How should Sylvia answer?

    a.   "It will increase hunger."
    b.   "It will decrease hunger."
    c.   "It will increase thirst."
    d.   "It will decrease thirst."

    (Conceptual, Obj. 2.1)

4. Which of the following is *false* regarding obesity?

    a.   It is predominantly affected by internal factors; external factors are minimal.
    b.   It is associated with higher levels of insulin.
    c.   It is associated with a lower calorie requirement to maintain weight.
    d.   It is associated with slow metabolism.

    (Factual, Obj. 2.2)

5. Once a virtuoso pianist has reached a high level of mastery on the piano, he or she tends to prefer new, complex pieces that will offer some new challenge to his or her skill. Which theory would explain this phenomenon best?

    a.   optimal-level theory   arousal: stimulation
    b.   opponent-process theory
    c.   drive-reduction theory
    d.   achievement motivation

    (Conceptual, Obj. 3.1)

6. TAT stories are used to score achievement imagery. Which of the following story themes is *not* indicative of a high achiever?

    a.   There is the pursuit of a long-term goal.
    b.   The main character is concerned with a high level of performance.
    c.   There is a desire to invent something or win an award.
    d.   There is a great fear of failure.

    (Factual, Obj. 4.1)

7. During "makeup" exam week, Curt's teacher gave him a choice of three different levels of test difficulty: easy, intermediate, and difficult. Although he has a low C average, Curt chose the most difficult makeup exam. Curt is probably:

   a.   a high achiever
   b.   a low achiever
   c.   intrinsically motivated
   d.   extrinsically motivated

   (Conceptual, Obj. 4.1)

8. The Kakinada Project was an attempt by McClelland and others to accomplish what in India?

   a.   to alter the diet and nutrition of the villagers
   b.   to raise achievement motivation levels among businessmen in the village
   c.   to implement a conservative family-planning program
   d.   to introduce modern agricultural methods

   (Factual, Obj. 4.1)

9. Some runners develop what they term a "positive addiction" for running and jogging, sometimes jogging far more than is practically healthy. What kind of motivation would you call this sort of behavior?

   a.   secondary drive
   b.   primary drive
   c.   fixed action pattern
   d.   homeostasis

   (Conceptual, Obj. 1.1)

10. Murray is best associated with what kind of motivation research?

    a.   thirst and hunger
    b.   metaneeds
    c.   self-esteem
    d.   social motives

    (Factual, Obj. 4.1)

11. Daniel has always enjoyed doing home improvement projects and spent a lot of his spare time pursuing such projects. When he started doing them professionally for money, however, he found his motivation diminishing. These kinds of projects weren't fun anymore. His intrinsic motivation was weakened by extrinsic motivation. This is a case of:

    a.   the illusion of control
    b.   self-handicap
    c.   incentive
    d.   the overjustification effect

    (Conceptual, Obj. 4.3)

12. _____ are needs that people seek to satisfy first and fundamentally:

    a.   Primary drives
    b.   Intrinsic motives
    c.   Basic needs
    d.   Metaneeds

    (Factual, Obj. 5.2)

■ ANSWER KEY ■

Concept 1

Manager 1: C
Manager 2: A
Manager 3: B

Concept 2

Factors indicative of normal-weight person: 3 and 5
Factors indicative of potentially obese: 1, 2, 4, and 6

Concept 3

1. B   3. A
2. A   4. B

Concept 4

Quadrant 1: C   Quadrant 3: B
Quadrant 2: A   Quadrant 4: D

Concept 5

1. Deficiency needs
2. Basic needs
3. Metaneeds

Chapter Exercise

1. Instinct
2. Motivation
3. Extrinsically motivated
4. Intrinsically motivated
5. Incentives
6. Metaneeds
7. Opponent-process theory

Practice Exam 1

1. c, p. 376
2. c, p. 378
3. b, p. 381
4. a, pp. 396–397
5. b, pp. 386–387
6. c, p. 387
7. d, p. 389
8. d, p. 392
9. d, p. 398
10. b, pp. 386–387
11. c, p. 393
12. b, pp. 399–400

Practice Exam 2

1. d, p. 376
2. a, pp. 389–391
3. c, p. 380
4. a, pp. 382–383
5. a, pp. 378, 385
6. d, p. 389
7. b, p. 389
8. b, p. 392
9. a, p. 377
10. d, pp. 387, 397
11. d, p. 393
12. c, p. 399

CHAPTER FOURTEEN
Sexuality and Love

KEY TERM ORGANIZER

Sexuality comprises all the factors that contribute to a person's ability to give and receive erotic pleasure. An important part of a person's sexuality is his or her sense of being male or female, a sense of *sexual identity*. *Transsexualism* is a rare condition in which people develop a sexual identity that is inconsistent with their genetic and anatomical sex.

In most species, sexual activity is tied to the female reproductive cycle, as in *estrus*. In humans, female hormones, principally *estrogens*, are unrelated to the female's sexual interests. A minimum amount of *testosterone*, the male hormone, seems to be needed for normal male arousal. Touch is the most obvious source of sexual stimulation. The *erogenous zones* are particularly sensitive to erotic touch.

According to Masters and Johnson, the human sexual response can be divided into four phases:

1. *Excitement phase:* body shows physiological signs of arousal.
2. *Plateau phase:* body reaches peak of sexual arousal.
3. *Orgasm:* waves of muscular contractions sweep over the body: in men, ejaculation causes a discharge of semen.
4. *Resolution phase:* body returns to the normal state; men now experience a refractory period.

Any problem that persistently prevents a person from engaging in sexual relations or from reaching orgasm during sex is known as a *sexual disorder*. The charts on the next page outlines the major sexual disorders.

Intimacy is the process by which people try to get emotionally close to each other. The emotion of *love* usually accompanies intimate relationships. Love is a feeling of deep affection for and attachment to another person.

Although the majority of adults are *heterosexual*, a good many people are either *homosexual* or *bisexual*. Psychologists have proposed the following hypotheses to explain the development of homosexuality:

	Erectile	Ejaculatory
M	Primary erectile failure: never achieved or maintained an erection	Premature ejaculation: ejaculating before he or his partner would like
A		
L	Secondary erectile failure: orgasmic in the past, but currently unable to acquire or maintain an erection	Inhibited ejaculation: inability to ejaculate during sex with a partner.
E		

[handwritten: cum 2 soon]
[handwritten: no cum]

	Vaginismus	Orgasmic
F		
E	Vagina involuntarily clamps shut so that penetration is impossible or extremely painful	Primary inhibited orgasm: never experienced an orgasm by any means
M		
A		Secondary inhibited orgasm: occasionally experiencing an orgasm, but not with present partner or not during intercourse
L		
E		

- *Biochemical:* level of sexual hormones determines sexual preferences.
- *Social learning:* stresses only learning; an early "homosexual event" occurs and is reinforced by subsequent masturbatory fantasies, by orgasmic pleasure, and even by peer groups.
- *Psychoanalytic:* male homosexuality results from a son's poor relationship with his father (too passive or too domineering).

Homosexuality is no longer regarded as a pathology in and of itself. Sex therapists focus more on helping persons cope with their sexual orientation in a more healthy and effective manner rather than on trying to change their sexual preference.

Some forms of sexual behavior strongly violate community norms and are considered criminally punishable:

- *Rape:* sexual intercourse with another person using physical force, threat, or intimidation. Most psychologists feel that the primary motive for rape is anger or the assertion of power. Studies of rapists tend to confirm this view.
- *Incest:* sexual activity between closely related persons. Incest cuts across all economic boundaries and family backgrounds. Incest is typically a strong indication of troubled family relationships and inadequacies. It is psychologically damaging to the child; generally the younger the child, the more serious the emotional consequences.

MAJOR CONCEPTS AND LEARNING OBJECTIVES

CONCEPT 1   Sexual identity develops from biological, genetic processes and social influences, and it evolves from the prenatal period on.

      1.1.   Define sexuality and sexual identity.

      1.2.   Identify and discuss the biological and the social influences on the
development of sexual identity.

Concept
Builder 1

*Directions: Match the following gender conditions with one
of the possible quadrants in the "gender matrix." The matrix
summarizes the relative strength of genetic/hormonal factors
versus social/cultural influences on gender development.
Some conditions may not fit "clearly" in one quadrant or
another, but do your best. The first question has been
completed for you as an example.*

Gender Matrix

	"Weak" influence of social/cultural factors	"Strong" influence of social/cultural factors
"Weak" influence of genetic/hormonal factors	A	B
"Strong" influence of genetic/hormonal factors	C	D

  _B_   1. Boy's genitals are accidentally mutilated; he is reared as a "girl."

  _____   2. Guevodoces syndrome

  _____   3. Overexposure to prenatal androgens in females, which results in "mas-
culinization"

  _____   4. Androgen insensitivity syndrome

  _____   5. Normal male (XY) or female (XX) gender development

---

CONCEPT 2   The human sexual response is affected by biological, individual, and social
factors. The sexual revolution gave great impetus to the study of the sexual
response, and includes the areas of dysfunction, therapy, and aging.

      2.1   Describe the roles of the reproductive system and hormones in sexual
behavior.

      2.2   Outline and describe the phases of the sexual response cycle for males
and females.

2.3   Describe the most common sexual dysfunctions and the therapeutic methods developed to treat them.

2.4   Describe the recent changes in our understanding of sexual behavior in later adulthood and in the elderly.

Concept Builder 2

Directions: Place the following physiological events under the correct phase of the human sexual response cycle.

Sexual Response Cycle

Excitement phase	Plateau phase	Orgasm	Resolution phase
F (sample)			

A.   Genitals fully engorged
B.   "Sex flush" appears
C.   Refractory period occurs here for men
D.   Women can experience multiple "climaxes" here
E.   Intense rhythmic contractions/muscle spasms
F.   Heart and respiration rate increases
G.   Genitals return to normal size

CONCEPT 3   Sexual behavior includes a diverse range of practices. These include, in addition to heterosexual behavior, masturbation, homosexuality, and sexual abuse.

3.1   Discuss the current views of masturbation and how these views have changed in the last several decades.

3.2   Identify and describe the various kinds of heterosexual and homosexual behavior and the prevalent attitudes and theories about homosexual behavior.

3.3   Identify and distinguish the types of sexual abuse and the frequency and psychological impact of the types.

3.4   Discuss the impact of the AIDS crisis on sexual behavior in America.

**Concept
Builder 3**

Directions: You write an advice column on sexuality entitled "Plain Talk." Read the following readers' questions and choose the most accurate reply (to be published) to their queries.

"Plain Talk"
Your Sexual Advice Column

1. My son has been arrested for rape. I was totally shocked and now would like to understand his crime better. What's the motive behind rape?

ANSWER A:
Rape is primarily sexually motivated; the rapist cannot get sexual satisfaction at home and tends to seek out a helpless victim when his frustration reaches a peak.

ANSWER B:
Rape is primarily motivated by anger or the assertion of power; evidence from convicted rapists shows that it is sometimes accompanied by physical assault, insults, and acts considered demeaning.

Your choice: _____

2. My coach says that we shouldn't have sex or masturbate during training season because it saps our strength. What's the scoop?

ANSWER A:
Tell your coach to go back to school— there's no evidence for this belief.

ANSWER B:
Sorry, but that's the truth. Having orgasms drains you physically.

Your choice: _____

3. My son had a "homosexual event" happen to him at summer camp this past year. I'm concerned that this may make him prefer a homosexual lifestyle now that he is dating. Could you give me some advice?

ANSWER A:
Although this early "event" is a common factor in the sequence of learning to be a homosexual (according to some theorists), you should not be overly concerned. These things happen to many children (both homosexual and heterosexual); there would have to be a consistent series of subsequent influences that reinforced this homosexual experience for it to become a lifestyle preference.

ANSWER B:
The evidence is very strong and clear on this issue. An early homosexual "event" is the first critical, and decisive, step toward becoming homosexual. Your son probably has fantasized about this event while masturbating, and his orgasms will only serve to reinforce his homosexual fantasies. His homosexuality is a certainty.

Your choice: _____

4. My brother-in-law has been diagnosed as being positive for the AIDS virus. We have a brand new baby in our household and I'm afraid to have my brother-law interact with our child in a casual, but socially contacting manner (feeding, kissing, cuddling, changing diapers, etc.). My wife says I'm wrong, even prejudiced in my thinking. Who's right?

ANSWER A:
AIDS cannot be transmitted by casual social contact. The only mode of transmission involves transferring the virus from the infected person to the blood system of another person. Your fears are unfounded and false. Don't deprive your child or your brother-in-law of the opportunity to have a meaningful, full relationship.

ANSWER B:
Don't take chances. A tiny trace of the AIDS virus could "accidently" be transferred to the baby via saliva or through hand-to-body contact. It's sad but necessary that your relative not touch the infant excessively. This is the only way to ensure a "safe" relationship.

Your choice: _____

CONCEPT 4

Sexual activity is an important component of our concepts of love and intimacy. The triarchic and the developmental theories of love and intimacy are two of the more recent developments in our understanding of love.

4.1 Give a detailed account of the triarchic theory of love and how it describes different types of relationships.

4.2 Describe the developmental perspective of love and attachment and discuss the advantages provided by the theory.

Concept Builder 4

Directions: Identify the following "equations" of love as described by Sternberg in his triangular theory of love by matching them to the appropriate concept.

The Mathematics of Love

_C_ 1. intimacy (alone)

_D_ 2. passion (alone), particularly "love at first sight"

_B_ 3. commitment (alone)

_E_ 4. intimacy + passion + (minimal) commitment

_G_ 5. intimacy + commitment

_A_ 6. passion + commitment

_F_ 7. intimacy + passion + commitment

a. fatuous love

b. empty love

c. liking

d. infatuation

e. romantic love

f. consummate love

g. companionate love

CHAPTER EXERCISE

Directions: The following test will measure two things about your knowledge of the chapter: (1) your ability to remember the key terms, and (2) your ability to identify these terms as applying to either the male gender, the female gender, or both (in common). Fill in the blanks, then insert each term in its proper place in the diagram. The first three examples have been worked for you. Try your knowledge!

What's Your Sexual Quotient?

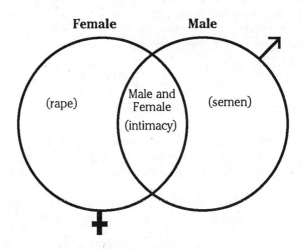

1. A discharged fluid containing sperm: (*semen*—see diagram)
2. Process by which people try to get emotionally close: *(intimacy)*
3. The sexual crime in which this gender is the usual recipient of force, assault, or coercion to have sexual intercourse *(rape)*

Now you try it:

4. A syndrome in which a fetus with an XY genetic background is reared as a girl: _____

5. Intense muscular contractions/spasms during the sexual response sequence: _____

6. This gender may have a multiple of these, one after another, without going through the resolution phase: _____

7. Areas of the body sensitive to touch: _____

8. The most prevalent complaint among male college students in terms of sexual dysfunction: _____

9. Involuntary muscle spasms making penetration during intercourse either painful or impossible: _____

10. Any problem preventing an individual from engaging in sexual relations or from having an orgasm during sex: _____

11. The "old" term for this is "impotence": _____

12. A sexual dysfunction that is a common complaint among female college students:

_____

13. A person whose primary source of sexual gratification is a member of the same sex:

_____

14. The period of time that must pass before this person can again become sexually aroused: _____

15. The readiness to mate in some species ("heat"): _____

PRACTICE EXAM 1

1. Nine out of ten genetic boys with androgen insensitivity syndrome who were reared as girls developed secure female gender identities

   a. true
   b. false

   (Factual, Obj. 1.2)

2. There is an interesting condition in cattle breeding in which a cow (female), called a "free-martin," acts and looks very much like a bull (male). This condition is caused by exposure to male hormones in the mother's womb from a fraternal twin brother. This condition is very similar to a human prenatal condition in which:

   a. females are born with only one X chromosome (Turner's syndrome)
   b. female fetuses are overexposed to prenatal androgens and act "masculinized"
   c. females are born with a male Y chromosome in addition to two X's
   d. females have Guevodoces syndrome

   (Conceptual, Obj. 1.2)

3. What is the most prevalent form of incest, according to court records?

   a. father-daughter
   b. father-son
   c. mother-son
   d. brother-sister

   (Factual, Obj. 3.3)

4. In trying to deter the violent act of rape, some states have suggested that a convicted rapist be castrated. If you were on the criminal justice research committee, what would your recommendation be?

   a. Yes; removal of the testes would lower sexual activity and the desire to rape.
   b. Yes; rapists would certainly see that rape is a severely punished crime.
   c. No; castration after 18 years of age would make no difference.
   d. No; the relationship between testosterone and sexual activity is only correlational; besides rape is a violent crime, not a sexual act.

   (Conceptual, Obj. 3.3)

5. In more than 70 percent of AIDS cases, a person found to have AIDS dies within _____ of diagnosis.

   a. 5 years
   b. 2 years
   c. 14 months
   d. 3 months

   (Factual, Obj. 3.4)

6. Lisa describes her new marriage as "perfect." She has intimacy and commitment from her husband, although they clearly don't (and never had) a passionate aspect to the relationship. How would Sternberg categorize this loving relationship?

     a.   as romantic love
     b.   as companionate love
     c.   as fatuous love
     d.   as empty love

                              (Conceptual, Obj. 4.1)

7. Erogenous zones of the body are areas that are particularly sensitive to:

     a.   touch
     b.   smell
     c.   heat
     d.   swelling

                                 (Factual, Obj. 2.2)

8. Tuesday is to Thursday as plateau phase is to:

     a.   excitement phase
     b.   refractory phase
     c.   orgasm phase
     d.   resolution phase

                                (Conceptual, Obj. 2.2)

9. According to the Kinsey surveys regarding elderly men and sexual activity, which of the following is false?

     a.   They average once a week for sexual intercourse.
     b.   They supplement intercourse with masturbation.
     c.   Most maintain a relatively active sexual life.
     d.   The intensity of orgasm grows with age.

                                 (Factual, Obj. 2.4)

10. Larry has been unable to achieve an erection for about seven months. His doctor tried several treatments but none were immediately successful. Then his doctor asked to monitor his penile activity while he slept for eight hours. What is his doctor trying to determine?

     a.   He is trying to see if Larry truly relaxes at night while he sleeps.
     b.   He is trying to determine whether Larry has a psychological or physiological dysfunction.
     c.   He is trying to see if Larry is experiencing nightmares that might be associated with nightly erections.
     d.   He is trying to see if Larry might be lying about his erectile failure.

                                 (Conceptual, Obj. 2.3)

11. Masturbation practices have changed since the days of Kinsey according to the 1974 Hunt survey. Which of the following statements is true?

     a.   Masturbation rates increased most among the elderly—82 percent say they masturbate regularly.
     b.   Most males feel it is normal; most females feel it is immature.
     c.   The masturbation rate doubled for men since Kinsey's survey.
     d.   Masturbation for the under-13 group increased dramatically.

                                 (Factual, Obj. 3.1)

12.   Alicia had been married for almost two years before she had an extramarital affair. This was a disturbing event for her so she decided to go to therapy with her husband. What would the current, up-to-date therapist already know about the probable cause of this infidelity?

a.   Women's sexual desires increase as they get older; men's don't.
b.   She is most probably dissatisfied with her marriage and the lack of emotional support.
c.   She is most probably sexually frustrated with her husband; her infidelity basically stems from boredom.
d.   There are a variety of reasons infidelity exists; there is no single factor.

(Conceptual, Obj. 3.2)

PRACTICE EXAM 2

1.   Mrs. Sanders found her 14-year-old son's diary while cleaning his room one day and started reading it. She was suddenly alarmed to read an excerpt that stated, "I'm very unhappy with my personal life; I have the strangest feeling that I'm a girl caught in a boy's body!" According to your text, this boy is showing the signs of:

a.   homosexuality
b.   androgen insensitivity syndrome
c.   transsexualism
d.   gender diffusion syndrome

(Conceptual, Obj. 1.2)

2.   A recently discovered condition in the Dominican Republic involves an enzyme deficiency in males in which they do not possess normal genitals at birth. They are reared as girls but at puberty, they "masculinize." This condition is called:

a.   Guevodoces syndrome
b.   transsexualism
c.   bisexuality
d.   androgen insensitivity syndrome

(Factual, Obj. 1.2)

3 .   Which of the following is *not* part of Sternberg's "consummate love"?

a.   intimacy
b.   passion
c.   commitment
d.   security

(Factual, Obj. 4.1)

4. ·   Jill has been involved in a string of short-term, unsatisfactory relationships. Whenever someone gets close to her, she becomes defensive and uncomfortable. She resents being "dependent" on someone else and eventually she ends the relationship (reluctantly). Using Haran and Shaver's "developmental perspective," what style of love does Jill exhibit?

a.   insecure
b.   anxious/avoidant
c.   anxious/ambivalent
d.   ambivalent/avoidant

(Conceptual, Obj. 4.1)

5. According to a rather prevalent stereotype about what turns men and women on, males are most aroused by explicitly sexual material, women by more romantic material. Hieman's research revealed:

    a.   this stereotype is still valid and strong
    b.   there has been an almost complete reversal in responses
    c.   most men and women find romantic stimuli most arousing
    d.   both men and women find erotic material most arousing

                                                    (Factual, Obj. 2.2)

6. Which of the following is associated with women more than men?

    a.   refractory period
    b.   plateau
    c.   multiple orgasms
    d.   resolution

                                                    (Factual, Obj. 2.2)

7. If Micah is experiencing a sexual problem, who would most likely be helpful in his treatment?

    a.   an endocrinologist, because hormonal factors are most important
    b.   a physician, because biological factors are most important
    c.   a sex therapist, because psychological factors are most important
    d.   a physiologist, because physiological factors are most important

                                                    (Conceptual, Obj. 2.3)

8. You view a pornographic movie featuring the male sexual athlete named "Orgasma-tron." He has the unusual ability to have multiple orgasms, one after another. His unique talent is due to an abnormality in the sexual response cycle. What is that?

    a.   an overabundance of semen
    b.   a prolonged orgasm phase
    c.   no apparent refractory periods
    d.   abnormally high levels of androgen

                                                    (Conceptual, Obj. 2.2)

9. Which one of the following conditions is *not* a characteristic of Masters and Johnson's sex therapy strategies?

    a.   Nondemanding sensual exercises such as massaging are prescribed.
    b.   The couple is asked to give each other honest feedback at home on sexual techniques that they like and don't like.
    c.   The couple is always treated by a pair of therapists, one male and one female.
    d.   The focus is on education of the couple and on the sexual relationship.

                                                    (Factual, Obj. 2.3)

10. After getting engaged, Barbara decided she wanted to have a sexual relationship with her fiance. To her frustration, she found that she could not allow penetration during intercourse because of extreme pain. Her vagina seemed to exhibit a constrictive muscle spasm each time she attempted to have sex. Barbara is most likely experiencing:

    a.   vaginismus
    b.   primary orgasmic disorder
    c.   secondary orgasmic disorder
    d.   inhibited orgasmic disorder

                                                    (Conceptual, Obj. 2.3)

11. According to research involving the motivation for rape, the primary motive is one of:

   a.   sexual lust
   b.   power or anger
   c.   impulsive sex
   d.   a pathological need for acceptance

(Factual, Obj. 3.3)

12. If you suspected that your son might be homosexual and you read some "social learning" literature on the subject, which of the following influences would you want to pay particular attention to?

   a.   the testosterone level in his bloodstream
   b.   peer group influences
   c.   father-son relationship
   d.   sperm count in the semen

(Conceptual, Obj. 3.2)

■   **ANSWER KEY**   ■

Concept 1

Quadrant 1: B   Quadrant 4: B
Quadrant 2: C   Quadrant 5: D
Quadrant 3: A

Concept 2

Excitement phase: F, B   Orgasm phase: D, E
Plateau phase: A   Resolution phase: C, G

Concept 3

1. B   3. A
2. A   4. A

Concept 4

1. c   5. g
2. d   6. a
3. b   7. f
4. e

Chapter Exercise

Male	Both	Female
1. semen	2. intimacy	3. rape
4. Guevodoces syndrome	5. orgasm	6. multiple orgasms
8. secondary erectile disorder	7. erogenous zones	9. vaginismus
11. male erectile disorder	10. sexual disorder	12. secondary inhibited orgasm
14. refractory period	13. homosexual	15. estrus

Practice Exam 1

1. a, p. 405
2. b, pp. 404–405
3. a, p. 423
4. d, pp. 408, 420–421
5. b, p. 424
6. b, p. 426
7. a, p. 410
8. d, pp. 411–412
9. d, pp. 414–416
10. b, p. 413
11. a, p. 416
12. d, pp. 417–418

Practice Exam 2

1. c, p. 406
2. a, p. 406
3. d, p. 427
4. b, p. 427
5. d, p. 415
6. c, p. 412
7. c, pp. 412–413
8. c, p. 412
9. b, p. 413
10. a, p. 412
11. b, p. 420
12. b, p. 420

CRITICAL THINKING ESSAY 4

Studying the Motivation to Avoid Success

Throughout the long history of achievement motivation (e.g., McClelland et al., 1953; Atkinson, 1958), research on the topic has focused primarily on men and their achievement motives (Alper, 1974). The few studies that involved female subjects suggested that women differ from men in their motive to achieve (e.g., Veroff, Wilcox, and Atkinson, 1953; French and Lesser, 1964). Women seem to be less responsive to cues that arouse achievement motives and more interested in interpersonal issues than intellectual or competitive ones. In an attempt to understand these sex differences, Matina Horner hypothesized that women may be just as motivated to achieve success as men but that perhaps another, competing motive may interfere with their achievement strivings. This other motive, which she conceptualized as a motive to avoid success, serves to inhibit achievement-related behavior. Horner described this motive as "a latent, stable personality disposition acquired early in life in conjunction with the standards of sex-role identity" (1972, p. 159).

HORNER'S RESEARCH ON FEAR OF SUCCESS

In 1964 Horner (1968) conducted a dissertation study to test her theory. Using the projective technique of achievement research, she instructed 90 women and 88 men at the University of Michigan to make up a story in response to each of six short cue statements. The stories were supposed to tell what the person in the cue was thinking about, how the person came to be in this situation, what would happen next, and so on. The critical cue statement was the last of the six. The women received the following critical cue: "After first-term finals, Anne finds herself at the top of her medical school class." The men received this cue: "After first-term finals, John finds himself at the top of his medical school class."

According to Horner, the presence of any of the following five themes in a subject's response to this statement would indicate a need to avoid success:

1. Conflict about the success
2. Existence or the anticipation of negative consequences of the success
3. Denial of effort or responsibility for the success
4. Denial of the cue itself
5. Bizarre or inappropriate responses

For the women, 59 of 90 responses (65.6 percent) showed one or more of these five themes; only 8 out of the 88 men (9.1 percent) wrote such responses.

In a second part of her test, Horner compared 30 women and 30 men from her original sample in competitive and noncompetitive situations. Consistent with her theory, most women who had shown a need to avoid success did more poorly in competition, whereas most women without this motive (and most men) did better in competitive situations.

Horner concluded that "most women have a motive to avoid success, that is, a disposition to become anxious about achieving success because they expect negative consequences (such as social rejection and/or feelings of being unfeminine) as a result of succeeding" (1972, p. 159). She also hypothesized that this motive is aroused in competitive circumstances in which women might expect negative consequences. Furthermore, she reasoned that this motive is more prevalent among high-ability, high-achieving women. Horner cautioned that the motive to avoid success is *not* a motive to fail; these women wish to succeed, but this competing motive inhibits their performance.

CRITICAL ANALYSIS OF HORNER'S RESEARCH

Soon after Horner submitted her dissertation in 1968, journalists and other researchers embraced her motivation construct, which became popularly known as "the fear of success." Dozens of scientific studies and countless articles in newspapers and magazines focused on this topic, which seemed to have benefited from its intuitive appeal and from Horner's simple (and therefore easily understood) methodology. Although Horner's idea of fear of success was widely recognized as important and valuable, other researchers (e.g., Robbins and Robbins, 1973; Hoffman, 1974) could not reliably replicate her findings and began to doubt the veracity of her theory. The criticisms centered on two fundamental aspects of her work: her measure of the motive and the conclusions she drew from her data.

Problems of Measurement. As we learned in Chapter 2, a psychological measure has to be both reliable and valid to be useful. Horner's measure, which was based on subjects' projective responses to a single critical cue, has been criticized for its inherent limitations in both of these areas.

Reliability. Horner's measure had several problems with reliability. First, it was only a single item. Subjects may have been responding to details of the item itself and not to the general psychological construct that it purported to measure. Would subjects respond differently to a change in phrasing—say, a different career or different names? Worse, male and female subjects responded to two different cues, which made direct comparisons between males and females impossible. In addition, her procedure could have introduced an experimenter bias, since the coder automatically knew the sex of the subject from the content of the response. To overcome this last

issue, other researchers (Robbins and Robbins, 1973; Monahan, Kuhn, and Shaver, 1974) presented both the "Anne" and "John" cues to both male and female subjects. Both studies found that the rate of fear-of-success imagery depended on the sex of the cue target, not the sex of the subject. That is, female subjects did not write more fear-of-success stories than men; all subjects wrote more fear-of-success stories about "Anne" than about "John."

A second problem concerns test-retest reliability. Because each response was unique, it was difficult to assess how well it related to an earlier response. Even when Horner's simple yes/no categorization was used, test-retest reliability was found to be poor (Zuckerman and Wheeler, 1975).

A third problem is that Horner's vague coding instructions made it difficult for subsequent investigators to apply her coding rules consistently (Ho and Zemaitis, 1981). Although reliability among judges *within* a study has been quite good, ranging between 80 and 100 percent agreement, the rate of agreement *between* studies is more problematic. A review of sixteen studies (Zuckerman and Wheeler, 1975) found that fear-of-success rates ranged from 20 to 89 percent for women and from 9 to 79 percent for men. As various investigators (Tresemer, 1974; Zuckerman and Wheeler, 1975; Griffore, 1977) point out, it is likely that different researchers interpret Horner's instructions differently.

Validity. Horner's measure has also received considerable criticism for its poor validity. First, it has not reliably predicted who would score high on fear-of-success measures or how these subjects would behave. The review of sixteen studies (Zuckerman and Wheeler, 1975) found no reliable sex differences; in fact, fear-of-success scores for male subjects were actually higher than those for females in seven of the sixteen studies. Other researchers (e.g., Hoffman, 1974; Pappo, 1983; Kearney, 1984) have failed to find sex differences in the motivation to avoid success. In addition, some researchers (e.g., Condry and Dyer, 1976; Zuckerman and Allison, 1976; Romberg and Shore, 1986) have not found reliable sex differences or differences between high and low fear-of-success subjects on a variety of behavioral tasks, including anagram solving and alpha-numeric substitution. Part of the problem may be that Horner never specified precisely which types of situations would arouse the success-avoidance motive (Zuckerman and Wheeler, 1975). Another part of the problem may be a lack of external validity: subjects may not find the experimental tasks to be relevant to them and therefore their motives would not be aroused. Recently some researchers (Gravenkemper and Paludi, 1983; Paludi and Fankell-Hauser, 1986; Romberg and Short, 1986) have recommended an idiographic approach, in which subjects are assigned tasks that are personally relevant for them. In general, Horner's original notion of a motive to avoid success has not been successful in predicting who will display the motive or how they will behave.

To address some of these problems of reliability and predictive validity, researchers (e.g., Good and Good, 1973; Zuckerman and Allison, 1976; Ho and Zemaitis, 1981; Pappo, 1983) have developed several objective measures of fear of success. Two studies (Griffore, 1977; Gelbort and Winer, 1985) compared several measures of this motive to assess the measure's concurrent validity. Both studies also compared these fear-of-success measures with measures of fear of failure, such as test anxiety (Alpert and Haber, 1960; Birney, Burdick, and Teevan, 1969), in order to assess the discriminant validity of the fear-of-success measures. That is, do fear-of-success subjects really fear success, or do they become anxious about any sort of evaluation? On the whole, both studies revealed small, insignificant correlations among the objective measures. The correlation between each of these measures and Horner's original test were particularly low. In contrast, relatively high correlations were obtained between the fear-of-success and fear-of-failure scales. Thus, the various measures of fear of success do not seem to tap the same construct, but they do seem to agree with tests for fear of failure. These results led researchers (e.g., Zuckerman and Wheeler, 1975; Sadd et al., 1978; Gelbort and Winer, 1985) to wonder whether tests of fear of success do measure a single construct and whether that construct really differs from

evaluation anxiety. However, others (e.g., Paludi, 1984) argue that Horner's original projective method should not be discarded until more reliable and valid measures are found.

Problems of Inference. Recall that Horner (1968, 1972) drew three basic conclusions from her data: (1) fear of success is a motive; (2) fear of success relates to avoiding achievement but not to desiring (or, for that matter, avoiding) failure; and (3) fear of success is more prevalent in women. The lack of reliability and validity of Horner's original projective fear-of-success measure (and the apparent lack of validity of later, objective fear-of-success measures) and the lack of reliable sex differences on these tests led other psychologists to doubt her conclusions. As one succinctly put it: "The 'motive to avoid success' may not be a motive and may have little to do with avoiding success. And it is by no means unique to women" (Tresemer, 1974, p. 82). But if fear of success is not women's avoidance of achievement, then what is it?

Some researchers consider fear of success to be a personality variable, but one that differs from Horner's conception. The fear of success may actually be a fear of failure (Shaver, 1976). Subjects who score high on fear-of-success measures also score high on fear-of-failure tests, indicating a high level of anxiety and concern over the possibility of failing. In fact, other researchers (e.g., Sadd et al., 1978) conclude that fear of success is simply test anxiety, at least in part.

Several researchers have investigated the relationship between sex roles and fear of success (e.g., Gayton et al., 1978; Kearney, 1982; Forbes and King, 1983; Cano, Solomon, and Holmes, 1984). Their findings indicate a negative relationship between masculinity and fear of success. That is, the more masculine a person is, the less fear of success the person shows. Contrary to Horner's theory, however, subjects' biological sex and self-rated femininity are unrelated to fear of success. These researchers conclude that fear of success in both men and women indicates a lack of typically masculine personality characteristics such as aggressiveness and competitiveness.

Other researchers see fear of success as a cognitive/situational variable—that is, a construct that is culturally based and affected by social and situational changes. It may be regarded as an awareness of the cultural expectations that males should succeed in competition whereas females should give more consideration to interpersonal concerns (Zuckerman and Allison, 1976). That is, "*Some* of what has been called fear of success may simply reflect realistic expectancies about the negative consequences of deviancy from a set of cultural norms for sex-appropriate behavior" (Condry and Dyer, 1976, p. 72). Longitudinal data seem to support this view. One team (Robbins and Robbins, 1973) reported that from the time of Horner's study to theirs (i.e., 1964–1972), survey data indicated that the value of success had increased for women and decreased for men. Similarly, it has been reported (Fiorentine, 1988) that women have shown an increase in the value they place on status-attained goals over the period from 1969 to 1984. (Interestingly, these surveys show no comparable decrease in the importance women attach to domestic-nurturant goals.) According to this view, the inconsistent findings in the fear-of-success literature may reflect changes in the value placed on career success. In short, fear of success may be not a motive, but rather an indication of an individual's values and his or her awareness of society's sex-role expectations.

The importance of social relationships for the individual has also been considered as a contributing factor in fear of success. One researcher (Balkin, 1986, 1987) found that family members and friends could affect a person's fear-of-success score. Thus, first-year college students were more likely to report fear of success if their parents did not attend college and if they had few or no friends going to college. Unfortunately, it is unclear from the data whether these subjects' fear-of-success scores reflected insecurity about succeeding in a new area or the interference of jealous or nonsupportive friends and relatives. The former would indicate a fear-of-failure motive; the latter would demonstrate the effect of situational variables on fear of success.

CONCLUSION: WHAT DO WE KNOW ABOUT THE FEAR-OF-SUCCESS MOTIVE?

It is difficult to draw concrete conclusions about a construct like fear of success because the available evidence is so mixed and inconsistent. One cause of this state of affairs is the impact of psychology's prevailing research climate. Horner was a student of John Atkinson, the most prominent motivation researcher in the nation at a time when motivation research was very prominent. It is likely that this training led her to conceptualize fear of success as an enduring, intrapsychic motive. By the same token, the increased prominence of cognitive psychology in the 1970s no doubt led many researchers to reformulate fear of success as a cognitive variable. In both instances the narrow focus on the topic may have limited researchers' interpretations of their data.

Another problem with the fear-of-success construct is, ironically, its popularity. The notion of fear of success clearly struck a cultural nerve when it first surfaced in the late 1960s. The public demand for such an idea may have led many journalists (and many psychologists) to indicate their acceptance of Horner's theory as fact by oversimplifying research results and overgeneralizing these results to different, untested populations (Tresemer, 1974). Without careful theory development and cautious data interpretation, it is little wonder that the field was marked by inconsistent findings.

Although the label "fear of success" has fallen out of public favor in recent years, the basic notion that psychological conflict results from the competing demands of interpersonal responsibility and individual achievement is still very much with us (e.g., Paludi and Fankell-Hauser, 1986; Coutts, 1987). With an ever-increasing number of personal and professional opportunities for women, these concerns are not likely to go away in the near future.

REFERENCES

Alper, T. G. Achievement motivation in college women: A now-you-see-it-now-you-don't phenomenon. *American Psychologist,* 1974, *29,* 194–203.

Alpert, R., and R. N. Haber. Anxiety in academic achievement situations. *Journal of Abnormal and Social Psychology,* 1960, *61,* 207–215.

Atkinson, J. W. (Ed.) *Motives in fantasy, action, and society.* Princeton, N.J.: Van Nostrand, 1958.

Balkin, J. Contributions of family to men's fear of success in college. *Psychological Reports,* 1986, *55,* 1071–1074.

Balkin, J. Contributions of friends to women's fear of success in college. *Psychological Reports,* 1987, *61,* 39–42.

Birney, R., H. Burdick, and R. Teevan. *Fear of failure.* New York: Van Nostrand Reinhold, 1969.

Cano, L., S. Solomon, and D. S. Holmes. Fear of success: The influence of sex, sex-role identity, and components of masculinity. *Sex Roles,* 1984, *10,* 341–346.

Condry, J., and S. Dyer. Fear of success: Attribution of cause to the victim. *Journal of Social Issues,* 1976, *32,* 63–83.

Coutts, J. A. Masculinity-femininity of self-concept: Its effect on the achievement behavior of women. *Sex Roles,* 1987, *16,* 9–17.

Fiorentine, R. Increasing similarity in the values and life plans of male and female college students? Evidence and implications. *Sex Roles,* 1988, *18,* 143–158.

Forbes, G. B., and S. King. Fear of success and sex-role: There are reliable relationships. *Psychological Reports,* 1983, *53,* 735–738.

French, E. G., and G. S. Lesser. Some characteristics of the achievement motive in women. *Journal of Abnormal and Social Psychology,* 1964, *68,* 119–128.

Gayton, W. F., G. Havu, S. Barnes, K. L. Ozman, and J. S. Bassett. Psychological androgyny and fear of success. *Psychological Reports,* 1978, *42,* 757–758.

Gelbort, K. R., and J. L. Winer. Fear of success and fear of failure: A multitrait-multimethod validation study. *Journal of*

Personality and Social Psychology, 1985, *48,* 1009–1014.

Good, L. R., and K. C. Good. An objective measure of the motive to avoid success. *Psychological Reports,* 1973, *33,* 1009-1010.

Gravenkemper, S. A., and M. A. Paludi. Fear of success revisited: Introducing an ambiguous cue. *Sex Roles,* 1983, *9,* 897–900.

Griffore, R. J. Validation of three measures of fear of success. *Journal of Personality Assessment,* 1977, *41,* 417–421.

Ho, R., and R. Zemaitis. Concern over the negative consequences of success. *Journal of Australian Psychology,* 1981, *33,* 19–28.

Hoffman, L. W. Fear of success in males and females: 1965 and 1972. *Journal of Consulting and Clinical Psychology,* 1974, *42,* 353–358.

Horner, M. S. Sex differences in achievement motivation and performance in competitive and non-competitive situations. Unpublished doctoral dissertation, University of Michigan, 1968.

Horner, M. S. Toward an understanding of achievement-related conflicts in women. *Journal of Social Issues,* 1972, *28,* 153–173.

Kearney, M. Are masculine trait-factors in women a help or a hindrance in dealing with fear of success? *Psychological Reports,* 1982, *51,* 558.

Kearney, M. A comparison of motivation to avoid success in males and females. *Journal of Clinical Psychology,* 1984, *40,* 1005–1007.

McClelland, D. C., J. W. Atkinson, R. A. Clark, and E. L. Lowell. *The achievement motive.* New York: Appleton-Century-Crofts, 1953.

Monahan, L., D. Kuhn, and P. Shaver. Intrapsychic versus cultural explanations of the "fear of success" motive. *Journal of Personality and Social Psychology,* 1974, *29,* 60–64.

Paludi, M. A. Psychometric properties and underlying assumptions of four objective measures of fear of success. *Sex Roles,* 1984, *10,* 765–781.

Paludi, M. A., and J. Fankell-Houser. An idiographic approach to the study of women's achievement striving. *Psychology of Women Quarterly,* 1986, *10,* 89–100.

Pappo, M. Fear of success: The construction and validation of a measuring instrument. *Journal of Personality Assessment,* 1983, *47,* 36–41.

Robbins, L., and E. Robbins. Comment on: "Toward an understanding of achievement-related conflicts in women." *Journal of Social Issues,* 1973, *29,* 133–137.

Romberg, D. L., and M. F. Shore. A test of two hypotheses of fear of success. *Sex Roles,* 1986, *14,* 163–180.

Sadd, S., M. Lenauer, P. Shaver, and N. Dunivant. Objective measurement of fear of success and fear of failure: A factor analytic approach. *Journal of Consulting and Clinical Psychology,* 1978, *46,* 405–416.

Shaver, P. Questions concerning fear of success and its conceptual relations. *Sex Roles,* 1976, *2,* 305–319.

Tresemer, D. Fear of success: Popular but unproven. *Psychology Today,* 1974 *7*(10), 82–85.

Veroff, J., S. Wilcox, and J. Atkinson. The achievement motive in high school and college age women. *Journal of Abnormal and Social Psychology,* 1953, *48,* 108–119.

Zuckerman, M., and S. N. Allison. An objective measure of fear of success: Construction and validation. *Journal of Personality Assessment,* 1976, *40,* 422–430.

Zuckerman, M., and L. Wheeler. To dispel fantasies about the fantasy-based measure of fear of success. *Psychological Bulletin,* 1975, *82,* 932–946.

RESPONDING TO CRITICAL ESSAY 4

1. Victor Hugo once remarked, "Nothing is so powerful as an idea whose time has come." This was certainly true for Horner's formulations of the "fear of success" notions. However, this popularity, ironically, came to be a problem with her research overall.

    Why might popularity eventually spell trouble for a psychological idea?

2. Matina Horner suggests that because women play two roles in our society (achievement versus femininity), they are motivated by a fear of success as well as a fear of failure. Indeed, her research has indicated women fear success more than men.

    How did later studies question the validity of Horner's basic premise?

3   Horner considered denial of effort or responsibility for success as a projection of the motive to avoid success.

    How might the differences in the motive to avoid success be *more* an indication of low-achievement rather than a motive that affects mainly women?

CHAPTER FIFTEEN

Infancy and Childhood

KEY TERM ORGANIZER

The universal process of age-related change over the life span is known as *development*. Several themes and issues are relevant to the study of development.

The first theme concerns the respective roles of nature and nurture. Each of us has a genetically programmed timetable for *maturation*. Although genes dictate a pattern of growth, the amount by which growth can vary is known as a *reaction range*.

The second theme has to do with whether people change radically as they develop, or tend to remain fairly stable. In some animals, there exist *sensitive periods* in which susceptibility to certain kinds of environmental influences increases. The most spectacular example of a sensitive period occurs through the process of *imprinting*.

The third theme concerns the nature of development: whether our skills and abilities develop in a smooth, continuous manner or go through a series of separate, distinct stages. In *stage theories*, like those of Piaget and Erikson, development proceeds in discrete steps that always occur in a given sequence.

The following chart summarizes the enduring themes and issues in development:

Development Theme	Development Concepts	Areas Addressed
Nature and nurture	Maturation Reaction range	Interaction of heredity and environment in development
Stability and change	Sensitive period Imprinting	Stability verses change in personality and abilities
Continuity and discontinuity	Stage theories (e.g., Piaget and Erikson)	Continuous, smooth development versus a series of differentiated stages

At the moment of conception, a predictable sequence of development begins, transforming the fertilized egg, or *zygote*, into a baby. The course of prenatal development falls into three basic periods. During the *germinal period*, the zygote begins the process of rapid cell division. Soon after the start of the *embryonic period*, the organism, now called an *embryo*, is connected to the mother's body by a flexible structure called the *placenta*. Once the major organs and physical features have taken shape, the developing organism is known as a *fetus*. During the *fetal period*, development shifts from forming organs to organizing their structures and establishing their functions.

Teratogens are agents that can alter or kill the developing organism. For example, alcoholic mothers often have babies with *fetal alcohol syndrome*, which is characterized by mental retardation, slowed growth, and physical malformation.

Human newborns are equipped with more than a dozen *reflexes*—unlearned responses to specific stimuli. Each baby has his or her own *temperament*, which consists of early, observable differences in emotional behavior, responsiveness to stimulation, and motor activity.

Piaget devoted his life to studying development, particularly cognitive development. Newborns begin almost immediately acquiring knowledge by acting on objects around them using recurrent action patterns called *schemes*. Through *assimilation*, a child adapts new information into a framework of existing schemes. Through *accommodation*, a child modifies existing schemes to make sense of new information.

Piaget proposed four progressive stages that all children go through. In the *sensorimotor stage*, knowledge is based on the infant's sensations and physical actions. Newborns lack *object permanence*, but they eventually develop *representational thought*, an ability to "think" about their actions. Representational thought provides the foundation for *deferred imitation*, the ability to mimic.

Once children can internalize schemes and think symbolically, they enter the *preoperational stage*. Preoperational thought is still immature. For example, children show *egocentrism*, an inability to comprehend another's point of view. Piaget maintained children of this age are not capable of mental *operations*—flexible, rigorous, and logical thought.

The *concrete operational stage* is marked by flexible, rigorous, and logical thought—but only in regard to concrete objects. One important principle schoolchildren come to understand is *conservation*. Children eventually reach the *formal-operational stage*, the fourth and final stage.

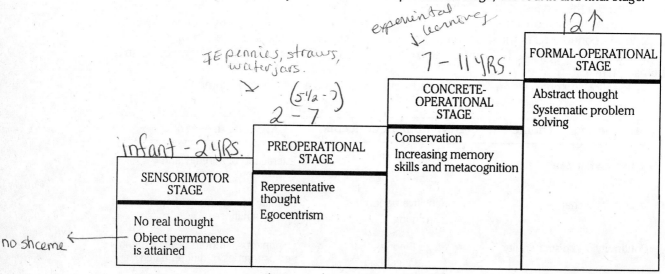

By their first birthdays, children have produced their first words. Their speech is marked by *overextension*, the stretching of the meaning of a word. Their speech resembles a telegram of short phrases, so psychologists call it *telegraphic speech*. Once they learn a rule of grammar, children apply it with rigid consistency, a phenomenon known as *overregularization*. Parents try to facilitate communication by using their own *motherese*.

The close relationship between caregiver and infant is called *attachment.* Attachment appears to go through four stages. At one point, once babies have become attached to their parents, they show *separation distress* when parted from their parents. Attachment studies are consistent with Erikson's views of early attachment. A basic conflict of early childhood, according to Erikson, is the conflict between shame (or doubt) and *autonomy,* the feeling of self-control and self-determination.

Once children begin to walk and talk, parents shift their emphasis from physically caring for the child to teaching the child to act in ways that society considers good or acceptable, a process known as *socialization.* The goal of *socialization* is *internalization*—incorporating society's values.

A central aspect of identity has to do with gender. Our *gender identity* is our unchanging sense that we are either male or female. Our *gender role* consists of the attitudes and patterns of behavior that society considers acceptable for our gender. By about the age of three, children understand what behavior is considered appropriate for girls and boys; these cognitive schemas are known as *gender schemas.*

MAJOR CONCEPTS AND LEARNING OBJECTIVES

CONCEPT 1   The major themes of development focus upon the nature and nurture issue, stability versus change, and continuity versus discontinuity.

1.1   Define development and discuss how the three themes of nature and nurture, stability and change, and continuity and discontinuity relate to development.

**Concept
Builder 1**

Directions: Look at the following four diagrams. Each graph depicts a different developmental function. Match each graph to its appropriate developmental function from the four listed below.

Plotting Development

a. maturation
b. heredity factors
c. reaction range
d. sensitive period

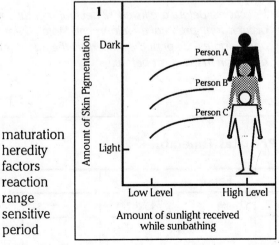

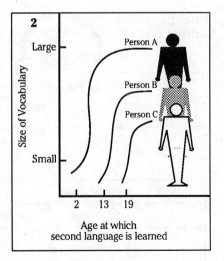

1. _____   2. _____

a. maturation
b. heredity factors
c. reaction range
d. sensitive period

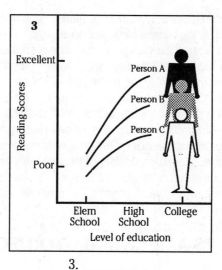

3. _____

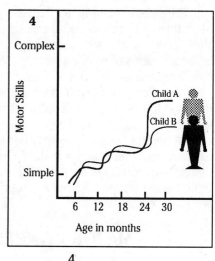

4. _____

CONCEPT 2

Prenatal and newborn development processes proceed through stages that are governed by genetics and the basic reflexes needed for survival at birth. Physical development in infancy and childhood involves both genetic and environmental factors.

2.1 Name and describe the stages of prenatal development and the hazards faced by the unborn.

2.2 Describe the sensory abilities of the newborn and how they work with the reflexes to enable survival.

2.3 Discuss how temperament affects development and the views regarding how temperament itself develops.

2.4 Outline and describe the progress of physical development from birth through childhood.

Concept Builder 2

Directions: Below are listed 12 developmental events that occur during prenatal development. Match them to the appropriate time period by inserting the number of the definition in the chart below.

Prenatal Timetable

Germinal	Embryonic	Fetal			Prebirth	
0	3 weeks	8 weeks	16 weeks	24 weeks	32 weeks	38 weeks

1. Fetus can cry, open and close its eyes, look up, down, sideways.
2. Fetus can bend fingers; curls toes in response to touch.
3. Zygote starts process of rapid cell division.
4. Three primary layers will eventually form various tissues and organs.
5. Kidneys, liver, and digestive tract have now appeared.
6 Sucks its thumb, yawns, and grunts.
7. Mother now notices spontaneous movements which are frequent and strong.
8. The face looks "human."
9. Rhythmic activity cycles develop; fetus appears to sleep and wake.
10. If born at this time, it may survive, though only with intensive medical care.
11. There is a spinal cord and a recognizable brain.
12. Organism most vulnerable to prenatal environmental influences.

CONCEPT 3

Cognitive development refers to the development of thought and the skills required to accumulate information. The best-known theory of cognitive development is that of Jean Piaget, who views cognitive development as a series of qualitative stages.

3.1   Define the basic concepts of scheme, assimilation, and accommodation used by Piaget.

3.2   Outline and describe the childhood stages of Piaget's theory and identify the basic skills acquired in each stage.

3.3   List and define the basic concepts of the information processing theory of development and distinguish this approach from that of Piaget.

3.4   Describe early communication and the development of first words and sentences and distinguish the views of Chomsky from those of the behaviorists on language development.

Concept Builder 3

Directions: Read the following words and phrases spoken by children and match them to the appropriate stage of language acquisition.

Out of the Mouths of Babes

☐   a. "Fall down. Hurt head."

☐   b. "Dinosaur." (while pointing at a picture of a dinosaur)

☐   c. "Dinosaur." (while pointing at a lizard on the garden gate)

☐   d. "Pah . . . gah . . . goo-goo . . . kee . . . kee."

☐   e. "Mommy shave legs."

☐   f. "I have a boo-boo."

☐   g. "Both my feets are cold."

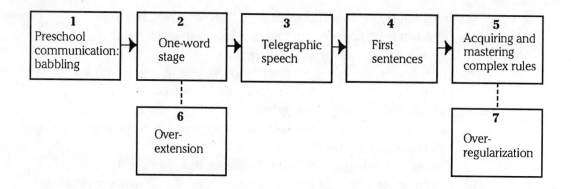

CONCEPT 4   Attachment is central to quality social development. The developmental views of Erikson begin with the basic trust that develops in this attachment. Many of our social behaviors are acquired during childhood.

4.1   Define attachment and discuss the process of its development.

4.2   Describe Erikson's four stages of psychosocial development that occur from birth through childhood.

4.3   Define socialization and discuss the importance of relationships with parents and peers during infancy and childhood.

4.4   Identify the factors that influence the development of gender identity and gender role and distinguish these two concepts.

**Concept
Builder 4**      *Directions: Look at the following schematic drawing of the factors that affect the learning of gender roles. Your task is to look at the key terms below, then insert the correct terms in each "block" of the drawing.*

Gender Links

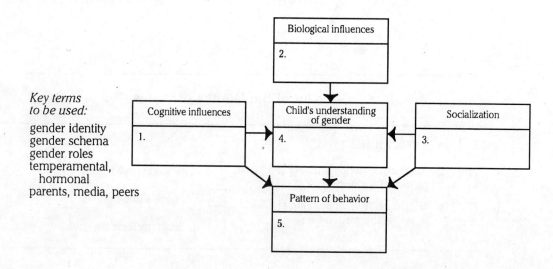

*Key terms
to be used:*

gender identity
gender schema
gender roles
temperamental,
   hormonal
parents, media, peers

CHAPTER EXERCISE

Directions: The schematic drawings below are graphic ways of depicting cognitive development. Your task is to read the definitions below and enter key terms described in the corresponding numbered blocks.

Diagramming Cognitive Development

Basic process

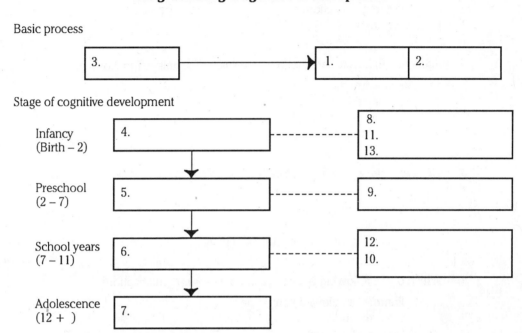

Key term definitions

1. The incorporation of new knowledge through the use of existing schemes.
2. The modification of existing schemes to incorporate new knowledge that does not fit them.
3. Gaining knowledge by acting on objects using recurrent action patterns.
4. The period of cognitive development in which the infant relies on action schemes.
5. The period of cognitive development characterized by the development of language and elaborate, symbolic play.
6. The period of cognitive development in which the child can use logical thought, but only in regard to concrete objects.
7. The stage of cognitive development typically reached in adolescence.
8. Thinking in which a person can mentally represent objects not directly in front of him or her.
9. The belief that everyone sees the world and responds to it the same as you do.
10. An understanding of one's own cognitive processes.
11. The awareness that objects continue to exist when out of sight.
12. The principle that irrelevant changes in the external appearance of objects have no effect on the object's quantity.
13. The ability to mimic in play on one occasion actions observed at an earlier time.

**PRACTICE
EXAM 1**

1.   Jeremy learns the word *bird* and refers to anything that flies as a bird, even though it may be a butterfly or duck. This is an example of:

   a.   overlearning
   b.   overextension
   c.   overregularization
   d.   telegraphing

   (Conceptual, Obj. 3.4)

2.   Egocentrism is associated with which stage of cognitive functioning?

   a.   sensorimotor
   b.   preoperational
   c.   concrete-operational
   d.   formal-operational

   (Factual, Obj. 2.4)

3.   The age at which children typically begin to talk in two-word sentences is:

   a.   1 year
   b.   18–30 months
   c.   3 years
   d.   dependent on the particular language

   (Factual, Obj. 3.4)

4.   Which of the following is a clear example of overregularization?

   a.   I and Mike followed you home.
   b.   Mommy book.
   c.   Doggie! (for a cat)
   d.   That boy runned fast.

   (Conceptual, Obj. 3.4)

5.   The fact that children exhibit overregularization in their speech is important because it shows that:

   a.   children are trying to use general rules and speak systematically
   b.   children learn speech by reinforcement
   c.   children learn speech by imitation
   d.   the general rules of language are almost always learned in school

   (Factual, Obj. 3.4)

6.   What is the best description of the relationship between heredity and environment?

   a.   Heredity is more important.
   b.   Environment is more important.
   c.   They interact with each other.
   d.   They seldom have any relationship to each other.

   (Conceptual, Obj. 1.1)

7.   Three-month-old Priscilla will start to cry and act distressed when her mother leaves the room for a minute, even though her mother continues to speak out loud to her. Priscilla has not yet attained what cognitive skill?

   a.   scheme of her mother
   b.   object permanence
   c.   conservation
   d.   accommodation

   (Conceptual, Obj. 3.2)

8. Which of the following terms does *not* belong with the others in describing the preoperational stage of thought?

    a. based on intuition
    b. representational
    c. logical
    d. egocentric

    (Factual, Obj. 3.2)

9. Bart, a four-year-old, tried to show a finger painting to his dad while his dad was underneath the family car changing the oil. Bart didn't comprehend that his dad couldn't see it; he kept explaining how he made the colors while his dad politely agreed from beneath the car. Bart's thinking shows an immaturity termed:

    a. complexive thinking
    b. object concept
    c. egocentrism
    d. representational thought

    (Conceptual, Obj. 3.2)

10. While buying groceries in the grocery store, Mindy passed by an adorable baby in a shopping cart, but as she approached the infant, the child looked terrified and started crying. What phase of attachment is this child in?

    a. first
    b. second
    c. third
    d. fourth

    (Conceptual, Obj. 4.1)

11. The goal of socialization is _____, or the child's incorporation of society's values.

    a. identity
    b. personality
    c. social cognition
    d. internalization

    (Factual, Obj. 4.3)

12. The minimum age of birth at which a fetus can survive has been established at _____.

    a. 23 weeks
    b. 25 weeks
    c. 32 weeks
    d. 36 weeks

    (Factual, Obj. 2.1)

PRACTICE EXAM 2

1. Most infants exhibit the following pattern of motor development: raising head and chin, sitting up, crawling, then first steps. This pattern can best be described as:

    a. a sensitive period
    b. maturation
    c. an established norm
    d. motor retardation

    (Conceptual, Obj. 1.1)

2. Infants begin life with a few simple, innate action patterns, such as grasping and sucking. Piaget calls these action patterns:

    a. assimilations
    b. reflexes
    c. fixed action patterns
    d. schemes

    (Factual, Obj. 3.1)

3. Monday is to sensorimotor as Wednesday is to:

    a. preoperational
    b. concrete operational
    c. formal operational
    d. postconventional

    (Conceptual, Obj. 3.2)

4. Germinal is to fetal period as Monday is to:

    a. Friday
    b. Tuesday
    c. Wednesday
    d. Saturday

    (Conceptual, Obj. 2.1)

5. Timing is especially important in determining whether an environmental influence will produce an abnormality in a fetus. During which period of pregnancy does the developing organism seem most vulnerable?

    a. embryonic period
    b. second trimester
    c. germinal period
    d. fetal period

    (Factual, Obj. 2.1)

6. On delivery one night, Susan, a midwife, delivered an infant that had multiple severe problems: cleft palate, kidney damage, and early signs of mental retardation. Susan suspected:

    a. thalidomide damage
    b. fetal alcohol syndrome
    c. DES tragedy
    d. environmental toxins

    (Conceptual, Obj. 2.2)

7. Even though Francine watches her mother make a sandwich, she insists that her mother not fold the bread in half. Francine claims that the folded sandwich is "less" than the open-face one. Francine doesn't understand:

    a. conservation
    b. assimilation
    c. equilibration
    d. transformation

    (Conceptual, Obj. 3.1)

8. Most infant response patterns, like reflexes, take a repetitive course of appearance, loss, and reappearance. What is the most plausible explanation for this pattern?

   a. It appears to be a built-in, reflexive pattern.
   b. It is a shift from an altricial to a precocial pattern.
   c. It may signify a shift from subcortical brain structures to the developing cortex.
   d. It is a shift from genetic to environmental control.

   (Conceptual, Obj. 2.4)

9. Hannah, an infant in the crawling stage, will crawl to the edge of her bed but will stop at the edge and look frightened of the height. This fear is extremely similar to the _____ experiments.

   a. foundling home
   b. visual preference
   c. "baby cliff"
   d. "visual cliff"

   (Conceptual, Obj. 2.2)

10. When Bill dances, he basically uses the same dance steps over and over, changing his speed but not his steps to fit the beat. When Lisa dances, she changes both her timing and her moves to fit the rhythm of the music. In Piaget's terms, Bill's dancing is close to _____ while Lisa's is more like: _____

    a. accommodation, assimilation
    b. accommodation, equilibration
    c. assimilation, accommodation
    d. assimilation, adaptation

    (Conceptual, Obj. 3.1)

11. If you worked in a hospital nursery that cared for premature infants, which of the following actions would be most beneficial to your baby patients?

    a. Avoid fondling them.
    b. Allow them lots of sleep and private time.
    c. Massage and rock them frequently.
    d. Wrap them tightly in warm clothing.

    (Conceptual, Obj. 2.4)

12. When Mrs. Copeland's kindergarten class returned to school after visiting the city zoo, she asked the students to pantomime their favorite animal. The children did so with great enthusiasm and humor. What cognitive ability did their mimicking involve?

    a. representational thought
    b. deferred imitation
    c. observational learning
    d. scheme attainment

    (Conceptual, Obj. 3.2)

■   **ANSWER KEY**   ■

Concept 1

1. b   3. c
2. d   4. a

Concept 2

1. fetal (24 weeks)   7. fetal (16 weeks)
2. fetal (9 weeks)   8. fetal (16 weeks)
3. germinal (0–2 weeks)   9. fetal (24 weeks)
4. germinal (0–2 weeks)   10. fetal (24 weeks)
5. embryonic (2–8 weeks)   11. embryonic (2–8 weeks)
6. prebirth (last 6 weeks) 12. embryonic (2–8 weeks)

Concept 3

1. d   5. f
2. b   6. c
3. a   7. g
4. e

Concept 4

1. gender schema   4. gender identity
2. temperamental, hormonal   5. gender roles
3. parents, media, peers

Chapter Exercise

1. assimilation   8. representational or symbolic thought
2. accommodation   9. egocentrism
3. schemes   10. metacognition
4. sensorimotor   11. object permanence
5. preoperational   12. conservation
6. concrete-operational   13. deferred imitation
7. formal-operational

Practice Exam 1
1. b, p. 454
2. b, p. 450
3. b, p. 454
4. d, p. 454
5. a, p. 454
6. c, pp. 435, 442
7. b, p. 448
8. c, pp. 449–450
9. c, p. 450
10. c, p. 457
11. d, p. 462
12. a, p. 438

Practice Exam 2
1. b, p. 434
2. d, p. 447
3. b, p. 450
4. c, p. 438
5. a, p. 438
6. b, p. 439
7. a, p. 450
8. c, p. 440
9. d, p. 443
10. c, p. 447
11. c, p. 445
12. b, p. 448

CHAPTER SIXTEEN

Adolescence and Adulthood

KEY TERM ORGANIZER

Adolescence is the period during which young people move out of childhood and get ready to take up adult lives. *Puberty* is a series of interrelated biological processes that change the immature child into a sexually mature person. The primary hormones involved in regulating physical changes during adolescence and adulthood are the *androgens* (male hormones) and the *estrogens* (female hormones).

The *adolescent growth spurt* brings children toward their adult height and weight. The *primary sex characteristics,* the sexual organs that are directly responsible for reproduction, reach maturity, and the *secondary sex characteristics,* such as breasts and body hair, which are not directly involved in reproduction, appear. *Menarche,* the first menstrual period, is often regarded as the true indicator of puberty in girls.

Adolescence also ushers in new ways of thinking about oneself and the world. Piaget described the ability to deal with abstractions and logical possibilities as the stage of *formal operations,* which he regarded as the culmination of cognitive development.

Children enter adolescence already possessing an *identity*—a coherent sense of individuality that encompasses thoughts and feelings about the self and provides a sense of personal continuity.

Most adolescents successfully resolve conflicts between their own needs and social demands. But a small percentage, who still have unresolved conflicts from earlier stages of development, may find old problems resurfacing. According to the *birth-cohort theory,* the more "crowded" a generation is, the higher the level of disturbance among its members.

Adulthood is the longest period of the lifespan. Traditionally, adulthood has been divided into three periods: young adulthood (18 to 40 years of age), middle adulthood (40 to 65 years of age), and late adulthood (65+ years of age). We seem to be moving toward an *age-irrelevant society,* in which major life events, such as marriage, parenthood, and retirement, are not closely tied to specific chronological ages.

The clearest biological marker of middle age among women is *menopause,* or the end of menstruation, which occurs gradually around the age of 50 when the ovaries cease producing estrogen.

Postformal thought emerges as adults learn through experience that their assumptions and ways of thinking influence the knowledge they glean from the world.

As people move through adulthood, they focus their energies and motivations on different emotional and social tasks. In Erikson's view, the major task facing young adults is the development of *intimacy,* in which they commit themselves to a close relationship that demands sacrifice and compromise. When people move into middle adulthood, the major conflict as described by Erikson is between generativity and stagnation. *Generativity* involves a concern for future generations. During the final stage of life, the central conflict is between *ego integrity,* which is a sense of the wholeness and meaningfulness of one's life, and despair.

Levinson sees development as an orderly sequence that alternates between stable and transitional stages. Levinson found that the transition to middle-adulthood is almost invariably accompanied with a *midlife crisis*—the state of physical and psychological distress that a man experiences when developmental tasks threaten to overwhelm his internal resources and social supports.

Some researchers believe that personality development in adulthood revolves around parenthood, and they call this shaping force the *parental imperative.* Once the children are grown, parents are free to indulge their individual desires, becoming more *androgynous,* embracing characteristics typical of both gender roles.

At one time, researchers believed that the typical pattern of adjustment to old age was *disengagement,* voluntarily withdrawing from social roles. Longitudinal studies, however, have found little evidence of disengagement and no sign that disengagement necessarily made later life satisfying. As part of this preparation for death, many old people turn inward. They may try to make sense of their lives through a process known as *life review,* a universal developmental process that is part of Erikson's final stage, the struggle between integrity and despair.

MAJOR CONCEPTS AND LEARNING OBJECTIVES

CONCEPT 1 The move from childhood to adulthood is marked by changes in physical characteristics and cognitive abilities. The major physical changes in adolescence begin with the onset of puberty. Movement from Piaget's stage of concrete operations to formal operations signals the cognitive changes of this age period.

1.1 List and describe the primary and secondary sex characteristics that are associated with the onset of puberty.

1.2 Describe the changes in problem-solving strategies that distinguish the stage of formal operations from that of concrete operations.

1.3 Outline the stages of moral development described by the work of Kohlberg.

Concept Builder 1

Directions: Following is an actual story used by Kohlberg as a "moral dilemma." His research focused on how subjects reasoned about the story. Read the sample responses that follow the story and identify the stage of moral reasoning it represents.

You Be the Judge

Stage 1: Avoid punishment.

Stage 2: Serve one's own needs and interests.

Stage 3: Be a good person in one's own and others' eyes.

Stage 4: Avoid breakdowns in the social system.

Stage 5: Sense of obligation to the social contract.

Stage 6: Belief in the validity of universal moral principles.

In Europe, a woman was near death from a special kind of cancer. There was one drug that the doctors thought might save her. It was a form of radium that a druggist in the same town had recently discovered. The druggist was charging ten times what the drug cost him to make. He paid $200 for the radium and charged $2,000 for a small dose of the drug. The sick woman's husband, Heinz, went to everyone he knew to borrow the money, but he could get together only about $1,000. He told the druggist that his wife was dying and asked him to sell cheaper or let him pay later. The druggist said: "No, I discovered the drug and I'm going to make money from it." So Heinz got desperate and broke into the man's store to steal the drug for his wife. Should the husband have done that? Why or why not? (Kohlberg: Development of character and moral ideology.)

_____ Subject 1: "Stealing is against the law. If everyone lived by his own private rules there would be chaos."

_____ Subject 2: "He should steal the drug because he needs his wife to clean his house for him."

_____ Subject 3: "In most instances it is probably best to obey the law, but here it might be right to steal because life is not the same as property and life takes precedence."

_____ Subject 4: "No, because he'll get caught and punished."

_____ Subject 5: "Yes, a human life takes precedence over any other moral or legal value, whoever it is. A human life has inherent value whether or not it is valued by a particular individual."

_____ Subject 6: "He should steal the drug if he truly loves his wife."

CONCEPT 2   Social development during adolescence involves adjustments to increasing independence, physical changes, and anxiety about the future. The formation of an identity is important for this period of life. Adolescents face a range of problems that have not been relevant in their childhoods.

2.1   Discuss the validity of the storm-and-stress view of adolescence.

2.2   Describe Erikson's stages that are relevant to adolescence and define the issues related to identity, including sexuality.

2.3   Describe the relationship between parents and adolescents.

2.4   List and describe the various problems faced by adolescents in contemporary society.

**Concept
Builder 2**

*Directions: Read each of the statements below made by
college students regarding their immediate career goals.
Match each to one of Marcia's categories:*

a. foreclosure   c. diffusion
b. moratorium   d. achievement

1. "I know exactly what I'm going to do. Even though Dad would love me to go into
    sales, as he did, I love engineering. I'm definitely going into mechanical engineering."

2. "I have no choice. The Bradfords have always been teachers. I'll follow suit. Easy
    choice because my career choice has already been mapped out for me!"

3. "I do love medicine, but med school is near impossible to get into. I love art and
    illustration as well, but it's difficult to make a profession out of either. Maybe I'll be a
    medical illustrator. Oh well, I'll stay in school for now—I haven't made my mind up."

4. "What do I want to be when I grow up? Hell's bells, I don't even know what to
    major in, much less pursue as a career. Bottom line is, I don't know—no comment.
    For now, my major will remain as Undecided." _____

CONCEPT 3   During adulthood, people reach physical and cognitive peaks in ability.
                     Though adults experience slow, subtle changes in these abilities which were
                     once considered deterioration, many adults continue to make significant
                     contributions into late adulthood.

                     3.1   Describe the major physical changes in adulthood.

                     3.2   Define postformal thought, crystallized and fluid intelligence, and
                           identify the characteristic changes in cognitive ability during adulthood.

**Concept
Builder 3**

*Directions: Respond to the following true-false test on
adulthood.*

Adulthood: Fact or Fiction?

_____   1. We seem to be moving toward an age-irrelevant society, in which life events
             and chronological age are loosely related.

_____   2. People reach their peak of physical agility, speed, and strength at middle age.

_____   3. Men go through a reproductive transition (in their fifties) equivalent to
             women's menopause.

_____   4.   Because of postformal thought, middle-age individuals can be more flexible, adaptive, and problem oriented than younger adults.

_____   5.   Verbal and reasoning skills increase through middle adulthood.

_____   6.   Highly practiced skills, such as those of a musician, show little or no slow-down with aging.

_____   7.   Short-term memory is unaffected by normal aging processes.

_____   8.   Recall memory is unaffected by the aging process.

_____   9.   Fluid intelligence tends to show a steady increase throughout the lifespan.

_____   10.   Cognitive decline on most IQ tests seems to be the result of mental disuse—not deterioration.

CONCEPT 4

Social development during adulthood requires skills for dealing with increasing responsibility and power over others, adjustment to life changes, and coping with realizations of mortality.

     4.1   Describe the stages of adulthood as defined by Erikson.

     4.2   Define midlife crisis and outline Levinson's stages of transition through adulthood.

     4.3   Describe the requirements of marriage, parenthood, work, and retirement and how these responsibilities change in late adulthood.

Concept Builder 4

Directions: Each picture below represents one of Levinson's stages of adult male development. Under each picture, write the name of the stage that it represents (become psychologically independent from parents; establishing one's self in the adult world; late twenties transition; consolidating one's career; midlife evaluation [possible midlife crisis]):

Snapshots of Adulthood

1. _____   2. _____   3. _____

4. _____   5. _____

CONCEPT 5   Just as life has its stages, death and dying involve stages of preparation and acceptance.

    5.1   Define life review and its role in the preparation for death.

Concept Builder 5

Directions: Read the following "diary" entries made by two elderly residents of a nursing home. Their "homework" was to start a life-review journal. Indicate which one reflects Erikson's integrity and which despair.

Looking Back

1.   Samuel: "Life has been a mixed blessing—full of laughter, full of tears. Now what plagues me are my regrets. Why didn't I spend more time with my children; why did I give my life to the store; it sucked the life out of me and I let it; why didn't I live life one day at a time rather than always thinking about tomorrow? Hell, tomorrow never comes. Now, I'm dying and what have I got to show?"

_____

2.   Estelle: "Life is so funny; and so simple once you 'give in' and enjoy it. Yeah, I wish I had gone into the theater. I was good—damn good. But I chose to start a family and, like the man said, 'Two roads diverged in a yellow wood . . .' Now, I know I was meant to be a mother—a damn good one! I've lived a rich life, and I have a lot to thank God for." _____

**CHAPTER
EXERCISE**

Directions: Read the brief definitions below and identify the key term they refer to. Then write that key term underneath the appropriate adult "model."

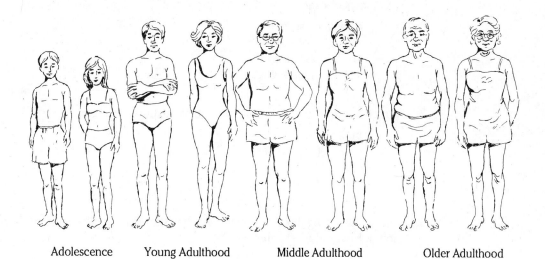

Adolescence   Young Adulthood   Middle Adulthood   Older Adulthood

1. Rapid increase in weight and height.
2. Voluntary withdrawal from society.
3. A sense of wholeness and meaningfulness in one's life.
4. Logical, abstract thought.
5. A concern for future generations.
6. Coherent sense of individuality.
7. Ability to commit the self to a close relationship.
8. The process of reflecting on the past.
9. Menarche.
10. Menopause.
11. Levinson's term for distress at middle adulthood.
12. Problem-oriented, flexible thought, characteristic of middle adulthood.
13. The sexual organs (maturation of _____).
14. The biological transformation into a sexually mature individual.
15. Sexual characteristics that have no direct reproductive function (appearance of _____).

PRACTICE EXAM 1

1. Elaine is 18 years old and a sophomore at Brainstorm University. What subphase of adolescence is she in?

    a.   early adolescence
    b.   middle adolescence
    c.   late adolescence
    d.   late-late adolescence

                                                              (Conceptual, Obj. 1.1)

2. Which of the following is *not* a secondary sexual characteristic?

    a.   pubic hair
    b.   breasts (for females)
    c.   genitals (both sexes)
    d.   underarm hair

                                                              (Factual, Obj. 1.1)

3. Jonathan is going through puberty and has started having "wet dreams" (nocturnal emissions). How old must Jonathan be?

    a.   12
    b.   13–14
    c.   15–16
    d.   17

                                                              (Conceptual, Obj. 1.1)

4. Which of the following students is likely to be most "popular" among his or her peers?

    a.   Joanne, a late-maturing female
    b.   Jeremy, a late-maturing male
    c.   Lori, an early-maturing female
    d.   Leroy, an early-maturing male

                                                              (Conceptual, Obj. 1.1)

5. When does the growth spurt peak for girls?

    a.   12 years
    b.   13 years
    c.   14 years
    d.   15 years

                                                              (Factual, Obj. 1.1)

6. In chemistry lab, the assignment is to analyze a "mystery" chemical to determine its composition. Bryan first tested all single possibilities from the six chemicals available—none yielded the right results. He then randomly tested a couple of two-chemical combinations and "accidently" discovered the correct combination. Bryan is probably functioning at the _____ level of thinking.

    a.   preoperational
    b.   concrete operational
    c.   formal operational
    d.   postformal operational

                                                              (Conceptual, Obj. 1.2)

7. Carol Gilligan modified Kohlberg's research to address female moral development more accurately. What did she *add* to Kohlberg's ethic of justice?

    a. the ethic of reciprocal altruism
    b. the ethic of caring
    c. the ethic of self-actualization
    d. the ethic of situational reasoning

    (Factual, Obj. 1.3)

8. You're a bright young attorney who knows that if you can "strike" (select) jury members who you know can reason at the principled level, your client will not receive the death sentence. Which of the following factors is *not* important in your selection?

    a. formal education of the jurors
    b. socioeconomic status of the jurors
    c. income level of the jurors
    d. age of the jurors

    (Conceptual, Obj. 1.3)

9. According to Erikson, society allows adolescents to "try on" a number of social roles and "experiment" with various beliefs and values. This period, which occurs during high school and college, is called:

    a. puberty
    b. identity diffusion
    c. psychosocial moratorium
    d. identity foreclosure

    (Factual, Obj. 2.2)

10. According to recent surveys, what percentage of adolescents say that their parents are satisfied with them?

    a. 15–20 percent
    b. 50–60 percent
    c. 75 percent
    d. 85–90 percent

    (Factual, Obj. 2.3)

11. Suppose a population expert predicts a new "baby boom" in the 1990s. Which of the following factors is likely to be *false* in the early part of the next century?

    a. The percentage of suicides will increase.
    b. Competition for good jobs will decrease.
    c. Burglary, auto theft, and robbery will increase.
    d. Competition for the "good" colleges will increase.

    (Conceptual, Obj. 2.4)

12. Which of the following groups is *highest* in the commission of crimes?

    a. young males (15–19)
    b. young adult males (25–29)
    c. young females (15–19)
    d. young adult females (25–29)

    (Factual, Obj. 2.4)

PRACTICE EXAM 2

1. A questionnaire is being constructed to try to identify probable alcohol and drug abusers. Which of the following is probably *not* very useful in identifying such a population?

   a. repeating a school grade
   b. crises and conflict with family members
   c. low achievers
   d. the ability to postpone gratification

   (Conceptual, Obj. 2.4)

2. Law-breaking that is the result of peer pressure is termed:

   a. social delinquency
   b. cohort delinquency
   c. peer-group delinquency
   d. socialized delinquency

   (Factual, Obj. 2.4)

3. Wilma's grandmother has lately been quite vocal in insisting that a "woman of 24" ought to be married and contemplating starting a family. Wilma's grandmother feels this way because she operates by:

   a. outdated norms
   b. a "social clock" that reflects her upbringing
   c. an appreciation of family values
   d. a knowledge of reproductive capacity

   (Conceptual, Obj. 3.1)

4. The clearest biological marker for middle-aged women is:

   a. menarche
   b. midlife crisis
   c. cohort effects
   d. menopause

   (Factual, Obj. 3.1)

5. If you were a researcher interested in studying age and cognitive functions, what kind of research design would you use to eliminate (or control for) "cohort effects"?

   a. longitudinal
   b. cross-sectional
   c. individual case studies
   d. field studies

   (Conceptual, Obj. 3.2)

6. Robert Browning once said, "Grow old along with me—the best is yet to be." He would be right *only* with respect to which of the following?

   a. memory tasks
   b. crystallized intelligence
   c. fluid intelligence
   d. recall rate

   (Conceptual, Obj. 3.2)

7. Which group consistently does better on any learning or memory task?

   a. young adults
   b. middle-age adults
   c. adolescents
   d. older adults

   (Factual, Obj. 3.2)

8. Suppose you are trying to promote a positive image of aging to your college freshman class. What aspect of the IQ and aging literature would you highlight?

   a. nonverbal, or performance-related data
   b. results of the WAIS tests
   c. longitudinal studies of intelligence
   d. hand-eye coordination studies

   (Conceptual, Obj. 3.2)

9. Hermon is at a point in his career where he would like to be a "mentor" to some of the younger employees. It's probably safe to assume that Hermon is at what stage of life, according to Erikson?

   a. identity
   b. intimacy
   c. generativity
   d. ego integrity

   (Conceptual, Obj. 4.1)

10. What is the major limitation of Levinson's transitional phases of adult development?

    a. It's limited to older adults (45+).
    b. It's limited to men only.
    c. It's limited to those individuals who have experienced midlife crisis.
    d. It's limited to college subjects.

    (Factual, Obj. 4.2)

11. Zachary is described as the ideal person. He not only loves his vocation as a carpenter, but he's a devoted family man and significantly shares in childrearing and household duties, such as cooking and sewing. What label best characterizes Zachary's social behavior?

    a. parental imperative
    b. androgynous
    c. postformal thought
    d. disengagement

    (Conceptual, Obj. 4.3)

12. What percentage of today's population is 65 or older?

    a. 4 percent
    b. 12 percent
    c. 20 percent
    d. 23 percent

    (Factual, Obj. 4.3)

■   **ANSWER KEY**   ■

Concept 1	Subject 1 - Stage 4 Subject 4 - Stage 1
	Subject 2 - Stage 2 Subject 5 - Stage 6
	Subject 3 - Stage 5 Subject 6 - Stage 3

Concept 2

1. d   3. b
2. a   4. c

Concept 3

1. T   6. T
2. F   7. T
3. F   8. F
4. T   9. F
5. T   10. T

Concept 4

1. establishing oneself in the adult world (early-mid 20s)
2. late twenties transition
3. midlife evaluation (possible midlife crisis; 40–45)
4. becoming psychologically independent from parents (18–20)
5. consolidating one's career (30s–early 40s)

Concept 5

1. Samuel: despair
2. Estelle: integrity

Chapter Exercise

Adolescence
1. adolescent growth spurt
4. formal thought
6. identity
9. menarche
13. primary sexual characteristics
14. puberty
15. secondary sexual characteristics

Young Adult
7. intimacy

Middle Adult
5. generativity
10. menopause
11. midlife crisis
12. postformal thought

Older Adult
2. disengagement
3. ego integrity
8. life review

Practice Exam 1

1. b, p. 470
2. c, p. 472
3. b, p. 472
4. d, p. 473
5. a, p. 472
6. b, p. 473
7. b, p. 475
8. c, p. 474
9. c, p. 476
10. d, p. 478
11. b, p. 479
12. a, p. 481

Practice Exam 2

1. d, p. 480
2. a, p. 481
3. b, p. 482
4. d, p. 483
5. a, pp. 487–488
6. b, p. 487
7. a, p. 486
8. c, p. 487
9. c, p. 489
10. b, pp. 475, 489–490
11. b, p. 493
12. b, p. 495

CRITICAL THINKING ESSAY 5

Studying the Effects of Divorce on Children

Over the past three decades the incidence of divorce has reached epidemic proportions. It is estimated that roughly half the couples married in the United States during the past decade will get divorced and that more than half the children born in the past decade will experience living with a single parent before their eighteenth birthday (Furstenberg et al., 1983). The American public is inclined to believe that divorce, like any other "epidemic," poses a threat to people's health and well-being and may leave them with lasting problems (Baydar, 1988; Wallerstein, 1989). No one doubts that divorce is an upsetting event for all family members; but are children from "broken homes" doomed to suffer long-term emotional problems? To answer this question, we must examine critically the research evidence on the adjustment of children in divorced families.

The first step in understanding the research in this field is to define two basic terms. First, *divorce* is used by most researchers to refer to the situation in which children live with only one of their parents as a result of a legal divorce or long-term separation. Some researchers, particularly those who use national surveys such as census reports, often use the term "single-parent family," though this may include situations other than divorce or separation (such as death of a parent, a never-married parent, or a change in custody for legal reasons).

A more difficult term to define precisely is *adjustment*. Researchers attempt to measure this variable in many ways: parent ratings of the child, teacher ratings, peer nominations and ratings, the child's self-ratings, parent and child behavior checklists, brief behavioral observations by researchers, indicators of

academic performance, and clinical impressions. Unfortunately, different investigators tend to use different measures, making direct comparisons across studies a tricky business. Emery (1982) and Demo and Acock (1988) have noted two other problems with measures of adjustment. First, researchers often employ unreliable or invalid measures such as subjective clinical impressions; occasionally the term "adjustment" is used without being defined at all (e.g., Rosen, 1979). Second, measures from different sources (such as parent, teacher, and child) frequently show poor intercorrelations. This may result either from the fact that different sources have access to different behavior or from the fact that raters' assessments are biased (for example, a mother's rating of her child may reflect her own maladjustment more than her child's).

Nevertheless, investigators tend increasingly to describe a child's adjustment in terms of four broad behavioral measures:

1. Externalizing problems (acting out, aggression)
2. Internalizing problems (withdrawal, depression, anxiety)
3. Social competence (popularity ratings by peers)
4. Academic performance (school grades, standardized test scores)

In addition, researchers are coming to view divorce as an ongoing process involving many complex interactions and adjustments, rather than as a single, time-limited event (Emery, 1982; Heatherington and Camara, 1984; Wallerstein, 1984, 1989; Kalter, 1987; Demo and Acock, 1988).

STUDYING ADJUSTMENT IN THE CHILDREN OF DIVORCE

Any discussion of methodology in this field should begin with a caveat: Since the primary independent variable of interest, divorce, cannot be manipulated experimentally (that is, we cannot randomly assign some children to divorced parents and others to intact families), the research is essentially correlational in nature. As we learned in Chapter 2, correlational designs merely show associations between variables and cannot directly assess cause and effect. Because of this basic limitation, no study is truly conclusive, and researchers in this area must rely on data gathered from different sources to overcome the pitfalls of each. Perhaps in recognition of this methodological limitation, the field has been characterized by a remarkable level of cooperation and conciliation.

Research Methodologies. Research on divorce tends to rely on three basic methodologies: limited studies of specific populations at one point in time, larger cross-sectional studies of different groups (usually children in different age groups) at one point in time, and longitudinal studies in which measures are recorded over several years.

Each of these methodologies has inherent weaknesses. Limited studies tend to focus on a narrow range of variables (e.g., custody arrangements or interparental conflict) or a particular sample (e.g., preschool children or adolescents). Controlling for one variable in a small sample often results in wide variability in other sample characteristics, a fact that complicates the interpretation of data. For example, Rosen (1979) studied children ten years after their parents' divorce. The children's ages ranged from nine to twenty-eight years, and their age at the time of their parents' separation ranged from three months to sixteen years. Cross-sectional analyses (e.g., Heatherington, Cox, and Cox, 1979a, 1979b, 1985; Kinard and Reinherz, 1984, 1986) measure a wide age range and separate the subjects into distinct groups. However, these researchers are left to deduce a developmental process by comparing different groups of subjects at different ages.

Longitudinal studies make it possible to follow developmental trends in the same subjects over time, but such studies are extremely costly and time-consuming. Furthermore, their cost usually limits researchers to gathering data on small samples, which may not be representative of the population (Heatherington and Camara, 1984).

Types of Samples. Three types of samples are typically employed in research on children of divorce: large representative samples, smaller samples of convenience, and clinical samples. Here, too, each category has inherent strengths and weaknesses.

Only large representative samples, such as census reports and national surveys (e.g., Furstenberg et al., 1983; Guidubaldi and Perry, 1984, 1985; Baydar, 1988), provide findings that can confidently be generalized to the population as a whole. Generalizability is crucial when we consider the potential influence that this research has on national policy. However, because these samples are so large, the data are often limited in detail. Superficial demographic information (status as divorced, separated, or remarried; age of children; and so on) is easily coded, but many of the complex factors in these family situations are not tapped by large-scale surveys (for example, was there interparental conflict, did the custodial parent date frequently or have a live-in lover, did the children share in the family responsibilities and decision making?). Worse, since these surveys are often conducted for other purposes, many important questions pertaining to children's adjustment are not asked, so that much of the most relevant information is simply not available.

While researchers who employ smaller samples of convenience are able to ask specific questions and can accommodate more detailed answers, it is unclear to what extent their data can be generalized to the population at large. These subjects are typically recruited through subject pools of college students, local school populations, court records, and newspaper advertisements, and the resulting samples are generally quite homogeneous in many respects. Researchers have reported on samples composed of students from upper-middle-class homes (Fishel, 1987), lower-middle-class homes (Shaw and Emery, 1987), and a private parochial school (Swartzberg, Shmukler, and Chalmers, 1983). One American sample (Rosen, 1979) had 44 percent of the children in the father's custody, which is quite high compared to the national rate of around 10 percent. Furthermore, subjects recruited through such means as newspaper advertisements are especially prone to volunteer bias. The researcher must make sure that those who participate in the study are not different on any important variables from those who decline to participate.

Clinical samples, recruited from among families in counseling programs, are usually small and could logically be expected to differ from the nonclinical population in important ways. Emery (1982) notes an additional problem with clinical samples: many subjects seeking counseling may exaggerate their problems in an attempt to rationalize being in therapy. Furthermore, the researchers who employ clinical samples (and who are, not surprisingly, usually professional clinicians themselves) often use less reliable measures, such as loosely structured interviews and clinical evaluations. This fact complicates any comparison between their results and those of other researchers. Paradoxically, this weakness is also the main strength of clinical samples. Because clinicians are able to conduct relatively lengthy individual interviews and to follow their subjects over a number of years, they are able to provide the field with rich, detailed, longitudinal information that is unavailable to other researchers.

CRITICAL ANALYSIS OF DIVORCE ADJUSTMENT

To put the strengths and weaknesses of these various methodologies into focus, we will look at two research programs that use very different research strategies. The first is a longitudinal project employing a clinical sample; the second is a series of limited studies using small samples of convenience.

A Study of a Divorced Family in a Counseling Program.   In 1971 divorced families from an upper-middle-class suburb in northern California were referred to a commu-

nity mental health program. Those families who had no overt signs of psychiatric problems (60 in all, with 131 children) were interviewed by a staff of five clinicians under the direction of Judith Wallerstein. Subsequent interviews were conducted one and a half years, five years, and ten years after the divorce. To date this research had generated a host of reports (e.g., Kelly and Wallerstein, 1976; Wallerstein and Kelly, 1976, 1980; Wallerstein, 1984, 1985, 1987). The data collected in these case studies are presented in the form of clinical impressions and quoted passages from subjects' responses. No standardized questionnaires or observations are reported, and no statistical analyses are performed.

One major flaw of this research program is in sample selection. The sample consists of families who chose to enter counseling at the time of their divorces. Does this group react to divorce differently from the majority of divorcing families who never seek any professional help? We simply do not know. In addition, this sample was from a mostly white, upper-middle-class community. Are they representative of minority families or families from less comfortable circumstances? Again, we do not know.

To complicate matters, Wallerstein breaks down her sample of 131 children into several groups according to their age at the time of their parents' divorce: young children, early latency, later latency, preadolescent, and adolescent—in effect creating a cross-sectional design. While this breakdown distinguishes children with important developmental differences, it also results in groups consisting of only 25 to 35 children each. Making generalizations from such small samples is risky.

Furthermore, this project includes no control group. Thus, it is impossible to compare these subjects with children from the same community whose parents were not divorced. Without information from a control group, we cannot know if this sample is worse off or better off than other children from the same community growing up at the same time.

A second major flaw is the method of data collection. Although lengthy interviews (usually lasting two to three hours) provide detailed data, this method is potentially subject to numerous biases. Since the interviewers knew the subjects personally, it is possible that their impressions (and perhaps even their questions) were biased by what they *expected* a child to say instead of what the child truly felt. Since the interviewers were professional clinicians, it is probable that they were especially sensitive to information that revealed some sort of symptomatology and may have interpreted many responses accordingly. For example, Wallerstein and Kelly (1976) interpreted the children's statements about their plans for the future as unconscious messages, commenting, for example, "Some seemed to be unconsciously extrapolating from these reconciliation wishes to plan future careers as repairmen, as bridge-builders, as architects, as lawyers" (p. 269). This interpretation is not necessarily wrong, but most other researchers would be unlikely to interpret a child's plan to become a lawyer or architect as a wish to reconcile divorced parents. We must also bear in mind that subjects who seek therapy may be more attuned to, or more willing to report, emotional problems (Emery, 1982).

Another problem relating to the data is that they are presented in a descriptive, as opposed to a statistical, format. No objectively collected data (questionnaire scores, test scores, and the like) are reported. Instead, clinical impressions and excerpts from subjects' responses are presented, leaving the reader to translate them into meaningful data that could be compared to other studies.

A Study of Adolescent Disturbance and Interparental Conflict.   The research of Nicholas Long and Rex Forehand and their colleagues (Long, et al., 1987; Long et al., 1988; Forehand et al., 1988) investigates a limited aspect of divorced families (interparental conflict) as it relates to a limited sample (adolescents) at one point in time (the first year following divorce). Although these studies are focused on a narrow list of independent variables, they assess adjustment through multiple dependent measures completed by the subjects, the parents, the teachers, and objective raters. These studies also compare the subjects with a control group. Moreover,

these studies examine equal numbers of male and female subjects in both the study group and the control group. Let's look at one study (Long et al., 1987) in more detail.

Long and his colleagues (1987), using court records, posted notices and advertisements in local newspapers, recruited 20 families that had been divorced in the past year. The target children in these families were 10 boys and 10 girls aged eleven to fifteen years. From a pool of 69 intact families who had volunteered to participate in a study, the families of 10 boys and 10 girls were matched to the divorced families in terms of family composition, social class, and other variables. These families served as controls.

To measure interparental conflict, the mothers completed a standardized questionnaire. In both the divorced and the married groups, half of the parents were considered "high conflict" and half "low conflict." To measure the children's adjustments, the mothers, the children's teachers, and the children themselves completed separate questionnaires concerning the children's cognitive and social behavior. The children also filled out a self-esteem inventory and brought in their last report cards to be used as a measure of their academic performance. In addition, the children and mothers were videotaped during a three-minute conversation about keeping their rooms clean (the most common issue between mothers and children at this age). The children's behavior during this interaction was coded by independent judges.

Like most studies of this kind, this one is well controlled. It clearly specifies the independent variables of interest, it uses dependent measures known to be reliable and valid, and it makes specific predictions that the research was intended to test. However, like most such studies, this one has many limitations. First, because it targets a particular age group, the results cannot be generalized to other age groups. Second, the study tested for disturbance only within the first year after divorce; longer-term problems were not assessed. Third, although this study did consider some mediating variables besides divorce per se (interparental conflict and social class), other mediating variables were not considered (such as the custodial parent's relationship with the noncustodial parent and the custodial parent's dating patterns). Had other dependent, independent, or mediating variables been chosen for study, the results might have been different. Finally, even though a control group was used (making it possible to assess the impact of divorce itself), we have no guarantee that this study's volunteer sample of convenience is representative of the general population.

CONCLUSION: WHAT DO WE KNOW ABOUT CHILDREN'S ADJUSTMENT TO DIVORCE?

Researchers in this field have used several different methodologies and many types of samples. They have investigated a number of mediating variables using a wide array of dependent measures. Somewhat surprisingly, the results they have reported have been quite consistent.

Findings. According to several researchers (Heatherington, Cox, and Cox, 1979a, 1979b; Kulka and Weingarten, 1979; Emery, 1982; Kinard and Reinherz, 1984, 1985; Demo and Acock, 1988), emotional disturbance in the children of divorce seems to be a direct reaction to the divorce itself and to occur during a "crisis period" of a year to eighteen months following the divorce. Afterward, most signs of disturbance gradually diminish. The pattern of disturbance seems somewhat different for boys and girls, though. Boys tend to have more externalizing problems (such as aggression), and their problems seem to be more disruptive and to last longer. Girls are more likely to have internalizing problems (such as depression), and there is evidence that they develop more problems with interpersonal relationships and promiscuous sexual activity in adolescence (Heatherington et al., 1985; Wallerstein, 1985; Cooney et al., 1987). In general, children who are between the ages of five and fifteen at the time of divorce seem to be affected most.

Differences in school performance do not seem to be caused by divorce. When such differences are found, they disappear once the family's social class is statistically factored out (Heatherington, Camara, and Featherman, 1983; Guidubaldi and Perry, 1984, 1985). Results concerning the correlation between divorce and a child's social behavior are inconsistent.

Several moderating variables seem to influence children's emotional reactions to their parents' divorce. First, social class, often measured by family income, accounts for much of the variance in children's adjustment. In light of this finding, it is regrettable that divorce often results in a significant lowering of social-class standing for mothers (who are usually awarded custody) and that the majority of fathers are unable or unwilling to pay child support, which would help to maintain the children's standard of living (Wallerstein, 1985).

A second moderating variable is interparental conflict. Several researchers (Rutter, 1971; Emery, 1982; Swartzberg et al., 1983; Long et al., 1987, 1988; Shaw and Emery, 1987; Forehand et al., 1988) have noted that interparental conflict, regardless of whether the parents are married or divorced, contributes to children's maladjustment as expressed in externalizing behaviors and feelings of inadequacy.

A third moderating variable appears to be the children's relationship with noncustodial parents and stepparents. Several investigators (Rutter, 1971; Hess and Camara, 1979; Fishel, 1987) have found that children who maintain a good relationship with their noncustodial parents (usually their fathers) experience fewer emotional problems than children who do not. Unfortunately, only about 15 percent of children of divorce have any regular contact with the absent parent (Furstenberg et al., 1983).

A fourth moderating variable that researchers have examined is remarriage. Although conventional wisdom claims that living in single-parent families is emotionally harmful to children, it appears that the custodial parent's remarriage also has its drawbacks for children, at least in the first year or so (Baydar, 1988). Boys seem to be affected more if remarriage occurs in their younger years, whereas girls experience more problems if the remarriage occurs during their adolescence.

Recommendations.   Although researchers in this area are hampered by methods that contain inherent weaknesses, they have been able to distill consistent results from all the available evidence. This consistency has enabled them to confidently recommend changes in public policy despite the limitation of their respective methodologies.

"Staying together for the sake of the children" is not necessarily the best strategy for married couples. If a separation or divorce will reduce interparental conflict without ending the relationship between the children and the noncustodial parent, then divorce seems to be preferable to a conflict-ridden marriage (Emery, 1982; Fishel, 1987). Of course, other factors (such as the loss of income in the single-parent family) must be considered in each case.

With these conclusions in mind, researchers have some suggestions for the U.S. legal system. First, the system's adversarial approach tends to promote interparental conflict and thus contributes to the children's maladjustment. Often, the noncustodial parent is stripped of any parental rights, such as access to school and medical records. A system that employed mediation instead of confrontation would seem to be in the children's best interest (Hess and Camara, 1979; Emery, 1982). Second, since economic loss is so devastating for many custodial parents, rulings on the noncustodial parent's financial responsibilities for child support and education should be enforced more strictly (Bane, 1976).

REFERENCES

Bane, M. J. Marital disruption and the lives of children. *Journal of Social Issues,* 1976, *32,* 103–117.

Baydar, M. Effects of parental separation and re-entry into union on the emotional well-being of children. *Journal of Marriage and the Family,* 1988, *50,* 967–991.

Cooney, T. M., M. A. Smyer, G. O. Hagestad, and R. Klock. Parental divorce in young adulthood: Some preliminary findings. *American Journal of Orthopsychiatry,* 1987, *56,* 470–477.

Demo, D. H., and A. C. Acock. The impact of divorce on children. *Journal of Marriage and the Family,* 1988, *50,* 619–648.

Emery, R. E. Interparental conflict and the children of discord and divorce. *Psychological Bulletin,* 1982, *92,* 310–330.

Fishel, A. H. Children's adjustment in divorced families. *Youth and Society,* 1987, *19,* 17–196.

Forehand, R., A. McCombs, N. Long, G. H. Brody, and R. Farber. Early adolescent adjustment to recent parental divorce: The role of interparental conflict and adolescent sex as mediating variables. *Journal of Consulting and Clinical Psychology,* 1988, *56,* 624–627.

Furstenberg, F. F., C. W. Nord, J. L. Peterson, and N. Zill. The life course of children of divorce: Marital disruption and parental contact. *American Sociological Review,* 1983, *48,* 656–668.

Guidubaldi, J., and J. D. Perry. Divorce, socio-economic status, and children's cognitive-social school entry competence. *American Journal of Orthopsychiatry,* 1984, *54,* 459–468.

Guidubaldi, J., and J. D. Perry. Divorce and mental health sequelae for children: A two-year follow-up of a nationwide sample. *Journal of the American Academy of Child Psychiatry,* 1985, *24,* 531–537.

Heatherington, E. M., K. A. Camara, and D. Featherman. Achievement and intellectual functioning of children in one-parent households. In J. Spence (ed.), *Assessing achievement.* San Francisco: Freeman, 1983, pp. 206–284.

Heatherington, E. M., and K. A. Camara. Families in transition: The processes of dissolution and reconstitution. In R. D. Parke (ed.), *Review of child development research: The family,* Vol. 7. Chicago: University of Chicago Press, 1984, pp. 398–439.

Heatherington, E. M., M. Cox, and R. Cox. Family interaction and the social, emotional and cognitive development of children following divorce. In V. Vaughn and T. Brazelton (eds.), *Family: Setting priorities.* New York: Science and Medicine Publishing Company, 1979a, pp. 8 9–128.

Heatherington, E. M., M. Cox, and R. Cox. Play and social interaction in children following divorce. *Journal of Social Issues,* 1979b, *35,* 26–49.

Heatherington, E. M., M. Cox, and R. Cox. Long-term effects of divorce and remarriage on the adjustment of children. *Journal of the American Academy of Child Psychiatry,* 1985, *24,* 518–530.

Hess, R. D., and K. A. Camara. Post-divorce family relationships as mediating factors in the consequences of divorce for children. *Journal of Social Issues,* 1979, *35,* 79–96.

Kalter, N. Long-term effects of divorce on children: A developmental vulnerability model. *American Journal of Orthopsychiatry,* 1987, *57,* 587–600.

Kelly, J. B., and J. S. Wallerstein. tTe effects of parental divorce: Experiences of the child in early latency. *American Journal of Orthopsychiatry,* 1976, *46,* 20–32.

Kinard, E. M., and H. Reinherz. Marital disruption: Effects on behavioral and emotional functioning in children. *Journal of Family Issues,* 1984, *5,* 90–115.

Kinard, E. M., and H. Reinherz. Effects of marital disruption on children's school aptitude and achievement. *Journal of Marriage and the Family,* 1986, *48,* 285–293.

Kulka, R. A., and H. Weingarten. The long-term effects of parental divorce in childhood on adult adjustment. *Journal of Social Issues,* 1979, *35,* 50–78.

Long, N., R. Forehand, R. Farber, and G. H. Brody. Self-perceived and independently observed competence of young adults as a function of parental marital conflict and recent divorce. *Journal of Abnormal Child Psychology,* 1987, *15,* 15–27.

Long, N., E. Slater, R. Forehand, and R. Farber. Continued high or reduced interparental conflict following divorce: Relation to young adolescent adjustment. *Journal of*

Consulting and Clinical Psychology, 1988, *56,* 467–469.

Rosen, R. Some crucial issues concerning children of divorce. *Journal of Divorce,* 1979, *3,* 19–25.

Rutter, M. Parent-child separation: Psychological effects on the children. *Journal of Child Psychology and Psychiatry,* 1971, *12,* 233–260.

Shaw, D. S., and R. E. Emery. Parental conflict and other correlates of the adjustment of school-age children whose parents have separated. *Journal of Abnormal Child Psychology,* 1987, *15,* 269–281.

Swartzberg, L., D. Shmukler, and B. Chalmers. Emotional adjustment and self-concept of children from divorced and nondivorced unhappy homes. *Journal of Social Psychology,* 1983, *121,* 305–312.

Wallerstein, J. S. Children of divorce: Preliminary report of a ten-year follow-up of young children. *American Journal of Orthopsychiatry,* 1984, *54,* 444–458.

Wallerstein, J. S. Children of divorce: Preliminary report of a ten-year follow-up of older children and adolescents. *Journal of the American Academy of Child Psychiatry,* 1985, *24,* 545–553.

Wallerstein, J. S. Children of divorce: Report of a a ten-year follow-up of early latency-age children. *American Journal of Orthopsychiatry,* 1987, *57,* 199–211.

Wallerstein, J. S. Children after divorce. *The New York Times Magazine,* January 22, 1989.

Wallerstein, J. S., and J. B. Kelly. The effects of parental divorce: Experiences of the child in later latency. *American Journal of Orthopsychiatry,* 1976, *46,* 256–269.

Wallerstein, J. S., and J. B. Kelly. *Surviving the breakup: How children and parents cope with divorce.* New York: Basic Books, 1980.

RESPONDING TO CRITICAL ESSAY 5

1. Studying children's adjustment to divorce is a very complex, but a critically important issue. However, there are few, if any, experimental studies that have directly assessed the effects of divorce.

    What basic methodological problem exists for all studies in this area?

2. According to researchers, emotional disturbance in the children of divorce seems to occur during a "crisis period" of a year to 18 months following the divorce.

    If you were speaking to an audience of parents, what would you tell them about recognizing emotional disturbance in their sons and daughters during the post-divorce period?

3. Research on divorce has relied on three basic methodologies.

    Compare and contrast the relative merits and inherent limitations of each method.

CHAPTER SEVENTEEN

Personality

KEY TERM ORGANIZER

Although there is no single definition accepted by all theorists, most would agree that *personality* consists of an individual's characteristic and distinctive patterns of thinking, feeling, and behaving.

PSYCHOANALYTIC THEORY

Sigmund Freud conceived the first comprehensive theory of personality. Freud theorized the existence of an aspect of personality, unknown to the conscious mind, that he called the *unconscious*, explored, in part, through the technique of *free association* (asking patients to say whatever comes to mind). The process devised by Freud to retrieve repressed memories and feelings, allowing them to be examined and understood, is known as *psychoanalysis*.

Dreams, according to Freud, were the "royal road to the unconscious." The *manifest content*, or the events the dreamer relates, is a kind of coded message from the dreamer's unconscious. The *latent content* is the underlying meaning of the dream, which can be decoded only through the process of analysis.

According to Freud, the personality includes three separate but interacting systems: the *id*, the *ego*, and the *superego*, which are described further in the following chart and graphic.

Structure Name	Basis in Personality	Level of Consciousness	Principle Followed	Process Used
Id	Biological drives and instincts	Unconscious	Pleasure-unpleasure principle	Primary process thinking
Ego	Control of individual actions	Mostly conscious	Reality principle	Secondary process thinking
Superego	Conscience and social inhibitions	Partly conscious; part unconscious		

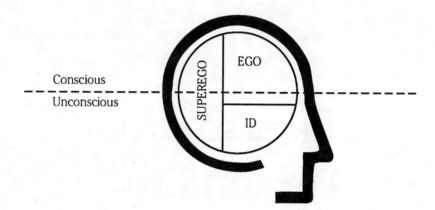

Freud saw the interplay of pulls and pushes among these three interacting systems as the primary determinant of human behavior and personality; he called it *psychodynamics.*

Anxiety is a state of psychic pain that alerts the ego to danger; it is akin to fear. When inner conflict is acute and anxiety threatens, the ego often tries to reduce the anxiety by means of irrational techniques known as *defense mechanisms.* The most fundamental mechanism, one that keeps threatening thoughts and memories from penetrating consciousness and pushes them back into the unconscious, is called *repression.* Freud saw this mechanism operating in the inability of patients recalling psychologically damaging, or *traumatic,* events. Another extremely common defense mechanism is *rationalization,* giving ourselves plausible explanations for unacceptable behaviors. Freud did identify one "positive" defense mechanism: *sublimation,* the diversion of erotic energy from its original source and toward a socially constructive activity.

Freud hypothesized that children pass through a series of five "psychosexual" stages, so named because the stages originate in the sexual instincts and within each stage a different part of the body becomes the focus of sensual pleasure:

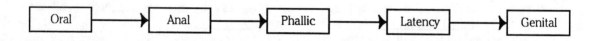

Some of Freud's followers extended this work into new areas. Carl Jung's analytic psychology included discussion of the collective unconscious as a vast storehouse of *archetypes*—myths, dreams, symbols, and other ideas and images shared by all humanity.

Karen Horney believed that childhood conflicts grew out of feelings of helplessness. Her theory revolved around what she called *basic anxiety* (feeling helpless and isolated in a potentially hostile world) and *basic hostility* (resentment over parents' indifference, inconsistency, and interference).

Several tests were developed to assess personality from the psychoanalytic perspective. Some clinicians use *projective tests,* in which subjects interpret ambiguous stimuli. Two of the most widely used projective tests are the *Rorschach inkblot test* and the *thematic apperception test* (TAT). Projective tests have problems of reliability and validity.

Most nonpsychoanalytic theories of personality deemphasize unconscious forces as determinants of personality and emphasize observable behavior, learning, cognitive processes, and biological factors.

TRAIT THEORIES

These theories are primarily descriptive, emphasizing the extent to which an individual possesses various traits (or predispositions to respond in a consistent way). Gordon Allport believed that traits can render different situations "functionally equivalent."

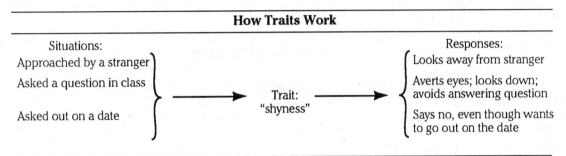

How Traits Work

Situations:		Responses:
Approached by a stranger		Looks away from stranger
Asked a question in class	Trait: "shyness"	Averts eyes; looks down; avoids answering question
Asked out on a date		Says no, even though wants to go out on the date

Allport classified traits into three categories: *cardinal traits, central traits,* and *secondary traits.* Any of these traits may be either *common traits,* which are seen to some degree in all individuals, or *individual traits,* which make each individual's behavior unique. The underlying tool in analyzing traits has been *factor analysis,* a statistical method that tries to quantify factors in a precise, scientific manner.

Allport's Approach

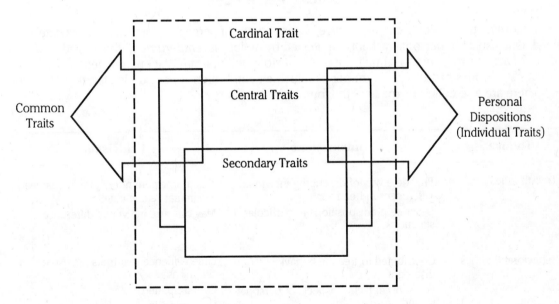

BEHAVIORAL THEORIES

These theories view personality as a set of learned responses. Dollard and Miller's behavior theory seeks to translate psychoanalytic phenomena into behavioristic terms. In this theory, neurotic conflicts are learned; they are characterized as extreme *approach-avoidance conflicts,* in which two motives clash so that satisfying one frustrates the other. B. F. Skinner's radical behaviorism analyzes behavior in terms of the external conditions that control it rather than paying attention to internal events of the person. Social-learning theorists believe that most new behavior is acquired through observational learning.

In the social-cognitive view, it is equally important to include the person who is performing the behavior. Bandura proposed a model of *reciprocal determinism,* in which each of the factors (environment, behavior, and person) influences and is influenced by the others. Social-cognitive theorists look at how people approach specific kinds of situations. For example, *self-efficacy,* which refers to our judgment of our own competence in a particular situation, becomes an important aspect of personality.

HUMANISTIC PERSPECTIVE

These theories emphasize creative potential and personal growth. Abraham Maslow based his theory on people who had achieved *self-actualization,* those who find fulfillment in doing their best. He identified two sets of human needs: basic, or *deficiency needs* (physiological and psychological needs), and *metaneeds,* or growth needs. Unfulfilled growth needs can lead to *metapathologies,* such as alienation. Carl Rogers believed that *conditional positive regard* in childhood leads to the denial and distortion of feelings so that we develop *conditions of worth* under which we know we will receive positive regard. Rogers' *self theory* suggests that people have an innate impulse toward becoming *fully functioning,* or psychologically adjusted. Rogers distinguishes between the *organism,* or the total range of possible experiences, and the *self,* or the recognized and accepted parts of experience.

BIOLOGICAL PERSPECTIVE

According to the biological perspective, some aspects of personality are biologically determined. One aspect of personality that is influenced by biology is *temperament,* the individual's pattern of activity, response to stimuli, susceptibility to emotional stimulation, and general mood.

These theories have made a number of valuable contributions to our understanding of personality. There are also criticisms made of the four approaches.

Theory	Contributions	Criticisms
Trait theories	Provide a way of describing individual differences in behavior Describe predispositions in particular situations	Trait names are not explanations; lead to circular reasoning May obscure individual differences
Behavioral theories	Contributed to treating behavior disorders Focus on objective aspects of personality and behavior	Little evidence that traits persist across situations Oversimplified Deterministic Can lead to totalitarianism
Humanistic perspective	Significant impact on therapy and research Positive focus on client growth Spawned the group therapy movement	Unscientific and subjective Lack neutrality
Biological perspective	Identified temperamental differences that exist from birth	Biological basis of personality not yet firmly established

MAJOR CONCEPTS AND LEARNING OBJECTIVES

CONCEPT 1   Sigmund Freud's theory of personality emphasizes the significance of child-hood experience and the role of unconscious motivation. His followers explored a number of variations of his views.

1.1   List and define the three basic structural concepts of Freud's view of the personality.

1.2   Identify and distinguish the function of defense mechanisms in their role of alleviating anxiety.

1.3   Outline and describe the five stages of psychosexual development and the focus anxiety in each stage.

1.4   Outline the views of post-Freudian psychoanalytic theorists Jung, Horney, Adler, and Fromm.

1.5   Discuss the problem of testing the basic concepts of psychoanalysis and the importance of its contributions.

Concept Builder 1

Directions: Match each situation described below to the defense mechanism that is being utilized.

Letting Your Defenses Down

_____   1. Mrs. Jacobs has always suspected her husband, Murray, of being unfaithful, but she won't acknowledge it. She pushes it out of her mind.

_____   2. Max has been told to take his heart medication. It's critical for his health, yet he refuses to do so.

_____   3. Julie hadn't wet her bed in years, but when she and her family moved recently, she started wetting her bed and sucking her thumb.

_____   4. Jeremy has channeled his desire to fight onto the football field. He's one of the meanest defensive tackles ever at Baytown High.

_____   5. Robert didn't get into Harvard Business School. Now he says he didn't want to anyway: "Harvard is too big; I want to go to a smaller school where I'll get a more personal education."

_____   6. Phil always picks on his brother after he has been disciplined. It's his way of taking out his frustrations.

_____   7. Mr. Williams is a fanatical crusader against homosexuality. He probably has tendencies toward homosexuality but doesn't outwardly show it.

_____   8. Carol accuses her best friend of being a rumor-monger. Actually, it's Carol who's the gossip.

a.   repression
b.   rationalization
c.   denial
d.   regression
e.   projection
f.   displacement
g.   reaction formation
h.   sublimation

CONCEPT 2   Trait theories of personality depend upon the view that personality can be described by a list of common traits. These traits are thought to exist in everyone and can be measured in individuals.

2.1   Outline and describe Allport's three kinds of traits and discuss the use of factor analysis to quantify the study of traits.

2.2   Discuss the methods of assessing and measuring personality traits.

2.3   Review the main issues of the person-situation debate as it presents a challenge to the trait approach to personality.

**Concept
Builder 2**

Directions: Read the following ads placed in the classified section of a school newspaper. These "personal ads" are meant to be very brief self-descriptions by people interested in meeting other people. Your task is to read each description and identify the kind of trait(s) being described according to the trait theorists.

Personal Ads—Love in the Classifieds

_____ 1. Janet Coleman, age 19. "I'm a psychology major (big fan of Eysenck's); I'm a person who is primarily interested in people and things outside my own world. Very outgoing."

_____ 2. Ted Ledbetter, age 25. "I took a personality test once that used some sort of fancy statistical technique—factor analysis, I think. Anyway, it summed me up very nicely: highly competitive."

_____ 3. Angela Capoletti, age 20: "I'm artistic, a little self-centered, sociable, and honest. I love Italian food and dance music."

_____ 4. April Taylor, age 18. "I'm pretty much like everyone else. Good-hearted, like to have fun, hard worker, and easy to talk to."

_____ 5. Steven Kandell, age 29: "Well, it's obvious that I'm too tall, too good-looking, and I've got way too much money. I know you're not interested in those little details, though. Here's what makes me unique: I've got the most beautiful smile and most unusual (some say warped) sense of humor of anybody I know!"

a. central and secondary traits

b. cardinal trait

c. individual traits (personal dispositions)

d. common traits

e. extrovert

CONCEPT 3   Behavioral theories consider personality to be the various ways individuals adjust to the demands of the environment. In the behavioral view, personality is learned.

3.1   Distinguish the radical behavioral approach from the social-cognitive approach and identify the basic concepts from each approach that are relevant to personality.

3.2   Discuss the ways in which behavioral approaches are oversimplified or deterministic and discuss the value of cognitive approaches in responding to these criticisms.

Concept Builder 3

Directions: Listen to Ralph as he talks about his ideas about looking for a job. Match his ideas with Mischel's concepts of observational learning.

Ralph's Job Search

_____ 1. "I want a job that will reward me for my work effort. Money (salary) is very important to me. If I work hard, I want the monetary payoff."

_____ 2. "My game plan is to be employed in three months. I'm going to take my time, go on as many interviews as possible, then make my decision after two months of looking. Then I'll vacation a month and start work!"

_____ 3. "I've got a damn good resume. I got professional help with it. It very clearly illustrates my unique skills and abilities, particularly in work situations."

_____ 4. "I've come to learn that making a good first impression in the interview is critical. Good eye contact and a smile get attention every time."

_____ 5. "I'm not afraid of answering the old 'How much salary do you require?' question; I view it as a challenge, a chance to negotiate."

a. competencies
b. encodings
c. expectancies
d. values
e. plans

CONCEPT 4   Humanistic theory emphasizes the unique potential of the individual for growth, creativity, and spontaneity and views the individual as capable of self-determination.

4.1   Define Maslow's concepts of self-actualization and metapathologies, and distinguish basic needs from metaneeds.

4.2   Define Rogers' concept of unconditional positive regard and its role in the development of the fully functioning person.

4.3   Outline the criticisms of humanistic theory and its contributions.

Concept Builder 4

Directions: Read the following story involving a counseling session with a student. As you read the story, you will be stopped at critical points and asked to identify the concept from Rogers' self theory that is being illustrated.

Helping Lance with Humanism

Lance, a college student, has been put on academic warning for two reasons: his grades are very low, and he was recently caught cheating on an exam. The school counselor asked Lance and his parents to come in and talk about what's going on with him right now. Here are some selected highlights of their conference:

a. conditional positive regard   d. self

b. unconditional positive regard   e. fully functioning person

c. conditions of worth

Counselor: "Lance, let's get straight to the point. Let's start with your getting caught for cheating. I get the feeling that that really hasn't sunk in just yet."

Lance: "Well, I really don't know what to say. . . . I don't know why I did it."

Counselor: "Lance, I think you really do know why. It's common to deny some aspect of your 'organism,' or range of experience, to avoid dealing with a problem."

Critical point 1: What aspect of Lance's person is working against the "organism"? ___

Lance: "Well, . . . I guess I do. There is so much pressure to make good grades and succeed. I really want to make myself, and particularly my folks, proud of me. I'm not blaming them, but I'm trying too hard and it's getting to me. I feel like I won't be a worthwhile person if I fail at school."

Counselor: "I know, Lance. Sometimes we try to strive toward some outside, extrinsic standard that has nothing to do with our self-worth as a person."

Critical point 2: What is the counselor referring to? ___

Lance's father: "It's true, Lance. Your mother and I have so overstressed grades and doing well that we have at times been insensitive and even rejecting of you as a person when you brought home bad grades."

Critical point 3: Lance has been treated by his parents as an object of

___

Counselor: "Lance, you may not feel this way now, but do you know that you are a valuable, worthwhile person whether or not you make good grades?"

Critical point 4: The counselor is giving Lance ___

Counselor: "Lance, it's my sincerest wish, and I think your parents' wish also, that you like yourself for yourself, that you not judge yourself based on just grades, that you not feel defensive about doing poorly in some classes, and that you have a harmonious relationship with your parents."

Critical point 5: The counselor is describing the characteristics of a ___

CONCEPT 5 Though a biological basis for personality has not been firmly established, there is evidence that temperament, task-orientation, and some personality traits may have biological foundations.

5.1 Describe the evidence for a biological basis to aspects of personality.

Concept Builder 5

Directions: Read the following descriptions of babies and their personalities. Identify the biological concept being illustrated.

Baby Biographies

_____ 1. "Laura has been shy since she was a three-month-old. She won't even look at strangers, and even if she knows you well, she'll still act inhibited and restrained."

_____ 2. "Butch is an irritable child (and irritating, I might add!). He fusses a lot, gets stressed out easily, and once he's worked up, there's almost nothing I can do to soothe him."

_____ 3. "Elliot has an incredible attention span. Whether he's studying a flower, or playing with his blocks, he'll stay focused on the situation at hand. He's tenacious!"

a. temperament
b. task-oriented behavior
c. personality traits

CHAPTER EXERCISE

Personality Match-up

Psychoanalytic theories

_B_ 1. Personality consists of eight stages
_C_ 2. Mediates between the id and reality
_E_ 3. A dream's underlying meaning
_D_ 4. Kind of unconscious that contains archetypes
_A_ 5. The name for "psychic pain"

a. anxiety
b. psychosocial
c. ego
d. collective unconscious
e. latent meaning

Trait theories

_C_ 1. Traits that reflect tastes and preferences according to Allport
_D_ 2. Another name for individual traits
_B_ 3. Habitual ways of responding to the world according to Allport
_A_ 4. A person who withdraws from social contacts and responsibilities.
_E_ 5. A person oriented toward the outside world; outgoing and sociable

a. introvert
b. central traits
c. secondary traits
d. personal dispositions
e. extravert

Behavioral theories

_a_   1. Should look at only two components of personality: environment and behavior

_B_   2. Should look at behavior, the environment, and
the person who is performing in order to explain
personality.

_D_   3. Personal judgment of one's own competence in
a specific situation

_C_   4. Interaction of environment, behavior, and the
person that determines behavior

a. Skinner's radical
behaviorism
b. social learning
theory
c. reciprocal determin-
ism
d. self-efficacy

Humanistic theories

_D_   1. The most basic psychological and physiological
needs, according to Maslow

_C_   2. The range of possible experiences, according to
Rogers

_E_   3. "Unfulfilled growth needs," according to
Maslow

_A_   4. People who are fulfilled doing their best,
according to Maslow

_B_   5. People who are psychologically adjusted, according to Rogers

a. self-actualized
b. fully functioning
c. organism
d. deficiency needs
e. metapathologies

PRACTICE EXAM 1

1.   In Allport's scheme of things, what kind of trait *cannot* be measured by a standardized test?

    a.   cardinal traits
    b.   secondary traits
    c.   common traits
    d.   personal dispositions (individual traits)

                                 (Factual, Obj. 2.1)

2.   Martin works for a film company. He was recently asked to develop and produce an
opening scene to a movie that would communicate the movie's scary, macabre tone.
Martin used a lot of dark, animalistic, shadowy figures. Jung would say that people would
respond to these images because they are:

    a.   archetypes
    b.   condensations
    c.   projections
    d.   free associations

                                 (Conceptual, Obj. 1.4)

3.   Which of the following is not a criticism of trait theories?

    a.   Providing a label does not provide an explanation.
    b.   Trait theories lure people into using circular explanations.
    c.   Traits emphasize individual differences too much.
    d.   There is little evidence that traits persist across situations.

                                 (Factual, Obj. 2.3)

4. Gilda is the kind of person who tends to think the worst possible thing will happen when something stressful occurs, such as losing her job or breaking off a romance. Pauline, on the other hand, views these situations as a potential challenge, a chance to make things better. What social learning concept might be used to "explain" these different personality reactions?

   a. competencies
   b. encodings
   c. values
   d. plans

(Conceptual, Obj. 3.1)

5. According to Dollard and Miller, conflict occurs:

   a. when avoidance and approach tendencies have equal strength
   b. when a person is under stimulus control
   c. when persons perceive an inconsistency between their behavior and their personality traits
   d. when a person is not fully functioning

(Factual, Obj. 3.1)

6. According to Skinner's radical behaviorism, to describe a person as "affectionate" is to describe what?

   a. a brief summation of this person's "nature"
   b. a common trait in this person
   c. this person's previous history of reinforcement
   d. a possible personal disposition in this individual *only*

(Conceptual, Obj. 3.1)

7. If a person fights frequently, Freud would say he or she has a strong aggressive instinct; if a person is promiscuous, Freud might say he or she had a strong sexual drive. This illustrates a problem in Freudian theory called a bias in:

   a. sample size
   b. inference/interpretation
   c. hindsight
   d. reifying of concepts

(Conceptual, Obj. 1.5)

8. Social learning theory uses a number of concepts to explain both a person's uniqueness and his or her consistency in behavior. What concept is defined as a unique set of skills for dealing with various situations?

   a. competencies
   b. encodings
   c. values
   d. plans

(Factual, Obj. 3.1)

9. Freud encountered many patients who seemed to have a neurological disorder, such as "glove anesthesia," for which he could find no known physical basis. Freud categorized these disorders as:

   a. nerve damage cases
   b. hysterical disorders
   c. psychosomatic symptoms
   d. anxiety disorders

(Factual, Obj. 1.2)

10. Frances is a caseworker who works with welfare clients. Although she's only been in the system one year, she's feeling alienated, apathetic, and cynical. Maslow would describe Frances' condition as:

    a.   being overwhelmed by deficiency needs
    b.   metapathological
    c.   conditional positive regard
    d.   not fully functioning

    (Conceptual, Obj. 4.1)

11. Which of the following is *not* a criticism of psychoanalysis?

    a.   It did not stimulate a lot of thought or research interest.
    b.   The basic concepts of the theory have been difficult to test.
    c.   The theory relies too heavily on inference and interpretation.
    d.   The theory was based on a small sample size.

    (Factual, Obj. 1.5)

12. Which of the following phrases *best* describes the major contribution Freud made to treating emotional problems in therapy?

    a.   He championed the "group approach."
    b.   He championed the "talking cure."
    c.   He championed the "medical approach."
    d.   He championed the "social approach."

    (Conceptual, Obj. 1.5)

PRACTICE EXAM 2

1. Before retiring to bed one night, Meryl turned up her electric blanket to the highest setting. She hopped into a toasty bed, fell asleep, and proceeded to dream about having a deadly fever in which she was in a lot of pain but her mouth was paralyzed and she couldn't call or scream to anybody. What is the *manifest* content of this dream?

    a.   Things are really "hot" in Meryl's life right now.
    b.   She feels helpless in her life right now and no one will help.
    c.   She would like to ask someone for help but just can't bring herself to do it.
    d.   She has a fever, is in pain, and can't call out for help because her mouth is paralyzed.

    (Conceptual, Obj. 1.1)

2. Which of the following is *not* an expression of the unconscious according to Freud?

    a.   dream content
    b.   slips of the tongue
    c.   jokes
    d.   basic hostility

    (Factual, Obj. 1.1)

3. Suppose you likened the personality structure, as Freud discussed it, to a horse that is being ridden by a rider. In this analogy, the horse would represent the _____ part of the personality.

    a.   id
    b.   ego
    c.   superego
    d.   all of the above

    (Conceptual, Obj. 1.1)

4. Freud identified one "positive" defense mechanism. What is that one?

    a.   rationalization
    b.   projection
    c.   sublimation
    d.   denial

                                                          (Factual, Obj. 1.2)

5. If you could describe Tony in one word, it would be ambitious. The way he approaches people, his job, even his family is in terms of how it will profit his future. We could say that this all-consuming "ambition" is a(n):

    a.   cardinal trait
    b.   central trait
    c.   secondary trait
    d.   individual trait

                                                      (Conceptual, Obj. 2.1)

6. Which of the following is *not* one of Eysenck's critical dimensions for understanding normal human behavior?

    a.   extroversion-introversion
    b.   neuroticism-stability
    c.   passiveness-aggressiveness
    d.   psychoticism–self-control

                                                          (Factual, Obj. 2.1)

7. Maslow described a hierarchy of personality needs that motivate the individual. The basic physiological and psychological needs, Maslow called:

    a.   deficiency needs
    b.   primary needs
    c.   metaneeds
    d.   growth needs

                                                          (Factual, Obj. 4.1)

8. Kirk's parents inadvertently tell him, "We *love* you so much when you get As on your report card." Rogers would describe this as:

    a.   metapathological
    b.   conditional positive reward
    c.   deficiency needs
    d.   conditions of worth

                                                      (Conceptual, Obj. 4.2)

9. Based on his notions of psychosexual development, what segment of the life span would Freud say was most critical to personality development?

    a.   first five years
    b.   the school years
    c.   adolescent sexually mature years
    d.   the total life span

                                                      (Conceptual, Obj. 1.3)

10. Which part of the mind corresponds to the hereditary aspect in Jung's scheme of things?

   a.   personal unconscious
   b.   collective unconscious
   c.   basic anxiety
   d.   basic hostility

(Factual, Obj. 1.4)

11. Which of the following is *not* a criticism voiced by Mischel against trait theories?

   a.   Correlations between personality trait measures and behavior rarely exceed 0.30.
   b.   Broad personality-trait measures are of little value in predicting behavior outside of test situations.
   c.   There is no reason to expect consistency across situations; people have been reinforced for particular responses in particular situations.
   d.   We pay more attention to later conflicting behaviors in people, not to first impressions.

(Factual, Obj. 2.3)

12. Glen would like to go to a critically acclaimed European movie playing exclusively at a downtown theater. However, it's in a bad section of town, he'll have to pay a parking fee, and the ticket prices are a bit high. What would you call this dilemma?

   a.   deficiency needs versus metaneeds
   b.   an approach-avoidance conflict
   c.   reinforcement control versus cognitive control
   d.   individual trait (or personal disposition) to avoid danger

(Conceptual, Obj. 3.1)

■   **ANSWER KEY**   ■

Concept 1

1.	a	5.	b
2.	c	6.	f
3.	d	7.	g
4.	h	8.	e

Concept 2

1.	e	4.	d
2.	b	5.	c
3.	a		

Concept 3

1.	d	4.	c
2.	e	5.	b
3.	a		

Concept 4

Critical point 1: d   Critical point 4: b
Critical point 2: c   Critical point 5: e
Critical point 3: a

Concept 5

1. c
2. a
3. b

Chapter Exercise

Psychoanalytic theories

1. b   4. d
2. c   5. a
3. e

Trait theories

1. c   4. a
2. d   5. e
3. b

Behavioral theories

1. a   3. d
2. b   4. c

Humanistic theories

1. d   4. a
2. c   5. b
3. e

Practice Exam 1

1. d, p. 515
2. a, p. 508
3. c, pp. 518–519
4. b, p. 521
5. a, p. 520
6. c, pp. 520–521
7. c, p. 512
8. b, p. 521
9. b, p. 503
10. b, p. 526
11. a, pp. 512–513
12. b, p. 513

Practice Exam 2

1. d, p. 503
2. d, p. 503
3. a, p. 504
4. c, p. 506
5. a, p. 514
6. c, p. 515
7. a, p. 526
8. b, p. 527
9. a, p. 507
10. b, p. 508
11. d, p. 519
12. b, p. 520

CHAPTER EIGHTEEN
Psychological Disorders

KEY TERM ORGANIZER

Within the field of psychology there are several ways of defining abnormality, illustrated in the following chart.

Approach	Definition	Example
Norm violation	Breaking or not observing the "rules of society" (usually bizarre violation)	Pedophilia
Statistical abnormality	Substantial deviation from a statistically calculated average	Scoring very low (or very high) on an IQ test
Personal discomfort	Judging one's own normality and expressing distress over one's behavior	Personal concern over a deep lack of assertiveness
Maladaptive behavior	Behavior that interferes with social and personal functioning	Severe obsessions
Deviation from an ideal	Deviating from some description of an ideal well-adjusted personality	Not feeling "self-actualized" or "fully functioning"

Societies have always explained and defined deviant behavior according to their own particular philosophical and religious outlooks. Typical explanations for psychological disturbances have been gods, demons, disease, and emotional stress. Theorists today tend to draw on both *biogenic* and *psychogenic* explanations.

The neuroscientific perspective focuses on genes, biochemistry, and neurological impairment, but it does not rely on the medical model or suggest that most abnormal behavior is the result of biological abnormality. For example, the *catecholamine hypothesis* views depression as a result of low brain levels of norepinephrine, and mania by high levels.

Theorists with a *psychoanalytic perspective* hold that mental disorders have their roots in childhood, when the structure of personality is formed. If the child fails to resolve life's early conflicts between pleasure and discipline, the balance among id, ego, and superego is disturbed, producing *anxiety*.

Historical Theory	Originator	Basic Assumptions	Modern-Day Perspectives
Biogenic theory	Kraepelin	Mental disorders have physiological causes	Neuroscience
Psychogenic theory	Mesmer	Mental disorders result from emotional stress	Psychoanalytic Behaviorial Humanistic-Existential Social-Cognitive

Theorists with a *behavioral perspective* believe that the learning principles of classical and instrumental conditioning can explain the development of abnormal behavior. They assume that abnormal behavior is learned in the same way as any other behavior.

Coming from a *social-cognitive perspective,* theorists view abnormal behavior in terms of learning theory *and* human thought processes. They believe that the way we interpret events may be even more important than the events themselves.

Theorists with a *humanistic-existential perspective* interpret psychological disorders as the result of an incongruence between the self and its goals that people have produced in order to gain the acceptance of others; existential theorists view disorders as the result of the anxiety that arises when people are unable to find meaning in their lives.

The generally accepted classification of abnormal behavior is that provided by the American Psychiatric Association in its *Diagnostic and Statistical Manual (DSM–III).* This manual, tied to the medical model, views psychological problems as diseases with specific symptoms, causes, predictable courses, and treatments. The *DSM–III* does not assume that these disorders have a biological cause. This labeling system has major advantages in both treatment and the advancement of knowledge. The disadvantages are the medical model's labeling of people as "sick," the illusion that naming a disorder explains it, the stigmatizing of people by attaching labels to their behavior, and the unreliability of diagnoses. However, the *DSM–III* provides the most practical classification system yet devised.

There are six major categories of psychological disorders.

Disorder	Definition	Types
Anxiety disorders	Feelings of apprehension that interfere with normal social and psychological functioning	Generalized anxiety disorders, free floating anxiety, panic disorders, obsessions, compulsions, phobias
Somatoform disorders	A display of symptoms with no apparent organic cause	Hypochondriasis, conversion disorders
Dissociative disorders	Splitting off certain kinds of behaviors that are normally integrated	Amnesia, fugue, multiple personality
Mood disorders	Severe mood disturbances	Major depression, bipolar disorder, dysthemia, cyclothymia
Schizophrenia (psychotic disorder)	Disintegration of the mind as an operating whole	Hebephrenic, catatonic, paranoid, undifferentiated, residual
Social disorders	Self-defeating, maladaptive personality patterns	Antisocial personality, sexual deviances, sociopaths, psychoactive substance abuse

Schizophrenia is one of the more common disorders studied. It is characterized by disordered thought (including *delusions, clang associations, perseveration,* and a *loosening of associations*), disordered perceptions (including *hallucinations*), and bizarre behavior.

Psychogenic and biogenic theories of abnormal behavior should be seen as complementary, providing an integrated perspective on the development of disorders. For example, genetic studies of schizophrenia, in which the disorder is traced in families and which uses studies of twins and of children adopted in infancy, indicate that heredity plays some role in schizophrenia. According to the *diathesis-stress model,* environmental stress allows a genetic predisposition (a diathesis) to schizophrenia to develop:

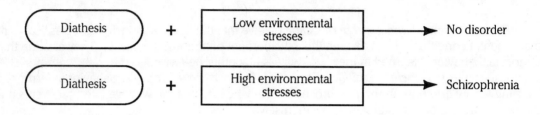

As for biochemical abnormalities, schizophrenics with positive symptoms may have abnormal levels of dopamine, a neurotransmitter (the *dopamine hypothesis*).

MAJOR CONCEPTS AND LEARNING OBJECTIVES:

CONCEPT 1   There are a number of definitions of abnormality, and each major perspective in psychology has its own approach to understanding the causes of abnormality.

                           1.1   Identify and distinguish the various definitions of abnormality.

                           1.2   Distinguish the neuroscientific, psychoanalytic, behavioral, social-cognitive, and humanistic-existential perspectives concerning abnormality.

                           1.3   Describe the classification scheme used by the *DSM–III.*

Concept Builder 1

Directions: Below are five comments from leading practicing psychologists on their definition of abnormality. Your task is to identify the criterion each is using to define abnormality from the list below.

        a.   norm violation
        b.   statistical
        c.   personal discomfort
        d.   maladaptive
        e.   deviation from an ideal

The Phyllis Donahue Show:
An Interview with Five Leading Therapists

Phyllis: "Thank you all for appearing here today on the Phyllis Donahue Show. Now, I wonder if you would each sum up your positions by giving the audience a one-sentence statement of your definition of abnormality."

Panelist 1: "Phyllis, I have a very fundamental definition. If you violate society's rules and expectations for behaving, then technically you're abnormal."

Criterion of panelist 1: _____

Phyllis: "But Dr. Breaker—may I call you Norm? Are you aware of a saying by gay people that goes, 'On Dec. 1, 1974, I was cured of my homosexuality,' reflecting the then-current DSM–II's dropping homosexuality as an inherent abnormality?"

Norm: "Yes, Phyllis, I am, but you see, the 'rules' society uses change."

Panelist 2: "Phyllis, I believe another way of defining abnormality is to call a behavior abnormal if it interferes with the person's social and personal functioning; this focuses on people's behavior in relation to others."

Criterion of panelist 2: _____

Phyllis: "Oh, I see, but there's a problem here; what if that person doesn't recognize that they have a problem, even though they are behaving dysfunctionally?"

Panelist 3: "That's why we need a more objective standard, one that bases abnormal classifications on scores obtained through a series of accepted psychological tests."

Criterion of panelist 3: _____

Phyllis: "Oh, the almighty test! Well, Professor Rorschach, that's no good. Would you believe that in college I took a career test and because of my low score, I was told that I probably would not succeed in any kind of entertainment field?"

Dr. Rorschach: "Yes, Phyllis, I would believe that."

Panelist 4: "Please, everyone. We now have many detailed personality descriptions of well-adjusted people. If a person deviates from this idealized profile, they may be experiencing some form of abnormality."

Criterion of panelist 4: _____

Phyllis: "So, if you're not a carbon copy of Sigmund Freud on two legs, you're imperfect, abnormal. Boy, now I know why they call you guys 'shrinks.'" *[Audience applauds.]*

Panelist 5: "Phyllis, all these points are debatable: we know that. My own criterion is simple: If a person judges his or her own behavior and expresses concern over some perceived behavior, then he or she is a candidate for therapy."

Criterion of panelist 5: _____

Phyllis: "Well Dr. Feelgood, let me tell you, after listening to these definitions of abnormality, I'm not feeling so normal myself."

Dr. Feelgood: "Well, Phyllis, I'm free after the show if you'd like to talk about it."

CONCEPT 2

Anxiety disorders, somatoform disorders, dissociative disorders, and major affective disorders are independent categories of the *DSM–III–R*. These are diagnostic labels that describe common patterns of abnormal functioning.

2.1 Describe anxiety and identify the major anxiety disorders.

2.2 Define somatoform disorders and describe hypochondriasis and conversion disorders.

2.3 Describe the three syndromes that are included in dissociative disorders.

2.4 Distinguish bipolar disorder from major depression and define dysthemia and cyclothymia.

2.5 Discuss the explanations for anxiety disorders, somatoform disorders, dissociative disorders, and affective disorders.

Concept Builder 2

Directions: Pretend that you are a volunteer working for your community mental health center's "hot line" service. As the calls are phoned in, it is your job to make a quick diagnosis based on the symptoms reported by the caller:

Hot Line

_____ 1. I feel completely worthless about myself; I don't feel attractive or bright; I've been contemplating suicide.

_____ 2. I just had a horrible experience that lasted for about 20 minutes. I felt an overwhelming sense of disaster overtaking me. My heart was pounding. I was sweating and shivering, and my breathing was very shallow and difficult.

_____ 3. I lost my sense of hearing this morning. My wife and I were bitterly arguing all night long about our upcoming divorce. My hearing came back as abruptly as it left, but I'm afraid it will go again.

_____ 4. I'm calling about my brother; he had been missing from home for three days and the police just found him. He claims he remembers nothing about his flight from home. He's very disoriented.

_____ 5. My moods lately have been like an elevator—up one minute, down the next. When I'm "up," I'm talking a mile a minute, can't sleep, and feel absolutely euphoric. Then I hit rock bottom, feeling totally depressed.

_____ 6. I have a persistent fear that I'm going to be left alone; I can't leave work or a party, or even get off the bus because I can't stand the thought of going home and being alone. Please don't hang up on me.

a. panic attack

b. phobic disorder

c. conversion disorder

d. fugue

e. major depression

f. bipolar disorder

CONCEPT 3   Schizophrenia is a severe disorder characterized by a generalized failure of functioning in thought, perception, adaptation. Between one and two percent of the population will have at least one episode of schizophrenia.

3.1   Define schizophrenia and describe the types of schizophrenia.

3.2   Outline and describe the major symptoms of schizophrenia.

3.3   Review the explanations of schizophrenia given by each perspective discussed in the text.

Concept Builder 3

Directions: You are a budding clinical psychologist serving your one-year internship in a mental hospital. You and the other residents are in an observation room, watching the chief psychologist and a schizophrenic patient. Identify the symptoms that are occurring as the interview proceeds.

a.   clang associations
b.   delusion of thought
c.   disorder of perceptions (hallucinations)

d.   disorders of mood
e.   disorder of motor behavior (catatonic stupor)
f.   perseveration

Portrait of a Schizophrenic

Doctor: "Victor, why don't you tell me what you've been doing all morning."

Patient: "Oh, scribbling and bibbling, bibbling and scribbling. Nibbling and cribbling."
    Symptom 1: _____

Doctor: "I don't understand, Victor."

Patient: "You see that picture on the wall?" *[points to mirror]* "It's telling me what to say, it's controlling me. It curses at me when I mess up."
    Symptom 2: _____

Doctor: "Victor, you've spent the last ten minutes tapping your head with both hands very hard. Do you have a headache?"
    Symptom 3: _____

Patient: "They're stealing thoughts out of my head. They go on cassette tape, in Dolby stereo, then they're played on rock videos for everyone to hear and see."
    Symptom 4: _____

Doctor: "Victor, you didn't start saying that until the horrible tragedy occurred—your parents dying in the house fire."

Patient: *[laughs uncontrollably]* "Boy, that was a good one, wasn't it, Doc?"
    Symptom 5: _____

Doctor: "Victor, would you like to go back to the ward now, or stay here and talk?"

Patient: "Stay here and talk, stay here and talk, stay here and talk . . ." (Victor repeats this phrase for five minutes.)
    Symptom 6: _____

CONCEPT 4   Social disorders include personality disorders, sexual disorders, and substance abuse disorders because they all involve long-standing habits of thought and behavior with social complications.

4.1   Define personality disorder and describe antisocial personality, or sociopath.

4.2   Describe how a sexual behavior may be classified as a sexual disorder.

4.3   Describe the effects of alcohol abuse and how substance use may be viewed as substance abuse.

Concept Builder 4

Directions: As a police officer, you encounter may suspects who are in need of psychological help. This week Sergeant Columbo from Vice Squad is briefing you on suspects that may also be sexually deviant. (Remember, this is a cop describing the deviances, not a psychologist.) What deviances is he describing?

Vice Squad: Profiles of Sexual Deviants

_____ 1. This individual is basically what you might call your "peeping Tom." He secretly watches others' sexual activities or secretly views their private body parts.

_____ 2. This individual, usually a man, gets his sexual gratification by dressing in "drag," or women's clothes.

_____ 3. We're finding more of this type of deviant in porno rings. He finds sexual pleasure through contact with children.

_____ 4. This next individual feels "trapped" in the wrong body; this feeling is so strong that the individual may have an operation to change gender.

a. fetishist
b. transvestite
c. transsexual
d. voyeur
e. pedophile
f. sadist
g. masochist

These next two personalities go together like a pair of bookends.

_____ 5. This person likes to be on the receiving end of pain while having sex.

_____ 6. This person likes to be on the giving end of pain during sexual expression.

_____ 7. Finally, this individual gets sexual gratification by touching or looking at some object; sometimes the turn-on is a specific part of the body other than the genitals.

CHAPTER EXERCISE   *Directions: Read the following definitions of the disorders covered in your text and fill in the appropriate terms from the key terms listed at the end of Chapter 18.*

DSM–III: A Mini-Version

Anxiety Disorders

1. When anxiety is an intense, irrational fear: _____

2. Panic attacks preceded by no specific stimulus: _____

3. An action that a person uncontrollably performs again and again: _____

Somatoform Disorders

4. The preoccupation with bodily symptoms as possible signs of serious illness:

   _____

5. Disorders in which an individual develops some physical dysfunction that has no organic basis and apparently expresses some psychological conflict:

   _____

Dissociative Disorders

6. Partial or total loss of memory: _____

7. A division into two or more complete behavior organizations, each well defined and highly distinct from the others: _____

Major Affective Disorders

8. One or more major depressive episodes with no intervening episodes of euphoria:

   _____

9. Disorder characterized by extreme moods, beginning with mania and followed by depression: _____

Schizophrenia

10. A tendency to dwell on the primary association to a given stimulus: _____

11. Illogical speech in which each sentence is generated from some mental stimulus in the preceding sentence: _____

12. Distortions of sensory perception: _____

Social Disorders

13. Another name for sociopath: _____

14. Inflexible and maladaptive personality traits: _____

15. Drug use that interferes with social and occupational functioning: _____

**PRACTICE
EXAM 1**

1. With the publication of the *DSM–III,* many "gay" people jokingly said that they were cured of homosexuality. That was when the American Psychiatric Association relaxed its standards about homosexuality because society regarded it more as an alternative "life-style" than an abnormality. This illustrates what criterion of abnormality?

   a. norms
   b. statistical abnormality
   c. personal discomfort
   d. maladaptive behavior

   (Conceptual, Obj. 1.3)

2. The *DSM–III* is tied historically to which person?

   a. Hippocrates
   b. Freud
   c. Kraepelin
   d. Mesmer

   (Factual, Obj. 1.3)

3. Jerrold, a psychiatric aide working in a mental ward, was asked why one of the patients had delusional thought patterns. Jerrold responded, "He's schizophrenic." How do you know he's schizophrenic?" he was asked in return. "Because he has delusions," was the reply. Jerrold is illustrating one problem in using psychiatric labels. What is that problem?

   a. Labels treat people as "sick."
   b. Labels give the illusion of explanation.
   c. Labels stigmatize people.
   d. Labels are unreliably applied.

   (Conceptual, Obj. 1.3)

4. Which of the most common phobias below exists in 3 to 6 percent of the population?

   a. speech phobia
   b. snake phobia
   c. hydrophobia, or fear of water
   d. agoraphobia

   (Factual, Obj. 2.1)

5. Inez, a woman in her early fifties, is frightened that she may have breast cancer. She has discovered a new "lump" in one of her breasts and is angry at her doctor for dismissing it as a harmless cyst. She's very well read on the subject of breast cancer and can tell you of the latest treatments. She's switching doctors again to see if she can't get the confirmation she knows to be true. Inez is probably developing:

   a. a conversion disorder
   b. hypochondriasis
   c. major depression
   d. psychosomatic illness

   (Conceptual, Obj. 2.2)

6. Which of the following is *not* a dissociative disorder?

   a. amnesia
   b. fugue
   c. multiple personality
   d. schizophrenia

   (Factual, Obj. 2.5)

7. The Troutmans' son committed suicide. In discussing their son's death, Mrs. Troutman told the psychologist that Sonny saw himself as not very attractive to girls; was fatigued most of the time; had been sleeping to excess in recent months; and did not spend any time working on his car, which he used to love to do. Sonny would have probably been diagnosed as developing:

    a.   generalized anxiety disorder
    b.   a panic disorder
    c.   major depression
    d.   bipolar disorder

                                                        (Conceptual, Obj. 3.4)

8. Schizophrenics often speak in rhymes or similar-sounding words. This disturbance of thought and speech is called:

    a.   clang association
    b.   perseveration
    c.   flattened affect
    d.   delusion

                                                        (Factual, Obj. 3.2)

9. Nurse Ratchett went to ask one of the schizophrenic patients what he wanted for lunch and the patient snapped back, "I can't make another decision today . . . decisions, decisions . . . they're too many . . . I can't . . ." This perseveration in the schizophrenic's behavior illustrates a disorder of:

    a.   perception
    b.   motor behavior
    c.   affect
    d.   thought

                                                        (Conceptual, Obj. 4.2)

10. Which form of schizophrenia is the most severe form of disintegration?

    a.   hebephrenic
    b.   catatonic
    c.   paranoid
    d.   undifferentiated

                                                        (Factual, Obj. 3.1)

11. You go to the library on campus and see that there is only one other person there (not surprising). He is wearing a trench coat and tennis sneakers. As you approach him to ask for the time, he "flashes" you. He is probably a(n):

    a.   sadist
    b.   librarian
    c.   exhibitionist
    d.   voyeur

                                                        (Conceptual, Obj. 4.2)

12. What percentage of people in the U.S. have had or will have at least one schizophrenic episode?

    a.   1–2 percent
    b.   5 percent
    c.   10 percent
    d.   17 percent

                                                        (Factual, Obj. 3.1)

PRACTICE EXAM 2

1. The diagnosis of mental retardation is most often made using the _____ criterion of abnormality.

    a. norm
    b. statistical
    c. maladaptive
    d. deviation from an ideal

    (Factual, Obj. 1.1)

2. Bonnie has been depressed ever since arriving at college. She aspires to be a physician but her mother keeps insisting that she be a nurse. Bonnie's unhappiness is spoiling her enthusiasm for classes, and her apathy is starting to jeopardize her grade point average. Bonnie decided her problems were getting to be overwhelming, so she went to the counseling center for help. This illustrates what criterion of abnormality?

    a. norm violation
    b. personal discomfort
    c. statistical abnormality
    d. deviation from an ideal

    (Conceptual, Obj. 1.1)

3. Which of the following is not an advantage of the *DSM–III–R* system of classification?

     a. The *DSM–III–R* provides a "special language" for behavioral disorders.
    b. The label attached to the abnormal behavior offers a useful explanation for it.
    c. If an individual's problem is accurately described, prognosis and treatment are more easily decided.
    d. A classification system makes possible advancements of knowledge about various disorders.

    (Factual, Obj. 1.3)

4. In the movie *The Caine Mutiny,* Humphrey Bogart played a Captain Quigg who was overbearing and highly suspicious of his crew members. Captain Quigg had an odd mannerism that he performed over and over again. He would uncontrollably fondle ball bearings in his hand, over and over. This ritualistic behavior illustrates:

    a. free-floating anxiety
    b. panic disorder
    c. an obsession
    d. a compulsion

    (Conceptual, Obj. 2.1)

5. People are sometimes mistakenly diagnosed as having a conversion disorder, when later it is discovered that they are developing:

    a. hypochondriasis
    b. an organic brain syndrome
    c. a neurological disorder
    d. a generalized anxiety disorder

    (Factual, Obj. 2.2)

6. The missing persons bureau picked up an older man who had been reported missing for six months by his family. The man had apparently left home and didn't come back. He had gotten a completely different job and had a totally different lifestyle. He remembered none of his "new" life when the police found him wandering around a vacant lot. It would appear that this man is suffering from:

   a. amnesia
   b. a fugue state
   c. multiple personality
   d. schizophrenia

   (Conceptual, Obj. 2.1)

7. Which disorder is the most frequent problem in outpatient clinics?

   a. depression
   b. bipolar disorder
   c. schizophrenia
   d. panic attack

   (Factual, Obj. 2.4)

8. Karen has been diagnosed as schizophrenic because of frequent delusions. Specifically, she believes that television editors are somehow stealing her ideas for new television shows and using them to make big money. They have some sort of technological radar-scanner that picks up her every thought. This illustrates the type of delusion involving:

   a. thought broadcasting
   b. thought transmission
   c. thought insertion
   d. thought withdrawal

   (Conceptual, Obj. 3.2)

9. Schizophrenics frequently show inappropriate emotional responses, or none at all. This disturbance indicates a disorder of:

   a. perception
   b. thought
   c. mood
   d. volition

   (Factual, Obj. 3.2)

10. During Frank's trial for the murder of his business associate, Frank's lawyer asked that he be placed under psychiatric observation. Frank showed no emotion or remorse over the murder, was impulsive, reckless, and did not honor his own financial obligations. Frank's lawyer suggested his defendant was a(n):

    a. schizophrenic
    b. sociopath
    c. amnesiac
    d. multiple personality

    (Conceptual, Obj. 4.1)

11. Which of the following is *false* regarding alcoholism?

    a. Alcoholism is the most serious drug problem in the United States.
    b. Alcohol is a stimulant.
    c. Alcoholics build up a tolerance for alcohol.
    d. Prolonged alcoholism leads to degenerative brain disease.

    (Factual, Obj. 4.3)

12. It is thought that many people harbor a variety of allergic susceptibilities (such as pollen, seafood, dog/cat dander), but that many people won't develop the allergic reactions provided the environmental stresses (or contaminants) are not present in high degrees. This disposition to develop allergies is remarkably similar to what concept (used to explain the development of schizophrenia)?

a. dopamine hypothesis
b. diathesis-stress model
c. psychogenic model
d. biogenic model

(Conceptual, Obj. 3.3)

■ ANSWER KEY ■

Concept 1

Panelist 1: a   Panelist 4: e
Panelist 2: d   Panelist 5: c
Panelist 3: b

Concept 2

1. e   4. d
2. a   5. f
3. c   6. b

Concept 3

Symptom 1: a   Symptom 4: b
Symptom 2: c   Symptom 5: d
Symptom 3: e   Symptom 6: f

Concept 4

1. d   5. f
2. b   6. g
3. e   7. a
4. c

Chapter Exercise

1. phobic disorder
2. panic disorder
3. compulsion
4. hypochondriasis
5. conversion disorder
6. amnesia
7. multiple personality
8. major depression
9. bipolar disorder
10. perseveration
11. loosening of associations
12. hallucinations
13. antisocial personality
14. personality disorders
15. psychoactive substance dependence

Practice Exam 1

1. a, p. 534
2. c, p. 536
3. b, pp. 539–540
4. d, p. 542
5. b, p. 546
6. d, pp. 546–547
7. c, p. 548
8. a, p. 553
9. b, p. 553
10. a, p. 553
11. c, p. 559
12. a, p. 552

Practice Exam 2

1. b, p. 534
2. b, p. 535
3. b, p. 539
4. d, p. 544
5. c, p. 546
6. b, p. 547
7. a, p. 548
8. d, p. 553
9. c, p. 554
10. b, p. 558
11. b, pp. 559–560
12. b, p. 557

CHAPTER NINETEEN

Approaches to Treatment

KEY TERM ORGANIZER

All therapies that focus on a dynamic interplay of conscious and unconscious elements are known as *psychodynamic therapies.* A wide variety of professionals treat mental disorders:

Type of Therapist	Therapeutic Settings
Psychiatrists	Private offices
Psychoanalysts	Hospitals
Clinical psychologists	Community mental health centers
Psychiatric social workers	Hot-line centers
Psychiatric nurses	Halfway houses
	Self-help group settings

As developed by Freud, psychoanalysis is both a theory of personality and a form of psychotherapy. In the initial phases of therapy, patients often show signs of *resistance,* or attempts to block treatment. As analysis progresses, the patient may respond to the analyst with strong feelings; this is evidence of *transference.*

In *behavioral therapy,* psychological problems are regarded as learned responses, and the primary target of therapy is the problem behavior itself. Many therapies are based on classical conditioning principles. *Systematic desensitization* is a procedure in which the client relaxes and then is gradually exposed to anxiety-producing stimuli. Clients unlearn anxiety through extinction. *Flooding* might be described as "cold-turkey" extinction therapy. Flooding involves continuous, intense exposure to the anxiety-provoking situation. Instead of using extinction, *aversion therapy* changes emotional responses by pairing the maladaptive response with an aversive stimulus, such as electric shock or nausea-producing drugs. An alternative to the use of painful shock is a technique called *covert sensitization,* in which clients visualize the behavior they are trying to eliminate and then conjure up the image of an extremely painful or revolting stimulus.

Therapists can also use instrumental conditioning principles to strengthen desirable behavior and to extinguish undesirable behavior. In a *token economy,* for example, a wide range of appropriate behaviors are rewarded with conditioned reinforcers (tokens) that can be used to "buy" secondary reinforcers. More recently, the role of cognition has received increasing emphasis. All varieties of *cognitive behavior therapy* attempt to change the way people think about themselves and the world. Therapists who specialize in *modeling* stress observational learning, in which people learn new behavior by watching another person. Some behavior therapists focus on clients' false assumptions about the world. In *cognitive restructuring,* the aim is to identify irrational assumptions and to subject them to the cold light of reason. Perhaps the oldest is *rational-emotive therapy (RET). Self-instructional training* focuses on what is termed "self talk." Instead of changing beliefs, this approach focuses on new ways of thinking and new ways of talking to oneself about the problem. Beck's *cognitive therapy* uses a questioning method that helps people discover for themselves how inappropriate their thoughts have been.

Therapy Based on	Type of Therapy
Classical conditioning and extinction	Systematic desensitization Flooding Aversion therapy Covert sensitization
Instrumental conditioning	Behavioral contracts Token economies
Behavioral and cognitive principles	Participant modeling or behavioral rehearsal Rational-emotive therapy Self-instructional training Cognitive therapy

In *humanistic therapies,* the goal is growth, not cure. The best-known variety of humanistic therapy is Rogers' system of *client-centered therapy,* which is sometimes called nondirective counseling. *Gestalt therapy* is a blend of Freudian concepts and humanistic philosophy. The goal of gestalt therapy is self-awareness and self-responsibility.

There are several types of family therapy. In the *family systems approach,* therapists see people as members of a family social system that consists of interlocking roles. In the *communications approach,* therapists assume that psychological disorder develops in a family whose members' subtle nonverbal signals directly contradict their verbal signals. *Behavioral family therapy,* too, emphasizes family interactions. During therapy, members are made aware of the way their actions reinforce one another's behavior.

Extensive reviews of psychotherapy have found strong evidence for its effectiveness; some reviews have found little difference among the various therapies in their effectiveness, and others have found behavioral therapy to be most effective. No one method has yet been found to be most effective in treating various disorders.

Neuroscience therapies aim at altering the central nervous system. The following are some drug therapies that have been used:

Antianxiety drugs: Mild tranquilizers, such as Valium, are prescribed for anxiety disorders, stress-related disorders, and withdrawal from alcohol.

Antipsychotic drugs: Major tranquilizers, such as Thorazine, are used to alleviate extreme agitation and hyperactivity in psychotic patients; they sometimes have a serious side effect, *tardive dyskinesia,* a muscle disorder.

Antidepressant drugs, such as imipramine, are used to regulate mood; antidepressants have also been helpful in treating depression.

An important aspect shared by all therapies is the relationship between therapist and client, known as the *therapeutic alliance* or the *therapeutic bond*. When the client perceives the therapist as helpful and sympathetic, the chances of substantial improvement or recovery increase.

Community mental health centers may provide outpatient services, inpatient services, emergency services, and training for community workers. Halfway houses can ease the discharged patient's transition into community life. The crisis hot line provides an inexpensive, immediate, effective way to deal with emergencies by telephone.

Nonprofessional interpersonal support for people with problems comes from family, friends, self-help groups, community workers, and paraprofessionals.

Psychologists try to prevent the development of disorder, to detect and treat minor disorders and keep them from becoming major, and to minimize the effects of major disorders on the patients and on society.

Four immediate targets for action toward prevention of psychological disorders include making sure all babies are wanted and healthy, preventing adolescent pregnancy, promoting academic and interpersonal skills, and providing social support for people in stressful situations.

MAJOR CONCEPTS AND LEARNING OBJECTIVES

CONCEPT 1   Psychotherapy is defined as a systematic series of interactions between a therapist trained to treat psychological problems and a person who is to be helped. Psychotherapy is a relatively formal arrangement with a paid professional. Psychodynamic therapy focuses upon the relationship between the unconscious and the conscious elements of the person.

1.1   Define psychotherapy and identify the differences among the professions of psychiatrist, psychologist, psychiatric social worker, psychiatric nurse, and psychoanalyst.

1.2   Define the concepts of resistance and transference and the role they play in psychoanalytic approaches to treatment.

Concept Builder 1

Directions: Read the following notes by a beginning therapist on her brief observations of various clients she has counseled that day. For each entry, identify the psychoanalytic concept being illustrated from the list supplied.

Therapy Log

_____ 1. I confronted Barbara today on her lack of accepting responsibility for her behavior and feelings. She became very perturbed; she started arguing with me, denying that it was true and doing anything to block getting on with today's session. I suspect she may even cancel next week's appointment.

a. repression
b. resistance
c. transference neurosis
d. free association

_____ 2. Walter and I got into a very productive argument today. I commented to him that he had a difficult time taking criticism from others. He asked me who the hell was I to be the almighty judge of mortals and he started criticizing me back. Then Walter had a valuable insight—he realized he had had this type of argument with his father a hundred times. I think we're at the stage now where he will start dealing with this problem in a much more realistic manner.

_____ 3. The session with Roseanne today was very painful. She had always referred to her mother as deceased but never mentioned how her mother had died. Through unrelenting probing on my part, she remembered her mother's death today, but recalled something she had never verbalized before. She finally acknowledged, out loud, that her mother committed suicide.

_____ 4. I asked Bianca to try a "new" technique with me today. I asked her to lie down on my couch and get comfortable. I then briefly asked her to think of her ex-husband and start saying words or phrases that came to mind without censoring them or "cleaning" them up. At first, she was hesitant, but then, the words came flowing forth.

CONCEPT 2   Behavior therapists regard psychological problems as learned responses, so therapy focuses on learning new, more appropriate response patterns.

2.1 Describe and distinguish among the therapies based upon classical conditioning: systematic desensitization, flooding, aversion therapy, and covert sensitization.

2.2 Describe token economies and the instrumental conditioning principles they utilize.

2.3 Describe how modeling and cognitive restructuring use cognition to achieve therapeutic goals.

Concept Builder 2

Directions: Read the various procedures described below for treating different problems and match them to the behavioral technique being used.

Behavior Therapy: Tools of the Trade

_____ 1. In treating a juvenile delinquent, one behavioral therapist in the correctional institution used plastic chips to reward "good" behavior (such as meeting curfew times, not cursing, etc.). The teenage offender could cash in the chips for recreation time, cigarettes, unstructured playtime, or other privileges.

_____ 2. One hospitalized patient had a cleanliness compulsion: she cleaned the floor of her room and disinfected the bathroom practically every hour. To treat this compulsion, she was required to cover the floor with dirt and soiled laundry and place dirty towels and litter in the bathroom. All cleaning materials were removed, and she was not allowed to use any cleaners. After repeated "contaminations" the anxiety normally elicited was completely extinguished.

_____ 3. An obese patient is treated by a technique in which she imagines herself sitting down to eat a huge meal. As she prepares to eat, she visualizes herself becoming violently nauseous. When she takes her first bite of food, she imagines the food swelling up three times its normal size, choking her. In her imaginary scenario her throat tightens up and finally she vomits all over her plate. She then visualizes a "relief" scene in which a decision not to eat is accompanied by pleasurable sensations.

_____ 4. In helping a client deal with the breakup of his marriage, the therapist asked the client to challenge some of his irrational beliefs—that being rejected by someone means that one is unlovable; that being rejected means one is not a worthwhile person. The therapist suggested that he say, instead, it's unfortunate that we broke up, but I'll meet someone new, maybe someone more to my liking, and I will love again.

_____ 5. A businessman who had a fear of flying was treated in several steps. Step one consisted of teaching him deep-muscle relaxation. Step two involved constructing a hierarchy of fears, from least frightening (going to the airport) to most frightening (sitting aboard an airplane accelerating for takeoff). In the final step he was instructed to relax as the therapist described the least anxiety-arousing scene and progressively moved up the hierarchy. At each point the client was instructed to relax until the anxiety diminished.

_____ 6. This procedure was used to help a client develop social skills in conversation. First, the therapist demonstrated verbal and nonverbal ways of dealing with silence, asking relevant questions, and building on information given to sustain conversations. Then the client tried the skills one at a time, starting with low-risk activities and building to high-risk, threatening social situations.

a. systematic desensitization

b. flooding

c. covert sensitization

d. token economies

e. participant modeling

f. rational-emotive therapy

CONCEPT 3   The goal of humanistic psychotherapy is growth, and humanistic therapists encourage clients to work to discover and then to fulfill their own potentials for health. Other therapeutic approaches employ combinations of approaches.

> 3.1   Describe Carl Rogers' system of client-centered therapy and its basic concepts.
>
> 3.2   Discuss the goals and methods of gestalt therapy, group therapy, and family therapy.
>
> 3.3   Review the evidence for the effectiveness of psychotherapy and the reasons for taking an eclectic approach to therapy.

**Concept
Builder 3**

Directions: Read the following phrases and words and identify the brief statement as belonging either to client-centered therapy (CCT) or to gestalt therapy (GT).

Buzz Words

1. Congruence, or genuineness: _____

2. Focus on the spatial: _____

3. Nondirective: _____

4. Empathy and intuition: _____

5. Focus on the act, not the fantasy: _____

6. Carl Rogers: _____

7. Empathic understanding: _____

8. Clients use first-person singular: _____

9. Unconditional positive regard: _____

10. Focus on now, not the past or the future: _____

CONCEPT 4   Biogenic therapy assumes that there are biological causes of mental disorders that can be treated with drugs, electroconvulsive therapy, or psychosurgery.

> 4.1   List and define the classes of drugs used in the treatment of mental illness or mental distress.
>
> 4.2   Distinguish the uses and effects of electroconvulsive therapy and psychosurgery.

**Concept
Builder 4**

*Directions: Pretend you work as an admissions psychologist
for a large psychiatric hospital. Your job is to read the
patient's symptoms and brief history and suggest a probable
treatment from the list of treatments your hospital specializes
in (given to the right).*

Admissions Report

_____ 1. John G. was diagnosed by his physician as depressed, possibly with bipolar disorder.

_____ 2. Sarah H. is severely depressed; she has a long history of medical admissions and treatment by Tofranil, Elavil, and Sinequan; none have given long-term relief of symptoms.

_____ 3. William F. reports that he is feeling an overwhelming sense of anxiety and tension; it may be in part related to his alcohol withdrawal symptoms (after being ordered to stop drinking by his family physician).

_____ 4. Michelle N. is possibly schizophrenic; she had a psychotic episode last night in which she was actively hallucinating and was very agitated.

a. drug therapy: antianxiety drugs

b. drug therapy: antidepressant drugs

c. drug therapy: antipsychotic drugs

d. electroconvulsive therapy (ECT)

CONCEPT 5   Community mental health services are a means of support for the mental patient who has returned to society and may continue to need help. The community service approach also seeks to find ways to prevent mental illness.

5.1   Distinguish the roles of community health service centers, halfway houses, and crisis hot lines.

5.2   Discuss the ways in which psychological disorders can be prevented.

**Concept
Builder 5**

*Directions: Several state legislators have met with a selected
group of community mental health officials to discuss the
future of mental health in their community. The health
officials have submitted four proposals. Read each plan and
identify its basic goal as it relates to the targets outlined by
the National Mental Health Association's Commission on the
Prevention of Mental-Emotional Disabilities.*

1. We would like to propose two elementary school programs. One program would be specifically designed for "latch-key" children. We feel that drug education is critical for this group since their parents work full-time and leave them at home, unsupervised, for two to three hours every evening. The second would be a program on how to play cooperatively with others, to try and reduce the early emphasis on aggressiveness and competitiveness. We would call it the "Everyone's a Winner" program.

   Target goal: _____

2. We would like to propose a community-based program that would deal comprehensively with family planning: parenting skills, prenatal care, and new baby nutrition and care.

   Target goal: _____

3. We would like to propose an intervention program for abused children and/or battered wives, particularly among the single-parent families. Our intervention teams would systematically make frequent home visits, talk with children and parents, provide training on problem-solving and coping skills, and make available support groups for family members where abuse and battering has been a problem.
   Target goal: _____

4. We would like to propose implementing a high school-based program designed to reduce the number of teen-age pregnancies. This program would include an after-school program for all interested teens on "Responsible Sex—Everybody's Business." We will also provide condoms and other contraceptives as part of the broad-based health services system.
   Target goal: _____

a. Make sure that all babies are wanted and healthy
b. Prevent adolescent pregnancy
c. Promote academic mastery and the psychosocial skills in the early school years
d. Provide social support for families in stressful situations

---

CHAPTER EXERCISE

Directions: Read the brief definitions below and fill in the correct terms from the key term list in your text.

Treatment Terminology

Practitioners

1. A professional who has earned a Ph.D. or Psy.D. in clinical psychology:

   _____

2. A person with special training in the technique of psychoanalysis:

   _____

3. A registered nurse who has specialized in psychiatric nursing: _____

4. An M.D. who specializes in treating mental illness: _____

Psychodynamic therapies

5. A client's attempt to block the therapist's treatment: _____

6. A client's transfer to the analyst of childhood feelings toward important people in his or her life, particularly parents: _____

7. Erikson's brand of psychodynamic thought: _____

Behavioral therapies

8. A procedure similar to participant modeling, but applied to social behavior:

    _____

9. People's beliefs that they can successfully execute whatever behavior is required to produce an outcome: _____

10. Clients unlearning anxiety through extinction: _____

11. "Cold-turkey" extinction therapy: _____

12. An alternative to aversion therapy without painful shock: _____

13. "Self talk" therapy: _____

14. Beck's therapy for depression: _____

Humanistic therapies

15. Another word for client-centered therapy: _____

16. Fritz Perls' blend of Freud and humanism: _____

17. The therapist's ability to see the world thorough the eyes of the client:

    _____

18. Continued support of a person regardless of what the person has said or done:

    _____

Family therapies

19. Therapy that sees family distress as result of "coercion": _____

20. Also known as the strategic approach to family therapy: _____

Biomedical therapies

21. The class of drugs to which Valium belongs: _____

22. The class of drugs that includes the tricyclics: _____

23. The class of drugs known as neuroleptics: _____

24. A muscle disorder in which patients grimace and smack their lips uncontrollably:

    _____

25. A shock treatment that induces convulsions: _____

PRACTICE
EXAM 1

1. Which of the following practitioners of psychotherapy *must* have a medical degree?

    a. psychiatrist
    b. psychiatric social workers
    c. clinical psychologist
    d. all of the above

    (Factual, Obj. 1.1)

2. In one of the initial therapy sessions, Tom's therapist suggested that he may have a problem expressing his anger. Tom immediately denied this and started arguing with the therapist, denying that anger was a problem (even though he was shouting at one point). This attempt to block treatment is called:

    a. transference
    b. transference neurosis
    c. resistance
    d. defensive blocking

    (Conceptual, Obj. 1.2)

3. Which of the following techniques might be described as "cold-turkey" extinction therapy?

    a. systematic desensitization
    b. flooding
    c. aversion therapy
    d. covert sensitization

    (Factual, Obj. 2.1)

4. Clinton has a hard time consistently doing his homework. To help him out, his school counselor suggested that for every 15 minutes Clint works on homework, his parents and teachers give a "plastic chip," which he could then exchange for things he likes, such as ice cream, extra recess time, or television privileges. This therapeutic approach is called:

    a. token economy
    b. modeling
    c. cognitive restructuring
    d. contracting

    (Conceptual, Obj. 2.2)

5. Which of the following is *not* a cognitive restructuring technique?

    a. rational-emotive therapy
    b. self-instructional training
    c. participant modeling
    d. cognitive therapy

    (Factual, Obj. 2.3)

6. Rather than condemn Stuart for having an extramarital affair, his therapist emphasizes that he is still a worthy person deserving support, even though he may have behaved in an irresponsible way. Stuart's therapist is demonstrating:

    a. congruence
    b. empathic understanding
    c. unconditional positive regard
    d. efficacy expectations

    (Conceptual, Obj. 3.1)

7. In the _____ approach to family therapy, it is assumed that family members fill certain roles, such as "weak" member, "strong" member, and "scapegoat."

   a. behavioral
   b. systems
   c. communications
   d. sociocultural

   (Factual, Obj. 3.2)

8. Mrs. Sawyer's child has a bed-wetting problem. What type of therapy would probably be most effective in treating this disorder?

   a. aversion therapy
   b. shock therapy
   c. drug therapy
   d. behavior therapy

   (Conceptual, Obj. 2.1)

9. What drug is the most frequently prescribed in the world?

   a. Valium
   b. Librium
   c. aspirin
   d. Thorazine

   (Factual, Obj. 4.1)

10. Which of the neuroscience methods of therapy would you want to avoid if you did *not* want to have irreversible effects produced by the therapy?

    a. shock treatment
    b. antipsychotic medication
    c. systematic desensitization
    d. psychosurgery

    (Conceptual, Obj. 4.2)

11. The Community Mental Health Centers Act of 1963 mandated one mental health center for every _____ members of the U.S. population.

    a. 10,000
    b. 50,000
    c. 100,000
    d. 500,000

    (Factual, Obj. 5.1)

12. Poindexter is terrified of telephoning a woman and asking her out for a date—so much so, that he decided to seek treatment for this social-skill deficiency. Which of the following treatments would be most appropriate?

    a. behavioral rehearsal
    b. modeling
    c. token economy
    d. covert sensitization

    (Conceptual, Obj. 2.3)

PRACTICE EXAM 2

1. Upon visiting her therapist for the first time, Joanna noticed several diplomas and certificate on the reception room wall. One of the certificates stated that Dr. D'Angelo had completed a one-year clinical internship. What kind of practicing therapist is Dr. D'Angelo?

   a. a psychiatrist
   b. a clinical psychologist
   c. a psychoanalyst
   d. a psychiatric social worker

   (Conceptual, Obj. 1.1)

2. According to Freudian psychoanalysis, the patient resorts to using a variety of defense mechanisms, the most important of which is:

   a. regression
   b. denial
   c. repression
   d. displacement

   (Factual, Obj. 1.2)

3. Michael is painfully shy. His therapist is using a technique in which Michael learns first to relax completely, then progressively imagine increasingly more anxiety-provoking scenes, such as approaching a woman to ask for a date, asking her for a date, then going on the date. This technique is called:

   a. covert sensitization
   b. aversion therapy
   c. flooding
   d. systematic desensitization

   (Conceptual, Obj. 2.1)

4. Although your text discusses six major types of treatment that are currently popular, how many distinct forms of psychotherapy have been catalogued?

   a. 25
   b. 50
   c. 100
   d. 1,000

   (Factual, Obj. 1.1)

5. Jan has been fearing statistics class for three quarters. On the first day of class, her instructor had her compute her grade point average and perform several other simple tasks. From then on Jan started believing that she could actually master statistics and be successful at it. A behavioral therapist would describe this change in behavior as the result of:

   a. positive reinforcement
   b. self-instructional training
   c. efficacy expectations
   d. rational-emotive therapy

   (Conceptual, Obj. 2.3)

6. One type of humanistic therapy requires that the clients use the first-person singular ("I am") to show that they take responsibility for their own actions and feelings. This therapy is called:

   a. gestalt therapy
   b. client-centered therapy

    c.   group therapy

    d.   cognitive restructuring therapy

(Factual, Obj. 3.2)

7. The Battered Women's Shelter runs a weekly meeting for abused women. This group offers the women social support from understanding peers and a chance to verbalize their feelings in a safe environment. This method of help would be most accurately described as:

    a.   gestalt therapy

    b.   a self-help group

    c.   client-centered group

    d.   a halfway house

(Conceptual, Obj. 5.1)

8. The first application of the group therapy concept was used on _____ patients.

    a.   obese

    b.   alcoholic

    c.   elderly

    d.   tubercular

(Factual, Obj. 3.2)

9. While touring her state's mental hospital, Melissa was a little disturbed at how the schizophrenic patients, who were on medication, behaved. Some grimaced and smacked their lips uncontrollably. She was later told this was called tardive dyskinesia, an unpleasant side effect of:

    a.   psychosurgery

    b.   shock therapy

    d.   antipsychotic drugs

    d.   aversion therapy

(Conceptual, Obj. 4.1)

10. The most appropriate use of electroconvulsive therapy (ECT) is in the treatment of:

    a.   schizophrenia

    b.   severe depression

    c.   extreme aggressiveness

    d.   amnesia

(Factual, Obj. 4.2)

11. When Marilyn's death was investigated, it appeared that she was drinking heavily and was on some type of medication, prescribed by her psychiatrist. The pill bottle was unmarked, but the medical examiner suspected:

    a.   antianxiety drugs

    b.   antipsychotic drugs

    c.   antidepressant drugs

    d.   antimanic drugs

(Conceptual, Obj. 4.1)

12. Halfway houses are successful in helping all but which of the following types of people?

    a.   drug addicts

    b.   former convicts

    c.   alcoholics

    d.   suicidal patients

(Factual, Obj. 5.1)

■ ANSWER KEY ■

Concept 1
1. b
2. c
3. a
4. d

Concept 2
1. d
2. b
3. c
4. f
5. a
6. e

Concept 3
1. CCT
2. GT
3. CCT
4. CCT
5. GT
6. CCT
7. CCT
8. GT
9. CCT
10. GT

Concept 4
1. b
2. d
3. a
4. c

Concept 5
Proposal 1: c
Proposal 2: a
Proposal 3: d
Proposal 4: b

Chapter Exercise
1. clinical psychologist
2. psychoanalyst
3. psychiatric nurse
4. psychiatrist
5. resistance
6. transference
7. ego psychology
8. behavioral rehearsal
9. self-efficacy
10. systematic desensitization
11. flooding
12. covert sensitization
13. self-instructional training
14. cognitive therapy
15. non-directive counseling
16. gestalt therapy
17. empathic understanding
18. unconditional positive regard
19. behavioral family therapy
20. communications approach
21. antianxiety drugs
22. antidepressant drugs
23. antipsychotic drugs
24. tardive dyskinesia
25. electroconvulsive therapy (ECT)

Practice Exam 1
1. a, p. 568
2. c, p. 570
3. b, pp. 572–573
4. a, p. 574
5. c, p. 575
6. c, p. 577
7. b, p. 579
8. d, p. 571
9. a, p. 584
10. d, p. 586
11. b, p. 587
12. a, p. 575

Practice Exam 2
1. b, p. 568
2. c, pp. 569–570
3. d, p. 572
4. d, p. 569
5. c, pp. 575–576
6. a, p. 578
7. b, p. 590
8. d, p. 579
9. c, pp. 584–585
10. b, p. 586
11. a, p. 584
12. d, pp. 588-589

CHAPTER TWENTY

Health Psychology and Adjustment to Stress

KEY TERM ORGANIZER

The view that mind and body are both involved in health and illness has led to the emergence of *health psychology,* the branch of psychology that deals with how people stay healthy, why they become ill, and how they react when illness develops. Health psychologists assume that biological, psychological, and social processes are all important influences on health and illness.

Establishing and maintaining health is known as *primary prevention:* research in primary prevention indicates that health habits are influenced by social, emotional, and cognition factors. Once established, health habits resist change. According to the *health belief model,* good health practices depend on whether we believe that we are vulnerable to illness and injury and whether we are convinced that changing our behavior will affect our health.

Some intervention strategies used by health psychologists are included in the following chart.

Those Focused on the Individual(s)	Those Based on Societal Action
Direct treatment	Social engineering
Media campaigns	
Workplace and school campaigns	
Community campaigns	

Stress is a pattern of disruptive physiological and psychological reactions to events that threaten our ability to cope. Stressful events appear to affect our health if they involve unpleasant change. The three basic approaches to the study of stress are illustrated in the following chart.

The impact of stress seems to depend on a person's *primary appraisal* (degree of perceived harm) and *secondary appraisal* (degree of perceived coping ability) of events. Hans Selye held that the body responds to stress in three stages: alarm, resistance, and, with continued stress, exhaustion.

Approach	Areas Emphasized	Representative Research
Identify environmental stresses	Change; separation and loss, occupational stress, traumatic events	Holmes and Rahne's SRRS
Analyze psychological and cognitive factors	Primary and secondary appraisal; predictability and control	Learned helplessness
Examine the physiological consequences of stress	Relationship of stress to hypertension, coronary heart disease, and possibly cancer	Selye's general adaptation syndrome Type A personalities

A connection has been found between general environmental stress and hypertension. Studies indicate that people with *Type A personalities* (impatient, competitive, hostile) are vulnerable to coronary heart disease but the same personality pattern may be associated with many different diseases. Intense stress appears to increase susceptibility to cancer by reducing the immune system's ability to function.

Successful *coping* depends on the ability to solve problems and to regulate one's own emotions by changing harmful aspects of the environment and by maintaining a positive self-image and satisfying interpersonal relationships. Some individuals have been termed "hardy" because they seem able to transform potentially stressful situations into less stressful experiences. Several techniques have been devised to help individuals who are not hardy deal more effectively with stress:

1. *Progressive relaxation:* the alternate tensing and relaxing of different muscle groups of the body in a specific sequence.
2. *Autogenic training:* a relaxation procedure that depends on self-suggestion and imagery.
3. *Biofeedback:* a form of operant conditioning designed to make people aware of an unconscious physiological response so they can learn to control it.

All three techniques are aimed at controlling physiological arousal. Other coping strategies involve stress management programs (workshops designed to alter cognitive and behavioral responses) and environmental interventions ("restructuring" the environment to increase control).

MAJOR CONCEPTS AND LEARNING OBJECTIVES

CONCEPT 1   Health psychology is the branch of psychology that deals with how people stay healthy, how they become ill, and how they react when illness develops.

1.1   Compare and distinguish between the health psychology model and the medical model of illness.

1.2   Define primary prevention and discuss the social, emotional, and cognitive influences on health.

Concept Builder 1

Directions: Read each of the following quotes and excerpts out of two medical books unearthed in the year 2000, then determine which book each statement came from: (a) the book written in 1950, based on the traditional medical model, or (b) the more recent book, written in 1990 and based on the health psychology model.

Medical Archives

_____ 1. "We believe that we have isolated the single critical factor in the development of coronary heart disease—blood cholesterol levels."

_____ 2. "Cancer seems to be the result of many factors operating together: a genetic predisposition; overexposure to radiation; one's overall psychological state (tendency to be depressed); and one's general ability to adapt to the social environment."

_____ 3. "The primary focus of our discipline is on pathology—that is, on illness and the factors that bring illness about."

_____ 4. "The disease of this century undoubtedly is stress; a person's biology as well as his or her psychological 'hardiness' determines the likelihood of suffering from stress."

CONCEPT 2   Programs aimed at promoting health have arisen in a number of contexts, at work, in the community, in the media, and at school.

2.1   Outline and described the health-promoting techniques of direct treatment, media campaigns, work and school programs, community program, and social engineering.

Concept Builder 2

Directions: The programs described below were designed to modify Americans' fitness habits to make the nation as a whole more healthy and increase the number of participants in the 1988 Olympics. Match each program to the intervention strategy being used.

The Fitness Revolution

_____ 1. One local high school offered a "fitness recess." Students were rewarded with two hours free time each week for every five hours of participation in a physical education/sports program.

_____ 2. The Olympic committee ran a series of frequent spot announcements on both radio and TV promoting the benefits of exercise, competition, and sports.

_____ 3. College-level physical education courses required their students to use "self-monitoring" along with contingency contracts that made students' grades contingent on their reaching specific fitness goals by the end of the semester.

_____ 4. The senator from Florida proposed a bill making it mandatory that five hours of physical education be given at all levels of public education. He reasoned that society needs to enforce healthy behavior and promote exercise as a way of maintaining health.

a. direct treatment

b. workplace and school campaigns

c. media campaigns

d. social engineering

CONCEPT 3   Stress and the symptoms of stress are very disruptive to health and are directly associated with a number of specific illnesses.

    3.1   Define stress and list and discuss the major sources of stress in the environment.

    3.2   Describe how the relationship between primary and secondary appraisal affects an individual's response to a stressful situation.

    3.3   Compare the effects of control and the effects of helplessness in the response to stressful situations.

    3.4   Outline Hans Selye's general adaptation syndrome and the illnesses that may result from physiological causes related to stress.

Concept Builder 3

Directions: As an actuary (statistician) for a life insurance company, it is your job to determine the "risk" an insurance applicant presents. You've discovered that the Social Readjustment Rating Scale (see Table 20.1 in the text) is a very reliable guide to a person's overall health and risk of being hospitalized for an illness. Which three of the following five applicants would you consider the best insurance risks?

The Actuary

Applicant A   Male who just moved to this area; was recently fired from his previous job, and as a consequence his wife has had to find a job.

Applicant B: Female, pregnant with her second child; has recently separated from her husband. She has been with a consulting firm for five years and has just won the "manager of the year" award.

Applicant C: Older male, two months into retirement; took out a $8,000 mortgage on his home so that he could "change his recreation" dramatically and start having fun with all his spare time.

Applicant D: Male who recently lost his wife; he found the recent Christmas holidays difficult without her.

Applicant E: Female who has had a history of trouble with her boss; recently she switched to a new line of work.

Your choices (3 out of 5): _____ , _____ , and _____

CONCEPT 4   Coping refers to the way of handling external and internal pressures that would otherwise lead to stress.

    4.1   Identify the characteristics of hardiness.

    4.2   Discuss how progressive relaxation, autogenic training, and feedback control the physiological response to stress.

    4.3   Distinguish the concept of stress management from that of environmental restructuring.

**Concept
Builder 4**

Directions: Sarah suffers chronic test anxiety. She experiences disabling levels of stress any time she has to take a test, whatever the subject matter is. She decides to go to her college counseling center for help before it's too late but is overwhelmed by the ways that are available to deal with her stress. Label each of the following techniques for reducing her physiological arousal.

Tackling Stress on Test Day

1. When you seat yourself on test day, sit quietly and repeat to yourself, "I'm very relaxed and at peace with myself, I will remain calm when I receive the test. I will proceed through the whole test in a calm manner and leave the class quietly, knowing I did the best I could."
   Name of technique: _____

2. This technique will require (initially) that you be hooked up to a small, portable blood-pressure sensing device. When your blood pressure reaches a certain level, a light will come on, signaling you to stop and relax. Once you learn to control your blood pressure consciously during test sessions, you will no longer need this device.
   Name of technique: _____

3. This technique requires that you participate in a weekly session of deep muscle relaxation. You will learn how to tense, then relax, all the muscles of your body in a certain sequence. This procedure will eventually allow you to completely relax in a very short time when you go into the classroom to take an exam.
   Name of technique: _____

**CHAPTER
EXERCISE**

Directions: In large blocks below are the letters that spell out "stress." Complete each of the phrases which follow by writing out the correct term in the blank spaces provided. Under some of the blanks you will find either an X or a +. The X means to cross out that letter in the box at the top of this exercise; the + means to write that letter in the appropriate box at the bottom of the exercise. The number in the block corresponds to the number of the definition.

Stamp Out Stress

1 S	2 T	3 R	4 E	5 S	6 S

1. Impatient, highly competitive individuals: (Sample)

   T y p e   A   p e r s o n a l i t y
   _____x_____+_____

2. A relaxation technique that involves self-suggestion:

   — — — — — — — — — — — — — — — —
        x   +

3. How a person initially perceives a stressful situation:

   — — — — — — — — — — — — — — —
      x   +

4. Based on the view that mind and body play equal roles in health.

   — — — — — — —   — — — — — — — — — —
   + x   +

5. Explains why some people feel overwhelmed by stressful events they cannot control:

   —
              +   x

6. Pattern of disruptive physiological and psychological responses:

   — — — — — — —
        +   x

4	6	3	1 L	2	5

PRACTICE EXAM 1

1. Which of the following does *not* belong with the other statements concerning the medical model?

   a.   focus on lower-level processes
   b.   illness viewed primarily as biological
   c.   single-factor explanations
   d.   social context important in understanding disease

   (Factual, Obj. 1.1)

2. In medical school, Joan is taught to pay particular attention to the patient's quality of home life, happiness at work, and attitudes toward life as well as the biological factors. Joan's curriculum has probably been strongly influenced by the:

    a.   medical model
    b.   biopsychological model
    c.   biological model
    d.   health belief model

                                                                  (Conceptual, Obj. 1.1)

3. Which of the following guidelines must a patient adhere to if he or she wishes to reduce the risk of a chronic illness?

    a.   The patient must rely on the physician's cure to get well.
    b.   He or she must accept the fact that most chronic illnesses cannot be controlled, even if one controls health behaviors.
    c.   The patient must be an active participant in regaining or maintaining his or her own health.
    d.   Modern diseases are not easily preventable; once chronic illness strikes, a normal life is very difficult to attain.

                                                                  (Conceptual, Obj. 1.2)

4. If adolescents are given "weak pressures" to engage in an unhealthy habit, they tend to develop counterarguments that protect them in the face of stronger social pressures later on. This social form of "immunization" is called:

    a.   autogenic training
    b.   social engineering
    c.   behavioral inoculation
    d.   psychoimmunization

                                                                  (Factual, Obj. 2.1)

5. Jennifer believes she is virtually immune to disease; she doesn't practice personal hygiene, she's unconcerned with her diet, and she believes in fate—if you're going to get seriously ill, there's nothing you can do to prevent it. Jennifer's health views reflect:

    a.   her sociocultural values
    b.   the health belief model
    c.   learned helplessness
    d.   hardiness

                                                                  (Conceptual, Obj. 1.2)

6. Primary appraisal depends on a person's motives and goals; secondary appraisal depends on a person's:

    a.   resources and ability to cope
    b.   emotional state
    c.   health beliefs
    d.   sociocultural values

                                                                  (Factual, Obj. 3.2)

7. There are some miraculous stories of young children accidentally falling into frozen lakes or streams and surviving, even after 30 minutes of submersion. At first their bodies go numb, then their autonomic nervous systems seem to slow down physiological processes so that they adapt to bitter cold for many minutes. It would appear that the _____ stage of Selye's general adaptation syndrome is operating.

    a. exhaustion
    b. resistance
    c. counterresistance
    d. alarm

    (Conceptual, Obj. 3.4)

8. The symptoms of stress include all of the following *except*:

    a. emotional upset
    b. cognitive disorganization
    c. coping mechanisms
    d. physiological arousal

    (Factual, Obj. 3.1)

9. Examine the following events from the SRRS: personal achievement, marital separation, Christmas, getting fired from work, pregnancy. What do they have in common?

    a. wear and tear
    b. lack of control
    c. intensity of emotional reaction
    d. change

    (Conceptual, Obj. 3.1)

10. Friedman and Rosenman identified Type A personalities as being more prone to developing:

    a. hypertension
    b. coronary heart disease (CHD)
    c. cancer
    d. post-traumatic stress syndrome

    (Factual, Obj. 3.3)

11. Paul, who is 19, recently went to a movie in which the central character was a Vietnam veteran who had difficulty adjusting to his family when he returned home after three years. The movie character had flashbacks of war, nightmares, startle reactions, and tended to be violent. This movie character is suffering from:

    a. Selye's general adaptation syndrome
    b. chronic hypertension
    c. excessive amounts of LCUs
    d. post-traumatic stress syndrome

    (Conceptual, Obj. 3.3)

12. Langer and Rodin worked with nursing home residents to make their environment less stressful. What factor produced the greatest change in happiness, health, and overall well-being?

    a. a sense of "control" over the environment
    b. a change to a protein-rich diet
    c. more recreation time outside the nursing home
    d. more frequent visits from family members

    (Factual, Obj. 3.3)

PRACTICE
EXAM 2

1. In the 1980s it became increasingly evident that most of the chronic illnesses were the result of:

    a. lifestyle factors
    b. infections
    c. poor sanitation
    d. contagious diseases

    (Factual, Obj. 1.2)

2. MADD (Mothers Against Drunk Driving) mounted a very effective campaign by publicizing their "don't drink and drive" message on radio, TV, and rock videos. Their inventive strategy illustrates:

    a. media campaigns
    b. direct treatment
    c. primary appraisal
    d. social engineering

    (Conceptual, Obj. 2.1)

3. What is the leading cause of death and chronic illness in the United States?

    a. coronary heart disease
    b. hypertension
    c. cancer
    d. infectious diseases

    (Factual, Obj.3.4)

4. Shakespeare once remarked that "There is nothing either good or bad but thinking makes it so." In which area of stress research would Shakespeare's observation have its most direct application?

    a. primary appraisal
    b. secondary appraisal
    c. hardiness
    d. meditation

    (Conceptual, Obj. 3.2)

5. According to Selye, the "fight-or-flight" syndrome occurs during the _____ stage of the general adaptation syndrome.

    a. alarm
    b. resistance
    c. appraisal
    d. exhaustion

    (Factual, Obj. 3.4)

6. Bryan and Susan both have to give speeches in their English courses for a substantial portion of their grade. Bryan worries about it all quarter, is constantly preoccupied with it, and can't sleep. Susan, on the other hand, views it as a challenge; she prepares all quarter for a chance to get up and really impress the rest of the class. The difference in their responses is best explained by which of the following statements?

    a. Susan has a Type A personality; Bryan doesn't.
    b. Susan exhibits the characteristics of biological adaptation. Bryan doesn't.
    c. Susan has had a lot of past experience giving speeches; Bryan hasn't.
    d. Susan's primary appraisal of the potential stressor differs from Bryan's.

    (Conceptual, Obj. 3.2)

7. Michael has developed a "phobia" about statistics. He's convinced he doesn't have the mind or the intellectual ability to grasp the basic concepts. His many hours of studying have been very frustrating; he continues to barely pass the course. Basically, he's given up, feeling he has no control over his performance in class. Michael's behavior could be best described as illustrating:

   a. Selye's general adaptation syndrome
   b. lack of hardiness
   c. traumatic experience
   d. learned helplessness

   (Conceptual, Obj. 3.3)

8. In the United States, which of the following groups is most affected by hypertension?

   a. white males
   b. black males
   c. white females
   d. black females

   (Factual, Obj. 3.4)

9. Dr. Kessler is doing his internship in emergency room medicine. He was chosen for this very stressful, intensive setting because of his commitment, involvement with patients, and his welcoming of changes in routine. Dr. Kessler's personality is best described as:

   a. Type A
   b. hardy
   c. health-belief oriented
   d. medical-model oriented

   (Conceptual, Obj. 4.1)

10. What do biofeedback, autogenic training, and progressive relaxation all have in common?

    a. All increase hardiness.
    b. All attempt to control physiological arousal.
    c. All are health belief models.
    d. All involve social engineering.

    (Conceptual, Obj. 4.2)

11. An abbreviated form of the progressive relaxation procedure is used in a behavior therapy called:

    a. biofeedback
    b. multimodal approach
    c. systematic desensitization
    d. social engineering

    (Factual, Obj. 4.2)

12. Which of the following is *not* one of the criticisms of biofeedback?

    a. Some experiments suggest that biofeedback is no more effective than simple relaxation techniques.
    b. The effects of biofeedback may be attributable to an enhanced "sense" of control or a placebo effect.
    c. Biofeedback is more expensive than simple relaxation techniques.
    d. The operant conditioning involved in the procedure is sometimes painful.

    (Factual, Obj. 4.2)

■   **ANSWER KEY**   ■

Concept 1
1. a   3. a
2. b   4. b

Concept 2
1. b   3. a
2. c   4. d

Concept 3

Applicants A (93 LCUs); C (81 LCUs); and E (59 LCUs)

Concept 4
1. autogenic training
2. biofeedback
3. progressive relaxation

Self-test
1. Type A personality   4. health psychology
2. autogenic training   5. learned helplessness
3. primary appraisal   6. stress

Practice Exam 1

1. d, p. 598
2. b, p. 599
3. c, p. 599
4. c, p. 605
5. b, p. 601
6. a, p. 613
7. b, pp. 615–616
8. c, pp. 615–616
9. d, pp. 607–608
10. b, p. 617
11. d, p. 610
12. a, p. 622

Practice Exam 2

1. a, pp. 599–600
2. a, pp. 602–603
3. a, p. 616
4 a, p. 613
5. b, pp. 615–616
6. d, p. 613
7. d, pp. 614–615
8. b, p. 616
9. b, p. 620
10. b, p. 620
11. c, p. 620
12. d, p. 621

CRITICAL THINKING ESSAY 6

Studying the Mind's Impact on Cancer

In 1964 Norman Cousins, a celebrated writer and long-time editor of the *Saturday Review,* was hospitalized because of a rapidly spreading paralysis. Specialists in collagen diseases (diseases of the body's connective tissue) informed him that his condition was advancing unchecked and that his chances of recovery were less than 1 in 500. Though paralyzed from the neck down, Cousins refused to accept this grim prognosis and took control of his treatment. He had himself discharged from the hospital to escape an atmosphere that he considered disrupting and anxiety-provoking. He took massive doses of Vitamin C, a treatment the experts warned was useless and perhaps even dangerous. Believing that positive, happy emotions would help him fight the disease, Cousins undertook a regimen of watching movie comedies and reading humorous books and magazines. Most of all, he refused to submit to his illness.

Almost immediately Cousins' symptoms began to subside, and over the next few months he gradually regained feeling in his body. Within six months he was back to normal. Over the next several years accounts of Cousins' experience spread throughout the medical community. Most physicians scoffed at the notion of "laughing away an illness," and many dismissed the story entirely. To clarify the issue, Cousins wrote an article describing his unique self-therapy in the *New England Journal of Medicine* (1976). Most medical professionals seemed to believe the events Cousins described, and many even wrote to agree that physicians and hospital staffers often overlook the psychological aspects of patient care. Still they doubted the veracity of a psychological cure for a pervasive collagen disease, calling Cousins' recovery "a massive

placebo effect" (Cousins, 1979). Cousins was not at all insulted by this interpretation, knowing that by placebo or some other means his mind had helped to cure his body.

Cousins' experience touched on a fundamental issue in both psychology and medicine: the interplay of psychological and physiological factors. This so-called *mind–body problem* has fascinated professionals for centuries, though areas of scientific research and medical practice devoted to this issue (such as behavioral medicine, psychosomatic research, psychoneuroimmunology) have been established only in the last few decades. Most researchers in these emerging fields study common types of disorders such as coronary disease, pain, and cancer. In this essay we focus on research into the question of whether the onset and course of cancer can be affected by psychological processes.

Interest in the effects of psychological variables on cancer has a long history (Greer, 1983). In the second century A.D., the Roman physician Galen wrote in *De Tumoribus* that sanguine (optimistic) women were less likely to develop breast cancer than were melancholic (depressed) women. Remission of cancer through hypnotism was reported by Elliotson (1848). More recently, cases of spontaneous cancer remission or cure associated with positive psychological factors have been reported by a number of clinicians (Everson and Cole, 1966; Weinstock, 1983; Mack, 1984; Muschel, 1984; Seigel, 1986), and treatment programs based on positive emotional states have been developed (e.g., Simonton, Matthews-Simonton, and Creighton, 1978; Siegel, 1986). Other clinicians have noted the impact of negative psychological factors on cancer. Feelings of interpersonal loss and an inability to express emotions have been found to be relatively more common among cancer patients (LeShan and Worthington, 1959; Bahnson and Bahnson, 1966; Greene, 1966). Though intriguing, these reports are based on uncontrolled clinical observations and are largely anecdotal.

STUDYING THE EFFECT OF PSYCHOLOGICAL VARIABLES ON CANCER

The preferred design for research in this area is a controlled experiment involving two groups of cancer patients closely matched on demographic variables (sex, age, occupation) and disease variables (type of cancer, tumor size, location, degree of spread). In addition to receiving the traditional medical treatments—radiation, chemotherapy, surgery—the treatment group would be exposed to pleasant experiences such as parties, frequent visits, comedies, and humorous books. They would be assured that they were in control of the course of their disease and thus encouraged to feel optimistic about their prognosis. The control group, in contrast, would be instructed to engage in neutral tasks such as watching TV or solving puzzles. The two groups would then be compared in terms of their psychological well-being (assessed via ratings of coping, depression, and so on), cancer morbidity (onset and progression, as measured by tumor size, spread of cancerous cells, and so on), and mortality (death) rates.

Despite the obvious advantages of this research paradigm, it has yet to be carried out. As Cousins found, medical professionals are skeptical about the idea that psychological factors can "cure" cancer, and research in this area receives little support. As a result, most studies of the connection between psychological and physiological factors in cancer have taken more roundabout approaches.

Research on the mind's role in cancer tends to follow four basic routes. *Animal studies* introduce cancer cells into host animals, which are then subjected to a variety of psychological manipulations, such as the inducement of stress. The researchers note the impact of these manipulations on the development and growth of cancerous tumors.

Retrospective studies look at smaller groups of human patients, often people undergoing biopsies (surgical removal of tissue to be tested for cancer), and compare the psychological profiles of those who have malignant tumors from those who have benign ones. *Prospective studies* examine large groups of cancer-free subjects over many years and compare the psychological characteristics of those who eventually develop cancer and those who do not.

A fourth line of research investigates ways to cope with the side effects of traditional medical treatments for cancer. For example, Redd and his colleagues (Redd, 1982; 1985–86; Redd and Andrykowski, 1982; Redd and Hendler, 1983) describe behavioral treatments to reduce the nausea, vomiting, and distress associated with chemotherapy. Katz and his colleagues study behavioral treatments that reduce the fear and pain of adolescents and children undergoing chemotherapy (Dolgin and Katz, 1988) and bone marrow aspirations (Katz, Kellerman, and Ellenberg, 1987). Although these studies demonstrate a connection between psychological treatment and cancer, they do not address the incidence of progression of the disease per se.

CRITICAL ANALYSIS OF RESEARCH ON THE MIND'S EFFECT ON CANCER

As with most areas of psychological research, studies on the psychosomatic aspects of cancer are carried out with varying degrees of experimental rigor (Fox, 1978; 1983). Although the studies described here suffer from a number of methodological flaws, a greater problem with this field is the incidence of exaggerated or unfounded claims based on inappropriate data. This essay focuses on the limitations inherent in the first three research approaches mentioned above (while also noting their advantages).

Analysis of Animal Research.   Several investigators (e.g., Riley, 1975; Temoshok, 1985) have studied the relationship between stress and cancer in rodent populations. In a prominent series of studies, Sklar and Anisman (1979; 1980; 1981) injected cancerous cells into mice and then subjected the mice to physical stress (electric shock) or social stress (isolation and crowding). They found that tumors developed faster and grew more quickly when the shock was inescapable. A single administration of shock resulted in earlier and faster tumor growth than a repeated series of shocks. This finding suggested that the animals somehow adapted to the shocks. Frequent changes in social situations (but not any particular situation itself) led to greater cancer morbidity. In general, it seems that uncontrollable stress and unstable social situations may hasten tumor growth. Sklar and Anisman claim that these results lend credence to human studies documenting a correlation between life stress and cancer morbidity and mortality.

Studies using animal subjects enjoy a number of methodological (as well as ethical) advantages over human studies. By injecting equal amounts of cancerous cells into cancer-free, genetically identical animals, researchers can maintain strict control over the initiation and probable course of the tumors. By assigning animals to certain cages and scheduling their sessions of shock, researchers can maintain control over the social and physical environments. In short, the *experimental validity* of animal studies is high.

However, animal studies suffer from limitations in *external validity,* and many writers urge caution in generalizing animal studies to human cancer. For example, Fox (1982; 1983) notes four limitations: (1) Animals and humans differ in how stress affects their immune systems, and it is hard to say how these differences affect the incidence and progression of cancer. (2) Animals used in research are from pure strains, and this high level of inbreeding may make them less resistant to cancer than humans, who are the products of much more genetic intermixing. (3) Animals and humans tend to suffer from different forms of cancer. Most animal cancers are viral, whereas only about 3 percent of human cancers are viral. Justice (1985) notes that viral and nonviral tumors respond differently to stress. (4) Electric shocks and overcrowded cages are only distant approximations of the complex psychological and social environments of humans, which involve a variety of physical, psychological, and social

stressors as well as innumerable environmental carcinogens.

Critical Analysis of Retrospective Studies.   A number of retrospective research programs have investigated the psychological factors associated with cancer in human subjects. These teams have typically focused on specific types of cancer, such as lung cancer (Kissen and Eysenck, 1962; Kissen, Brown, and Kissen, 1969; Abse et al., 1974), uterine cervical cancer (Schmale and Iker, 1966), testicular cancer (Edwards, DiClemente, and Samuels, 1985), skin cancer (melanoma) (Kneier and Temoshok, 1984; Temoshok, 1985; Temoshok et al., 1985), and breast cancer (Kircaldy and Kobylinska, 1987). Perhaps the most prolific research program has been the investigation of breast cancer by a team at the University of London (e.g., Greer and Morris, 1975; Greer, Morris, and Pettingale, 1979; Pettingale, Watson, and Greer, 1984; Watson, Pettingale, and Greer, 1984; Pettingale, Burgess, and Greer, 1988).

One retrospective study conducted by this team involved 30 women with breast cancer (Pettingale et al., 1984; Watson et al., 1984). Within three months after having a mastectomy (surgical removal of all or part of a cancerous breast), each patient was given questionnaires that measured her emotional expressiveness, anxiety, degree of repression, and current mood. The women then watched two stressful videotapes and one neutral tape. The women's heart rate and skin conductance were measured continuously while they watched the videotapes. Afterward they rated their moods again and described their reactions to the tapes. A control group of twenty-seven healthy women went through the same procedure. In comparing the two groups, the researchers noted that the cancer patients expressed less anxiety and anger in both their questionnaires and reactions to the tapes, but they showed *more* autonomic arousal than the control group. The investigating team concluded that cancer patients tend to repress their emotions and try to appear nice and cooperative. They speculate that an inability to express negative emotions and a tendency to be compliant and to conform to social standards constitute a "Type C," or "cancer-prone," personality. This personality-related vulnerability to cancer corresponds to findings from several other studies and clinical reports involving many types of cancer (e.g., LeShan, 1959; Kissen and Eysenck, 1962; Edwards et al., 1985; Temoshok, 1985).

The University of London study examined the reactions of women who already had cancer. The most obvious advantage of this procedure over animal studies is that studying human subjects enables researchers to be more confident in generalizing their results to the broader population of human cancer victims. In addition, using human subjects, particularly a small, select sample, allows researchers to employ a wide variety of sophisticated objective, projective, and observational measures and interviews in assessing subjects' personalities and reactions to complex situations.

Retrospective studies also have inherent limitations. Because it is obviously unethical to infect healthy human subjects with cancerous cells, retrospective studies are by necessity correlational in design. For this reason the direction of causality is always open to interpretation. Thus, perhaps the cancer causes the Type C personality, rather than vice versa; or perhaps a third, unknown genetic or environmental factor causes both the cancer and the Type C responses.

Another problem involves the timing of the onset of cancer in the sample. To examine economically a sample large enough to produce reliable results, investigators who conduct retrospective studies recruit subjects who are already identified as cancer victims or potential victims. The University of London study examined the responses of breast cancer victims who had recently undergone surgery. It is possible that their ratings and reactions were influenced by their awareness of their condition (including their recent operations) and thus did not reflect their precancer personalities. To get around this problem, many researchers (e.g., Abse et al., 1974; Greer and Morris, 1975; Gorzynski et al., 1980) study patients admitted for biopsies, thus measuring their personalities and responses before their diagnoses are known. However, the stress of biopsy (and the looming risk of cancer) may

still affect subjects' responses. Moreover, Fox (1978) warns that most cancerous tumors begin to form years before they are detectable, and it is probable that undetected tumors have already had an impact on patients' immune, endocrine, and other physiological systems; these changes may in turn have affected patients' psychological responses. Thus, retrospective studies look at subjects' responses to an existing cancer, even if that cancer has not yet been diagnosed.

Critical Analysis of Prospective Studies.   As Fox (1978) suggests, to measure the psychological factors of subjects *before* they develop cancer, researchers must study them years before they are identified as cancer victims. Furthermore, since only a small percentage of the general population contracts cancer, only a small proportion of a random sample could be expected to do so; thus, large samples of randomly chosen, cancer-free subjects are required. Several researchers (e.g., Thomas and Duszynski, 1974; Shekelle et al., 1981; Grossarth-Maticek et al., 1983; Persky, Kempthorne-Rawson, and Shekelle, 1987; Hahn and Petitti, 1988; Kaplan and Reynolds, 1988; Zonderman, Costa, and McCrea, 1989) have conducted long-term (ten to twenty years) prospective studies of large samples (1,337 to 8,932 subjects). Subjects are given questionnaires (and in some cases a physical examination) as part of an ongoing project. At periodic intervals (usually every five years or so), the health status of the subjects is documented and the questionnaires are readministered. Finally, the responses of those who contracted cancer or died of the disease during the interval are compared to the rest of the sample.

The logistical problems involved in prospective studies are immense, and it takes ambition and determination to undertake these large, long-term projects. Unfortunately, these massive efforts have not yielded a corresponding rich store of results, and the findings that do emerge are inconsistent. For example, after following 2,020 male employees at a Western Electric plant in the Midwest for 17 years (Shekelle et al., 1981) and 20 years (Persky, Kempthorne-Rawson, and Shekelle, 1987),

Shekelle and his colleagues found that those who died from cancer showed slightly higher scores on the Minnesota Multiphasic Personality Inventory-Depressed subscale (MMPI-D) during the initial screening. Statistically controlling for subjects' age, history of tobacco and alcohol use, family history of cancer, occupational status, and serum cholesterol level did not alter these results. No measure other than depression predicted cancer mortality.

In contrast, Zonderman, Coster, and McCrea (1989) found *no* association between depression and cancer. These investigators surveyed a nationally representative sample of men and women on a variety of health and nutrition variables, including two measures of depression: the Center for Epidemiologic Studies Depressed scale (CES-D, 2,814 subjects) and the Depressed subscale of the General Well-Being Schedule (GWS-D, 6,913 subjects). They found no association between either of these measures and cancer morbidity or mortality. Again, these results were unaffected by statistically controlling for subjects' age, sex, marital status, tobacco and alcohol use, family history of cancer, hypertension, and serum cholesterol level.

There are several possible reasons for the disagreement between these two studies. First, they employed different samples. A sample of 40- to 55-year-old men working at a single utility plant in the Midwest might well be different from a national sample of civilian men and women aged 25 to 75. Second, the two studies used different dependent measures. The 60-item MMPI-D is a gross screening measure designed to differentiate clinical and nonclinical samples. It is not particularly sensitive to small, nonclinical variations, such as those shown in the Western Electric data. In contrast, the 20-item CES-D and the 4-item GWS-D are designed to detect differences in symptoms of depression in normal samples. One could overcome this problem by comparing the Western Electric study to one conducted by Hahn and Petitti (1988), which also used the MMPI-D. Unfortunately, Hahn and Petitti studied an entirely female sample, and this sex difference may account for the fact that they found no correlation between MMPI-D scores and cancer morbidity. Third, Shekelle

and colleagues used cancer *mortality* (deaths) as their dependent variable, while the other two studies chose cancer *morbidity* (onset) as their dependent variable. This difference may account for the inconsistent results. (In fact, Persky and colleagues examined both morbidity and mortality and found that MMPI-D scores predicted cancer mortality—but *not* morbidity—in follow-up studies over 10 years.) In short, while these prospective studies may seem similar in their superficial characteristics, their numerous differences make direct comparisons difficult.

The fact that prospective studies are based on large-scale surveys gives rise to a number of other limitations (Fox, 1978; Temoshok and Heller, 1984). First, the measurement items must be kept short and superficial, which makes it impossible to use the more detailed measures necessary to pick up the Type C personality pattern. Second, the purpose of the study is often not directly relevant to psychological factors and cancer. For example, Thomas and Duszynski (1974) were initially interested in hypertension and coronary disease, and Hahn and Petitti (1988) were looking at patterns of contraceptive use. Thus, the measures reported in prospective studies are frequently "tacked on" to a larger study; they may even be adapted from other fields of research or based on different psychological constructs. This calls into question their validity in a population of cancer patients. Third, since each survey uses multiple measures, it is quite likely that researchers will find a "significant" result on one of the measures. For example, if a researcher administers 20 measures, he or she would expect to get a "significant" result (at the .05 level) on one of them just by chance. Researchers must be careful to statistically control for this problem. Fourth, data on life events (such as illnesses and hospitalizations) should be confirmed through a check of written records; forgetting and distortion are common when subjects attempt to report the events of the past several years. Finally, because prospective studies are longitudinal, the researcher is "stuck" with the initial measure, even if it proves to be unpopular with other researchers or to be invalid for a population of cancer patients.

CONCLUSION: WHAT DO WE KNOW ABOUT THE MIND'S EFFECT ON CANCER?

Considering the way interest in the psychological aspects of cancer has burgeoned in the past few years, we know surprisingly little about the mind's effect on cancer. One obstacle is the indifferent (and occasionally hostile) attitude of the medical community. As Cousins (1979) noted, many of these concerns are well placed. Oncologists (cancer specialists) fear that popular belief in a "laughing cure" for cancer will raise the hopes of many patients unrealistically and that some patients will put off or even refuse the uncomfortable and painful medical treatments that are currently available. This negative attitude seems to be rooted in the tendency of medical professionals to dismiss the influence of psychological factors on physical illnesses. In one recent survey (Ray, 1986), for example, a majority of oncologists acknowledged that they pay too little attention to their patients' psychological well-being.

Another obstacle to clarifying the relationship between the mind and cancer is the lack of consistency in research methods. Investigators have examined cancers of different types, stages, and sites in a variety of sample populations using a bewildering array of psychological and physiological measures. According to Temoshok and Heller (1984), comparing these different studies is like comparing apples, oranges, and fruit salad. It is little wonder, then, that the research yields such mixed results.

Despite this diversity, one trend seems to be emerging. Many reports from a variety of retrospective studies and clinical observations have confirmed the existence of a Type C personality, which represses emotions and complies with social expectations. However, no cause-and-effect relationship has been established: it is unclear whether this personality pattern is a marker for future cancer or merely a reaction to an existing condition. In any case, not everyone who displays this personality pattern will get cancer. Nor is it valid or fair to assume that people who develop cancer have somehow "brought it on themselves" through their emotionally repressed and socially compliant personalities. Only carefully designed prospective studies will provide conclusive data concerning the question of causality. Even then, we will not know if laughter can cure cancer; but we will know if a positive outlook and a willingness to express our emotions can help us ward off the disease.

REFERENCES

Abse, D. W., M. H. Wilkins, R. L. Van de Castle, W. D. Buxton, J. P. Demars, R. S. Brown, and L. G. Kirschner. Personality and behavioral characteristics of lung cancer patients. *Journal of Psychosomatic Research,* 1974, *18,* 103–113.

Bahnson, C. B., and S. B. Bahnson. Role of ego defenses: Denial and repression in the etiology of malignant neoplasm. *Annals of the New York Academy of Sciences,* 1966, *125,* 827–845.

Cousins, N. Anatomy of an illness (as perceived by the patient). *New England Journal of Medicine,* 1976, *295,* 1458–1463.

Cousins, N. *Anatomy of an illness (as perceived by the patient).* New York: Norton, 1979.

Dolgin, M. J., and E. R. Katz. Conditioned aversions in pediatric cancer patients receiving chemotherapy. *Journal of Developmental and Behavioral Pediatrics,* 1988, *9,* 82–85.

Edwards, J., C. DiClemente, and M. L. Samuels. Psychological characteristics: A pretreatment survival marker of patients with testicular cancer. *Journal of Psychosocial Oncology,* 1985, *3,* 79–94.

Elliotson, J. *Cure of a true cancer of the female breast with mesmerism.* London: Walton & Mitchell, 1848.

Everson, T. C., and W. H. Cole. *Spontaneous regression of cancer.* Philadelphia: Saunders, 1966. [CT6]

Fox, B. H. A psychological measure as a predictor of cancer. In J. Cohen, J. W. Cullen, and L. R. Martin, (eds.), *Psychological aspects of cancer.* New York: Raven Press, 1982, pp. 275–295.

Fox, B. H. Current theory of psychogenic effects on cancer incidence and prognosis. *Journal of Psychosocial Oncology,* 1983, *1,* 17–31.

Gorzynski, J. G., J. Holland, J. L. Katz, H. Weiner, B. Zumoff, D. Fukushima, and J. Levin. Stability of ego defenses and endocrine responses in women prior to breast biopsy and ten years later. *Psychosomatic Medicine,* 1980, *42,* 323–328.

Greene, W. A. The psychological setting in the development of leukemia and lymphoma. *Annals of the New York Academy of Sciences,* 1966, *125,* 794–801.

Greer, S. Cancer and the mind. *British Journal of Psychiatry,* 1983, *143,* 535–543.

Greer, S., and T. Morris. Psychological attributes of women who develop breast cancer: A controlled study. *Journal of Psychosomatič Research,* 1975, *19,* 147–153.

Greer, S., T. Morris, and K. W. Pettingale. Psychological response to breast cancer: Effect on outcome. *Lancet,* 1979, *2,* 785–787.

Grossarth-Maticek, R., D. T. Kanazir, H. Vetter, and P. Schmidt. Psychosomatic factors involved in the process of cancerogenesis: Preliminary results of the Yugoslav Prospective Study. *Psychotherapy and Psychosomatics,* 1983, *40,* 191–210.

Hahn, R. C., and D. B. Petitti. Minnesota Multiphasic Personality Inventory–rated depression and the incidence of cancer. *Cancer,* 1988, *61,* 845–848.   [CT6]

Justice, A. Review of the effects of stress on cancer in laboratory animals: Importance of time of stress application and type of tumor. *Psychological Review,* 1985, *98,* 108–138.

Kaplan, G. A., and P. Reynolds. Depression and cancer mortality and morbidity: Prospective evidence from the Alameda County Study. *Journal of Behavioral Medicine,* 1988, *11,* 1–13.

Katz, E. R., J. Kellerman, and L. Ellenberg. Hypnosis in the reduction of acute pain and distress in children with cancer. *Journal of Pediatric Psychology,* 1987, *12,* 379–394.

Kircaldy, B. D., and E. Kobylinska. Psychological characteristics of breast cancer patients. *Psychotherapy and Psychosomatics,* 1987, *48,* 32–43.

Kissen, D. M., R. I. F. Brown, and M. Kissen. A further report on personality and psychosocial factors in lung cancer. *Annals of the New York Academy of Sciences,* 1969, *164,* 535–544.

Kissen, D. M., and H. J. Eysenck. Personality in male lung cancer patients. *Journal of Psychosomatic Research,* 1962, *6,* 123–127.

Kneier, A. W., and L. Temoshok. Repressive coping reactions in patients with malignant melanoma as compared to cardiovascular disease patients. *Journal of Psychosomatic Research,* 1984, *28,* 145–155.

LeShan, L. Psychological states as factors in the development of malignant disease: A critical review. *Journal of the National Cancer Institute,* 1959, *22,* 1–18.

LeShan, L., and R. E. Worthington. Some recurrent life history patterns observed in patients with malignant disease. *Journal of Nervous and Mental Disease,* 1959, *124,* 460–465.

Mack, R. M. Lessons from living with cancer. *New England Journal of Medicine,* 1984, *311,* 1640-1644.

Muschel, I. J. Pet therapy with terminal cancer patients. *Social Casework,* 1984, *65,* 451–458.

Persky, V. W., J. Kempthorne-Rawson, and R. B. Shekelle. Personality and risk of cancer: 20-year follow-up of the Western Electric Study. *Psychosomatic Medicine,* 1987, *49,* 435–449.

Pettingale, K. W., C. Burgess, and S. Greer. Psychological response to cancer diagnosis: I. Correlations with prognostic variables. *Journal of Psychosomatic Research,* 1988, *32,* 255–261.

Pettingale, K. W., M. Watson, and S. Greer. The validity of emotional control as a trait in breast cancer patients. *Journal of Psychosocial Oncology,* 1984, *2,* 21–30.

Ray, C. The surgeon's dilemma in the management of the patient with breast cancer. In M. Watson and S. Greer (eds.), *Psychosocial issues in malignant disease.* Proceedings of the first annual conference organized by the British Psychosocial Oncology Group. London, 7–8 November, 1984. Oxford: Pergamon Press, 1986, pp. 29–34.

Redd, W. H. Behavioural analysis and control of psychosomatic symptoms of patients receiving intensive cancer treatment. *British Journal of Clinical Psychology,* 1982, *21,* 351–358.

Redd, W. H. Use of behavioral methods to control the aversive effects of chemotherapy. *Journal of Psychosocial Oncology,* 1985–86, *3,* 17–22.

Redd, W. H., and M. A. Andrykowski. Behavioral intervention in cancer treatment: Controlling aversion reactions to chemotherapy. *Journal of Consulting and Clinical Psychology,* 1982, *50,* 1018–1029.

Redd, W. H., and C. S. Hendler. Behavioral medicine in comprehensive cancer treatment. *Journal of Psychosocial Oncology,* 1983, *1,* 3–17.

Riley, V. Mouse mammary tumors: Alteration of incidence as apparent function of stress. *Science,* 1975, *189,* 465–467.

Schmale, A. H., and H. P. Iker. The affect of hopelessness and the development of cancer: I. Identification of uterine cervical cancer in women with atypical cytology. *Journal of Psychosomatic Research,* 1966, *28,* 714–721.

Seigel, B. *Love, medicine, and miracles: Lessons learned about self-healing from a surgeon's experience with exceptional patients.* New York: Harper & Row, 1986.

Shekelle, R. B., W. J. Raynor, A. M. Ostfeld, D. C. Garron, L. A. Bieliauskas, S. C. Liu, C. Matiza, and O. Paul. Psychological depression and 17-year risk of death from cancer. *Psychosomatic Medicine,* 1981, *43,* 117–125.

Simonton, O. C., S. Matthews-Simonton, and J. L. Creighton. *Getting well again: Self-help to overcoming cancer for patients and their families.* Los Angeles: J. P. Tarcher, 1978.

Sklar, L. S., and H. Anisman. Stress and coping factors influence tumor growth. *Science,* 1979, *204,* 513–515.

Sklar, L. S., and H. Anisman. Social stress influences tumor growth. *Psychosomatic Medicine,* 1980, *42,* 347–365.

Sklar, L. S., and H. Anisman. Adaptation to the tumor-enhancing effects of stress. *Psychosomatic Medicine,* 1981, *43,* 331–342.

Temoshok, L. Biopsychosocial studies on cutaneous malignant melanoma: Psychosocial factors associated with prognostic indicators, progression, psychophysiology, and tumor-host response. *Social Science and Medicine,* 1985, *20,* 833–840.

Temoshok, L., and B. W. Heller. On comparing apples, oranges, and fruit salad: A methodological overview of medical outcome studies in psychosocial oncology. In C. L. Cooper (ed.), *Psychosocial stress and cancer.* London: Wiley, 1984, pp. 231–260.

Temoshok, L., B. W. Heller, R. W. Sagebiel, M. S. Blois, D. M. Sweet, R. J. DiClemente, and M. L. Gold. The relationship of psychosocial factors to prognostic indicators in cutaneous malignant melanoma. *Journal of Psychosomatic Research,* 1985, *29,* 139–153.

Thomas, C. B., and K. R. Duszynski. Closeness to parents and the family constellation in a prospective study of five disease states: Suicide, mental illness, malignant tumor, hypertension, and coronary heart disease. *The Johns Hopkins Medical Journal,* 1974, *134,* 251–270.

Watson, M., K. W. Pettingale, and S. Greer. Emotional control and autonomic arousal in breast cancer patients. *Journal of Psychosomatic Research,* 1984, *28,* 467–474.

Weinstock, C. Further evidence on psychobiological aspects of cancer. *International Journal of Psychosomatics,* 1983, *31,* 20–22.

Zonderman, A. B., P. T. Costa, and R. R. McCrea. Depression as a risk for cancer morbidity and mortality in a nationally representative sample. *Journal of the American Medical Association,* 1989, *262,* 1191–1195.

RESPONDING TO CRITICAL ESSAY 6

1. Medical historians have noted that the history of medicine has been a history of placebos. That is, the *belief* that a cure will occur is powerful and therapeutic in and of itself, whether or not there is a sound medical basis.

    If medicine is indeed such a living testament to the power of the placebo effect, why is the medical community so skeptical of Cousins' recovery, calling it "a massive placebo effect"?

2. The so-called "mind-body problem" has fascinated professionals for centuries. Indeed, many modern medical specialties devote themselves to this issue (e.g., psychoneuroimmunology, behavioral medicine, psychosomatic research). The common focus is the interplay of psychology and medicine.

    What parallel do you see between the focus of this essay and the discussion of the "diathesis-stress model" presented in Chapter 18 of your text (Psychological Disorders)?

3. Some research indicates that there may be a "cancer-prone" personality, the so-called Type C personality. Many retrospective studies and clinical observations confirm the existence of the Type C personality.

    What is a major problem in inferring that the Type C personality causes cancer to develop in an individual?

CHAPTER TWENTY-ONE

Attitudes, Social Cognition, and Interpersonal Attraction

KEY TERM ORGANIZER

In psychological terms, an *attitude* is an evaluative response to a particular object, idea, person, or group of people. Traditionally, attitudes are considered to have three components: an affective (emotional) component (how we feel about the attitude object); a behavioral component (how we act toward the object); and a cognitive component (our knowledge, beliefs, and thoughts about the object). The relationship of the components is illustrated below:

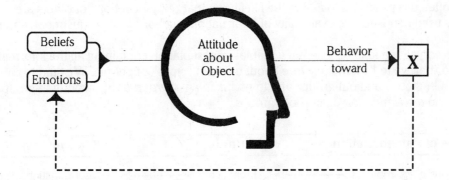

Many factors affect the development of an attitude. Emotional responses may be the product of classical conditioning. An affective response may also be the result of the *exposure effect*, in which repeated neutral encounters produce positive feelings toward the object. Behavioral responses to "attitude objects" are often learned through instrumental conditioning.

Cognitive dissonance theory holds that an inconsistency between two of our attitudes or between our attitudes and our behavior produces an unpleasant state of arousal that motivates us to re-establish consistency by changing either an attitude or a behavior.

Self-perception theory holds that we change our attitudes when we perceive them to be inconsistent with our behavior, without necessarily experiencing unpleasant arousal. Some researchers argue that attitude change is motivated primarily by people's need for affirmation of themselves as good and worthwhile.

Attitudes may be changed through persuasion in two major ways:

- *Central route to persuasion:* the message recipient evaluates the quality of the arguments presented;

- *Peripheral route to persuasion:* the recipient uses heuristic thinking, previous experiences, or some other method other than evaluation of the quality of the arguments.

The degree of consistency between attitudes and behavior is influenced by the amount of direct experience a person has with the object of the attitude, by social norms and the person's self-consciousness, and by personality type (especially the extent to which the person is self-monitoring, trying to match his or her behavior to the situation regardless of his or her attitude).

Social cognition refers to the way we think and reason about ourselves as social beings, about other people, about relations between people, and about the various groups to which we and other people belong.

According to the "naive scientist" model of social cognition, people are rational processors of information, trying to make the best possible and most intuitively logical social judgments about themselves and others by analyzing behavior for distinctiveness and consensus.

In making inferences about social relations, we apply heuristics (rules of thumb) that result in social schemas. These cognitive frameworks are subject to causal attribution biases:

1. We may reject consensus information (a general agreement about the appropriate response to a social stimulus) because we perceive it as irrelevant to our own situation.
2. We may commit the *fundamental attribution error,* ascribing another person's behavior to the person rather than to the situation.
3. The actor-observer bias may cause us to see other people's behavior as revealing what they are really like but to see our own behavior as resulting from the situation.

We often use heuristics to assess the likelihood that our perceptions of others are accurate. Frequently used heuristics are availability of information, anchoring and adjustment, and representativeness.

A *stereotype* is a kind of schema, a mental representation containing all the information that we know or believe to be generally true about different "types" of people. We tend to categorize people into in-groups and out-groups and to maintain an *in-group bias,* favoring in-groups through *prejudice* and *discrimination* against out-groups.

Type of Categorization	**Attitude**	**Behavior**
Stereotype (Example: "My race is superior; my sex is superior.") ⟶	Prejudice (Racist or sexist attitudes) ┈┈┈⟶	Discrimination (Segregation, harassment, oppression, ridicule, etc.)

Prejudice and discrimination can generate a *self-fulfilling prophecy,* whereby an out-group member behaves in a way that confirms the initially false expectations of an in-group member. Stereotypes are difficult to change. There are several major forces that affect liking and attraction toward other people:

Social Factor	Nature of Influence on Attraction
Proximity	How close together people live and work plays a major role in friendship formation.
Similarity	Couples tend to share the same race, religion, educational level, and economic status.
Effects of approval	Constant approval seems to produce less favorable attitudes than does approval that follows criticism.
Need structures	Both complementary and compatible needs affect friendship and romantic relationships.

MAJOR CONCEPTS AND LEARNING OBJECTIVES

CONCEPT 1   An attitude is an evaluative response toward a particular object, person, or group of people. Psychologists are concerned with measuring and predicting attitudes, and whether attitudes are consistent with one another and with behavior.

1.1   Outline and describe the three-component model of attitudes and attitude formation.

1.2   Define cognitive dissonance and discuss how dissonance leads to self-justification behavior.

1.3   Discuss the challenges to cognitive dissonance from self-perception theory and the view that people seek to maintain the integrity of their self-systems.

Concept Builder 1

Directions: The following statements and questions are meant to measure your attitude toward the study guide you are using and at the same time illustrate components of an attitude. For each question, identify the component of the attitude being illustrated from the supplied list.

a. cognitive component
b. affective component
c. behavioral component

1. On a scale of 1 to 7, check how much you like the study guide so far:

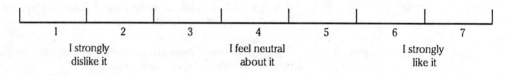

| 1 | 2 | 3 | 4 | 5 | 6 | 7 |

I strongly   I feel neutral   I strongly
dislike it   about it   like it

This measures the _____ of your attitude.

2. Read the following statements:

I believe using this study guide will help me learn more from this course.

I think the concept builders are excellent ways to make the information relevant.

In my opinion, the writer of this study guide will become a legend in his own mind!

This is called the _____ of your attitude.

3. This study guide provides a strong incentive to study in order to prepare for class-room examinations. If this statement reflects your situation, then it may be an illustration of the _____ of your attitude.

CONCEPT 2   Other causes of attitude change include persuasive communication and factors like experience, the strength of the attitude-behavior link, and person-ality factors.

2.1   Define and distinguish the central route to persuasion and the periph-eral route to persuasion, and discuss the influences at work in each route.

2.2   Identify the factors in individual experience that influence the strength of the attitude-behavior relationship.

2.3   Explain how self-consciousness and personality type may influence the attitude-behavior link.

**Concept
Builder 2**

Directions: The problem of drug use in our society has become epidemic. A number of television commercials have attempted to change our attitudes about the dangers and futility of drug use. Read each of the following commercial messages and identify the mode of persuasion being used.

C = central route to persuasion
P = peripheral route to persuasion

Just Say No

1. This ad, repeated frequently, shows a sizzling frying pan with hot oil; the narrator says, "These are drugs." An egg drops into the pan and immediately crackles and fries from the searing heat. The narrator says, "These are your brains on drugs."

    _____

2. Mothers Against Drunk Driving (MADD) tries to educate people by providing accurate facts about alcohol's effects on our bodies; MADD proponents hope that the misinformed or uninformed will be more receptive to MADD's message.

    _____

3. This commercial shows an unkempt, poorly dressed, and "dull" looking teen-ager smoking pot. The camera pans in closely and the narrator says, "Now I know why they call it dope." _____

4. This commercial features a highly recognizable, and highly popular, athletic figure discussing the problems and hellish conflicts that cocaine inflicted upon his life.

    _____

5. The surgeon general appears on one TV ad and summarizes some astounding statistics about fetal alcohol syndrome. He shows, through animated graphics, how alcohol enters the fetus's bloodstream via the placenta of a drinking mother.

    _____

6. This ad shows an electroencephalograph (EEG) with nine needles tracing wavy lines. The narrator says, "This is the brain activity of a normal 14-year-old." Then the needles stop, scribing virtually straight lines. The narrator says, "This is the brain activity of a 14-year-old on marijuana." _____

CONCEPT 3   Social cognition refers to the ways we think and reason about ourselves, others, relations between people, and the groups to which we belong. The naive-scientist model suggests that we attempt to process information about others in a rational way.

3.1   Review and distinguish causal attribution, the fundamental attribution error, and the actor-observer bias.

3.2   Identify and define the way heuristics of availability, representativeness, and anchoring affect our perceptions of others.

Concept Builder 3

Directions: Look at the following matrix that summarizes how observers and actors explain the causes of behavior. Notice that different causes are attributed for misdeeds and mistakes than for achievements and laudable deeds. After looking at the chart, use the quadrant designations to identify the kind of attribution being made for the four situations that follow.

Attribution: A Matter of Perspective

Causes of Behavior

		Misdeeds/ mistakes	Achievement/ laudable deeds
Social-Cognitive Perspective	Observer	I. Dispositional cause	II. Situational cause
	Actor	III. Situational cause	IV. Dispositional cause

 1.   Professor Brainbuster gave a particularly poor lecture on social psychology. He recognized his poor performance and explained that he just didn't have the time to prepare for this lecture because he was trying to finish his new book.

 2.   Professor Brainbuster's students explained the poor lecture differently. They say he lacks expertise in the social psychology area; after all, his specialty is neuroscience.

 3.   When Professor Brainbuster gave his students an exam on the social psychology chapter, they did great. He commented that either the students were lucky or he must have given them an easy exam.

 4.   The students, however, explained their good test scores differently. They said that in spite of a poor lecture, their hard studying and test-taking skills paid off.

CONCEPT 4   Our "categories of people" are complex mental representations of different types of people containing all the information we believe to be true of members of that category. These categories form stereotypes that define in-groups and out-groups and create self-fulfilling prophecies.

4.1   Define stereotype and discuss the way stereotyping leads to in-group and out-group distinctions.

4.2   Discuss how an initially false expectation leads one to behave in accordance with a self-fulfilling prophecy.

4.3   Identify the conditions under which stereotypes change.

**Concept
Builder 4**

Directions: Look at the following flow chart. It represents the major factors that result from social categorization. Your task is to fill in the names of the major social categorization processes in the right-hand column.

Anatomy of Social Categorization

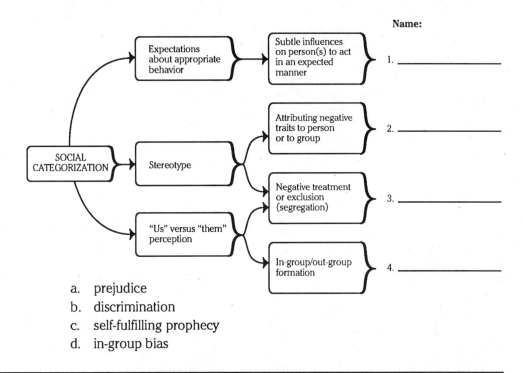

a. prejudice
b. discrimination
c. self-fulfilling prophecy
d. in-group bias

CONCEPT 5   Similarity of attitudes, appearance, and background influence interpersonal attraction. Social psychologists have investigated effects of similarity, complementarity, and proximity on attraction.

5.1   Summarize the effects of similarity on attractiveness and friendship.

5.2   Describe how complementary and compatible needs and proximity affect attractiveness.

Concept Builder 5

Directions: Read the following statements made by various couples as they describe the basis of attraction that led to a relationship and eventually to marriage. Match each couple's statement to the attraction factor being illustrated.

Reasons for Marriage: The Attraction Factor

_B_ Couple 1: Well, we were alike in many ways; we're both tall, were born in the same month, and come from the same middle-class backgrounds; we both valued a relationship that would allow us to pursue our careers.

_C_ Couple 2: We hated each other when we first met. I thought, what a dork he was, but a cute dork! Gradually, we both quit criticizing each other and started to compliment each other. Our liking for each other kept growing.

_E_ Couple 3: I think our attraction had a lot to do with the fact that we both wanted a good, strong, loving family. That was really confirmed when we had our first child. Family values are very important to us.

_a_ Couple 4: We were essentially childhood sweethearts. I grew up just two houses from my spouse; we went to the same elementary school and same high school. During my senior year, she transferred to my college. I just couldn't get rid of her!

_D_ Couple 5: He jokes that we have a "fifty-fifty" relationship. I cook, he eats. I wash the clothes, he wears them. Actually, he is the kind of person who has to have someone take care of him, and I'm the nurturing type. I like taking care of him; he likes being taken care of.

a. proximity
b. similarity
c. effects of approval
d. complementary needs
e. compatible needs

CHAPTER EXERCISE

Directions: Below are ten brief definitions (forty letters or less) of key words in the text. Your task is to write in the appropriate key term for each of the following clues.

Password

Clues: Key terms:

1. False expectations ultimately confirmed: _self-fulfilling prophecy_
2. Motivates a person to re-establish consistency: _cognitive dissonance_
3. Three-component evaluative response: _attitude_
4. "Us" vs. "them" thinking: _in group bias_
5. Repeated neutral encounters: _exposure effect_
6. Changing attitudes through a "quality" argument: _central route_
7. Mental representation of "types" of people: _stereotypes_
8. Physical nearness: _proximity_
9. Message recipient's use of heuristic thinking: _peripheral route_
10. Way we think and reason about ourselves: _social cognition_

**PRACTICE
EXAM 1**

1. The simplest way to think about attitudes is to view them as:

    a.   opinions
    b.   values
    c.   morals
    d.   preferences or aversions

    (Factual, Obj. 1.1)

2. Bennie was eating lasagna at a friend's house one night when the hostess asked how he liked the dish; he replied that it was great. Then the hostess revealed that the meal was made with venison rather than hamburger. Bennie didn't feel so good about what he had just eaten after hearing this news. What component of his attitude showed an abrupt change?

    a.   cognitive
    b.   affective
    c.   behavioral
    d.   motivational

    (Conceptual, Obj. 1.1)

3. Which of the following statements is *true* regarding the exposure effect?

    a.   We need only one positive experience to develop a liking toward something previously considered negative.
    b.   Repeated neutral encounters will not cause a person to develop positive attitudes.
    c.   Encounters must be aversive to produce negative responses.
    d.   Simple repeated encounters lead to negative attitudes.

    (Factual, Obj. 1.1)

4. Earl knows that if he acts very interested in his job as bank teller, is on time every day, and agrees with his boss's opinions, he may be promoted to assistant manager. Earl's theory of attitude formation is based on:

    a.   inoculation
    b.   operant conditioning
    c.   self-monitoring
    d.   classical conditioning

    (Conceptual, Obj. 1.1)

5. According to cognitive dissonance theory, the smaller the reward offered, the _____ the shift in attitude.

    a.   smaller
    b.   greater
    c.   slower
    d.   faster

    (Factual, Obj. 1.1)

6. Kyle's parents have been playing classical music for him since he was an infant. They believed he would learn to like this music because of his repeated encounters with it. What concept are his parents using?

    a.   exposure effect
    b.   proximity effect
    c.   reinforcement theory
    d.   involuntary conditioning

    (Conceptual, Obj. 1.2)

7. Which of the following statements illustrates the affective component of an attitude?

    a.   "I detest wrestling."
    b.   "I know the exam is scheduled for next week."
    c.   "I think these prices are too high."
    d.   "President Bush is an honest man."

                                                        (Conceptual, Obj. 1.1)

8. Which of the following is *not* a component of attitudes listed in your text?

    a.   the affect component
    b.   the behavioral component
    c.   the perceptive component
    d.   the cognitive component

                                                        (Factual, Obj. 1.1)

9. Many advertisers believe that playing an ad over and over again will develop a positive attitude toward a product. What principle is this based on?

    a.   cognitive dissonance
    b.   reinforcement theory
    c.   message saturation
    d.   exposure effect

                                                        (Conceptual, Obj. 1.1)

10. After pondering his choices for three months, Willard finally selected a personal computer to purchase. Just two weeks after buying it, he read in *Byte* magazine that the PC he purchased would be discontinued because of design problems. Willard immediately canceled his subscription to the magazine and raved about how great his PC worked. What is Willard experiencing?

    a.   cognitive dissonance
    b.   attribution error
    c.   self-fulfilling prophecy
    d.   self-monitoring

                                                        (Conceptual, Obj. 1.2)

11. The major point of LaPiere's classic study using a Chinese couple during the 1930s was that:

    a.   Chinese prejudice led to discrimination in jobs
    b.   anti-Oriental attitudes were virtually nonexistent in the 1930s
    c.   people's behavior is sometimes inconsistent with their attitudes
    d.   affective and cognitive aspects of attitudes are very different from each other

                                                        (Factual, Obj. 2.2)

12. If you wanted your newly elected official to be true to his words, act on his verbalized attitudes, and not worry about making a good impression, what kind of trait should this person exhibit?

    a.   low post-decisional dissonance
    b.   high post-decisional dissonance
    c.   low self-monitoring
    d.   high self-monitoring

                                                        (Conceptual, Obj. 2.3)

**PRACTICE
EXAM 2**

1. When prejudice is expressed in behavior, we call it:

   a.   stereotyping
   b.   discrimination
   c.   racism
   d.   attribution

   (Factual, Obj. 4.1)

2. Eddie is a waiter in a local restaurant. He thinks he's pretty good at "sizing" up customers by the way they look, dress, and act when they enter the establishment. If they look like "poor" tippers, he doesn't spend much time with them; if they look like they might be generous, he gives them a lot of personal attention. For the most part, Eddie's tips confirm his reading of people. What might Eddie be inadvertently creating in these situations?

   a.   a prejudicial attitude
   b.   a keen perceptual sense
   c.   a self-fulfilling prophecy
   d.   attribution error

   (Conceptual, Obj. 4.2)

3. "Us" versus "them" categorizations tend to create intergroup conflict. Part of the reason stems from the fact that a group may view itself positively and view other groups negatively. These groups are called:

   a.   in-groups and out-groups
   b.   dominant groups and subordinate groups
   c.   positive groups and negative groups
   d.   valued groups and devalued groups

   (Factual, Obj. 4.1)

4. The single most important factor in friendship is:

   a.   physical proximity
   b.   similarity
   c.   exposure effects
   d.   approval

   (Factual, Obj. 5.1)

5. In terms of needs, what seems to be associated with harmonious marriages?

   a.   complementary needs
   b.   compatible needs
   c.   high affiliative needs
   d.   low dominance needs

   (Factual, Obj. 5.2)

6. Paul and Paula have been dating for three months now and feel that they can really depend on each other. They enjoy sharing activities, such as camping out and having small dinner parties. What is the basis for their attraction?

   a.   proximity
   b.   exposure effects
   c.   compatible needs
   d.   high affiliative needs

   (Conceptual, Obj. 5.1)

7. Privately, Norman dislikes and has a negative opinion of most other ethnic groups, particularly Hispanics. But publicly he does not show it, and by law, he is required to show that he has a fair balance of Hispanics and whites in his company. Norman's private ideas illustrate:

   a. discrimination
   b. stereotyping
   c. cognitive dissonance
   d. prejudice

   (Factual, Obj. 4.1)

8. Experimenter bias is an example of:

   a. stereotyping
   b. self-fulfilling prophecy
   c. prejudice
   d. attributional error

   (Conceptual, Obj. 4.2)

9. Lester believes that drug-use is highest among inner-city Blacks, mainly because that's what TV news broadcasts most frequently. If it is revealed that TV newscasts show these Black populations disproportionately, what heuristic is Lester's social perception being based upon?

   a. self-fulfilling prophecy
   b. availability
   c. anchoring
   d. actor-observer bias

   (Conceptual, Obj. 3.2)

10. The affective component of attitude is to classical conditioning as the _____ component is to instrumental conditioning.

    a. behavioral
    b. cognitive
    c. emotional
    d. evaluative

    (Conceptual, Obj. 1.1)

11. How does cognitive dissonance differ from self-perception theory in explaining the results of dissonance studies?

    a. Self-perception requires an unpleasant state to explain attitude change.
    b. Cognitive dissonance addresses attitudes; self-perception addresses behavior.
    c. Self-perception has no affective component.
    d. Cognitive theory requires an unpleasant state to explain attitude change.

    (Factual, Obj. 1.3)

12. When is the central route to persuasion most effective?

    a. when the target's motivation to think about an issue is high
    b. when motivation or ability to think about the arguments is low
    c. when persuasion lends itself well to an emotional appeal
    d. when credibility of the communicator is an issue

    (Factual, Obj. 2.1)

■ ANSWER KEY ■

Concept 1
1. b
2. a
3. c

Concept 2
1. P
2. C
3. P
4. P
5. C
6. P

Concept 3
1. III
2. I
3. II
4. IV

Concept 4
1. c
2. a
3. b
4. d

Concept 5
Couple 1: b
Couple 2: c
Couple 3: e
Couple 4: a
Couple 5: d

Chapter Exercise
1. self-fulfilling prophecy
2. cognitive dissonance
3. attitude
4. in-group bias
5. exposure effect
6. central route to persuasion
7. stereotypes
8. proximity
9. peripheral route to persuasion
10. social cognition

Practice Exam 1
1. d, p. 628
2. b, p. 629
3. c, p. 629
4. b, pp. 629–630
5. b, pp. 630–631
6. a, p. 629
7. a, p. 629
8. c, p. 628
9. d, p. 629
10. a, pp. 630–631
11. c, p. 636
12. c, p. 638

Practice Exam 2
1. b, p. 645
2. c, p. 646
3. a, p. 645
4. a, p. 653
5. b, p. 652
6. c, p. 682
7. d, p. 645
8. b, p. 646
9. b, p. 642
10. a, pp. 629–630
11. d, pp. 631–632
12. a, p. 634

CHAPTER TWENTY-TWO

Social Influence and Group Processes

KEY TERM ORGANIZER

Social facilitation, or enhanced performance in the presence of others, occurs whenever people work on simple tasks or on tasks they have already mastered. This appears to come about because the presence of others increases arousal and leads to an increase in *dominant responses.* On easy tasks, dominant responses are usually correct, but on difficult or new tasks, they are likely to be wrong.

The norms of a culture are social forces that exert a powerful, although often unrecognized, pressure on individuals to conform. A *social norm* is a shared standard of behavior, a guideline people follow in their relations with others. *Conformity* can be defined as the tendency to shift one's view or behavior closer to the norms expressed by other people. The following key experiments have contributed to our knowledge about conformity:

Conformity	Effect on Social Behavior
Sherif's experiment	Used the "autokinetic effect," a perceptual illusion involving movement, to examine conformity.
Asch's experiment	Naive subjects yielded to group pressure in the "line-judging" task.
Zimbardo's prison experiment	Subjects adopted the social roles of guards and prisoners without being coached on how to behave.
Obedience	
Milgram's experiments	Dramatic illustration of the pressure to comply to an authority figure's request to shock a "learner" in a mock learning experiment.

Obedience is any behavior that complies with the explicit commands of a person in authority. Factors which can lead to disobedience include lack of direct confrontation with authority, and nearness of the subject to the victim. Conformity to peers can also override the demands of authority.

People are pushed to conform to unanimous opinion of others by two forces:

- *Normative influence:* agreeing with the expressed judgments of others even though we know they are wrong;

- *Informational influence:* relying on the responses of others as a source of information about reality.

Both animals and human beings behave in altruistic ways, and altruism appears to have both social and biological bases. According to sociobiologists, organisms are motivated to protect their genes, not their lives. The application of this concept to human beings has not been established, although it may work through *reciprocal altruism,* in which reinforcement need not be direct. In emergencies, the presence of bystanders appears to inhibit people from giving aid. The explanation of this inhibiting effect includes the following:

Audience inhibition: normative influence of bystanders that inhibits response in an emergency;

Diffusion of responsibility: the diminishment of personal responsibility caused by the presence of others, which inhibits response in an emergency;

Social influence: the informational influence of bystanders that inhibits response in an emergency.

Any act that is intended to cause pain, damage, or suffering to another is an act of interpersonal *aggression*. The following factors affect aggression:

Factor	Nature of Influence
Biological influence	No strong biological evidence has been found; where it has been implicated, the environment still exerts a profound influence.
Social-learning theory	Aggressive "models" can exert a powerful influence on imitation; there are many reinforcers for behaving in an aggressive manner.
Situational factors	Frustration-aggression hypothesis; uncontrollable stress; level of anger.

The choice between cooperation and self-interest in daily life has been studied by using the Prisoner's Dilemma game. Despite the fact that a strategy of cooperation helps both players, most people choose self-interest. The most effective strategy in continuing games is tit-for-tat. Although threats are not very effective in games based on the Prisoner's Dilemma, people use threats when they are available.

Individual choices can have serious social consequences, as in the *tragedy of the commons.* The tragedy of the commons is an example of a social trap. Social traps develop because the immediate consequences of an action (personal gain) outweigh long-term outcomes (social harm). It has been suggested that only mutually agreed-upon coercion, which makes antisocial action difficult or expensive, will get people out of social traps.

When working cooperatively, a group can accomplish much more than a single individual. Yet, a group member puts out less effort in a group than when working alone. The decreased effort occurs because, as *social impact theory* predicts, the impact of social forces affecting the situation is spread out over the entire group.

Although social impact theory assumes that social loafing is the result of the diffusion of responsibility for the group's work, the opportunity for self-evaluation can reduce social loafing as effectively as evaluation by others.

The physical environment has a powerful influence on social behavior. The distress that is associated with crowds depends not on *physical density* (number of people in a given space), but on the psychological experience of *crowding* (perception of restricted space). The distress of crowding depends on increased arousal, combined with a lack of perceived control.

MAJOR CONCEPTS AND LEARNING OBJECTIVES

CONCEPT 1 Social facilitation, the simplest form of social influence, refers to enhanced performance in the presence of others. This enhancement depends upon dominant responses and arousal.

1.1 Define social facilitation and describe the concept of dominant processes.

1.2 Discuss the effect of arousal on social facilitation.

Concept Builder 1

Directions: The following diagram depicts the chain of events involved in social facilitation, with each step labeled. After studying this diagram, read the story that follows, then list the correct sequence of letters that best describes the chain of events at the two pianists' performances.

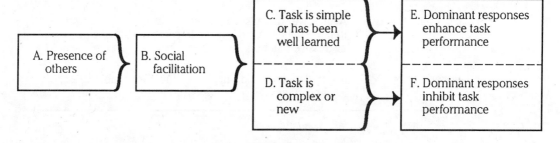

A Tale of Two Students

Once upon a time, there were two music students, Treble and Bass. Both were told at the end of the quarter, they would be required to give a public recital of some new piece of music. Treble chose a complex piece by Mozart and worked hard on it throughout the quarter. She practiced diligently, committing new passages to memory and replaying each one daily. Bass also chose a difficult piece by Salieri, but he didn't practice as often. He reasoned that the composition was very close to the Salieri composition he had worked on in his previous piano course.

When recital day arrived, Treble's composition seemed like a breeze; she whipped through it beautifully, and was given a standing ovation.

Bass, on the other hand, had relied too heavily on his false sense of confidence. The piece was just too difficult to perform in front of others and he messed up several times, stopping at one point.

Moral of the story: Practice makes perfect.

1.   List the four steps that occurred to Bass: ____ ____ ____ ____

2.   List the four steps that occurred to Treble: ____ ____ ____ ____

CONCEPT 2   Conformity and obedience to authority are two forms of social influence that induce people to act against their beliefs or moral standards.

2.1   Define "social norm" and "conformity."

2.2   Give a detailed account of Sherif's, Asch's, and Zimbardo's experiments on conformity.

2.3   Outline and describe the effects of situational variables and minority influences on conformity, and distinguish normative and informational influence on conformity.

2.4   Outline Milgram's experiments on obedience and summarize the factors that influence obedience.

2.5   Discuss the role of hidden influences on compliance.

Concept Builder 2

Directions: When Brad was interviewing with the corporate giant I.B.N., several things stuck in his mind. When Brad returned home to his apartment, he mentally replayed the interview. Match each statement he recalled to the social influence concept being illustrated.

Social Influence at I.B.N.

_____ 1.   "We expect you to believe in the I.B.N. philosophy, to adhere to the company's norms and values, and to fit in with the team concept."

_____ 2.   "We do have a dress standard here: gray pinstripe suits, yellow ties, and 12-pound wing-tip shoes."

_____ 3.   "We want to emphasize the importance of complying with the demands and directives of management and chief executive officers. This is essential to our harmony here at I.B.N."

_____ 4.   "If you are unclear about what to do, look to me—I'll teach you the ropes."

_____ 5.   "We have no problem doing business in South Africa. We hope you don't have a problem with that." (You privately do believe doing business with an apartheid state is wrong.)

a.   social norm

b.   conformity

c.   informational influence

d.   obedience

e.   normative influence

CONCEPT 3 Helping behavior is classed as prosocial behavior because it benefits another person or group. Psychologists have studied both helping and failure to help in order to understand prosocial behavior.

    3.1   Define "altruism" and "reciprocal altruism."

    3.2   List and describe the factors that aid or inhibit the tendency to help in emergency situations.

Concept Builder 3

Directions: A number of explanations have been put forth to explain the failure of bystanders to respond to an emergency. Read the following recommendations that are meant to encourage people to help others and to get involved in crisis or emergency situations. Then match each recommendation to the factor being countered.

When Will People Help?

_____ 1. "Don't assume that someone has already called the police or ambulance. Even if that were true, it's very important that you act as if it is your responsibility to get help to the victim."

_____ 2. "Don't be afraid of doing something that could turn out to be embarrassing in front of others, such as overacting or acting on a false alarm. You may do something that's foolish, but that's only temporary. Not taking a potential, life-saving action could be fatal for someone, and that's permanent."

_____ 3. "When a potential emergency occurs, but the situation is ambiguous, interpret it as an emergency. Don't wait for others to define the situation as an emergency for you. Interpret it as serious; if you err, err in favor of the potential victim."

Reasons for not responding

a. audience inhibition

b. social influence

c. diffusion of responsibility

CONCEPT 4 Aggression is classed as an antisocial behavior because the intention to cause pain, damage, or suffering to another has social costs. Aggression has both biological and learned components. Attempts to explain aggressive behavior fall into three categories: biological, social learning, and situational explanations.

    4.1   Describe the evidence for the biological basis of aggression.

    4.2   Discuss the roles of modeling and reinforcements in the social-learning view of aggression.

    4.3   Explain the frustration-aggression hypothesis and the way frustration arises in situational contexts.

Concept Builder 4

Directions: Below are five strategies recommended to a prison warden for decreasing inmate aggression. Read each proposed strategy and match it to the type of explanation it seems to be reflecting.

_____ 1. Decrease the level of frustration for the prison inmate. Do not thwart prisoner's attempts to meet their basic physiological and psychological needs.

_____ 2. Screen all inmates, using medical procedures to detect any chromosomal or brain abnormalities. If such aberrations are detected, label those prisoners "high risk" for aggression and give them extra medical attention.

_____ 3. Have well-liked guards and certain trustees "model" good behavior for other prisoners. Have these models of good behavior in highly visible roles in cell blocks.

_____ 4. Make deliberate attempts to reward "good" or "cooperative" behavior in inmates. At the same time, make sure that bad or aggressive behavior isn't inadvertently rewarded with attention, even negative attention.

_____ 5. Reduce the forms of uncontrollable stress, such as unannounced bed checks, unexpected work details, and unplanned transfers to new dorms.

a. biological explanations

b. social learning explanations

c. situational explanations

CONCEPT 5

Group processes can be facilitated or debilitated by the strategies that individual group members adopt, such as cooperation and competition. Environmental psychology involves the study of how individuals are affected by physical environments.

5.1 Discuss how the Prisoner's Dilemma game illustrates the problem of the choice between cooperation and competition.

5.2 Describe the tragedy of the commons and identify some strategies for breaking out of social traps.

5.3 Explain how social impact theory accounts for decline in performance in groups.

5.4 Discuss impact of crowding and density on an individual's experience of the environment.

Concept Builder 5

Directions: One way to look at the possible problems that could develop between the United States and the Soviet Union is to use the Prisoner's Dilemma model to describe several possible scenarios. Look at the dilemma in the following diagram. After studying the diagram, answer the questions that follow with the quadrant number(s) that are most appropriate.

Missile Negotiations

U.S.S.R.

	Freeze current number of warheads	Add new warheads
Freeze number of warheads	I. Nuclear threat suspended	II. U.S.S.R gains advantage
Add new warheads	III. U.S. gains advantage	IV. Runaway escalation

U. S. (labeled at left)

1. Which choice is the most cooperative option? _____

2. Which choice(s) reflects high self-interest? _____

3. Which choice is most competitive, and dangerous, in the long run? _____

4. If a tit-for-tat strategy is used, what should the United States do after the Soviet Union announces it will increase its number of warheads (strategy II)? _____

CHAPTER EXERCISE

Directions: Below are five major social behavior categories corresponding to the major concepts of this chapter, followed by brief definitions of the key terms of this chapter. Your task is to identify the key terms for each definition, then place each term under the appropriate heading.

Key Term Review

Social Facilitation	Conformity/ Obedience	Helping	Aggression	Group Processes

1. The interference with goal-directed behavior: _____

2. The impact of social forces affecting the situation is spread out over an entire group:

   _____

3. Enhanced performance in the presence of others: _____

4. Concern about others' evaluation of our behavior: _____

5. Aggression is always the result of frustration: _____

6. The tragedy of the commons is an example of this: _____

7. The responses most likely to be made in a particular situation: _____

8. Tendency to shift views or behavior closer to the norms followed by other people:

   _____

9. Waiting for others to define a situation as an emergency: _____

10. Any behavior that complies with the explicit commands of an authority figure:

    _____

11. Spreading the responsibility for intervening over all the bystanders: _____

PRACTICE EXAM 1

1. Social facilitation states that the presence of others has an arousing effect, and when we are aroused, our _____ responses are enhanced.

   a.   competitive
   b.   dominant
   c.   simple
   d.   complex

   (Factual, Obj. 1.1)

2. Larry is a good racquetball player. Recently, however, he played unusually well before a large crowd in the playoffs. He attributed his exhibition to the presence of people watching him, spurring him on. This effect illustrates:

   a.   social facilitation
   b.   reciprocal altruism
   c.   exposure effect
   d.   arousal effect

   (Conceptual, Obj. 1.2)

3. Behavior that is most important to the community is generally regulated by:

   a.   customs
   b.   law
   c.   norms
   d.   morals

   (Factual, Obj. 2.1)

4. Which of the following newspaper headlines would *best* describe Zimbardo's experiment on social roles?

   a.   "Blind Obedience Common in America"
   b.   "Minority Influence Powerful"
   c.   "We Are Conforming Animals"
   d.   "Prison Brutality Out of Hand"

   (Conceptual, Obj. 2.2)

5. Moscovici states that minority dissent exerts its influence on an individual's private _____, shifting them away from the majority position.

   a. attitudes
   b. beliefs
   c. behaviors
   d. values

   (Factual, Obj. 2.3)

6. As Chuck was walking along a busy city street, he saw a middle-aged man staggering about and eventually stumbling and falling. Chuck was concerned, but when he looked around, everyone else seemed nonchalant, so Chuck shrugged his shoulders and walked on. What factor is operating to keep Chuck from intervening?

   a. audience inhibition
   b. social influence
   c. diffusion of responsibility
   d. conformity

   (Conceptual, Obj. 3.2)

7. Trivers proposes that when a person performs an altruistic act, he or she increases the chances that the person who is helped will one day help the helper or the helper's kin. This concept is called:

   a. social influence
   b. sociobiology
   c. reciprocal altruism
   d. social impact theory

   (Factual, Obj. 3.1)

8. Janet has no problem being "packed" in among a large number of people at a music concert. However, she feels panic when she is surrounded by others on a elevator. What is Janet experiencing?

   a. physical density
   b. crowding
   c. social trap
   d. social impact

   (Conceptual, Obj. 5.4)

9. According to some psychologists, the key situational factor predicting aggression is not frustration, but _____; this may be provoked by frustration or other experiences, such as verbal attacks.

   a. anonymity
   b. loss of individuality
   c. loss of reinforcements
   d. level of anger

   (Factual, Obj. 4.3)

10. Jason and Marty are playing a video game called "Ambush," which pits two players against each other. They're both being stalked by the FBI in this game, and the major play options involve variations of either cooperating with each other to avoid ambush or competing with each other to see who gets ambushed first. Examine the first three moves of each player:

	Marty's moves	Jason's moves
1.	cooperative	cooperative
2.	competitive	competitive
3.	cooperative	cooperative

Jason's play strategy illustrates:

a. tit-for-tat
b. the common good
c. cooperation
d. blind self-interest

(Conceptual, Obj. 5.1)

11. Garrett Hardin suggests that the only way to get people to break out of social traps is to:

a. use a tit-for-tat strategy
b. deprive people of all freedom
c. use mutually agreed-upon coercion
d. limit communication between people

(Factual, Obj. 5.2)

12. It has been observed that work performance and quality suffer in organizations with many people who produce work anonymously. Which theory would explain this effect most clearly?

a. reciprocal altruism theory
b. "hidden influence" theory
c. normative influence theory
d. social impact theory

(Conceptual, Obj. 5.3)

PRACTICE EXAM 2

1. Suppose you supervise factory workers who assemble circuit boards for computers. The workers' job is very simple and repetitive—at times, even boring. What can you do to boost their performance on this task?

a. have workers work alone
b. add bright room colors and background music
c. have several people work openly in front of each other
d. schedule frequent work breaks

(Conceptual, Obj. 1.1)

2. The presence of others enhances the performance of which of the following behaviors?

a. complex tasks
b. new skills
c. recently learned skills
d. well-learned responses

(Factual, Obj. 1.1)

3. Which of the following is the best example of a norm?

a. sleeping, lying down, in a bed
b. wearing fashionable clothing
c. social pressure from friends
d. obeying an authority figure

(Conceptual, Obj. 2.1)

4. In investigating conformity, Sherif used the _____ effect as the basis for making judgments.

    a.   exposure
    b.   social facilitation
    c.   autokinetic
    d.   social trap

                                                                    (Factual, Obj. 2.2)

5. What do the Nazi atrocities, the My Lai massacre, the Jonestown tragedy, and Milgram's experiments have in common?

    a.   All involve the lack of altruism.
    b.   All involve dominant responses.
    c.   All involve obedience to authority.
    d.   All involve conformity to social roles.

                                                                    (Conceptual, Obj. 2.4)

6. Among the 40 subjects participating in the Milgram experiment, what percentage obeyed the experimenter to the very end of the experiment?

    a.   20
    b.   50
    c.   65
    d.   90

                                                                    (Factual, Obj. 2.4)

7. Which of the following observations would argue against the biological basis of aggression in human beings?

    a.   According to Freud, we are driven to aggression by the death instinct.
    b.   Some prison inmates have been found to have XYY chromosomes.
    c.   There is a consistent linkage of televised violence and aggressive behavior.
    d.   Violent behavior has been linked to various types of brain damage.

                                                                    (Conceptual, Obj. 4.1)

8. Which of the following is *not* a social learning explanation for aggressive behavior?

    a.   Frustration and anonymity promote aggression.
    b.   Most aggressive behavior requires intricate, learned skills.
    c.   Aggression is related to exposure to models of violent behavior.
    d.   Reinforcement for aggressive acts explains why people attack one another.

                                                                    (Factual, Obj. 4.2)

9. Tiffany is in a relationship in which her attempts to receive love and recognition keep getting blocked and thwarted. She reached a point, one day, where she could no longer stand it, so she lashed out at her boyfriend, telling him off, throwing her ring back at him, and leaving. What factor best describes Tiffany's aggressive reaction?

    a.   uncontrollable stress
    b.   a punishing role model
    c.   frustration-aggression
    d.   buildup of the death instinct

                                                                    (Conceptual, Obj. 4.3)

10. The most commonly chosen strategy in the Prisoner's Dilemma game is:

   a. tit-for-tat
   b. blind self-interest
   c. cooperation
   d. the common good

(Factual, Obj. 5.1)

11. Sometimes a region or community goes through a long water drought, and residents are asked not to use water for any nondrinking purposes (washing cars, watering lawns, etc.). What would Garrett Hardin suggest as a strategy for preventing a social trap from developing?

   a. advertise heavily about the harm that will be caused if everyone uses water
   b. ask people to take their cars to car washes and use paper plates
   c. ration water to everyone
   d. put a heavy, temporary tax on water use

(Conceptual, Obj. 5.2)

12. Just as the presence of bystanders diffuses responsibility, so the presence of several participants in a joint endeavor reduces the individual contribution of each. This is called:

   a. the Prisoner's Dilemma
   b. social impact theory
   c. the social trap
   d. the tragedy of the commons

(Factual, Obj. 5.3)

■ ANSWER KEY ■

Concept 1   Bass: A, B, D, F
                  Treble: A, B, C, E

Concept 2   1. b   4. c
                  2. a   5. e
                  3. d

Concept 3   1. c
                  2. a
                  3. b

Concept 4   1. c   4. b
                  2. a   5. c
                  3. b

Concept 5   1. strategy I   3. strategy IV
                  2. strategies II and III   4. add warheads

Self-Test   *Social Facilitation:* 3. social facilitation; 7. dominant responses
                  Conformity/Obedience: 8. conformity; 10. obedience
                  Helping: 4. audience inhibition; 9. social influence; 11. diffusion of responsibility
                  Aggression: 1. frustration; 5. frustration-aggression hypothesis
                  Group Processes: 2. social impact theory; 6 social trap

Practice Exam 1

1. b, pp. 658–659
2. a, pp. 658–659
3. b, p. 661
4. d, p. 666
5. a, p. 665
6. b, p. 672
7. c, p. 670
8. b, p. 683
9. d, p. 678
10. a, p. 679
11. c, pp. 680–681
12. d, pp. 681–682

Practice Exam 2

1. c, pp. 658–659
2. d, p. 659
3. b, pp. 660–661
4. c, p. 662
5. c, p. 666
6. c, p. 667
7. c, pp. 674–675
8. a, pp. 675–676
9. c, p. 677
10. b, p. 679
11. d, p. 681
12. b, pp. 681–682

CHAPTER TWENTY-THREE

Industrial/Organizational Psychology

KEY TERM ORGANIZER

Industrial/organizational (I/O) psychology has its roots in industrial engineering, personnel psychology, and the human relations movement. Frederick Taylor, an industrial engineer, called on management to redesign work methods to make them more efficient, a system known as *scientific management.*

In matching workers to jobs, many employers rely on psychological tests as predictors of job performance and on nontest predictors, such as interviews. To be useful, a test must be both reliable and valid. Furthermore, it should have predictive validity; unfortunately, most tests are only moderate predictors of success on the job. If a test has an *adverse impact* on members of a protected minority, it may be found to violate the Civil Rights Act. Interviews may lack validity because of the biases and backgrounds of the interviewer and applicant or because of the structure of the interview itself.

Work motivation affects how long employees stay with a company, how dependably they perform their duties, and how innovative they are on the job. Theories of motivation can be divided into three areas, as follows:

Need Theories	Cognitive Theories	Reinforcement Theory
Maslow's Need Hierarchy—fundamental, psychological, metaneeds	Expectancy theory: motivated by our goals and how attainable we think goals are	Operant learning principles applicable in the workplace
McClelland's research—socialized and personalized power	Equity theory: motivated to remove perceived inequities	
	Goal-setting theory: motivated by conscious intentions to attain a goal	

Job satisfaction reflects the match between what workers want from a job and what they get. The relationship between job satisfaction and performance is apparently circular, with the perception of good performance initiating the cycle. Employees who feel *organizational commitment* display helpful and cooperative behaviors at work.

I/O psychologists take four basic approaches to the question of what makes a leader effective:

Approach	Definition	Organizational Success
Trait	Effective leadership depends on personal characteristics.	Depends on selection of leader
Behavioral	Effectiveness depends on what leaders do (leadership style).	Depends on training of leader
Situational	Effectiveness depends on situation (task, organization, work group).	Depends on economic trends
Contingency	Leadership is contingent on combinations of traits, behavior, situations.	Depends on appropriate combinations, given a specific situation

There are a number of contingency theories:

Theory	Theorists	Definitions of Leadership
Cognitive resource theory	Fiedler	Situation determines how leadership style and traits are related to performance of the work group
Life-cycle theory	Hersey & Blanchard	Leadership is the ability to foster maturity and responsibility in group members
Vroom-Yetton-Yago model	Vroom, Yetton, & Yago	Leadership varies by the situation; leaders alter style to fit situation at hand
Path-goal theory	Evans & House	Leader's role is to influence group members' expectations
Transformational leadership	Bass	Leadership produces large-scale organizational change

Norms set by the work group can strongly influence a worker's behavior on the job. When a group's task requires cooperation and interdependence, then a system that rewards individual efforts will be counterproductive. External pressures and external stress can enhance group cohesiveness and motivation, but they can sometimes lead to "groupthink"—a phenomenon in which members suspend their own ability to think critically, thus compromising the group's decision-making ability. Group cohesiveness can increase productivity if the group has productivity as a strongly held norm.

MAJOR CONCEPTS AND LEARNING OBJECTIVES

CONCEPT 1   Industrial/organizational (I/O) psychology is concerned with human behavior in the workplace. One of the major concerns of I/O psychology is to find workers who fit the demands of the job. Psychological tests and interviews are used as predictors of performance.

    1.1   Discuss the early psychological studies in industrial settings.

    1.2   Outline and describe the psychological and legal issues concerning the use of psychological tests as predictors of job performance and fit.

    1.3   Discuss the advantages and disadvantages of interviews in the selection process.

    1.4   Define the "realistic job preview" and discuss its merits for job selection.

Concept Builder 1

Directions: Read the following statements concerning interviewing as a selection tool. For each statement, indicate whether the observation or the technique would lead to a valid interview or an invalid interview.

| | Potential Source of: | |
	Validity	Invalidity
1. Interviewers should have an "ideal" applicant against which to evaluate the people they interview.		
2. Interviewers should be given feedback on later successes or failures of the applicants they hire.		
3. Interviewers should give more weight to unfavorable information than to favorable information.		
4. Interviewers should receive training on how to conduct an interview.		
5. Interviewers should rely more on an applicant's body language than on the words he or she uses.		
6. The interviewer should use a structured format.		
7. Interviewers should not worry about the cues (words, appearance, behavior) they use when interviewing an applicant.		
8. Interviewers should (and it's only natural to do so) rate applicants who are of the same ethnic and social background as themselves more highly than other applicants.		
9. Interviewers should ask only those questions that reveal pertinent information about job duties.		
10. Interviewers should request personal information such as marital status, child-care arrangements, and spouse's salary.		

CONCEPT 2   Work motivation affects how long employees stay with a company, how dependably they perform their duties, and how innovative they are on the job. Need theories, cognitive theories, and reinforcement theories have been offered to account for motivation.

> 2.1 Discuss how needs for self-actualization and achievement predict motivation and distinguish socialized power from personalized power.
>
> 2.2 Distinguish the expectancy theory from the equity theory of work motivation and define the basic concepts of each.
>
> 2.3 Contrast the use of goal-setting and the use of reinforcement to achieve worker motivation.

Concept Builder 2

Directions: Assume that you are an interviewer in the personnel department of a large company and you are conducting "exit" interviews with employees who have decided to leave the company. Your job is to decide which motivational theory best explains their reason for leaving.

Exit Interview: Reasons Why Workers Leave Their Jobs

_____ 1. I'd have to say my main reason for quitting is that I see absolutely no connection between how much effort I put into my job in the credit office and my ultimate job performance. I can only process what customer service can get to me on a daily basis. I could do a lot more, but they forward only 20 to 30 applications a day. I have no control over them, so why should I knock myself out to process 20 to 30 applications before lunch?

    a. expectancy theory
    b. equity theory
    c. goal-setting theory
    d. reinforcement theory

_____ 2. I'm quitting because the company withdrew a very good incentive program last month. As you know, my salary isn't that great, but the fringe benefits were fantastic; tuition payback program, free dental and medical insurance, and a free corporate membership to the health club. I didn't mind their increasing the deductibles on the dental/medical program. But when the company dropped its tuition payback program, that did it.

_____ 3. I'm quitting because of favoritism. I came here about the same time as Joan. We're both data processors, doing about the same kind of work, but she gets almost $200 a month more than I get. First I asked for a raise, but I didn't get one. Then I decided, I won't get mad, I'll get even, so I slowed my production down. That didn't work so I tried to change my attitude, and I stopped comparing myself to Joan, but the unequal pay thing kept gnawing away at me. It's just not fair and it's not going to change.

_____ 4.   I'm quitting because I never got any feedback on how well
I was doing. I work in inventory, cataloguing and keeping
track of all merchandise. I never knew if I was filling orders
too slowly, too quickly, too anything! There were never
any definable goals set for performance. I need tangible
goals to work toward and to gauge my progress.

CONCEPT 3   Motivation of workers depends heavily on the attitude held by employees,
especially job satisfaction and organizational commitment.

    3.1   Define job satisfaction and discuss the relationship between satisfaction
and performance.

    3.2   Identify the factors that influence organizational commitment.

**Concept
Builder 3**

*Directions: The figure below depicts job satisfaction and
organizational commitment as two main dimensions of
work-related attitudes. Read the ten statements beneath the
diagram and identify each as characteristic of job satisfaction
(JS), organizational commitment (OC), or a combination of
the two (JS + OC):*

Work-Related Attitudes

_____ 1.   Avoiding conflicting or ambiguous work roles
_____ 2.   Turning down an attractive offer to go with a competitor
_____ 3.   "Personality" of worker
_____ 4.   "Direct assistance" to fellow employees (helping them when they have a
problem)
_____ 5.   Complying with company policies, such as being punctual, or not wasting
time
_____ 6.   Associated with lower absenteeism and turnover
_____ 7.   Level of satisfaction with previous jobs
_____ 8.   Defending one's company when others make critical remarks
_____ 9.   Working late; volunteering for difficult projects
_____ 10.   Willing to change companies, but committed to one's career

CONCEPT 4   As leaders, managers play a role in shaping employees' attitudes and behavior. However, workers are social beings, so the group to which a person belongs also exerts a strong influence on behavior on the job.

> 4.1 List and describe the four approaches to the study of leadership and review the criticisms of each.
>
> 4.2 Identify and describe the three characteristics of transformational leadership.
>
> 4.3 Outline and describe the major variables in influencing group effectiveness

Concept Builder 4

Directions: Read the following classified ads from the job section of the paper. Each one is soliciting for a management position, yet each ad is basing its idea of a good manager on a different criterion of leadership. Your task is to identify the leadership criterion being sought in each ad.

Position Available: Manager

_____ 1.   Sales firm seeking a natural leader; must be aggressive, dominant, bright, self-disciplined, and have charisma. If you possess these qualities, you have a future with us.

_____ 2.   The time could not be better for you to join Mr. Fixit's. We need an opportunistic individual to join a rapidly expanding do-it-yourself chain of hardware stores. We are opening a new store in the northside area, guaranteed to be a million-dollar grosser. Come join a winning team!

_____ 3.   We need a take-charge person who will command respect from employees. The job is very clearly defined: supervise a road gang of asphalt pourers. You will be given authority to hire and fire as well as set salary rates. If this sounds like a perfect combination of factors to you, contact us immediately.

_____ 4.   We are seeking a doer, someone with proven managerial and leadership skills in the health-care field. We don't care about your personality as much as your ability to exercise an appropriate leadership style, given the situation. That might mean being "task-centered" one day, and then "employee-centered" the next. If you can perform, give us a call.

a.   trait approach

b.   behavioral approach

c.   situational approach

d.   contingency approach

CHAPTER EXERCISE

Directions: Read the following excerpts from the notebook of a modern-day industrial psychologist. She has consulted on a number of projects and has jotted down brief remarks. Your task is to identify the "key term" to which the remark relates.

Notes from an I/O Consultant

1. I applied the four-fifths rule, and I have determined a discriminatory effect exists here at the factory.

   Key term: _____

2. I have determined that Jack doesn't really care if he gets fired. His work valence is negative and low.

   Key term: _____

3. I definitely feel employees here are underpaid; however, because they are given lofty job titles, they work hard to live up to the implications of those titles even though the ratio of inputs to effort is not equal.

   Key term: _____

4. Upper management is interested in formulating an MBO philosophy. I've given them a book by Edwin Locke.

   Key term: _____

5. I have recommended that people working "on the line" not be paid hourly, but rather on a fixed-ratio schedule, or piecemeal rate.

   Key term: _____

6. Unlike other companies I've visited, employees at this company really do identify with their organization. They participate actively in company-sponsored programs and events.

   Key term: _____

7. The president and founding father of this company really stimulates loyalty and trust from his employees. He's very charismatic and conveys a tremendous sense of confidence in his "family" that they *can* excel and achieve.

   Key term: _____

8. One reason the company's CEO is so successful is that he can execute a range of successful leadership behaviors; he can be directive, participative, supportive, or achievement-oriented, depending upon the situation.

   Key term: _____

9. One problem for some of the lower-level supervisors is that they are unaware of their subordinates' maturity level; they continue to use a directive and task-oriented approach even though their work group is more mature and responsible.

   Key term: _____

10. I'm going to recommend a training program for these supervisors. It's fairly new and based on Fiedler's work on how situation, traits, and leadership style interact.

    Key term: _____

**PRACTICE
EXAM 1**

1. In 1927 industrial psychologists conducted a series of experiments that revealed an interesting phenomenon: no matter how working conditions are manipulated, workers' productivity increases after the intervention. They named this effect:

    a. adverse impact
    b. expectancy theory
    c. the Hawthorne effect
    d. reinforcement theory

    (Factual, Obj. 1.1)

2. The personnel department at Widgets, Inc., needs to fill a supervisory position and will be interviewing a large number of applicants. Which group intelligence test would you recommend to personnel?

    a. the Stanford-Binet
    b. the Otis Self-Administering Test of Mental Ability
    c. the MMPI
    d. the Rorschach inkblot test

    (Conceptual, Obj. 1.2)

3. An interview is a complex, dynamic process. What is the current feeling about the validity of the interview process by I/O psychologists?

    a. The typical interview does not validly predict an applicant's potential.
    b. Interviews are the best possible tools for selecting future employees.
    c. Interviews are valid only if interviewers compare the interview to an "ideal" applicant profile.
    d. Interviews are valid if interviewers pay more attention to the applicant's gestures, facial expressions, and posture than to his or her words.

    (Factual, Obj. 1.3)

4. At Upstate Teacher's College, all students are required to spend three quarters as student teachers in a public school. The reason for this is to give the potential teacher a realistic introduction to teaching. This requirement is very similar to the technique your text labeled:

    a. career entry introduction (CEI)
    b. realistic job preview (RJP)
    c. new job orientation (NJO)
    d. first-time apprenticeship (FTA)

    (Conceptual, Obj. 1.4)

5. According to Maslow, workers have a need for companionship and self-esteem in their work. This would correspond to the _____ level in the hierarchy.

    a. fundamental need
    b. valence
    c. metaneed
    d. existence

    (Factual, Obj. 2.1)

6. Suppose an employee were to ask you, "Does my promotion to assistant manager depend on the quality of work I'm doing now?" According to expectancy theory, what factor is being illustrated?

    a.   valence
    b.   expectancy
    c.   equity
    d.   instrumentality

    (Conceptual, Obj. 2.2)

7. Management by objective (MBO) is a popular organizational technique used to in-creased performance in corporations. MBO is based on the _____ theory of work motivation.

    a.   ERG
    b.   expectancy
    c.   goal-setting
    d.   reinforcement

    (Factual, Obj. 2.3)

8. Daniel is an I/O psychologist. Daniel's specialty, however, is to study and consult on collective bargaining and negotiation. What subspecialty of I/O psychology does Daniel practice?

    a.   personnel and human resources management
    b.   organization development
    c.   industrial relations
    d.   engineering psychology

    (Conceptual, Obj. 1.1)

9. What kind of psychological tests are among the better predictors of job performance?

    a.   perceptual accuracy tests
    b.   intelligence tests
    c.   motor ability tests
    d.   career interests inventories

    (Factual, Obj.1.2)

10. Victor Hugo once remarked that "nothing is so powerful as an idea whose time has come." If we were to apply this idea to the concept of leadership, which theory would it come closest to describing?

    a.   trait
    b.   behavioral
    c.   situational
    d.   the "great man" theory

    (Conceptual, Obj. 4.1)

11. Which type of test validity is most important in testing for complex tasks?

    a.   predictive
    b.   content
    c.   construct
    d.   concurrent

    (Factual, Obj. 1.2)

12. Some historians believe that the failure to be prepared for the surprise attack on Pearl Harbor was the result of a decision made by a small, highly cohesive group of individuals. They were relatively insulated from outside advice and, in a misguided attempt to maintain an atmosphere of congeniality, were not aggressive in expressing individual doubts about the wisdom of their plan not to act to protect this naval base. Janus would call such a fiasco an example of:

   a.   conformity
   b.   groupthink
   c.   discretionary stimuli
   d.   adverse impact

   (Conceptual, Obj. 4.3)

PRACTICE EXAM 2

1. Prof. Otis teaches a college course called Industrial/Organizational Psychology. He says that he has been teaching this particular course since 1970, the year he graduated from graduate school. When he was taking this course as an undergraduate, it was called:

   a.   Industrial Psychology
   b.   Personnel Psychology
   c.   Scientific Management
   d.   Human Relations

   (Conceptual, Obj. 1.1)

2. How can a plaintiff in a civil rights suit prove adverse impact?

   a.   by presenting test-job performance correlations
   b.   by applying the "four-fifths" rule
   c.   by demonstrating that interviewers are typically white
   d.   by showing the invalidity of the interview technique

   (Factual, Obj. 1.2)

3. When Buddy arrived for his interview at a local department store, he was surprised to find out that he was going to be interviewed in a "structured" manner. What's the purpose of this?

   a.   to make the interview more valid
   b.   to counteract first impressions
   c.   to see how an applicant will react under pressure
   d.   to see if the applicant will lie

   (Conceptual, Obj. 1.3)

4. Which approach to the study of leadership would heavily emphasize selection—finding the *right* individuals to fill openings within the organization?

   a.   the behavioral approach
   b.   the situational approach
   c.   the contingency approach
   d.   the trait approach

   (Factual, Obj. 4.1)

5. Bob manages a firm of professional psychologists. These individuals have a strong sense of personal control and are motivated by being consulted on everyday matters. What style of leadership would work most effectively with this group?

   a.   achievement-oriented
   b.   participative

c.   directive
d.   charismatic

(Conceptual, Obj. 4.1)

6.   What work motivation theory looks at whether we believe we are being treated fairly on the job?

a.   equity theory
b.   expectancy theory
c.   reinforcement theory
d.   goal-setting theory

(Factual, Obj. 2.2)

7.   "Workaholics" are people who are overmotivated to perform their job. They work extra hours, take work home with them, and seem all consumed with their profession. Work must be extremely rewarding to these people. Which theory might address the apparent reward aspects of this form of motivation?

a.   expectancy theory
b.   equity theory
c.   goal-setting theory
d.   reinforcement theory

(Conceptual, Obj. 2.3)

8.   The major source of worker dissatisfaction is:

a.   lack of creativity in jobs
b.   poor working conditions
c.   ambiguous or conflicting work roles
d.   routine work

(Factual, Obj. 3.1)

9.   "Great leaders are born, not made." What theory would be most supportive of this statement?

a.   trait theory
b.   behavioral theory
c.   situational theory
d.   contingency theory

(Conceptual, Obj. 4.1)

10.   Howard's company has been undergoing some organizational change lately and has just installed a new "cafeteria compensation" program. What theory is at the foundation of such programs at major companies like Howard's?

a.   equity theory
b.   expectancy theory
c.   goal-setting theory
d.   reinforcement theory

(Conceptual, Obj. 2.2)

11.   Benny "accidentally" opened his workmate's paycheck and noticed that his friend's check was $200 more than his own. Benny was outraged; he stomped into his boss's office and demanded a raise; after all, his workmate was hired after Benny and does essentially the same job. What label might best describe Benny?

a.   He is "equity sensitive."
b.   He is experiencing "adverse impact."

c.   He is a "benevolent" altruist.
d.   He is an "entitled" employee.

(Conceptual, Obj. 2.2)

12. When members of a group find that belonging to the group helps them to achieve their goals, and if group members like each other, the group will stay together. This defines the level of _____ in a group.

a.   cohesion
b.   homogeneity
c.   uniformity
d.   conformity

(Factual, Obj. 4.3)

■ ANSWER KEY ■

Concept 1   Potential sources of invalidity: 1, 3, 5, 7, 8, and 10
Potential sources of validity: 2, 4, 6, and 9

Concept 2
1.	a	3.	b
2.	d	4.	c

Concept 3
1.	JS	6.	JS
2.	OC	7.	JS
3.	JS	8.	OC
4.	JS + OC	9.	OC
5.	OC	10.	JS

Concept 4
1.	a	3.	d
2.	c	4.	b

Chapter Exercise
1.	adverse impact	6.	organizational commitment
2.	expectancy theory	7.	transformational leadership
3.	equity theory	8.	path-goal theory
4.	goal-setting theory	9.	life-cycle theory
5.	reinforcement theory	10.	cognitive resource theory

Practice Exam 1	Practice Exam 2
1. c, p. 689	1. a, p. 689
2. b, p. 690	2. b, p. 693
3. a, pp. 694–695	3. a, p. 695
4. b, p. 696	4. d, p. 706
5. c, p. 696	5. b, p. 708
6. d, p. 698	6. a, pp. 699–700
7. c, p. 701	7. d, p. 701
8. c, p. 690	8. c, p. 703
9. b, pp. 690–692	9. a, p. 706
10. c, p. 707	10. b, p. 698
11. c, p. 693	11. a, p. 700
12. b, p. 711	12. a, p. 710

CRITICAL THINKING ESSAY 7

Does Absence Make the Heart Grow Fonder—Or Go Wander?

Absence makes the heart grow fonder.
—Thomas Haynes Bayle

If you can't be with the one you love,
Honey, love the one you're with.
—Stephen Stills

For centuries poets, authors, songwriters, and their audiences have been keenly interested in the effect that a prolonged absence has on an ongoing romantic relationship. Specifically, people wonder how the stress of a separation will affect their relationship. As the two quotations above illustrate, people have come to very different conclusions about this question.

Surprisingly, psychologists have virtually ignored this topic, and as a result we know very little about which of these lay conjectures is more accurate. A search of the personality and social psychology literature published over the last fifteen years failed to find any study that examined the effect of a prolonged separation on the quality of a relationship. (In contrast, many studies have examined the reverse aspect of the topic—that is, which qualities in a relationship affect the decision to stay together or to separate.) We must look at this question indirectly, by turning to applied psychology in the areas of industrial/organizational (I/O) psychology, marital therapy, and military psychology.

STUDYING THE EFFECTS OF SEPARATION ON RELATIONSHIPS

I/O Psychology: Business-Travel Separations.   A few I/O psychologists have studied the impact of the corporate executive's heavy travel schedule on his or her spouse. For example, Boss, McCubbin, and Lester (1979) distributed questionnaires to the spouses (all wives) of business executives attending a company retreat at a luxury resort. Of the 66 respondents, those who reported coping successfully with their husbands' frequent absences shared the following characteristics: they identified with the corporate lifestyle; they developed their own interests through membership in clubs and groups; and they relied on their sense of independence.

Gullotta and Donohue (1983) found essentially identical results in their investigation of couples who were frequently separated as a result of business relocations. They also found that couples who were dissatisfied with their situations reacted in predictable ways. Husbands often used their business travel as a way to escape the strains in their marriages; wives escaped through alcohol and drugs. Many of these husbands and wives reported engaging in extramarital affairs during the prolonged separations.

Marital Therapy: Structured Separations.   Voluntary separations have also been examined. Recently, Granvold and Tarrant (1983), following the lead of Toomin (1975), suggested that structured separations can be helpful in marital therapy. As these researchers state, "The purpose of structured separation is to interrupt dysfunctional marital interactions as a means of facilitating the decision to either divorce or maintain the marriage" (p. 197).

In another aspect, Baxter and Wilmot (1984) interviewed 90 undergraduates involved in opposite-sex relationships to discover what "secret tests" they may have used to understand their relationships. One category of such tests was the "separation test." Simply put, students saw a partner's willingness to endure a separation yet remain in the relationship as a sign of the partner's commitment to that relationship. In a second sample of 91 students, 24.4 percent (30 percent of the women, 10 percent of the men) reported having used a "separation test" in their present relationship.

Military Psychology: Overseas Tours of Duty and Prisoners of War.

The bulk of the available information on separations comes from studies of military families. These studies have concentrated on separations resulting from extended overseas tours of duty and from situations in which one spouse has been a prisoner of war (POW).

The first type of separation was studied by Beckman, Marsella, and Finney (1979). Their subjects were 56 wives of U.S. Navy personnel assigned to nuclear submarines based in Hawaii. Submarine personnel alternated 12-week tours of sea duty and shore duty. Thus the wives alternated three-month periods of being with their husbands and being separated from them. The wives completed depression questionnaires during the fifth week of sea duty and again during the fifth week of shore duty. Perhaps not surprisingly, the researchers found that wives reported feeling more depressed when their husbands were away. Though straightforward and topical, this study showed only that separations are stressful; it could not reveal *how* the stress of the separation affected these navy marriages or how the wives coped with this stress. Furthermore, officers in the submarine service make an elite and atypical sample, so the study shed no light on how regular navy personnel and their families react to separations.

To remedy these deficiencies, Patterson and McCubbin (1984) conducted a more in-depth study of 82 male navy personnel and their wives. The husbands were assigned to surface assault ships that were scheduled for eight-month deployments (alternating with eight-month periods in port). Both spouses were given structured interviews and a battery of questionnaires one to four months before separating. The wives repeated this procedure four to six months after the separation began. Finally, both spouses participated in follow-up structured interviews one to three months after their reunion. The same procedure was followed for a control group of families of seamen who were in port during this time.

The interviews and the questionnaires were designed to tap several factors that were thought to be relevant to the wives' separation experience, including their attempts to cope with the separation; their perceptions of themselves, their marriages, and the navy; and their level of depression. Patterson and McCubbin found that the wives admitted to higher levels of depression beginning about a month before the separation and lasting until shortly before the reunion. In addition, most wives felt a great deal of stress during the separation. Nevertheless, some wives showed relatively little subjective distress during the separation. These wives tended to be characterized by acceptance of their navy lifestyle, optimism, high self-esteem, and self-reliance. The investigators also found that reunions were more successful when the family made an effort to allow the husband and father to maintain his family roles during and after the separation through letters, special tasks reserved for him, and so on. This "open ranks" approach led to a more satisfying reunion than did a "closed ranks" approach in which the absent spouse was excluded from his family duties and roles for the duration of the separation (Hill, 1949/ 1971).

Perhaps the most thorough study of military separation was conducted by the Center for Prisoner of War Studies (CPWS) from 1971 to 1978 (Hunter, 1986). When the United States and North Vietnam began to negotiate an exchange of prisoners in 1971, the Department of Defense authorized the CPWS to get in touch with 100 families of servicemen who had been classified as missing in action and who were eventually released in 1973. The navy was the only service branch that decided to follow up on returned POWs, so the final sample for study consisted of 60 navy officers (all members of flight crews) and their families. The control group consisted of the families of 60 navy officers who had not been taken prisoner but who were matched to the sample on variables such as age, rank, total flight hours, and type of aircraft flown.

These 120 families were studied at the time of the prisoners' reunion with their families and once a year for the next five years. On each occasion the CPWS interviewed both spouses and gave them questionnaire packets to be returned by mail. The information gathered concerned the couples' methods of coping with the absence and the reunion, the quality of the marriage, patterns of family interaction, personal adjustment, and self-esteem. Additional material was obtained from the officers' service files and psychological examinations conducted upon their return.

Although most families reported a euphoric "honeymoon effect" immediately after the reunion, during the first year many ex-POWs and their families found it difficult to adjust to being back together. Renegotiating family roles and reconciling disparate methods of disciplining the children were frequently cited problems. As one manifestation of the severity of these difficulties, 30 percent of the ex-POWs and their wives got divorced. Although this divorce rate was much higher than that of the control group (11.5 percent), it was close to the rate for the general population. Apparently, however, these difficulties were transitory for most couples. After two years, the POW group and the control group did not differ significantly on any of the variables studied (Nice, McDonald, and McMillian, 1981; Hunter, 1984; 1986).

From the interviews and questionnaires administered before the reunion, at the time of the reunion, and one year after the reunion, McCubbin and colleagues (1975) found that three factors reliably predicted positive family adjustment: the number of years the couple had been married before the husband was taken prisoner; the wife's perception of the quality of the marriage before her husband was taken prisoner; and the absence of any emotional dysfunction in the wife.

Similar results were reported in a study of 135 men who served in World War II. Hill (1949/1971) and his colleague Boulding (1950) found that the best predictor of a positive

reunion after the war was a positive marriage before the war. An egalitarian family structure (which required less renegotiation of roles and duties after the serviceman's return) also boded well for a satisfactory reunion. Current researchers have found that the stress of periodic separations is reduced if the wife identifies with the military lifestyle (Amen, et al., 1988), especially if she is able to obtain social support from other military wives (Rosen and Moghadam, 1988).

CRITICAL ANALYSIS OF RESEARCH ON SEPARATION

Research on separations of couples in ongoing relationships is hampered by two fundamental limitations: investigators must employ correlational designs, and they must make use of special samples. Because of these restrictions, it is virtually impossible for researchers to make any determination of causality and to generalize their claims to broader populations.

To require randomly chosen couples to separate for long periods would be ethically indefensible, even if it were possible. Thus, researchers are constrained to study people who are already undergoing prolonged separations in an attempt to associate their separation with some measure of the quality of their relationship. This correlational design makes it difficult to determine the directionality of any observed effects. Take the case of a couple who felt that their relationship had been strengthened as the result of a voluntary separation. Did absence improve the relationship, or did their strong relationship make the absence bearable? Perhaps some other variable was affecting both their decision to separate and the quality of their relationship. This possibility was raised by McCubbin and his colleagues (McCubbin et al., 1975; Boss, McCubbin, and Lester, 1979; Patterson and McCubbin, 1984), who found that commitment to a chosen lifestyle, the wife's psychological and social resources, and the quality of the relationship before the separation were factors that mediated the effect of a prolonged absence.

Collecting longitudinal data is one way to address this problem. While longitudinal correlational research cannot show causality, it can reveal patterns of association over time. So, for example, if relationship variables (such as ratings of the quality of the marriage and desire for the partner) improve over time, this would indicate that absence is associated with increased fondness. Unfortunately, the only longitudinal data available, the CPWS data (Hunter, 1984, 1986), are unable to answer these questions. No data were gathered between the initial contact and the reunion, so little is known about how the wives' perceptions of their relationships changed over time. Furthermore, the honeymoon effect of the reunion may have inflated ratings of the relationships at the time of the husbands' return. Most disappointing to those looking for a causal connection between long separations and marital satisfaction, the data showed no significant differences between the separated group and the control group.

Another problem facing researchers is the rarity of prolonged separations in ongoing relationships among the general population. Consequently, sample populations that would naturally undergo separations—especially military and corporate families, as we have seen—have become the focus of study. Although these samples provide investigators with reliable data at relatively little cost, generalizations based on this research must be made with caution.

First and foremost, researchers must watch for a *self-selection bias*. For the most part, the subjects used in the research described here voluntarily chose occupations or lifestyles that require one spouse to be absent frequently. As a result, their reaction to separations may reveal more about the type of people they are than about the effects of the separations themselves. For this reason, the study of World War II veterans was particularly useful. These men were more or less randomly selected from a group of 82,000 Iowa males drafted for military service. Because they did not volunteer for service, their reaction to separation (as distinct from their willingness to be separated) can be assessed more directly. Unfortunately for researchers (but fortunately for the general population!), the type of large-scale involuntary induction seen in World War II is very uncommon.

A second problem also pertains to the representativeness of the research sample. Military personnel and business executives who travel a lot are likely to possess unique skills that are considered valuable. The importance of the task requiring separation and the camaraderie common among groups of specialists may influence how these people view their separations. Their spouses, too, may have atypical characteristics that suit them to the military or corporate way of life. To complicate this problem, most researchers rely on data gathered almost exclusively from the partner who stayed behind, almost always the wife. A wife's perception may be very different from her husband's, a possibility that further limits the generalizability of the data.

In addition, as we indicated earlier, at least some members of the sample population may actively seek "enforced" separation. Recall that Cullotta and Donohue (1983) found that many couples use business travel as a temporary escape from their marriages. Similarly, Jensen, Lewis, and Xenakis (1986) report that some military personnel may volunteer for unaccompanied overseas duty as a way of separating from their families without seeking a divorce. This desire for situations that require separation probably influences these people's perceptions of their relationships and makes them less similar to the general population.

Jensen, Lewis, and Xenakis (1986) discuss other ways in which military personnel may not accurately represent the civilian population. For most military personnel, particularly officers, a stable marriage is essential for career advancement. This is less true for most civilians. In addition, most soldiers and seamen are closely supervised, and careful screening procedures remove people who are judged unfit for duty. These practices (and the personalities of those who accept them) may well influence the typical perception of separation held by military personnel and their spouses.

One sample population that experiences frequent enforced separations may be the most convenient group for psychologists to study:

college students. Since many college students attend institutions far away from their home towns, many are involved in long-distance romances. In addition, the long breaks and summer vacations of the college schedule require couples who met in school to separate for extended periods. Although college students thus constitute a sample of convenience, it is a much broader sample (and thus more easily generalizable) than special groups such as traveling corporate spouses, navy personnel, and prisoners of war. Despite these advantages, the effects of absence on college relationships have, surprisingly, not been studied to any great extent.

CONCLUSION: WHAT DO WE KNOW ABOUT THE EFFECTS OF ABSENCE ON RELATIONSHIPS?

Psychologists have conducted very little research even remotely related to the effects that separation has on relationships. What little we do know about this topic comes from small, mostly nonrandom samples drawn from self-selected populations. Clearly, this evidence must be interpreted with great caution.

Nevertheless, the results gathered from groups as divergent as the families of Vietnam POWs, corporate executives, and people contemplating divorce have been remarkably consistent. One general finding is that a strong relationship before the separation is the best predictor of a strong relationship after the separation. A commitment to the lifestyle that requires frequent absences and the partners' ability to develop as individuals during separations also predict a positive reunion. Conversely, limited evidence suggests that partners who are not strongly committed to each other or to their lifestyle may grow distant as a result of frequent absences; some spouses, it seems, seek enforced separations as a substitute for divorce. As Baxter and Wilmot (1984) suggest, some couples by design or by accident use separation as one test (among several) of the quality of their relationship. Toomin (1975) and Granvold and Tarrant (1983) recommend structured separations for couples who cannot decide whether to divorce. While all separations are seen as stressful, strong unions survive (and may even be strengthened by) the hardship of separation, whereas weak relationships are often destroyed by it. The seventeenth-century French philosopher La Rochefoucauld provided perhaps the most eloquent expression of this idea:

> Absence diminishes little passions and increases great ones, just as the wind blows out a candle and fans a fire.

REFERENCES

Amen, D. G., L. Jellen, E. Merves, and R. E. Lee. Minimizing the impact of deployment separation on military children: Stages, current preventive efforts, and system recommendations. *Military Medicine,* 1988, *153,* 441–446.

Baxter, L. A., and W. W. Wilmot. "Secret tests": Social strategies for acquiring information about the state of the relationship. *Human Communication Research,* 1984, *11,* 171–201.

Beckman, K., A. J. Marsella, and R. Finney. Depression in the wives of nuclear submarine personnel. *American Journal of Psychiatry,* 1979, *136,* 524–526.

Boss, P. G., H. I. McCubbin, and G. Lester. The corporate executive wife's coping patterns in response to routine husband-father absence. *Family Process,* 1979, *18,* 79–86.

Boulding, E. Family adjustments to war separation and reunion. *Annals of the American Academy of Political Social Science,* 1950, *272,* 59–67.

Granvold, D. K., and R. Tarrant. Structured marital separation as a marital treatment method. *Journal of Marriage and Family Therapy,* 1983, *9,* 189–198.

Gullotta, T. P., and K. C. Donohue. Families, relocation, and the corporation. *New Directions for Mental Health Services,* 1983, No. 20, 15–24.

Jensen, P. S., R . L. Lewis, and S. N. Xenakis. The military family in review: Context, risk, and prevention. *Journal of the American Academy of Child Psychiatry,* 1986, *25,* 225–234.

Hill, R. *Families under stress*. New York: Harper and Row, 1949; Westport, Connecticut: Greenwood Press, 1971.

Hunter, E. J. Treating the military captive's family. In F. Kaslow and R. Ridenour (eds.), *Treating the military family: Dynamics and treatment*. New York: Guilford Press, 1984, pp. 167–196.

Hunter, E. J. Families of prisoners of war held in Vietnam: A seven-year study. Special issue: The development and evaluation of human service programs in the military. *Evaluation and Program Planning*, 1986, *9*, 243–251.

McCubbin, H. I., B. B. Dahl, G. R. Lester, and B. A. Ross. The returned prisoner of war: Factors in family reintegration. *Journal of Marriage and the Family*, 1975, *37*, 471–478.

Nice, E., B. McDonald, and T. McMillian. The families of U.S. Navy prisoners of war five years after reunion. *Journal of Marriage and the Family*, 1981, *43*, 431–437.

Patterson, J. M., and H. I. McCubbin. Gender roles and coping. *Journal of Marriage and the Family*, 1984, *46*, 95–104.

Rosen, L. N., and L. A. Moghadam. Social support, family separation, and well-being among military wives. *Behavioral Medicine*, 1988, *14*, 64–70.

Toomin, M. K. Structured separation for couples in conflict. In A. S. Gurman and D. G. Rice, (eds.), *Couples in conflict*. New York: Jason Aronson, 1975, pp. 353–362.

RESPONDING TO CRITICAL ESSAY 7

1.   Your critical essay opened with two popular observations about the nature of absence: one referred to the belief that absence makes the heart grow fonder; another popular maxim is "out of sight, out of mind."

     Based upon the research cited in the essay, which proverb do you feel is most supportable?

2.   Research on separations of couples has not been able to make any determination of causality or to generalize its claims to a broader population.

     What has methodologically hampered basic research on separation?

3.   Studying the "special" populations, referred to in question 2, does limit the generalizability of such studies.

     What additional methodological problem do such populations pose for the researcher, particularly about the nature of the "volunteers"?

APPENDIX

Using Statistics in Research

KEY TERM ORGANIZER

Researchers generally analyze data by means of statistics. When studying the behavior of a group on a single variable, a *frequency distribution,* or a representation showing the number of subjects who obtain each given score, is often used. A frequency distribution may be symmetrical or skewed. Another way of summarizing a frequency distribution is with a *measure of central tendency,* which may be the *mode,* or most frequently obtained score; the *mean,* or arithmetic average; or the median, or the score that falls in the exact middle of the distribution. Measures of *variability* indicate how closely clustered the distribution of scores is. The simplest measure of variability is the *range.* More reliable is the *standard deviation (S.D.),* a value that indicates the extent to which figures in a given set of data cluster around the mean. In a curve of *normal distribution,* the mean, median, and mode fall at the same point, and the curve has a smooth bell shape. *Correlation coefficients* show the extent to which a relationship between two variables can be predicted. When two variables change in the same direction, there is a *positive correlation* between them; when one variable increases and the other decreases, there is a *negative correlation.* A correlation coefficient is expressed as a number ranging from –1 to +1. *Scatter plots* are used to display correlations in graphic form.

MAJOR CONCEPTS AND LEARNING OBJECTIVES

CONCEPT 1   Researchers analyze data by means of statistics. Statistics reduce masses of data to simpler and more informative numbers. Statistics are basically tools.

1.1   Describe how statistics are used in research and the characteristics of a frequency distribution.

1.2   Compare the characteristics of the three measures of central tendency.

1.3   Outline the procedures used to measure variability and describe the curve of normal distribution.

1.4   Define linear relationships and scatter plots; describe how correlations are measured.

**Concept
Builder 1**

Directions: Read the following story about the dean of Scatter Plot College, Dean Wormer, who must review the year's statistics on his teaching faculty to make recommendations for next year's salaries.

Let the Numbers Tell the Story

As Dean Wormer is leafing through his massive computer printouts, he flips to a summary chart entitled "Teacher Evaluation Data." This frequency distribution summarizes the overall scores the teachers received from their student evaluations (overall scores range from 1 to 10). Here is the summary chart:

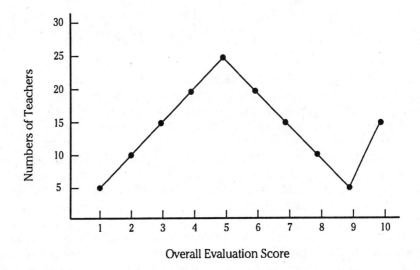

Dean Wormer considered evaluation scores of 1–3 to be "poor"; 4–6 to be "average"; 6–9 to be "excellent"; and 10 to be "outstanding." Dean Wormer knew nothing about statistics and numbers, so he called in his assistant, you, to answer the following questions:

1. "First of all, what kind of graph is this?"

    Your answer: _____

2. "The printout says I have 140 teachers altogether; the overall scores for all of them add up to 775. Now how do I get an average?" "What kind?" you ask. "A mean, median, or mode?" Looking very bewildered, Dean Wormer says, "A mean, I guess."

    Your answer: _____ (round off to nearest tenth of a point)

3. "Oh," says the dean. "Well, how about the mode then?" Without having to add any numbers, you look at the chart and answer,_____.

4. Then the dean says, "Listen, 15 of my teachers got a 10 overall; they're considered my outstanding teachers and I don't think it would be fair to compare everyone else with them. If I drop the '10s' off, look how nice that distribution looks! What is that called, the shape of the curve, I mean?"

    Your answer: _____

5. "Now, the printout has S.D. = 2.44. What's that mean?"

    You answer: S.D. stands for _____

6. "Thanks again. So, if I wish to use this S.D. stuff, here's what I think I'll do. I will not give a raise to those below one standard deviation (-1 S.D.) at all next year; I will give a 5% raise to those above one standard deviation (+ 1 S.D.). Now tell me, what are the critical numbers needed on the evaluation scores that are one above and one below the average?"

    Your answer: –1 S.D. would equal _____; +1 S.D. above would equal _____
    (Hint: use the mean computed above in questions 2 and 5)

7. By the way, Dean, what were your old evaluation scores when you were a teacher? "Get back to work, knave; you know numbers don't mean everything."

CHAPTER EXERCISE

Directions: Match the brief definition on the left side of the page with the key terms on the right-hand side. Note: Not all terms on the right will be used.

Statistical Jargon

_____ 1. A graph of summary data

_____ 2. The largest score minus the smallest score

_____ 3. The degree of relationship between two variants

_____ 4. The middle score of a distribution

_____ 5. Accounts for chance results

_____ 6. Identical mean, median, and mode

_____ 7. The average score

a. mean
b. mode
c. median
d. range
e. standard deviation
f. histogram
g. linear function
h. correlation coefficient
i. statistical significance
j. normal distribution

PRACTICE EXAM

1. Suppose I discover that as I eat more vegetables, my body weight decreases. I have demonstrated:

    a. a positive correlation
    b. a negative correlation
    c. a cause-and-effect relationship
    d. random sampling

    (Conceptual, Obj. 1.4)

2. In an unbalanced distribution, which measure of central tendency is least biased?

    a.   mean
    b.   median
    c.   mode
    d.   all are equally biased

                                                                (Factual, Obj. 1.2)

3. The average extent to which all scores in a particular set vary from the mean is the:

    a.   standard deviation
    b.   central tendency
    c.   probability statistic
    d.   statistical significance

                                                                (Factual, Obj. 1.3)

4. Which of the following is *not* true regarding the curve of normal distribution?

    a.   It reflects many of the characteristics found in life.
    b.   68.2 percent of the cases lie within one standard deviation of both sides of the mean.
    c.   The mean and the median are the same; only the mode differs form the other two.
    d.   The curve helps researchers determine whether the outcome of an experiment was due to chance or to the independent variable.

                                                                (Factual, Obj. 1.3)

5. Jack Templeton, a baseball contract negotiator, represents the players' association for the New Bedford Pirates. He is arguing for an increase in every active player's salary. Most players receive very similar salaries; however, the salaries of a pitcher and a third-baseman are practically double the others' salaries. What measure of central tendency would Jack find most effective in presenting his case?

    a.   mean
    b.   median
    c.   mode
    d.   any of the above would suffice

                                                                (Conceptual, Obj. 1.2)

6. If there is a positive correlation between participating in extracurricular activities and popularity, what does that mean?

    a.   Highly popular people also participate in a lot of extracurricular activities.
    b.   Participating in extracurricular activities causes people to be more popular through increased exposure.
    c.   Unpopular people probably spend more time studying or working, not participating in extracurricular activities.
    d.   As popularity increases, participation in extracurricular activities decreases.

                                                                (Conceptual, Obj. 1.4)

7. The linear function is represented graphically as a:

    a.   normal distribution
    b.   histogram.
    c.   "scatter plot"
    d.   straight line

                                                                (Factual, Obj. 1.4)

Look at the following normal curves of distribution:

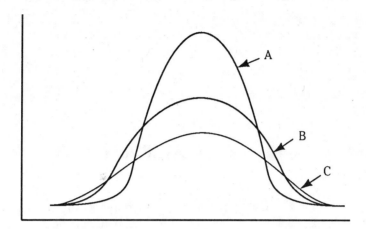

8. Which curve represents the least variability?

    a. a
    b. b
    c. c
    d. either b or c

                                                (Conceptual, Obj. 1.3)

9. The _____ is the measure of central tendency most used by psychologists.

    a. mode
    b. mean
    c. median
    d. range

                                                (Factual, Obj. 1.2)

10. When Professor Brainbuster posted his grades for the final, he constructed a "frequency polygon" showing the distribution of scores. It was not a normal distribution in that there were a disproportionate number of Ds and Fs, which made the distribution look lopsided. This distribution would be described as being:

    a. symmetrical
    b. pathetic
    c. skewed
    d. low in variability

                                                (Conceptual, Obj. 1.1)

11. Given the following set of scores—3, 4, 5, 5, 6, 6, 6, 8, 10—what is the range?

    a. 5
    b. 5.9
    c. 6
    d. 7

                                                (Conceptual, Obj. 1.3)

12. Suppose that, generally speaking, the taller people are, the more they weigh. Which of the following is the best estimate of the correlation coefficient between height and weight?

a. +.63
b. −.11
c. 0.00
d. −.77

(Conceptual, Obj. 1.4)

■ **ANSWER KEY** ■

Concept 1

1. frequency polygon
2. 5.5
3. 5

4. symmetrical distribution
5. standard deviation
6. −1 S.D. = 3.06
    +1 S.D. = 7.94

Chapter Exercise

1. f
2. d
3. h
4. c

5. i
6. j
7. a

Practice Exam

1. b, p. 727
2. b, p. 721
3. a, p. 722
4. c, pp. 722–724
5. b, p. 721
6. a, pp. 726–727
7. d, p. 726
8. a, p. 721
9. b, p. 720
10. c, p. 718
11. d, p. 722
12. a, p. 727

Thinking Critically: A Psychology Student's Guide

ROBERT S. FELDMAN AND STEVEN S. SCHWARTZBERG
UNIVERSITY OF MASSACHUSETTS AT AMHERST

WHAT'S IN IT FOR YOU:
AN INTRODUCTION TO CRITICAL THINKING

Maria smokes a pack of cigarettes a day. Concerned about her health, you would like her to quit. You tell her that doctors think smoking is a dangerous habit, but she answers that doctors have been wrong before, so why should she believe them . . . and furthermore, why should she believe you? Even after this rebuff, you are still concerned. How would you try to convince her to stop smoking?

Betty has just bought a new compact disc by her favorite artist, and she is eager to listen to it. She gets home, flips on the power switch of the stereo, and . . . nothing happens. She again turns the power button off and on, but still nothing happens. What should she do next?

Wade Boggs, the star player of the Boston Red Sox, performs an elaborate set of pre-game and midgame rituals throughout the baseball season. According to one news report, "he eats specific foods on specific days, leaves for the ball park at the same time each day, takes the same number of practice grounders from the same coach, runs his sprints at the same time, runs to his position retracing his exact footprints, and draws the Hebrew symbol *chai* ("life") in the dirt each time he steps up to home plate" (*Boston Globe Magazine*, April 9, 1989, p. 44). Boggs believes that he needs to complete these exacting rituals in order to play the game successfully. How would you assess the logic of his claim?

What do these scenarios have in common? They all involve situations that invite *critical thinking*. Whether evaluating a scientific research experiment or figuring out what might be wrong with a broken home appliance, critical thinking is an important and common tool of everyday life. Don't let the term frighten you; its applications are endless, it is a skill that can be practiced and honed, and it is extremely likely that you already do it, without realizing it, in many situations.

What characterizes critical thinking? People who think critically scrutinize the assumptions that underlie their decisions, beliefs, and actions. When presented with a new idea or a persuasive argument, they carefully evaluate it, checking for logical consistency and listening for tacit assumptions that may distort the central point. They pay attention to the context in which ideas or actions are implemented. Wary of "quick-fix" solutions and absolute claims, critical thinkers are skeptical of simple answers to complex questions. And rather than accepting pat, stock, or proverbial answers, critical thinkers attempt to develop alternate ways of understanding situations and taking action.

Although it may at first sound daunting, consistent application of critical thinking can be learned quite readily. The reason is that the ability to think critically is not something that a person is innately born with and it is not equivalent to measurable intelligence. Instead, it is a *process* of thinking, in which a few basic principles can be applied to a vast array of situations. Like versatile tools with many uses, the principles of critical thinking can serve as a kind of cognitive tool-kit. With a little practice, you can use these guidelines flexibly and creatively to tackle everyday problems, clarify your own position on difficult social issues, evaluate scientific research, and become a more educated consumer of the information you hear and read.

Your understanding of the world probably already embodies some of these basic principles of critical thinking. For example, consider the situation faced by Betty, whose stereo is malfunctioning. What would be your next step?

After determining that the stereo *should* be working (and questioning basic assumptions such as this is often the first step of critical thinking), you would probably try to define the problem as precisely as possible. For example, you might first try to determine if the electricity is out by turning on a lamp or looking at an electric clock to make sure other electrical appliances are working. (If they are not, you would need to explore a new set of questions, focusing more on the larger situation than on the stereo: Is it a blown fuse? Is it just one room, or the whole apartment, or the entire street?).

If the other appliances are working, you might then investigate if the electric socket is defective. To do this, you might plug the functioning lamp into the stereo socket. If the lamp works, you might then plug the stereo into the socket where the lamp had been, and—if the stereo still doesn't work—you would know that the electricity works and the socket works, but the stereo does not.

Critical thinking, unfortunately, wouldn't be able to help you fix the complex circuitry inside the stereo, and you would have to take it to a repair shop. But approaching the problem critically does play a vital role in identifying the source of the problem. By examining assumptions about whether the stereo should be working, and by logically and systematically exploring various possibilities of what might be wrong, the problem can be defined as precisely and appropriately as possible.

This simple example illustrates just one way of thinking critically in everyday life. As we will see, the same principles involved in diagnosing the stereo problem can also be applied to many other situations.

CRITICAL THINKING AND PSYCHOLOGY

Because of the nature of the field, psychology requires the consistent use of the principles of critical thinking. For one thing, psychology is a discipline that examines human phenomena at different *levels of analysis*. A brief glance through any introductory psychology textbook indicates the enormous breadth of the field, ranging from the microscopic study of a nerve cell and the analysis of human social behavior in emer-

gency situations to teaching language to chimpanzees and the theoretical rationales for psychotherapy. At times, then, psychologists attempt to answer questions that are *molecular*—extremely specific and detailed. At other times, they must take a *molar* view, examining the "big picture" rather than isolated details. When studying psychology, then, the following questions, central in critical thinking, must always be asked: What is the level at which this topic is being discussed? How would the same topic look from a different level?

Furthermore, psychologists hold a unique vantage point on human nature (Winter, 1984). The psychological conception of humankind differs from the view of other disciplines—for example, the economic view of people as rational actors, the legal view of a "reasonable or just person," or the theological view of humanity in the context of religion. Psychology offers a specific—and unique—perspective on human behavior. As you will learn, psychologists differ greatly in their theories regarding why humans function the way they do. At the same time, psychologists also share certain common beliefs. As you study the field, it is crucial that you are able to identify what those shared beliefs are, and challenge them to see if they fit with your experience.

Finally, psychology is a discipline committed to scientific research. Yet research—in the field of psychology, in other sciences, and in the general culture—can easily be misapplied, misinterpreted, or taken out of context. Critical thinking will help you evaluate the merits and dangers of scientific research. Some educators believe that learning to evaluate research critically is one of the most important skills that an introductory course in psychology can teach (e.g., Winter, 1984).

To aid your critical thinking skills, we will describe what critical thinking is, highlight the ways in which you already think critically, and point you in the right direction to further develop the requisite skills. Of course, learning to think critically won't happen without effort and practice, and there are no easy solutions. (Remember: Critical thinkers reject quick-fix solutions and are skeptical of simple answers to complex questions.) While the concepts presented here should all be easy to understand, you need to experiment with them, to try them out on your own, and to apply them to different situations.

SOME BACKGROUND ON CRITICAL THINKING

Before actually discussing the specific principles involved in critical thinking, an important question needs to be asked: Can critical thinking be taught at all? A brief look at changing ideas about education over the past 100 years can help provide an answer.

Had you completed your secondary education in the mid to late nineteenth century, the philosophy guiding your schooling would have been fundamentally different than the one which is guiding your more contemporary education. While one of the primary goals of education—teaching students to think critically—has remained the same throughout, beliefs about how to accomplish this goal have changed dramatically.

Until the early twentieth century, educators believed in the "formal discipline" of the mind. By studying certain fields, such as logic, grammar, and mathematics, it was felt that a person's intellect could be flexibly developed across a range of situations and disciplines. The idea was somewhat similar to the way one engages in physical exercise to gain muscular strength. Specific intellectual capacities, such as memorization, were treated analogously to muscles—the more one exercised them, the theory went, the stronger they became.

For example, students were taught Latin because it is a complex language requiring a great deal of memorization. Educators believed that this helped students' intellectual abilities in many different situations. Latin was not taught because of its everyday importance; it was taught so that the skills developed from learning it could be transferred to other intellectual pursuits.

Despite the appeal of the notion that the mind could be exercised to gain strength like a muscle, psychologists in the early 1900s adamantly rejected this long-standing principle

(James, 1899; Thorndike, 1906, 1913). They argued that intellectual abilities were highly task-specific and that skills did not transfer from one field of study to another. Largely through their influence, twentieth century school curricula moved away from the idea of formal discipline, which had been the cornerstone of educational philosophy (Nisbett et al., 1987).

Recently, however, psychologists and educators have begun reexamining the potential value of learning specific cognitive strategies that can be broadly applied (e.g., Brookfield, 1987; Nisbett et al., 1987; Sternberg & Caruso, 1985; Sternberg & Wagner, 1986). Current research (e.g., Lehman, Lempert, & Nisbett, 1988; Nisbett et al., 1987; Sternberg & Wagner, 1986) suggests that certain aspects of the formal discipline model deserve to be salvaged and that some skills (such as using inductive reasoning and applying abstract logic to pragmatic situations) can transfer across situations.

While it may or may not be the case, then, that learning Latin will make you more intelligent, there *are* benefits to learning abstract, general concepts that can transfer to different academic and practical tasks. In other words, the skills of critical thinking can be learned, and individuals can improve their abilities to think logically, coherently, and critically.

However, before considering these specific principles of critical thinking, we need to consider the ways in which people come to know the things they know.

KNOWING WHAT WE KNOW: SOURCES OF OUR KNOWLEDGE

Obesity is bad for your health. The earth revolves around the sun. 6 x 5 = 30. A picture is worth a thousand words.

All of us know a great deal of information. Some of it has been learned formally, in school. Some we have learned through the media—television, movies, newspapers. And for many other things, although we feel we "know" them, we're not sure where or how they were learned. How does a person come to believe that something is true?

Around the turn of the century, the American philosopher Charles Peirce theorized that there are four ways in which individuals come to "know" something (Peirce, 1960). He labeled these four means of knowing as the method of tenacity, the method of authority, the a priori method, and the scientific method.

METHOD OF TENACITY

According to the method of tenacity, a person believes certain ideas to be true primarily because those ideas have been around for a long time. Rather than questioning an idea's validity or testing its merit, the idea is accepted because of its longevity—if it has survived so long, it must be true.

From the vantage point of critical thinking, tenacity is a poor method to determine if something is true. Simply because a person has always held a certain belief is not, by itself, a reason to continue believing it. (People continued to believe that the sun revolved around the earth long after Copernicus proved that the reverse was true.) Yet why do people cling to old beliefs?

One reason may be that our cognitive systems are actually biased toward remembering and preferring information that we already know. Psychologists use the word *schema* to mean the organized and stored knowledge that a person holds on a given topic. Each of us has many cognitive schemas, ranging from what we may know about football and how much we like certain foods to perceptions of our own physical appearance. Research on schemas indicates that they are very resistant to change (for a review, see Fiske & Taylor, 1984). Because of schemas, we encode new information in a framework that is strongly influenced by what we already know. Old ideas, then, aren't discarded easily, and people have a tendency to continue to believe what they've always believed.

METHOD OF AUTHORITY

A second way of knowing something is the method of authority. People judge certain information to be true because it comes from a source of authority—a scientist, the government, a parent, a teacher, an expert of some sort. Advertisers easily take advantage of the method of authority to help sell their products; how much more likely we are to buy something that "leading experts" use, "four out of five doctors recommend," or "scientists have proven" to be superior to the competition!

While you may be thinking, "I'm too smart for that—I'm not going to believe something just because someone in authority tells me it's so," the method of authority is actually much more influential in our lives than you might at first acknowledge. As an example, think for a moment about something you most likely take for granted: that cigarette smoking is unhealthy. Ask yourself *why* you believe that it is unhealthy. If you answered "because it causes cancer and other diseases," then ask yourself *how* you know that it causes diseases. Most likely, the answer is that scientists, the U.S. Surgeon General, and maybe teachers and your parents have told you it is unhealthy. In other words, you believe cigarettes are unhealthy because voices of authority have said that it is so.

In fact, cigarette smoking *is* related to many adverse health effects, and physicians have accrued overwhelming evidence which links cigarettes with a variety of diseases. But you shouldn't rely on their word for it. As a critical thinker, you need to draw an important distinction: Cigarette smoking is not unhealthy because medical experts say it is unhealthy. Instead, it is unhealthy because scientific data have been gathered to implicate it in life-threatening illnesses. To determine for yourself whether smoking is unhealthy, then, you may want to read the actual scientific reports, or at least summaries of the reports, on the subject.

As with the method of tenacity, critical thinkers regard the method of authority as an unsatisfactory means of determining if something is true. Of course, what an expert in a certain field tells us may very well be true, but it is not going to be true simply because of the person's stature. In fact, here is what a medical guidebook for pregnant women had to say about cigarette smoking in 1957, advice that sounds startling to modern ears:

> By no means try to give up [ciga-rette smoking] in pregnancy. There is no surer way of upsetting the nerves at a period when you should be calm . . . even the most inveter-ate smoker can usually be content with a package a day or somewhat less, and if you arrange this there is no great cause for concern (East-man, 1957, p. 78).

A PRIORI (OR INFORMAL OBSERVATION) METHOD

Peirce's third method, which he labeled the "a priori" method, is knowledge based on informal observation. With this method, a person assumes that a cause-and-effect relationship exists between two variables or speculates about a general rule based on a particular incident. Something is deemed to be true based on informal and uncontrolled observation.

For example, Maria worked as a sales assistant in a gardening store. She was in a particularly good mood one day and smiled a great deal. At the day's end, she realized that she had sold more merchandise that day than ever before, and she decided that the custom-ers had bought more because she had been smiling. She further decided that salesclerks should always smile.

Maria is reasoning based on informal observation. She has taken a specific event—her smiling at customers—and decided that this caused the increase in sales. It might have . . . but can she be sure? Perhaps that day would have been a record sales day anyway, whether or not she had been smiling. Or, perhaps Maria was doing something in addi-tion to smiling that helped sales, such as flattering the customers. In other words, Maria is basing her decision on uncontrolled observa-tion, and although she may be right, it also may be that her smiling was irrelevant.

Maria also believed that her smiling (a particular incident) would increase sales for all salespeople (a general rule). This, again, is an example of informal observation.

Informal observation is more sophisti-cated and involves thinking more critically than the methods of tenacity or authority because it relies on observation and the forming of hypotheses. But it still lacks the rigor and control of the scientific method (discussed next). Because it is done informally, without any way to check or verify the information, it can easily lead to wrong conclusions. Reason-ing by the informal observation method is at the heart of many superstitious beliefs. And sometimes, it can lead to "logical" conclusions that are silly or absurd.

For example, let's return to the case of Wade Boggs. He believes that the elaborate rituals he performs daily throughout the baseball season make him a better ballplayer. While he is unquestioningly a superb hitter, it may be that he's only batting average when it comes to critical thinking. Boggs is reasoning from the informal observation method; he has informally observed two events and concluded that a causal relationship exists between them. He believes that variable A (his ritualized routines) cause variable B (his success at the game). While his superstitious actions have likely become habitual, his deduction that they cause his success is probably false. Only the scientific method can accurately determine if this is the case.

SCIENTIFIC METHOD

The scientific method relies on critical thinking and is the soundest means of deter-mining if something is true. It involves con-trolled experimentation and reaching conclu-sions that are rational and supported by evidence. But don't get the idea that the scientific method is something limited to crusty, humorless scientists tediously working in some antiseptic laboratory. It is a way of knowing or determining something to be true that has everyday applications.

Let's go back to Maria's conclusion that because she smiled, she sold more merchandise. She wondered if this belief was accurate or not, and so in order to find out, she designed a little experiment.

Maria conducted her experiment at the store. Because she knew that the busiest shopping hours were between two and four o'clock every afternoon, she selected that time for her study. She decided that on certain days (chosen randomly), during those hours, she would continually smile. On certain other days, she would not smile at all during those same hours. Except for changing her smile, she attempted to present herself the same way in all other regards. At first, she thought she might only do this for a few afternoons, but then realized that this would not be enough time to establish a consistent trend. So she conducted her experiment for two weeks, at the end of which she compared her total sales for the two-hour block on the smiling and nonsmiling days.

Let's say that Maria's total sales were significantly higher for the smiling days than for the non-smiling days. Assuming that she had kept everything else the same and had randomly chosen the days when she was or wasn't smiling, she would be in a much stronger position to claim that her smiling had led to increased sales than before.

Now imagine a slightly different scenario. Let's say that Maria had not been purposely changing her smile in a systematic way. However, at the end of each workday, she noted in her diary whether or not she had been smiling. After two weeks, she read her diary and discovered that on days she had been smiling, she had sold more merchandise. In this case, could she determine that her smiling caused the increased sales?

No. If this were all the information Maria had, she might be able to determine that smiling and increased sales were related to one another, but she could not say which caused which. Her smiling might have led to increased sales, but it is also possible that good sales days caused her to smile more.

Frequently, two events that are correlated are interpreted as having a cause and effect relationship. However, *correlation is not the same as causality*. Determining that one event has caused another is more difficult than determining that they are related.

What is needed to determine cause and effect between two variables? According to the philosopher John Stuart Mill, three conditions must ideally be met to determine causality. Without them, the cause and effect of two variables (here labeled A and B) can be guessed at, but not proven. These three conditions are:

1. B does not occur until after A.
2. It can be demonstrated that A and B are related.
3. Other explanations of the relationship between A and B can be ruled out.

What happens when we apply these criteria to Wade Boggs's elaborate behaviors? Boggs believes that his rituals (variable A) cause him to be a good hitter (variable B). In this case, Mill's first condition is met: B does not occur until after A. So far, so good. But can Boggs demonstrate that A and B are related? For example, is retracing his exact footprints as he runs to his position or fielding exactly the same number of practice grounders in pre-game warm-up necessary for him to hit well? Most likely, there is no relationship between these rituals and his batting ability. And given that the events aren't necessarily related, Mill's third condition cannot even be applied. So much for Boggs's beliefs.

How about Maria? In the situation where she systematically varied her smile, Maria meets Mill's three conditions: Variable B (the sale) occurs after variable A (her smiling); she has determined that the two events are related; and, by controlling other factors, she has attempted to rule out other explanations for the relationship. However, in the second situation, in which Maria found a relationship between smiling and increased sales in retrospect after reading her diary, she cannot meet Mill's first condition: She does not know if variable B followed variable A, or vice versa. Hence, she cannot determine cause and effect.

In your study of psychology, the distinction between correlation and causality will arise again and again. As a brief example, let's look at theories about the cause of schizophrenia, a mental disorder that involves serious disturbances in people's perceptions of reality and their ability to think and act rationally.

Although there is no cure for schizophrenia, the symptoms frequently can be alleviated by medication. The medication works by affecting a chemical in the brain called dopamine. By blocking the brain's receptor sites for dopamine, the drugs reduce the amount of dopaminergic (the adjective form of "dopamine") activity. Because reducing the brain's transmission of dopamine alleviates schizophrenic symptoms, people thus assume that schizophrenia is caused by an excessive transmission of dopamine.

Yet such an assumption may be wrong. While the effects of the medication indicate that a relationship exists between dopamine and schizophrenia, the discovery of a relationship between two variables is not enough to prove causality. It may be, for example, that the drugs have some additional unknown effect that influences both dopamine functioning and schizophrenic symptoms. Or, it may be that dopamine transmission does affect schizophrenic symptoms, but in a complex way that goes beyond measuring the amount of dopamine transmission. Further, there is as yet no direct evidence that schizophrenics show higher levels of dopaminergic activity than nonschizophrenics. So at the current time, the best that can be said is that dopamine functioning is related to schizophrenia. The true cause (or, more accurately, causes) of schizophrenia remains unknown (Strauss & Carpenter, 1981).

By this point, you may be realizing that you have accumulated your wide array of knowledge in many different ways. Actually, very little of what we "know" personally is based on a rigorous scientific method. Some ideas we believe because of their tenacity. Others we believe because an authority figure has told us they are true. Still others we take for granted or assume to be true, without having challenged or tested them. And while it is not always feasible to conduct well-controlled experiments in our daily life, we *can* become more attentive to the fallacies and gaps in our own logical thinking. This can be accomplished by learning to think critically.

SOME PRINCIPLES OF CRITICAL THINKING

To learn to think critically, you need to familiarize yourself with four fundamental principles that characterize the process. Each of these principles can be regarded as a thinking skill or a set of related thinking capabilities. Honing these skills takes time and practice, but you may be surprised how quickly you can start mastering them and applying them to your course work, practical problems that arise in daily living, and your personal beliefs about complex social issues.

The four main principles that underlie critical thinking are: (1) identifying and challenging underlying assumptions; (2) checking for factual accuracy and logical consistency; (3) accounting for the importance of context; and (4) imagining and exploring alternatives. While we do not mean to suggest that this is an exhaustive list or that it is the only available strategy for learning critical thinking, these principles do lay a strong foundation for the critical evaluation of new information.

1. IDENTIFYING AND CHALLENGING ASSUMPTIONS

Every statement, every argument, every research proposition, no matter how factual or objective it may sound, has embedded within it certain assumptions. These assumptions may be quite subtle and difficult to recognize. Learning to identify and challenge the assumptions that underlie a statement is one of the most crucial components of critical thinking.

What do these assumptions consist of? They may be ideas that people take for granted, perhaps commonsense beliefs that seem beyond questioning. Alternately, they may represent values that you grew up with and that you believe are commonly shared. Or they could be facts that you automatically accept as "given" without challenging them. Assumptions can be found in little truisms or proverbs that you find meaningful, in stereotypes, and in the beliefs that help create your views of life and the world.

Each of us has an enormous store of personal knowledge, some of which is shared by others, but much of which is unique to ourselves. This knowledge is an integral part of how we make sense of the world around us. Yet, when we stop and think about it, much of this "knowledge" is not factual but based on beliefs and assumptions. We usually consider these beliefs to be self-evident and only become aware of them through careful examination or when they are challenged. This fund of information, sometimes called "implicit personal knowledge" or the "assumptive world" by psychologists, shapes our ideas and perceptions about the world (Janoff-Bulman, 1989; Polyani, 1962).

Identifying and challenging assumptions means two things, then. First, it involves looking at the assumptions that are hidden in somebody else's presentation of facts, a speaker, an author, a classmate, a professor, a politician. Second, it means becoming aware of how our assumptions affect our own thinking. Our assumptions even act like a filter, guiding and shaping the information that we take in.

When presented with new information or when examining their own ideas and beliefs about a topic, critical thinkers attempt to identify the assumptions that color and shape the information. Put simply, challenging assumptions means learning to separate opinion from fact. It is as if critical thinkers act like mental surgeons, operating on the facts they hear to "cut away" unwanted opinions and assumptions.

Even the statement "It's a beautiful day!" has an underlying assumption. (Before reading ahead, try to think about what it may be.) If the day in question is sunny and warm with a gently billowing breeze, you may be likely to concur; in other words, you share with the speaker an assumption that weather of this sort is, indeed, "beautiful." It may seem such a factual and automatic response that you don't realize you are assuming anything. Yet the belief that such weather is "beautiful" is subjective, and represents an assumption.

Imagine, for example, that you have a friend for whom such "beautiful" days are extremely unpleasant. On cold and rainy days

he is free to do as he pleases, but when the weather is temperate, he must engage in laborious and tedious chores around the house. He dreads days that you consider beautiful, but feels joyous and carefree on rainy days. So when he greets you on a cold, damp day with a gleeful smile and a cheery "It sure is a beautiful day!" it becomes apparent that even simple interchanges about the weather can be clouded by underlying assumptions.

The fact that "it's a beautiful day" has a hidden assumption may seem to be relatively insignificant, and, on one level, it is. Critical thinking does not necessarily involve analyzing every casual sentence in conversation for flaws and hidden opinions. On a more complex level, though, assumptions about what is "right" influence our beliefs and actions on everything ranging from interpersonal relationships and how to spend leisure time to serious societal issues such as race relations, the environment, abortion, artificial parenthood, and on and on.

Additionally, identifying and challenging the assumptions that underlie statements of "fact" is often a crucial component of scientific progress. One example drawn from the field of psychology is how ideas about homosexuality have changed in the past two decades.

Until 1973, the American Psychiatric Association considered homosexuality a mental disorder. It no longer does. What is different now? Early psychological theories of homosexuality made the assumption that homosexuality was "abnormal" by adopting, without challenging, the prevalent cultural attitude. (The idea of homosexuality as abnormal is a good example of Peirce's method of tenacity; psychiatrists judged it to be deviant, in large part, because this had been a tenacious and long-standing belief in western culture.) But when researchers identified this as an assumption rather than fact and designed experiments that set out to challenge the assumption, they found that a belief in the abnormality of homosexuality was unwarranted (see, e.g., Bell, Weinberg, & Hammersmith, 1981; Hooker, 1957, 1968; Saghir & Robins, 1971, 1973).

For example, in one study, psychiatrists looked at the results of psychological tests taken by homosexual and heterosexual men, without knowing whose test they were examining. The psychiatrists were then asked to determine which tests were those of gay men and which were those of straight men. Until that time, psychiatrist had argued that homosexual men, because of their mental disturbance, could be distinguished from heterosexual men on the basis of psychological tests. However, the psychiatrists were unable to determine which tests had been taken by which group. In fact, psychiatrists' performance was no better than chance (Hooker, 1957). Similarly, several other studies have been unable to distinguish gay and straight men on the basis of psychological functioning.

Therefore, the psychological community has moved away from the assumption that homosexuality is inherently disturbed. Still, because the method of tenacity is so strong, the culture at large sees this as a controversial issue. Remember the discussion of tenacity and schemas: It is only slowly that long-held beliefs are relinquished.

***

How can you learn to *identify* and challenge assumptions? To *identify* them, you can simply start by asking yourself what assumptions an author or speaker is making. (As an example, this booklet makes many assumptions, including the belief that critical thinking can be taught and is worth knowing. What other assumptions are being made?)

Yet this process of direct questioning is not always as simple as it sounds. To make it easier, try asking questions that are as specific as possible. Rather than looking at an overall topic and wondering if a specific conclusion is right or wrong, look at how the conclusion was derived. Ask yourself whether specific points represent "facts" or if they are assumptions. Remember, most statements of "fact" involve assumptions. These assumptions can be opinions, or they can be value judgments that inadvertently bias how the facts are presented.

To *challenge* assumptions after identifying them, ask yourself a different set of questions: Is this assumption justified, and is it

reasonable? Why or why not? Do I agree with this assumption? What would happen if a different assumption were made?

Often, assumptions are uncovered when contradictions arise. Perhaps some new information or a new experience contradicts something you had previously believed. In such an instance, examine both the old and new information carefully, for you may discover that the discrepancy is based on differing assumptions. Similarly, if you read or hear something with which you disagree, this is a good clue that you and the author or speaker have differing assumptions underlying your viewpoints.

Finally, try to identify your own values and beliefs. Again, this is not as simple as it sounds. But as an exercise, spend a few minutes examining how you feel about a controversial social issue, such as abortion, surrogate motherhood, or capital punishment. After clarifying your stance, write down what you think is fact and what you think is opinion. Then do the same thing with a topic in your daily life—perhaps why someone should attend college or what makes a good relationship. After you have done this for both topics, write down points of view that support the *opposite* position. (Don't cheat—construct a good argument!) You may discover that your values and beliefs include many more assumptions and opinions than you had previously considered.

2. CHECKING FOR FACTUAL ACCURACY AND LOGICAL CONSISTENCY

In addition to identifying and challenging hidden assumptions, critical thinkers examine the rationality of an argument or statement. This process involves two main questions: (1) How factually accurate is the information, and (2) is the argument logical and consistent, or is there a fallacy in the reasoning?

Checking for Factual Accuracy. At its most basic level, checking for factual accuracy means verifying that information is true. Is the speaker or author making a clear and obvious factual error? Can the facts of an argument or statement be substantiated? What is the source of the information? In other words, critical thinkers pay careful attention to the evidence upon which an argument or claim is being supported.

But checking for accuracy involves more than just verifying the validity of factual statements. Often, what is *not* said in a claim is as important as what is said. Facts can be distorted to mislead; they may be presented in such a way as to imply or suggest a conclusion that is unwarranted. When confronted with factual information, critical thinkers allow for the possibility that an important point might be missing from the presentation.

For example, a manufacturer proudly advertises that its brand of laundry detergent is "preferred by a 4-to-1 ratio." With such a claim, you are being led to believe that this product is the most popular and effective detergent. However, important information has been left out of the claim. Even if the 4 to 1 ratio is factually correct, with the specified product preferred four times as much, what is it being compared to? The advertiser doesn't say. It may be in comparison with other leading detergents, but it also may be compared to something that is an irrelevant or inappropriate basis of comparison. Because important information is missing, the claim is meaningless.

An incomplete presentation of facts, such as in the case above, is a common rhetorical device. Politicians on the campaign trail, advertisers, lawyers trying to convince a jury —many persuasive individuals will use facts in a way that is technically not false, but is nonetheless misleading. And the method isn't limited to people in authority; it is a frequently used technique to make something sound more factually based than it actually is.

A factual presentation of information can also be distorted by misusing charts and pictures. Often, a visual, pictorial representation can help convey an idea clearly and succinctly. Graphs and charts can be used to clarify a topic that would otherwise be too cumbersome to express—but such visual props can also mislead.

Imagine, for example, that the number of applicants to a large state university has increased steadily and consistently over the past seven years. In 1982, the school received 24,550 applications, and by 1989 the number of applicants had risen to 27,630. (This represents an increase of approximately 15 percent over the seven year span).

Now look at the first three graphs on the next page (Figures 1, 2, and 3). They all present the same information: the university's steady increase of applicants over the seven years. But how different they look! Figure 1 presents what might seem to be the "truest" picture; visually, we read it as if a slight but steady increase has occurred. But by altering the units of measurement (Figure 2) and the minimum value on the *y* axis (Figure 3), dramatically different pictures emerge, quite literally. While they all present the same "facts," the visual impact of each leads to different interpretations.

Similarly, graphs that don't tell you exactly what they are measuring are useless. For example, perhaps the manufacturer of the laundry detergent just discussed is eager to show how popular its brand has become. In advertisements, the manufacturer uses the graph shown in Figure 4 to demonstrate the product's increasing popularity. Very eye-catching and impressive . . . but meaningless, for it is never stated what the unit of measurement is. Each notch on the graph could represent 50 new customers, or 50,000.

Checking for Logical Consistency. Sometimes, the facts of a claim may be correct and fully presented, with no deception and nothing omitted. Yet still a claim may be wrong. After checking for accuracy, critical thinkers ask a second question: Are the conclusions derived logically and consistently from the facts?

One type of logical fallacy is called a *tautology*, or circular reasoning. A tautology is a statement that is true by definition: Depressed people are sad. Good students achieve academic success. Fish are good swimmers because . . . well, because they're fish, so they have to be good swimmers. Such reasoning is circular because it "proves" what it is *assumes* to be true, with the "proof" only being a further extension of the assumption.

Many impressive sounding, but false, claims are based on tautological reasoning.

Figure 1
Number of Applicants to State U.

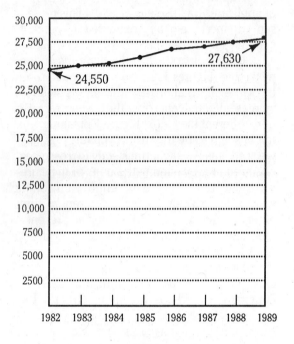

Figure 2
Number of Applicants to State U.

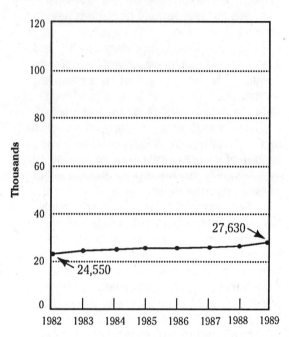

Figure 3
Number of Applicants to State U.

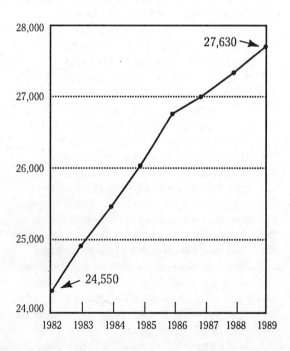

Figure 4
Increased Sales of
"Our Brand" Detergent

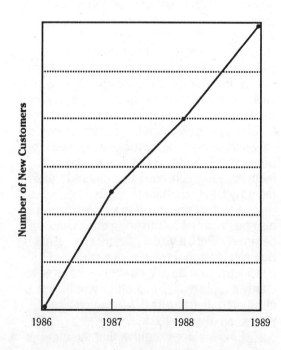

This faulty logic is also used frequently in humor. An example is a joke Woody Allen tells in the movie *Annie Hall*: My brother has a problem; he thinks he's a chicken. We'd take him to a psychiatrist . . . except that we need the eggs. If you analyze the "logic" of the joke, you will find that it is based on a tautology: It circularly assumes its absurd premise to be true.

Another way to think critically about whether a conclusion is accurately reached from a set of facts is to determine if a causal relationship has been inferred when only a correlation exists. Remember, as discussed previously, *correlation is not causality*. To prove causality between two variables is a specific and exacting process, but many correlational claims can misleadingly sound as if they are causal.

Take, for example, a study that relates back to the educational concept of formal discipline and the potential value of teaching Latin and Greek. A group of researchers in the early 1980s demonstrated that high school students who studied one of these two languages scored an average of 100 points higher on the verbal SAT than students who did not (cited in Lehman, et al., 1988). Given these results, a newspaper editorial suggested that Latin or Greek should be taught to all students because these dramatic results indicated that studying one of these languages obviously helped make pupils smarter (Costa, 1982).

Can you identify the editorialist's mistake? He took two bits of information that were related—studying Latin or Greek and a high SAT score—and assumed that one caused the other. It sounds plausible, yet such an assumption is unjustified and perhaps mistaken.

For example, it may be that only exceptional students decided to study Latin or Greek in the first place; in that case, they may have excelled on the SATs regardless of studying the language. It may also be that schools that offered Latin or Greek courses were generally of a higher academic caliber than schools that did not, and actually taking Latin or Greek was less important than attending a school that offered these courses. Whatever the reason (or, more likely, combination of reasons), a critical thinker would dismiss the editorialist's

claim because the conclusion is not logically derived from the evidence.

In summary, checking for factual accuracy and logical consistency involves asking yourself several questions. Are the facts accurate, and verifiable? Is important information missing, so that the facts that are presented are misleading? Does an argument or statement make logical sense? Is a conclusion based on circular (tautological) reasoning—in other words, is it defining its answer in terms of its unquestioned assumptions? And finally, can it be demonstrated that one event caused another to happen, or are they only related to one another?

3. CONSIDERING THE IMPORTANCE OF CONTEXT

A recent book on creative problem solving offers the following puzzling "letter" (Bransford & Stein, 1984, p. 51):

> Dear Jill,
>
> Remember Sally, the person I mentioned in my last letter? You'll never guess what she did this week. First, she let loose a team of gophers. The plan backfired when a dog chased them away. She then threw a party, but the guests failed to bring their motorcycles. Furthermore, her stereo system was not loud enough. Sally spent the next day looking for a "Peeping Tom," but was unable to find one in the yellow pages. Obscene phone calls gave her some hope until the number was changed. It was the installation of blinking neon lights across the street that finally did the trick. Sally framed the ad from the classified section and now has it hanging on her wall.
>
> Love,
>
> Bill

Reading this letter, it is difficult to comprehend what Bill is trying to communicate. The words make sense, as do the sentences. Grammatically the writing is fine, but what does it mean? Is it simply gibberish?

The meaning of the letter becomes much clearer when one understands the context of Sally's unusual actions: She dislikes her next-door neighbors and wants them to move away. Knowing this, go back and read the letter again. While you might not approve of her devious schemes, the meaning of her behavior is much more comprehensible!

Appreciating the importance of contextual information is a primary feature of critical thinking. Ideas are rarely context-free; the same fact or set of facts can have tremendously different meanings in different contexts. A child's shrieking at the top of her lungs, for example, could indicate that she feels great distress—but if she is at an amusement park, sandwiched into a roller-coaster car with her best friends and careening down the track at breakneck speed, it could signify utter delight. Similarly, getting a C on an exam could be terribly disappointing to a student accustomed to earning straight A's but a welcome sign of progress for a student who regularly fails his courses.

Psychologists are well aware of the importance of context in determining human behavior. For example, in a series of classic experiments, Asch (1951) demonstrated the enormous effect of the social influence of peers, even on such matters as how people perceive unambiguous visual stimuli. Asch's experiments are important because they reveal the extreme influence of context: If you are in a room full of people, all of whom perceive something differently from you, you are apt to change your perception to match theirs. Psychologists have also demonstrated that how people respond to "emergency" situations also varies significantly depending upon the context of the emergency (e.g., Darley & Latané, 1968; Latané & Darley, 1976).

When presented with new information or ideas, then, critical thinkers ask themselves in what context (or contexts) the information makes sense. They consider if the information applies universally, in every situation or if it applies only in very specific circumstances. In addition, they try to determine if there are cases in which the facts do not apply—where, in fact, the same facts mean something else.

The importance of context in determining the validity of a proposition also suggests that absolute or dogmatic statements should be treated with extreme caution. Sentences that begin with "People always . . ." or "It is never the case that . . ." usually ignore the importance of the context in which the supposed "always" or "never" takes place. Furthermore, many sentences don't explicitly state the "always" or "never" but imply it between the lines. Critical thinkers try to hear when an absolute claim is being implied and then sort out the contexts and situations in which the claim may be true.

As an example of ignoring the importance of context, consider proverbs. With catchy phrasing and a succinct message, the lessons that proverbs teach are easy to learn. But if you think for a moment about the proverbs you know, you may discover that for each "truth" a proverb reveals, a second proverb offers a "truth" exactly opposite the first!

For example, a well-known saying tells us that "absence makes the heart grow fonder"—but an equally popular proverb warns us, "Out of sight, out of mind." And we all know that "too many cooks spoil the broth," but at the same time, "many hands make light work." And imagine how difficult it is to live boldly, since "opportunity knocks only once" and "nothing ventured, nothing gained," while simultaneously trying to live cautiously because "it is better to be safe than sorry." (Try to think of some more pairs of proverbs that offer opposing and contradictory "truths.")

Critical thinkers are wary of proverbial sayings because they leave out as much as they include, failing to take context into account. Most proverbs do have some wisdom to offer regarding the human condition, but they present only part of the picture. Taken individually, any proverb is incomplete because it offers its "truth" in a more absolute manner than actually fits the wide breadth of human functioning (listen for the implied "always" or "never" that remains hidden).

Cultural Relativity. So far, the importance of context has been discussed in terms of identifying different meanings for the same facts and in rejecting the absolutism of all-or-none claims. One more feature is necessary to appreciate the importance of context for critical thinking: the cultural relativity of ideas.

It may be difficult to imagine that many of the ideas and beliefs that you hold as important are not universal but are instead, shaped and defined by cultural influences. When considering their core beliefs, people tend to feel that all individuals must feel the same way or that their beliefs must be absolute rather than relative. Yet many of the ideas we hold, the actions we take, and the emotions we display are shaped by cultural guidelines and expectations.

For example, consider how people grieve in response to the death of a loved one. Our culture has many unstated "rules," or social norms, regarding how to mourn the death of a loved person. These norms include such things as who is permitted (or expected) to grieve, how long the period of grief should last, what emotions the grieving person can display, and how the bereaved person should act. Imagine how odd it might seem for a man who was recently widowed to be laughing and cavorting about in public, or parents who had recently lost a child to mourn for four days and then never publicly mention their child again, or a recently widowed woman to take a knife and inflict wounds on herself.

Yet these mourning practices are considered "normal" in other cultures. Although crying appears to be the most common cross-cultural response to the death of a loved one, in Balinese society, bereaved individuals never cry in public. Instead, they act in a friendly and jovial nature (Rosenblatt, Walsh, & Jackson, 1976). The Hopi Indians of North America have a grief period of four days, after which the bereaved person is expected to return to the tasks of daily life and make no mention of the departed person (Miller & Schoenfeld, 1973). And self-infliction of injury is a mourning ritual practiced in several cultures (see Pollock, 1972, for a review). From the perspectives of these other cultures, crying in public, elaborate mourning rituals, or acting depressed for many months after a loss seems unusual and "abnormal."

For a person who is grieving in our culture, the emotional experience of grief may seem so dramatic and vivid that it does not seem shaped by cultural rules. Yet grieving must be culturally shaped, given the evidence that other cultures handle loss differently. To understand a psychological phenomenon such as grief, then, it is important to think critically about the cultural context in which it occurs and to determine how one's own ideas and beliefs about the phenomenon might be defined by one's own culture.

4. IMAGINING AND EXPLORING ALTERNATIVES

So far, we've discussed the importance of several skills for critical thinking: (1) identifying and challenging assumptions in your own thinking and that of an author or speaker; (2) checking for factual accuracy and logical consistency; and (3) taking into account the context of a set of facts. But these guidelines are only part of the picture. They all require you to act somewhat like a strict interrogator; your task is to detect flaws in logic, uncover lurking opinions, debunk erroneous assertions, and reject claims that are too extreme. A fourth component of critical thinking, imagining and exploring alternative solutions, calls instead for creative ingenuity. In many situations, it is not enough simply to point out the shortcomings or inconsistencies in an idea or argument; critical thinking also involves generating new ideas, alternative explanations, and more viable solutions than those that are presented.

Like the other components of critical thinking, the skills involved in generating creative and fresh alternatives can be honed through practice. The following strategies will help you develop the ability to imagine and explore creative alternatives to problems.

1. Simplify Complex Information. It is obviously helpful to have a full grasp on a problem or issue before tackling it. However, complex topics are, by definition, difficult to understand. Cognitive psychologists have demonstrated that there is a limited amount of material a person can comprehend at once; it is easy to get "overloaded" by too much information. Therefore, when presented with a barrage of facts, or when you feel there is too much information to easily make sense of, try organizing it into a simpler form before generating alternative ideas.

One way to simplify complex information is to systematically break it down into component parts. If you play a musical instrument, for example, you probably have a different approach to learning an easy piece of music than to learning one that is long and challenging. With an easy piece, you may try sight-reading it, playing the whole composition at once. But with a more complex piece, you would likely try to learn it a bit at a time. You might concentrate on one movement or section until you have mastered that and then go on to the next section. Only after approaching it in its components might you attempt to interpret or understand it as an entire piece.

The same principle can be applied to complex ideas. It is often helpful to divide a large problem into simpler components, making sense of them individually before attempting to master the larger phenomenon. And it is often easier to think of changes at the component level of a problem than to confront it as a whole.

A second strategy to simplify information is to visualize it. Rather than hold a complex problem in your head, write out its components. For example, make a list of pros and cons or strengths and weaknesses of a proposition, and compare the two. Or, perhaps the information lends itself well to charts or other pictorial representations. Sometimes it is helpful to write an outline of an argument or idea, to be able to "see" if the logic is consistent.

Because organizing complex information into a visual model simplifies it, it helps you to imagine and explore alternatives. To further generate new ideas, after organizing the information, try to organize it again—differently. Any pie can be sliced in a number of ways; what happens when you take the same information but organize it in a different method?

A third way of simplifying complex information is to try to understand it by means of an analogous everyday example. Bring things into your own frame of reference. This might mean substituting simple words for complicated scientific or technical language. It might mean thinking of an experience you've had that typifies a larger concept. Or it might involve providing specific details to an idea that is only presented as an abstraction.

For example, imagine the following problem. Four cards are placed in front of you displaying an A, a B, a 4, and a 7. Every card has a letter on the front and a number on the back. Your instructions are to turn over only the cards necessary to establish this rule: If there is a vowel on the front, then there is an even number on the back. What cards do you turn over?

Most adults do not correctly complete this task (Wason, 1966). However, here is an analogous example, with more familiar, less abstract terms (D'Andrade, 1982). Instead of four cards, you have four receipts. Two are facing up: One for $25, the other for $15. The other two face down: One has a signature, the other one does not. Your instructions are to turn over only the receipts necessary to establish that if a receipt is for more than $20, then it has a signature on the back. Which receipts do you turn over?

If you answered that you need to turn over two receipts—the one for $25 (to make sure it is signed) and the receipt that is unsigned (to make sure it is not for an amount larger than $20), you reasoned correctly. By similar logic, with the first task you need to turn over the A and the 7. When the same conceptual problem is applied in more familiar terms, subjects find the second task easier than the first (D'Andrade, 1982).

2. Redefine the Problem. Redefining a problem involves trying to look at it from a fresh perspective. Often, a problem and its components have been defined in a certain way. What happens if those definitions are stretched, altered, or abandoned altogether? Trying to conceptualize a problem or argument from different vantage points can lead to new ideas.

For example, in one experimental situation, subjects were presented with a candle, a large box of matches, and several thumbtacks (Duncker, 1945). Their task was to mount the candle on the wall so that it could be used for illumination. No other tools or objects could be used. How could this be done? (Sorry—the thumbtacks were not big enough to fit through the candle.)

Most subjects were unable to figure out how to accomplish the task. But there is a simple solution, which involves redefining the possible function of one of the objects: the matchbox. By emptying out the matches, the box can be tacked to the wall and converted into a candle holder.

What many people fail to see in approaching this situation is that the matchbox can be used as anything other than a matchbox. This is an example of a phenomenon called *functional fixedness*: It is difficult to look at familiar objects in a novel or unfamiliar way.

The same is true when approaching complex problems. We often become locked into seeing something from only one perspective or vantage point. However, overcoming this "cognitive fixedness" can allow us to explore solutions to problems with creative ideas that otherwise would not have occurred to us.

3. Brainstorming. Brainstorming is usually thought of as a group activity. However, the principles involved can also be practiced by a single individual attempting to imagine and explore novel solutions to problems.

The technique of brainstorming (Osborn, 1963) begins by defining a problem that needs to be addressed. After the problem is defined, the next step is to think of as many solutions as possible, with one important condition: the newly generated ideas are not critiqued or judged. For brainstorming to be effective, it is necessary to suspend the immediate judgments that new suggestions sometimes elicit. There are no such things as "good" ideas or "bad" ideas in brainstorming. No matter how seemingly outlandish, farfetched, or insignificant, all possible solutions to or redefinitions of the problem are encouraged.

As you might guess, the purpose of brainstorming is to overcome or circumvent some of the other problems that have already been discussed. By generating new ideas in a way that encourages creativity and novelty,

ideas may germinate and take root that would otherwise be quickly dismissed. Even the most preposterous suggestion may have within it a kernel of truth or the key to unraveling a knotty problem.

After the new ideas have been generated in a judgment-free manner, they are then evaluated one by one to determine their helpfulness. In this process, the evaluation proceeds as does the evaluation of any new ideas or propositions: with the guidelines for critical thinking already discussed.

4. Switching Roles. One of the ways we mentioned to simplify a complex argument was to write it down. Not only does this allow you to organize the material visually, it can also help you try to reconstruct and understand the logic of a different viewpoint.

When you are presented with an idea or an argument with which you disagree or that you cannot follow, try to construct, step by step, how the authors or speakers have reached their conclusions. Try to follow their logic, attempting to see the situation from their eyes. Imagine that you have to agree with, and defend, their conclusion in a debate; how would you convince somebody of their point?

In the process of hypothesizing how someone reached a conclusion other than your own, several things may happen. You may uncover questionable assumptions in their (or your) logic. You may be able to isolate specifically where the point of disagreement is. And, in a creative way, you may be able to take the strongest points of both arguments and forge a new, flexible alternative.

As we mentioned earlier, a valuable exercise is to spend a few moments looking at a social issue that you have strong feelings about, but imagining that you need to defend the *opposite* view from the one you hold. (Most complex issues have adherents on either side, many of whom have struggled with their choices.) Can you identify the differing assumptions in the different views, and come up with any novel solutions?

* * *

These strategies are just a few of the several ways to creatively explore alternative options. The process of creating new possibilities goes hand in hand with the other steps of critical thinking; after potential alternatives are generated, they can be subject to the same critical scrutiny as any other proposition.

One impediment to critical thinking is an overly strong attachment to one's own ideas. People often find it easier to practice the skills of critical thinking in dissecting someone else's argument, than in thinking critically about their own views. But critical thinkers maintain the same questioning attitude toward their own ideas as toward those of others. They approach all ideas, both their own and others', with a stance of "reflective skepticism" (Brookfield, 1987), meaning that they greet all challenging ideas or information with serious, but cautious, consideration.

When people learn to relinquish their investment in the rigid maintenance of their own beliefs, they can also allow for a potentially valuable source of new information: making mistakes. Part of imagining and exploring creative options is learning from things that have gone wrong. In sum, don't be discouraged or disheartened about having made mistakes; use them as an education.

A FINAL COMMENT ON THE PRINCIPLES OF CRITICAL THINKING

These four principles—identifying and challenging assumptions, checking for factual accuracy and logical consistency, looking at context, and imagining and exploring alternatives—form the foundation of critical thinking. Taken together, these guidelines will help you think critically about information you learn in school, read in the newspaper, hear on television, or glean from casual conversations with friends or family. They will assist you in examining some of your own ethical positions on difficult social problems. And these guidelines can even help win arguments with your friends!

Critical thinking will also help you evaluate the merits of research, as you encounter it in academic settings and in the culture in general. It is to this application of critical thinking that we now turn our attention.

THINKING CRITICALLY TO EVALUATE RESEARCH

We live in a research-oriented society. From the pioneering breakthroughs on the cutting edge of medical science to the semiannual choices network executives agonize over regarding what television programs to air, research is a fact of modern life. We rely on it, and with this reliance comes an inherent danger, for research findings can be easily misused, distorted, or taken out of context to say something other than what they are meant to.

Thinking critically goes hand in hand with developing an appreciation of the enormous benefits, and inherent dangers, of scientific research. Research is a double-edged sword; when misapplied, its ability to obscure knowledge is as great as its ability to illuminate. Research that is soundly conducted can answer difficult questions with more certainty and objectivity than any other method of inquiry, but the casual reporting of research can be fraught with distortions that, intentionally or unintentionally, mislead an unsuspecting public. Studies may be poorly designed or conducted, findings can be taken out of context and misapplied, and "results" can be carefully worded so as to subtly, but wrongly, imply the truthfulness of a dubious claim.

As we've already mentioned, the field of psychology has as one of its cornerstones a commitment to empiricism, or the research-based validation of its concepts. As such, the study of psychology is a particularly helpful context in which to hone your skills of assessing and evaluating the merits of research.

Psychologists say many things about human nature, based on the research they conduct. However, rather than believing something simply because a psychologist says it (beware the method of authority), critical thinkers carefully scrutinize research to determine, for themselves, how sound it is.

Six steps characterize the research process in the field of psychology (Winter, personal communication). Each step is associated with particular issues relevant to critical thinking.

Step 1: The Idea

Psychological research begins with an *idea*. This idea may relate to a practical or societal problem that needs a solution. It may be a casual observation of human behavior that warrants closer examination. Conversely, it may be derived from a specific theory and represent a test of the theory's power to predict certain outcomes.

Step 2: The Question

The researcher's idea leads to the development of a specific *question*. This question, sometimes stated as a formal hypothesis, should be framed in a way that allows it to be tested—in other words, it has to be asked so that it can be answered, so that the experiment will support or negate it.

Step 3: The Method

To answer the question, the experimenter devises a scientific method that "translates" the question into a research procedure. By developing an experimental model or a means of systematic observation, the experimenter attempts to answer the experimental question as accurately and specifically as possible.

Applying Critical Thinking:

When assessing a single experiment or a program of research (a series of studies that are unified by the same theme), first try to identify the underlying idea or theory on which the experimenter is basing his or her study. What are some of the assumptions the experimenter is making? If the idea for the study is derived from a larger theory, is it logically consistent with the theory? If the study relates to a social or practical problem, is the problem being defined in a way that makes sense? Is the context of the problem being taken into account?

Applying Critical Thinking:

First, identify as specifically as possible the question that is being asked in the experiment. After you have identified it, ask yourself if this question is logically derived from the idea that guides the experiment and is a testable (answerable) question. Further, consider if the way in which the question is framed introduces any hidden assumptions about what the outcome of the study will be. Is the experimenter introducing any bias into the study?

Applying Critical Thinking:

Again, the first step is to identify the procedure that the experimenter has employed to test the question. Does the approach make sense to you? Is it logically derived from, and consistent with, the experimental question?

In the leap from hypothetical question to experimental design, research studies can sometimes develop a crucial gap in logic. In some cases, a laboratory-designed study does not accurately capture the "real world" phenomenon it is trying to examine, and so the results of the study, however interesting, will be of little relevance to the original situation. At other times, a research design may introduce new variables that inadvertently distort the experimental question. In these cases, the results cannot be associated, with certainty, with the original question of interest.

Thus, two crucial questions must be asked of any research design: (1) Does the research design adequately capture the real-world phenomenon or theoretical concept that it is attempting to examine? (2) Has the design introduced any unwanted and irrelevant features that distort the experimental question?

Step 4: The Experiment

Once an experimenter has an idea, a testable question, and a procedure to test the question, the next step is to conduct an initial experiment. The results of the experiment will confirm or refute the question asked.

Applying Critical Thinking:

At this step in the process, critical thinking follows two paths. First, are the results accurate? Are they presented in a complete and detailed manner, without any significant omissions or gaps in logic?

Second, are the results being presented in an appropriate context? Or has the experimenter taken accurate results but applied them in a way that extends beyond the limitations of the experimental design? Remember that the results relate to the experimental situation but not necessarily to the "real world." Are the results reported in a fashion that is too global, too inclusive, or too absolute?

It is also important to consider the results in the context of other scientific inquiries on the same topic. Single studies seldom prove a point decisively, and it is rare for scientific progress to hinge on a single, monumental experiment. In most cases knowledge accrues slowly, as consistent research findings gradually accumulate. Therefore, when faced with the results of a single study, critical thinkers ask themselves: What is *not* being reported? Are these results consistent and expected with what is already known, or is this the only study to produce the results it did, whereas many others produced opposing results?

Step 5: Criticism

After the results of an initial study are made known, the next step in the research process is *criticism*.

Other members of the scientific community examine the study and its conclusions. The criticisms might focus on the experimental design or methodology (in which case, they would echo the critical questions discussed above). Frequently, other researchers will question not the results themselves, but how the experimenter explains or interprets them. Approaching the same experimental phenomenon from a different angle, or with a different theoretical idea, other researchers will propose alternative explanations for the findings.

Applying Critical Thinking:

Researchers do not present experimental results in a vacuum; they also explain what they think the results mean or indicate. At this step, then, think critically not only about the results but also about the explanation offered for them. Does the explanation make sense? Is it the only possible explanation for those results? If not, could you generate alternative explanations?

Also important at this stage of the process is carefully examining the assumptions that are embedded in the explanation. Probably more so here than at any other point in the scientific process, assumptions can be uncovered that affect the interpretation of the results. What is the researcher presenting as fact that might be an opinion or a personally held, subjective value?

Step 6: Further Studies

After other researchers suggest alternative explanations for the results, they in turn conduct *further studies* to support or disconfirm the new interpretations. In this manner, the cycle of research and the gradual accrual of knowledge continues. Previous findings are either replicated or refuted, new findings lead to new questions, which in turn beget new findings, and old theories are strengthened, modified, or discarded.

Applying Critical Thinking:

Often at this point in the scientific process, different researchers will argue that the same facts mean entirely different things. To think critically, evaluate the different explanations. Do they make sense individually? Is one better than the others? Why or why not? Can you synthesize differing points of view to generate a creative new alternative?

Earlier, we mentioned that psychology is a discipline that looks at phenomena at different levels of analysis, from the microscopic to the molar. Is there a way in which differing explanations could be approaching the same phenomenon at varying levels of analysis? If so, how could one or more views be integrated?

***

Understanding and practicing these guidelines for critically evaluating research will help you in your introduction to the field of psychology. But, in all likelihood, the gain will extend beyond that. Pick up a newspaper, turn on the radio, watch the advertisements on television—the casual reporting of research findings permeates our culture. And the more you know about the mechanics of sound research, the more mental ammunition you'll have to determine, for yourself, what research claims you choose, or don't choose to believe.

A FEW CONCLUDING COMMENTS

Earlier in this booklet, we mentioned that the skills of critical thinking can be likened to a cognitive toolkit. Tools take time to master; anyone can hold a hammer, but only with practice can you learn to hit a nail consistently on the head. So it is, too, with the critical thinking skills discussed here. Don't be discouraged if you don't immediately fully integrate these guidelines into your style of thinking and become a critical thinking "whiz." With time, patience and practice, you can develop your ability to think critically. These guidelines can become a familiar, and useful, means of evaluating new information.

Teaching students to think critically is currently a major focus of higher education, and we do not suggest that the system presented here is the definitive one, or that it is the only way for you to learn critical thinking skills. But we do believe that the four principles we discuss—identifying and challenging assumptions, checking for factual accuracy and logical consistency, accounting for the importance of context, and imagining and exploring alternatives—provide a strong foundation. These guidelines can strengthen your ability to evaluate factual-sounding claims made by professors, friends, politicians, and advertisers. They can also help you clarify your personal beliefs on difficult social topics, and judge fairly those beliefs that differ from your own.

One final note: Critical thinking can be fun. Rather than approaching these skills as a burdensome task, think instead of the pleasure associated with implementing a creative new idea, solving a complex problem, or understanding, for the first time, an idea that had always mystified you. Broadening one's intellectual abilities can be enormously rewarding in its own right, and critical thinking can be a valuable source of intellectual enrichment, personal growth, and pride in your own cognitive abilities.

REFERENCES

Asch, S. E. (1951). Effects of group pressure upon the modification and distortion of judgments. In H. Guertzkow (Ed.), *Groups, leadership, and men*. Pittsburgh: Carnegie Press.

Bell, A., Weinberg, M., & Hammersmith, S. (1981). *Sexual preference: Its development in men and women*. Bloomington: Indiana University Press.

Bransford, J. D., & Stein, B. S. (1984). *The ideal problem solver: A guide for improving thinking, learning and creativity*. New York: W. H. Freeman.

Brookfield, S. D. (1987). *Developing critical thinkers*. San Francisco: Jossey-Bass.

Costa, R. M. (1982, March 6). Latin and Greek are good for you. *The New York Times*, p. 23.

D'Andrade, R. (1982). Paper presented at the Symposium on the Ecology of Cognition: Biological, Cultural, and Historical Perspectives, Greensboro, N.C.

Darley, J. M., & Latané, B. (1968). Bystanders' intervention in emergencies: Diffusion of responsibility. *Journal of Personality and Social Psychology*, 8, 377-383.

Duncker, K. (1945). *On problem solving* (L. S. Lees, Trans.). *Psychological Monographs*, 58.

Eastman, N. J. (1957). *Expectant motherhood*, 3rd rev. ed. Boston: Little, Brown.

Fiske, S. T., & Taylor, S. E. (1984). *Social cognition*. Reading, Mass.: Addison-Wesley.

Hooker, E. (1957). The adjustment of the male overt homosexual. *Journal of Projective Techniques*, 21, 18-31.

Hooker, E. (1968). Homosexuality. In *International encyclopedia of social sciences*. New York: Macmillan.

James, W. (1899). *Talks to teachers on psychology; and to students on some of life's ideals*. New York: Holt.

Janoff-Bulman, R. (1989). Assumptive worlds and the stress of traumatic events: Application of the schema construct. *Social Cognition*, special issue: "Social Cognition and Stress."

Latané, B., & Darley, J. M. (1976). Help in a crisis: Bystander response to an emergency. In J. W. Thibaut, J. T. Spence, and R. C. Carson (Eds.), *Contemporary topics in social psychology*. Morristown, N.J.: General Learning Press.

Lehman, D. R., Lempert, R. O., & Nisbett, R. E. (1988). The effects of graduate training on reasoning. *American Psychologist*, 43, 431-442.

Miller, S. I., & Schoenfeld, L. (1973). Grief in the Navajo: Psychodynamics and culture. *International Journal of Social Psychiatry*, 19, 187-911.

Nisbett, R. E., Fong, G. T., Lehman, D. R., & Cheng, P. W. (1987). Teaching reasoning. *Science*, 238, 625-631.

Osborn, A. F. (1963). *Applied imagination: Principles and procedures of creative problem solving* (3rd revised Ed.). New York: Scribner's.

Peirce, C. S. (1960). In C. Hartshorne and P. Weiss (Eds.), *Collected Papers: Vol. 5: Pragmatism and pragmaticism*, 2nd ed. Cambridge: Harvard University Press.

Pollock, G. (1972). On mourning and anniversaries: The relationship of culturally constituted defense systems to intrapsychic adaptive processes. *Israeli Annals of Psychiatry*, 10, 9-40.

Polyani, M. (1962). *Personal knowledge: Towards a post-critical philosophy*. Chicago: University of Chicago Press.

Rosenblatt, P. C., Walsh, R. P., & Jackson, D. A. (1976). *Grief and mourning in cross-cultural perspective*. New Haven: Yale: HRAF.

Saghir, M., & Robins, E. (1971). Male and female homosexuality: Natural history. *Comprehensive Psychiatry*, 11, 503-510.

Saghir, M., & Robins, E. (1973). *Male and female homosexuality: A comprehensive investigation*. Baltimore: Williams & Wilkins.

Sternberg, R. J., & Caruso, D. (1985). Practical modes of knowing. In E. Eisner (Ed.), *Learning the ways of knowing*. Chicago: University of Chicago Press.

Sternberg, R. J., & Wagner, R. K. (1986). *Practical intelligence*. Cambridge: Cambridge University Press.

Strauss, J. S., & Carpenter, W. T., Jr. (1981). *Schizophrenia*. N.Y.: Plenum.

Thorndike, E. L. (1906). *Principles of teaching*. New York: A. G. Seiler.

Thorndike, E. L. (1913). *The psychology of learning*. New York: Mason-Henry.

Wason, P. C. (1966). Reasoning. In B. M. Foss (Ed.), *New horizons in psychology*. Harmondsworth, England: Penguin.

Winter, D. G. (1984). Reconstructing introductory psychology. In K. I. Spear (Ed.), *New directions for teaching and learning*, no. 20 (pp. 77-88). San Francisco: Jossey-Bass.